Women and Leadership

Women and Leadership

Transforming Visions and Diverse Voices

Edited by

Jean Lau Chin, Bernice Lott, Joy K. Rice, and Janis Sanchez-Hucles

© 2007 by Blackwell Publishing Ltd

except for editorial material and organization © 2007 by Jean Lau Chin,
Bernice Lott, Joy K. Rice, and Janis Sanchez-Hucles

BLACKWELL PUBLISHING
350 Main Street, Malden, MA 02148-5020, USA
9600 Garsington Road, Oxford OX4 2DQ, UK
550 Swanston Street, Carlton, Victoria 3053, Australia

The right of Jean Lau Chin, Bernice Lott, Joy K. Rice, and Janis Sanchez-Hucles
to be identified as the Authors of the Editorial Material in this Work has been
asserted in accordance with the UK Copyright, Designs, and Patents Act 1988.

First published 2007 by Blackwell Publishing Ltd

1   2007

Library of Congress Cataloging-in-Publication Data

Women and leadership : transforming visions and diverse voices/edited by
Jean Lau Chin, Bernice Lott, Joy K. Rice, and Janis Sanchez-Hucles.
    p. cm.
    Includes bibliographical references and index.
    ISBN-13: 978-1-4051-5582-3 (hardcover : alk. paper)
    ISBN-13: 978-1-4051-5583-0 (pbk. : alk. paper)   1. Leadership in women.
2. Feminism.   3. Women civic leaders.   I. Chin, Jean Lau.   II. Lott, Bernice E.
III. Rice, Joy K.   IV. Sanchez-Hucles, Janis, 1951–

HQ1111.W72 2007
305.4201—dc22

2006024429

A catalogue record for this title is available from the British Library.

Set in 11/13pt Baskerville
by Graphicraft Limited, Hong Kong
Printed and bound in Singapore
by C.O.S. Printers Pte Ltd

The publisher's policy is to use permanent paper from mills that operate
a sustainable forestry policy, and which has been manufactured from
pulp processed using acid-free and elementary chlorine-free practices.
Furthermore, the publisher ensures that the text paper and cover board
used have met acceptable environmental accreditation standards.

For further information on
Blackwell Publishing, visit our website:
www.blackwellpublishing.com

Contents

Notes on Contributors

Coeditors

Jean Lau Chin, EdD, ABPP is Professor and Dean of Derner Institute for Advanced Psychological Studies, Adelphi University, Garden City, NY. As past-president of the Society for the Psychology of Women, American Psychological Association, she led a presidential initiative on Feminist Leadership. She has held leadership/management roles for the past 35 years including Systemwide Dean, California School of Professional Psychology at Alliant International University, and President, CEO Services.

Bernice Lott, PhD is Professor Emerita of Psychology and Women's Studies at the University of Rhode Island and is former Dean of its University College. She received her university's Excellence Award for scholarly achievement, served as president of the American Psychological Association's Division on the Psychology of Women, and has been honored for scholarly, teaching, and social policy contributions. In 1999, she was awarded the honorary degree of Doctor of Humane Letters by the University of Rhode Island.

Joy K. Rice, PhD is a clinical psychologist, Clinical Professor of Psychiatry at the University of Wisconsin Medical School and Professor Emerita of Educational Policy Studies and Women's Studies at the University of Wisconsin-Madison. Among her many publications, she initiated and coauthored a 2001 position paper to APA Council on Cultural and Gender Awareness in International Psychology.

Janis Sanchez-Hucles, PhD is Professor and Chair of Psychology at Old Dominion University, Norfolk, VA, and works part time as a clinical psychologist, consultant, and trainer. Dr. Sanchez has become a national speaker and trainer in the areas of diversity and cultural competence. Among her numerous publications is her book *The first session with African Americans: A step by step guide* (2000) and a journal article on racism as a form of emotional abuse and trauma.

Authors

Judith E. N. Albino, PhD is President Emerita, Professor of Craniofacial Biology and Clinical Professor of Psychiatry, at the University of Colorado. She is a consultant with the Academy for Academic Leadership and works with nonprofit organizations in organization planning and leadership development. She is president of the Society of Psychologists in Management.

Asuncion Miteria Austria, PhD is Professor, Chair, and Director of Clinical Training, Graduate Program in Clinical Psychology, Cardinal Stritch University, Milwaukee. She served on the American Psychological Association's governance boards, and was past president of two APA sections of Clinical Psychology. She has numerous awards for humanitarian service, mentoring, and outstanding contributions to the clinical psychology of women.

Roya Ayman, PhD is Professor at Illinois Institute of Technology, Institute of Psychology where she is the director of the Industrial and Organizational Psychology program. She was coeditor of *Leadership theory and research* (1993) and has had extensive publications on issues related to leadership, culture, and gender.

Nancy L. Baker, PhD, ABPP is on the faculty of Fielding Graduate University, Santa Barbara, CA. She has battled for women's rights for over 30 years, having served on the National Executive Board of the Coalition of Labor Union Women, as Chairperson of the Committee on Women in Psychology, and as President of the Society for the Psychology of Women within the American Psychological Association.

Mary B. Ballou, PhD, ABPP is Professor and Program Coordinator of Counseling Psychology at Northeastern University, involved with the Boston Consortium of Graduate Women's Studies Programs, and Chair of the Feminist Therapy Institute. Her publications in feminist mental health theory include *The foundation and future of feminist therapy* (2005) and *Personality and psychopathology: Feminist reappraisals* (1992).

Martha E. Banks, PhD is a research neuropsychologist at ABackans DCP, Inc. She was Professor of Black Studies at the College of Wooster in Ohio, and served in leadership roles within the American Psychological Association. She has published widely in books and journals, including *Cultural Diversity and Ethnic Minority Psychology*, and is editor of *Women with visible and invisible disabilities: Multiple intersections, multiple issues, multiple therapies* (2003).

Dolores S. Bigfoot, PhD is an enrolled member of the Caddo Nation of Oklahoma and Assistant Professor of Research in the Department of Pediatrics, Oklahoma University Health Sciences Center. She is Director of the Indian Country Child Trauma Center, and is recognized for her efforts to bring traditional Indian practices and beliefs into formal teaching and instruction for those working with Indian populations.

A. Toy Caldwell-Colbert, PhD, ABPP is Vice Chair for Psychological Services and Professor, Department of Psychiatry, Howard University College of Medicine, Washington, DC, and Consultant to the President. Her 27-year administrative/management posts in higher education include Provost and Associate Vice President at Howard, University of Illinois, and Indiana State University. She is President of the Society for the Psychological Study of Ethnic Minority issues.

Dorothy W. Cantor, PsyD is in private practice in Westfield, NJ. As author of groundbreaking books, including *Women in power: The secrets of leadership* (1992) and *What do you want to do when you grow up?* (2001), she appears frequently on television and radio, and lectures nationally to corporate audiences. A leader in American psychology, she was the eighth woman President of the American Psychological Association.

Lillian Comas-Díaz, PhD is Executive Director of the Transcultural Mental Health Institute, a Clinical Professor at George Washington University Psychiatry Department, and maintains a private practice in Washington, DC. She is former director of the American Psychological Association's Office of Ethnic Minority Affairs, and of the Hispanic Clinic at Yale University School of Medicine.

Jessica Henderson Daniel, PhD is Director of Training in Psychology, Department of Psychiatry, Children's Hospital, Boston. She is on the board of directors of the American Psychological Association, and was honored for her mentoring of Psychology Fellows at Harvard University's teaching hospitals. She identifies herself as being both an African American woman and a woman of color; her interests include media images of women, inclusion/exclusion of women of color in discussions about development and trauma, and the importance of women's lives in context—including race/ethnicity, class and locale.

Florence L. Denmark, PhD is the Robert Scott Pace Distinguished Research Professor at Pace University, New York. An internationally recognized scholar and researcher, her most significant research emphasized women's leadership, interaction of status and gender, and aging women. She is a past president and fellow of the American Psychological Association, and her numerous national and international awards include the 2004 American Psychological Foundation Gold Medal for Lifetime Achievement in the Public Interest.

Alice Eagly, PhD is a Professor of Psychology at Northwestern University, Evanston, IL. Her leadership roles include President of the Society for Personality and Social Psychology. Her awards include the Carolyn Wood Sherif Award of the Society for the Psychology of Women for contributions as a scholar, teacher, mentor, and leader.

Edna M. Esnil, PsyD is Director of Training at Notre Dame de Namur University, Belmont, CA, and is also in private practice. Her interests include gender and multicultural issues. She is currently Program Cochair for APA's Society for the Psychology of Women, and served on the Board of Directors of the Asian American Psychological Association.

Marlene G. Fine, PhD is Professor of Communications at Simmons College in Boston. Her previous positions include Dean of Graduate Studies at Emerson College and Associate Dean, Director of the MBA Program, and Chair of the Department of Marketing and Communications in the College of Management at the University of Massachusetts, Boston.

BraVada Garrett-Akinsanya, PhD is President of Brakins Consulting and Psychological Services in Minnesota. She is also President of the Multi-Cultural Specialty Providers Mental Health Network dedicated to culturally competent mental health services. Her unique style of combining humor with education and sound clinical skills has made her much sought after for her expert summary by the media, including *Star Tribune, Insight Health*, the *Art Cunningham Show, TIPical MaryEllen*, and KMOJ 99.1 FM radio.

Beverly Greene, PhD, ABPP is Professor of Psychology at St. John's University and a practicing clinical psychologist in New York City. She is a Fellow in seven of APA's divisions and currently serves on APA council. She is recipient of many national awards including the 2006 Florence Halpern Award for Distinguished Professional Contributions to Clinical Psychology.

Ruth L. Hall, PhD is an African American licensed psychologist and Professor of Psychology at the College of New Jersey. Her presentations and publications focus on African American women, sport and exercise, and sexual orientation. She is a Fellow in Divisions 35, 45, and 47 in APA.

Diane F. Halpern, PhD is Professor and Chair of Psychology and Director of the Berger Institute for Work, Family, and Children at Claremont McKenna College in California. She has been president of several professional organizations including the American Psychological Association. She has more than 350 publications including *From work–family balance to work–family interaction: Changing the metaphor* (2005). Her many awards for teaching and research include 2002 Outstanding Professor Award from the Western Psychological Association.

Jeanette Hsu, PhD is Training Director for the psychology internship and postdoctoral training programs at the VA Palo Alto Health Care System. She has served on the boards of the Asian American Psychological Association, Society for the Psychology of Women, and currently of the Association of Psychology Postdoctoral and Internship Centers (APPIC).

Michael Hucles, PhD is an Associate Professor of History at Old Dominion University. He is currently working with two other scholars on writing a complete history of the Norfolk, VA, African American population. Included among his publications is "Mary E. Cary Burrell" in *Black women in America: An historical encyclopedia* (1994).

Phillip Hucles is a first year law student at The University of Virginia. He graduated from the College of William and Mary with a BA in Economics and a minor in Business with a concentration in Marketing. Phillip plans to combine his legal career with his finance background and go into entertainment law with expertise in handling contracts and personal finances.

Norine G. Johnson, PhD is President of ABCS Psych Resources. She was 2001 President of American Psychological Association, President, Women in Psychology; and Board of Visitors, Wayne State University, 2002–5. She was awarded Distinguished Leader for Women in Psychology in 1998. Her publications focus on adolescent girls, psychology and health, and feminist psychology.

Deborah Jones-Saumty, PhD is Chief Executive Officer of the American Indian Associate in Talihina, OK.

Debra M. Kawahara, PhD is Assistant Professor, California School of Professional Psychology at Alliant International University-San Diego. Her interests include feminist leadership and its development in Asian American women, the mental health of minorities and women, and cultural competency. She coedited a special issue of *Women & Therapy*, focusing on Asian American women.

Gwendolyn Puryear Keita, PhD is Executive Director of the Public Interest Directorate of the American Psychological Association. Her past positions include Director of the Women's Programs Office, and Assistant Director, Howard University Counseling Services in Washington, DC. She has written extensively on women and depression, violence against women, and women's health.

Clara Sue Kidwell, PhD is Director of the Native American Studies program and Professor of History at the University of Oklahoma in Norman. She has published *Choctaws and missionaries in Mississippi, 1818–1918* (1987) and articles on American Indian women, education, and systems of knowledge.

Karen Korabik, PhD is Professor at the University of Guelph, Ontario, CN where she is the research director for Women and Work at the Centre for Families, Work, and Well-Being. She is a Fellow of the American Psychological Association and has published extensively on issues related to gender dynamics in organizations.

Jennifer M. Leigh, PhD is a research fellow at the Center for Health Quality, Outcomes, and Economics Research in Bedford, MA, and a clinical psychologist in private practice. Her work emphasizes promoting change through relationships with the intersection of culture, relational patterns, and approaches to healing; and is aimed at improving patient outcomes by emphasizing organizational cultural competence and relationship-centered management.

Margaret E. Madden, PhD is Provost and Vice President for Academic Affairs at Potsdam College, State University of New York. Her passion for undergraduate teaching led her career to focus on academic administration in small, teaching-oriented, undergraduate colleges including Long Island University, Lawrence University, and Franklin Pierce College. Her scholarly work includes a feminist analysis of women's administrative styles in higher education, and developing a management philosophy based on feminist values and social psychology principles.

Sanjay C. Mehta is a graduate student in the Virginia Consortium Program in Clinical Psychology. He received his bachelor's degree in psychology from the State University of New York at Binghamton. He is also a member of the Psi Chi national honor society. His major clinical interests are therapy with Asian Americans, psychological interventions with medical disorders, and neuropsychology.

Linda R. Mona, PhD is Staff Psychologist at the VA Long Beach Health Care System in the spinal cord injury service. She has advocated for the inclusion of disability in university diversity curriculum, effected changes for students with disabilities, and conducted research at the World Institute on Disability leading to national recognition by the American Psychological Association, and Association on Higher Education and Disability.

Natalie Porter, PhD is Professor at California School of Professional Psychology, Alliant International University, and former Vice President of Academic Affairs there. Feminist clinical psychology education, supervision, and ethics have been her particular areas of interest with numerous publications including chapters on "Covision: Feminist supervision, process, and collaboration" (1997) and "Integrating anti-racist, feminist, and multicultural perspectives in psychotherapy: A developmental supervision model" (1996).

Penny Sanchez, MBA is Vice President, Relationship Manager for APAC Customer Services, Inc. and is responsible for a $12 million Healthcare client where she led a Six Sigma Project Team to automate and deliver key performance metrics. Prior to this, she was Regional

Vice President at Xerox Services where she managed a $125 million Operations and Technical service support unit.

Ester R. Shapiro, PhD is Associate Professor of Psychology, University of Massachusetts, Boston and Research Associate, Gaston Institute for Latino Public Policy. A Cuban immigrant and daughter of Eastern European immigrants to Cuba, she studies resilience-building interventions using cultural creativity to promote health and equality. She is author of *Grief as a family process: A developmental approach to clinical practice* (1994), and coproduced an award-winning documentary on domestic violence with Cuban film maker Lizette Vila.

Karen L. Suyemoto, PhD is Assistant Professor in Clinical Psychology and Asian American Studies at University of Massachusetts, Boston. Her research and teaching focus on bridging multicultural psychology and ethnic studies and particularly on the social constructions of racial and ethnic identities (especially in relation to Asian American and multiracial individuals and communities), and interventions for promoting social justice action.

Melba Vasquez, PhD, ABPP is in independent practice in Austin, TX. Her numerous publications on professional ethics, ethnic minority psychology, and psychology of women include *Ethics in psychotherapy and counseling* (2nd ed., 1998). She is past President of Texas Psychological Association (2006), and past President of two APA Divisions, Psychology of Women and Counseling Psychology. Her numerous awards include the James M. Jones Lifetime Achievement Award, APA 2004.

Diane J. Willis, PhD is Professor Emerita, Department of Pediatrics, University of Oklahoma Health Sciences Center and a consultant to the Indian Health Service and Choctaw Nation CARES Project. She is past president of the Division of Clinical Psychology, APA, and president of the American Orthopsychiatry Association.

Ann S. Yabusaki, PhD is in private practice and consults to programs and organizations on culturally sensitive psychological services. She was president and dean of several professional schools of psychology, and participated in the design and implementation of a Doctor of Psychology program based on principles of cultural competence.

Foreword

Alice Eagly

When the modern feminist movement emerged, it did not feature much discussion of leadership. There was virtually no analysis of what feminist leadership might entail. Because leadership had been largely a privilege of men, and feminism focused on women, it is understandable that the study of leadership did not have much salience. Feminists wanted to understand women's experiences and the roots of women's oppression. Psychologists in particular had neglected the study of women. Therefore, new topics emerged—sexual harassment, rape, math anxiety, family violence, menstrual cycle effects, and the politics of reproductive rights, to name just a few. To study leadership, be it in organizations or in politics, would have meant focusing on men. Feminists had other priorities. The discovery and development of women-focused topics made good sense.

Much has changed. Women are now far more common in the ranks of leaders. For example, women occupy 24% of all chief executive positions in the United States (U.S. Bureau of Labor Statistics, 2006, Table 11). They constitute 44% of school principals (U.S. National Center for Education Statistics, 2005), and 21% of college and university presidents (Corrigan, 2002). It makes sense that feminists find the study of leadership appropriate now that it addresses the experiences of women as well as men. Although women remain rare in the top ranks of corporate leadership and greatly underrepresented in the Congress, women's increasing presence in these and other leadership roles raises many questions about their functioning as leaders. Feminist psychologists are beginning to answer these questions.

There are more important reasons for feminists to study leadership than the fact that women now have much greater access to leadership roles. These other reasons have to do with the power of leaders to produce social change. Feminism is a social movement that has social change as its goal—change that yields greater equality between women and men. Reaching this goal requires effective feminist leadership within all sectors of society. Gender equality cannot be achieved unless a commitment to equal opportunity spreads throughout society and influences all societal institutions. Because leaders have the potential not merely to influence others but to shape institutions and the society at large, they have the capability to foster gender equality as they carry out their roles.

Let us take the example of the president of a university, who is in a position to initiate policies that increase the representation of women and minorities on faculties and in decision-making roles throughout the university. University presidents can encourage practices that are supportive to women and minorities in academic fields in which they are traditionally underrepresented. They can initiate a parental leave policy where none existed and make sure that health plans include contraceptive coverage. In hundreds of ways, a university president can change the practices and the culture of a university to make it as welcoming to women as to men. Leadership thus opens up opportunities to act on feminist goals. Without the power inherent in such a role, it is far more difficult to bring about change. The presence of many women, especially feminist women, in leadership roles throughout societal institutions can greatly speed the pace of social change toward gender equality.

Women's occupancy of positions of leadership that entail substantial authority makes it very important to address the question of how feminist leaders should proceed. How can these individuals be effective yet true to their feminist values? The chapters of this book provide many thoughtful answers. Central to these answers is the belief that leadership style should be collaborative rather than top-down, command-and-control. This view is understandably popular with feminists, given that command-and-control leadership styles are prototypically masculine. Moreover, women were historically at the bottom of hierarchies, under the control of others. Feminist leaders do not want to reproduce oppressive hierarchies by exerting command-and-control leadership over subordinate groups. Therefore, democratic, weblike, collaborative relationships seem more attractive than autocratic, hierarchical relationships. Nevertheless, feminists need to keep in mind that some situations call for the clear-cut exercise of authority. Leaders who are inflexibly collaborative can be poorly prepared to exert directive, autocratic leadership when it is needed. In a crisis, for example the Hurricane Katrina disaster, the quick, decisive exercise of centralized authority could have saved lives but was tragically absent.

Because leadership has generic features, some of the recommendations about feminist leadership provided in the chapters of this book resemble the advice that emerges from what can be considered the mainstream leadership literature, which gives little explicit consideration to gender issues. For example, many leadership researchers would agree with the approval of transformational leadership that is found in some of the chapters of this book. Transformational leadership as well as the rewarding aspects of transactional leadership are likely to be effective in a wide range of settings (e.g., Avolio, 1999; Judge & Piccolo, 2004).

An emphasis on values also emerges from the chapters of these books. This theme has become very important in leadership researchers' recent discussions of authenticity in leadership. Authentic leaders "know who they are, what they believe and value, and . . . act upon those values and beliefs while transparently interacting with others" (Avolio, Gardner, Walumbwa, Luthans, & May, 2004, p. 803). Leadership theorists assume that this self-aware, value-oriented behavior ordinarily produces positive outcomes in followers' attitudes, behavior, and performance by acting through mediational processes that involve followers' trust, hope, and other positive emotions. Feminist leaders would do well to contemplate authenticity in leadership and to realize that achieving authenticity can be a more difficult matter for female than male leaders (Eagly, 2005). The challenges lie in gaining the legitimacy that allows a leader's values to be accepted by others. Moreover, feminist values are not necessarily widely endorsed throughout an organization, contributing to a feminist leader's potential difficulties in achieving authenticity.

To the extent that feminist analysts of leadership take the complexities of women's leadership into account, they are not merely rediscovering what makes leaders effective in general. Even though transformational and authentic leadership are advantageous for leaders of both sexes, leadership remains a different experience for women and men. When women enter male-dominated leader roles, they face expectations that have been shaped by these prior male occupants of the roles. Traditions are masculine, and women are at risk for seeming unqualified and having others resist their efforts to exert influence. This realization is threaded through the chapters of this book. Gaining leadership roles and performing effectively in them is challenging for women, especially in roles that have been dominated by men. Good research on these issues can help women understand these challenges and overcome them to become effective leaders. The chapters of this book are an important step along the route to this understanding.

References

Avolio, B. J. (1999). *Full leadership development: Building the vital forces in organizations*. Thousands Oaks, CA: Sage.

Avolio, B. J., Gardner, W. L., Walumbwa, F. O., Luthans, F., & May, D. R. (2004). Unlocking the mask: A look at the process by which authentic leaders impact follower attitudes and behavior. *The Leadership Quarterly*, *15*, 801–823.

Corrigan, M. E. (2002). *The American college president: 2002 ed*. Washington, DC: American Council on Education, Center for Policy Analysis.

Eagly, A. H. (2005). Achieving relational authenticity in leadership: Does gender matter? *Leadership Quarterly*, *16*, 459–474.

Judge, T. A., & Piccolo, R. F. (2004). Transformational and transactional leadership: A meta-analytic test of their relative validity. *Journal of Applied Psychology*, *89*, 901–910.

U.S. Bureau of Labor Statistics. (2006). *Household data: Annual averages, 2005 from the Current Population Survey*. Retrieved February 12, 2006 from http://www.bls.gov/cps/home.htm

U.S. National Center for Education Statistics. (2005). *Digest of education statistics, 2005*. Washington, DC: Author. Retrieved August 2, 2006 from http://165.224.221.98/programs/digest/d05/tables/dt05_083.asp

Overview: Women and Leadership: Transforming Visions and Diverse Voices

Jean Lau Chin

As the number of women increases in the workforce and in leadership roles, it is important to have the models to understand the intersection of gender and leadership. What is effective and successful leadership in women? Do the leadership styles of women differ from those of men? Although there is general agreement that women face more barriers to becoming leaders than men do, especially for leader roles that are male-dominated (Eagly & Johannesen-Schmidt, 2001), there is much less agreement about how women actually lead. Much of the existing leadership literature has been created by men and studied men in leadership roles.

Women's roles have evolved dramatically in the last 30-plus years with equal opportunity legislation, affirmative action principles, women's movement and feminist thought affecting both scientific and popular interest in women leaders. As the U.S. population becomes increasingly more diverse through rapidly changing demographics, individuals and organizations are attempting to address issues of diversity in a culturally competent manner. Women have embraced feminist principles of inclusion, gender equity, collaboration, and social justice. Feminists are concerned with how differential power and oppression contribute to the unequal status of women compared to men in all realms of work, family, and social environments.

This book challenges us to transform existing models of leadership to incorporate gender, and to draw on the diverse voices of women leaders to transform our visions of effective leadership styles. We look at how diverse women lead, how feminist principles contribute to leadership, and the barriers that women face as leaders.

Indvik (2004) points to the scarcity of women in higher levels of corporate leadership. While women make up 46.6% of the workforce in the US, they filled only 15.7% of corporate officer positions in 2002. She discusses the sex differences in worldview, socialization, and life experience that may result in different mental models or "implicit theories" of leadership among women. There is much to suggest that women lead differently from men, and feminist leadership styles are different and more collaborative despite significant overlap between the leadership styles of men and women. The intersection of identities across race, ethnicity, gender, class, and profession, that is, diverse women leaders, contribute additional dimensions that may influence differences in leadership styles.

The Process: A Presidential Initiative

As President of Division 35, the Society for the Psychology of Women of the American Psychological Association (APA) during 2002–3, my presidential initiative to study women and leadership, titled *Feminist Visions and Diverse Voices: Leadership and Collaboration*, began a yearlong web-based dialogue among feminist psychologist leaders to identify how women and feminist women lead. We sought to construct new models of feminist leadership considering the influence of gender and contexts on women in leadership roles.

Models of Feminist Leadership and Management Styles constituted Section I, with Bernice Lott as the leader. Its major challenge was to define, discuss, and dissect the central constructs of "feminist" and "leadership." Collaboration as a Feminist Process constituted Section II, with Joy Rice as the leader, focused on the process of leadership and the use of collaboration among feminist women as leaders within APA, nationally and internationally. Diverse Feminist Groups constituted Section III, with Janis Sanchez-Hucles as the leader. Issues for women in leadership roles were seen as more complex, with the intersection of identities associated with race, ethnicity, ability status, and sexual orientation.

Telecommunication technology was used as an innovative process to promote scholarship through 15 web-based discussion boards. We sought to enhance a feminist process of collaboration, to convene a scholarly dialogue, and to publish on women and leadership. Over 100 women psychologists were invited and agreed to participate in this initiative. Many were feminists; many were women psychologists holding different positions of leadership including management positions as a university president, provost, and department chair. Many were women leaders in American Psychological Association governance including APA president, Council of Representatives, division presidents, state leadership, chairs of APA committees and division executive committees. Many viewed their leadership roles as social change agents, policymakers, advocates, or community leaders.

A brief discussion introduced each web-based discussion board on some aspect of leadership, and was made public and available to all Division 35 members. The dialogue has been archived on the www.feministleadership.com website, with Marlene Maheu serving as e-editor. Since this venue was unfamiliar to many of the women, participation on the web-based forums needed to be nurtured. Several teleconferences helped to synthesize themes and to promote further dialogue on the web. Several face-to-face meetings were also convened to promote networking and collaboration made more difficult by a web-based format. We created emails with thought-provoking questions about leadership to direct participants to the website discussion boards. While this was facilitative, many also found responding to these questions too demanding as they attended to their routine of answering emails.

Context of the feminist leadership initiative

My presidential year began with the anniversary of the September 11, 2001 terrorist attack on the World Trade Center and ended with the SARS epidemic threatening the physical and psychological health of all. During that year of 2002–03, the rapid rise and fall of dot-com companies and the stock market resulted in a downturn of our economy that was unparalleled since the depression of 1929; many lost their fortunes and retirement savings.

These events created a sense of crisis among all of us; many experienced a threat to their personal safety and personal fortunes. We were all forced to re-examine how small our global environment really is, how interdependent and vulnerable we really are in the scheme of things. The events fueled a dialogue among the participants about the contexts of leadership and the leadership styles needed during times of crisis.

3

There was an initial rise in popularity ratings for President Bush with his aggressive and authoritarian leadership style as he declared war on Iraq. We also witnessed a rise in patriotism with support for his strong, visible, and decisive leadership. However, as the war continued, many in the US began to criticize President Bush's unilateral stance in declaring war without the support of the United Nations, viewed by some as an unwillingness to work as a team player. There was increased discontent with President Bush's authoritarian style of leadership, and whether it was indeed good or necessary during times of crisis. Many feminists questioned whether a more collaborative style of leadership consistent with feminist principles would have led to different outcomes.

While many of the feminist women participating in the initiative had played prominent roles as advocates for women's issues and social change, that is, "getting a seat at the table"; promoting a feminist agenda, that is, feminist policy; infusing feminist principles in service, training, and research; and managing organizations, institutions, and departments; few viewed themselves as leaders. Fewer had engaged in discussions of what constituted feminist leadership.

What is Feminist Leadership?

My presidential initiative raised many questions: What is feminist leadership? How do feminist women lead? Do women lead differently from men? Are there feminist principles that can contribute to effective leadership models? Are there differences in the leadership styles of men, women, and feminist women? Is there such a thing as good feminist leadership or is it just good leadership? Are there feminist models of leadership? What would be considered a feminist style of leadership? How do we know when feminist leadership is effective?

Given the paucity of literature on feminist leadership, it became apparent that we needed to capture the experiences of women and feminists as leaders in addition to empirical studies. We also needed to deconstruct existing theories and principles of feminism and leadership to understand effective leadership styles among women, and their intersection with feminist principles.

Several approaches characterize the literature on leadership. Some emphasize characteristics residing in a leader, for example, leadership traits, skills, or styles, while other approaches examine the contexts of leadership, for example, situations in which leadership is exercised, rewards and punishments of leadership. Still others emphasized the interpersonal process between leaders and who they lead, for example, power relationship between leader and follower, and leader as a servant of his or her followers (i.e., servant leader). These are important to review to identify how gender and leadership intersect, and how they are relevant to women in leadership roles.

Leadership Characteristics

"Great man" theories: trait approach

The trait approach identifies the personality characteristics of a leader. Early leadership studies focused on identifying those qualities that made for great leaders. These trait approaches suggest that individuals have special innate characteristics that make them leaders, for example, "He is born to be a leader" or "He is a natural leader" (Northouse, 2004), and concentrated on those traits that differentiated leaders from followers (Bass, 1990). These approaches typically identified great men leaders; some traits associated with great leaders have included intelligence, dominance, confidence, and masculinity (Lord, DeVader, & Alliger, 1986).

Charismatic leadership has been a trait frequently found and associated with great men leaders; consequently, effective leadership has been associated with "masculine traits," and characterized the leadership of men within male-dominated contexts. Because there have been few women leaders, this approach has been criticized for its inattention to gender and the leadership styles of great women. Gender biases would favor the leadership of men as more effective, and their masculine traits as more expectable indicators of good leadership.

Competencies of leadership: skills approach

The skills approach identifies the essential competencies of good and effective leadership, and focuses on the measurement and development of those competencies. Northouse (2004) defines three competencies of leadership: problem-solving skills, social judgment skills, and knowledge, while Bennis (1984) describes four competencies of leadership: management of attention (giving the message), management of meaning (developing the vision), management of trust (interpersonal connectedness), and management of self (knowledge of one's skills).

5

How do women and feminists manage these competencies? The recurring answer among the participants was that women tend to be more collaborative. This competency was further defined as having social judgment and interpersonal connectedness, skills commonly associated with feminist relational styles. The use of a collaborative process as a skill and competency of leadership lies in women "being" feminist, and using "the self " to promote an effective leadership style. The skill approach is promising for women because it suggests that leadership skills are competencies that can be acquired.

Leadership styles: process approach

The style approach focuses exclusively on what leaders do (behavior) and how they act (process), where style is understood as relatively stable patterns of behavior. Northouse (2004) defines leadership as a process whereby an individual influences a group of individuals to achieve a common goal, emphasizing process or a transactional event over the traits or characteristics residing in the leader. Leadership is composed of task behaviors that focus on goal accomplishment or relationship behaviors that help subordinates or followers feel comfortable with themselves, the situation, and each other.

Two styles of leadership have received considerable attention in the literature. Transformational leaders act as catalysts of change (Aviolo, 1994) and tend to be visionary (Tichy & Devanna, 1986), with a holistic picture of how the organization should look when meeting its stated goals, while transactional leaders are focused on getting things done, that is, they are task-oriented, act with directedness, and use rewards to achieve an organization's stated goals (Bennis, 1984; Sergiovanni, 1984).

Several studies (e.g., Bass & Avolio, 1994) found women to be more attentive than men to "the human side of enterprise" (McGregor, 1960), suggesting that female leaders tend to base judgments more on intuition and emotions than on rational calculation of the relationships between means and ends. Other studies identify women's management styles as more democratic and participatory than those typically adopted by men (Mertz & McNeely, 1997).

However, it is not that simple. A meta-analysis by Eagly and Johnson (1990) of research comparing the leadership styles of women and men found both the presence and absence of differences between the sexes. Female and male leaders did not differ in their use of an interpersonally oriented or task-oriented style in organizational studies (i.e., holding leadership roles). However, women were somewhat gender stereo-typic, using an interpersonal-oriented style in leadership studies using laboratory experiments and assessment studies. In general, women tended to adopt a more democratic or participative style and a less auto-cratic or directive style than did men on all types of studies.

A meta-analysis of transformational, transactional, and laissez-faire leadership styles among women (Eagly, Johannesen-Schmidt, & van Engen, 2003) found that female leaders were more transformational than male leaders and also engaged in more of the contingent reward behaviors that are a component of transactional leadership. Male leaders were generally more likely to manifest the other aspects of transactional leadership (active and passive management by exception) and laissez-faire leadership. Although these differences were small, the implications are encouraging because it identifies areas of strength in the leadership styles of women. A transformational style is also consistent with fem-inist principles of inclusion, collaboration, and social advocacy.

Contextual Leadership

While studies have documented differences in the management styles of women compared to men (e.g., Eagly & Johnson, 1990), the different findings suggest that situational contexts may well influence leadership styles. Margaret Madden urged us during the web dialogue to recog-nize that "leadership is contextual"; to understand feminist leadership, we need to examine the contexts in which they lead. Behavior occurs within a context and is influenced by the power relationships among the participants.

Gender role biases in appraisals and expectations of women leaders

Eagly and Karau (2002) suggest that perceived incongruity between the female gender role and leadership roles leads to two forms of prejudice: (a) perceiving women less favorably than men as potential occupants of leadership roles, and (b) evaluating behavior that fulfills the prescriptions of a leader role less favorably when it is enacted by a woman. One con-sequence is that attitudes are less positive toward female than male leaders. Other consequences are that it is more difficult for women to become leaders and to achieve success in leadership roles.

7

Eagly (1987) also found that women leaders were evaluated differently than men, and were expected to engage in activities and actions congruent with their culturally defined gender roles; leadership was typically not one of them because of stereotypes about women. Forsyth, Donelson, Heiney, and Wright (1997) found that group members favor men over women when selecting and evaluating leaders, even when actual leadership behaviors are held constant in a variety of group settings. They examined this role-incongruence hypothesis in small groups led by women who adopted a relationship- or task-oriented leadership style. Group members with liberal attitudes regarding women's roles responded positively to both leadership types. Group members with conservative attitudes felt the task-oriented leader was more effective, but they also rated her more negatively on measures of collegiality. These results suggest that individuals' reactions to women leaders are tempered by expectations about the role of women and men in contemporary society.

Masculinized contexts and feminist leadership

Theorists have suggested that leadership involves managing the benefits to the organization and realizing its purpose. Therefore, it is important to look at the organizational cultures, that is, the contexts in which leadership occurs. Often women leaders must manage within organizational cultures that tend to be masculinized, and believe that they must adapt their leadership style accordingly. Women leaders are often bound by these perceptions that constrain them to their gender roles and influence their leadership styles and behaviors. At the same time, these same behaviors may be defined as signs of ineffective leadership. Kolb and Williams (2000) argue for a fundamental change in organizational cultures, away from masculinized contexts toward creating gender-equitable work environments.

Karakowsky and Siegel (1999) found that the proportion of men and women in a work group, along with the gender orientation of the group's task, can significantly influence the kind of leadership behavior exhibited in group activity. Using feminist principles to deconstruct principles of leadership, Joyce Fletcher (2002, 2003) makes the distinction between feminist attributes and feminist goals. While organizations may have feminist attributes such as relational and collaborative processes, environments that ignore gender and power dynamics do not have feminist goals. She advocates trying to create more egalitarian environments, but suggests that organizations need to challenge the power structure and masculinized frameworks in which it operates to do so. Without that recognition, the rhetoric may sound feminist, but the goal is not there to make it feminist. Consequently, a feminist leadership model needs to have the achievement of feminist values as its goal.

Interpersonal Process of Leadership

Power, hierarchical structures, and feminist leadership

We need to examine the power structures inherent in leadership roles, and if a collaborative process is possible within hierarchical structures and masculinized contexts. While power appears inherent in the dominance of leader to follower, others have attempted to be more egalitarian by defining the relationship as that of a servant leader.

There is an old Chinese saying: "Women hold up half the sky" to suggest the amount of power that women carry. This power is both feared and revered; if we remember the Amazon women warriors who once ruled the earth, it was men's fear of them that may have led to their destruction. Indvik (2004) suggests that men's discomfort with women leaders takes many forms. Research has shown that women perceive a need to adapt their behavioral style so that men can avoid feeling intimidated (Ragins, Townsend, & Mattis, 1998), and that a narrower range of acceptable behavior exists for female leaders than for male leaders (Eagly, Makhijani, & Konsky, 1992).

Jacobs and McClelland (1994) found that two distinct styles of power-related themes distinguish successful men from successful women leaders. Successful male managers were more likely to use reactive power themes, while successful female managers were more likely to use resourceful power themes. Differences between the sexes in the power themes were less pronounced among those who remained in lower levels of management.

Collaborative process as feminist leadership

With advances in technology and communication, businesses and corporations increasingly engaged in an international and global economy, which resulted in an examination of the transferability of leadership and management practices across cultures. Western businesses observed high

9

levels of productivity in collective societies and diverse ethnic cultures, for example in Japan, and began an examination of these management practices and leadership styles with the goal of importing them to Western businesses and organizations. At the same time, non-Western businesses, in a race for a place in the international marketplace, sought to import and emulate Western business management practices. This resulted in identifying dimensions of team and collaborative leadership different from those observed in the US. More recently, non-Western businesses have shifted from merely adopting Western theories and practices to cherishing their unique social and cultural factors when applying Western theories of management (Kao, Sinha, & Wilpert, 1999).

Participants in the initiative also viewed a collaborative style and process as essential to a feminist leadership style. Feminist principles dictate that all will be involved in planning and decision making, and consensus building is valued. The feminist literature has shown that women tend to use nurturance to engage, communicate, and lead. The use of a collaborative process is viewed as leveling the playing field between leader and follower, and to create more egalitarian environments; these collaborative and egalitarian processes have been described as "shared leadership."

Collaborative leadership has emerged recently as essential to the skills and processes of the "modern" leader (Cook, 2002). Raelin (2003) introduces the Four Cs of "Leaderful Practice," and says that leadership in this century needs to be concurrent, collective, collaborative, and compassionate. While he recommends a process closely akin to a feminist process, he does not view gender as essential to the process nor does he introduce feminism as among its principles. Feminist women have noted that women emphasize planning and organizing work using an empathic approach, while placing less emphasis on the "need to win at all costs" compared to men ("Women May," 1997).

Rawlings (2000) suggests that current business trends of globalization, accelerated growth, and re-engineering require more cross-functional collaboration and integrated strategies across organizations. Senior and middle management teams are being asked to work together with more interdependence, with shared accountabilities outside their own functions, and with higher levels of trust and participation. This advent of the strategic leadership team does not fit neatly with traditional beliefs about the autocratic nature of teams and team building—these differences have been dichotomized as democratic versus autocratic styles.

Reflective leadership: strategic planning from the heart and soul

Looman (2003) suggests that to cope with current complex and volatile environmental and cultural trends, leaders must integrate their cognitive and emotional mental-processing systems and function from a metacognitive perspective. They must turn from a profitability-at-all-costs focus toward a focus on environments that encourage development of individual minds and problem solving through humanitarian collaboration and evolutionary progress. Looman identifies important changes in the environment that call for a more reflective style of leadership and suggests internal characteristics needed by leaders who can make careful long-range plans for the future that integrate human potential rather than splinter it.

Diversity in feminist leadership

Diverse feminist groups differ in their leadership styles, since the issues they face as leaders are influenced by and made more complex when considering race, ethnicity, ability status, and sexual orientation. For example, an African American woman may identify with the values of straightforwardness and assertiveness in her leadership style. An Asian American woman may identify more with values of respectfulness and unobtrusiveness. Others may perceive the African American woman to be intimidating and deem the Asian American woman passive.

Interpretation of the behaviors of diverse women leaders may vary depending on the different ethnic and contextual perspective from which it is viewed. Women leaders having multiple identities associated with race, culture, gender, disability, and sexual orientation face additional challenges to their leadership roles.

Women as Leaders

Some core questions are: What is the influence of perceptions about women on their leadership styles? What are effective leadership styles among women leading within masculinized contexts? Can women leaders gain respect and credibility if they lead with "feminist styles of leadership"? Clearly, expectations and perceptions drive how women

11

leaders behave. A look at some women leaders in the public eye is instructive. How did these women lead? How were they allowed to lead?

The First Lady is by definition a leader, but only because her husband is elected as President. Hillary Clinton, as First Lady, was characterized alternately by her unfeminist "stand by her man" stance in supporting her husband and by her "unfeminine" behavior perceived as opportunistic motives for the presidency. Few would question her brilliance. Her Health Care Reform proposal during her days as First Lady was one of the most comprehensive and complex ever proposed. However, it failed perhaps because the United States could not accept having its First Lady advocating for substantive policy reform; nor could it accept her use of her role to further her political aspirations. With the exception of Eleanor Roosevelt, most first ladies focused on more modest goals such as beautification projects.

Another prominent leader, Dr. Jocelyn Elders, was characterized by her controversial stands on health policy during her days as US Surgeon General.

> It didn't take long for Dr. Jocelyn Elders, the first black and second woman to hold the position of U.S. Surgeon General, to stir up controversy. In fact, this determined woman in the uniform of a three-star admiral did it less than a year into Bill Clinton's presidency, speaking out on drug legalization (she's for it) and abortion rights (she wants to keep coverage in the Clinton health plan). Elders has also been just as critical of the tobacco industry as her predecessor, a Reagan appointee, C. Everett Koop. (Motavalli, 1994)

Yet, Dr. Koop did not receive anything like the criticism Dr. Elders received for speaking out on similar issues.

Both Jocelyn Elders and Hillary Clinton were limited by the expectations of how women should behave. While they chose to define policy in their roles of leadership, and were outspoken, they violated the norm of silent, passive, and conforming women.

Andrea Jung, described as an Asian American Wonder Woman, is CEO of Avon Products. She has demonstrated, and has been accepted for, a leadership style that is both assertive and feminist. Perhaps it is because the business that she leads is viewed as "feminine" (i.e., context) or because she did not behave outside the expectations of the public (i.e., perceptions). In 2001, she was named by *Fortune* magazine for the fourth year as one of the 50 most powerful women in American business.

Jung (2002) found that businessmen had limited insight into women's abilities. Most men still considered women as fragile vessels whose self-confidence could be shattered with a well-delivered put-down and whose strength would be depleted after eight hours of high-powered deal making. Jung realized that men refused to recognize their own limitations, while women did that all too well. Jung thought that businesswomen needn't dwell in this world of delusion, and recognized that the corporate landscape is sculpted by male values. "Women don't support other women as well as they should," Jung says, and chose to remedy the situation by adopting strategies typically used by her male colleagues while refusing to accept the limitations placed upon her by virtue of her gender. "Some people just wait for someone to take them under their wing," Jung says. "I've always advised that they shouldn't wait. They should find someone's wings to grab onto" (Jung, 2002). As a woman leader, she was not afraid to seek out mentors and heed their advice.

Women leaders face a complexity of issues that include continuing perceptions and expectations that often limit their roles and behaviors. In the US Congress, House Democrats elected Nancy Pelosi of California as House minority leader in 2002; she was the first woman ever to head a party in either chamber of the legislature. Yet she was still described within a masculinized context. In a *Boston Globe* column, McGrory (2002) wrote, "He is called the Hammer. She's a velvet hammer. He is Tom DeLay, the newly elected House majority leader, who is all coercion and threat. She is Nancy Pelosi of California, who is all persuasion and smiles." This description of our House leaders reflects the gender bias and differential language we use describing women leaders in masculinized contexts. While the description points to the collaborative and interpersonal strengths of Nancy Pelosi, it also reflects the tendency to "feminize" women leaders in ways that suggest weakness or to suggest incredulity when women behave as decisive and effective leaders.

It suggests the need for us to move toward a context that celebrates women's strengths in a gender-equitable work environment. It also suggests the additional burdens, stressors, and challenges faced by women leaders. Diane Halpern, President of APA in 2002, sums it up with her statement on the feminist leadership website:

One example of what I mean by additional stressors for women leaders is the concern that I am not being "feminist" enough, especially when I don't see the benefit in finding consensus for all issues (e.g., when it means compromise to my values). I am free in this context (an on-line project on feminist leadership) to think about ways stress may vary for women and men leaders. But in other psychology-related areas, it seems as though talk about these possible differences is not compatible with being a feminist.

Stresses for feminist leaders

Many feminist leaders participating in the initiative felt that they were expected to behave in ways consistent with "feminine roles." Some felt marginalized if they behaved in ways associated with gender since they were then viewed as weak. Many felt there was a gender bias influencing expectations of how they should behave as women leaders, thereby creating no-win situations that became impediments to effective leadership.

Many women commented about how they are diminished when they demonstrate "feminine traits" in their leadership styles. They also felt constrained by how they should behave given the gender attributions placed on their behaviors. All too often, behaviors associated with femininity are rated as negative with respect to leadership. Tears signal weakness while nurturing leadership styles are viewed as lacking in substance. Conversely, women are also viewed negatively when they adopt styles and traits characteristic of men leaders. An aggressive and direct man is often viewed as forthright and taking charge as a leader while the same behavior in a woman is viewed as overbearing and angry.

The challenge women and feminist leaders grapple with is how to conform to what is "expected" while still retaining their credibility and effectiveness as leaders. Must they change themselves, that is, who they really are, to gain credibility as leaders? Can they use feminist principles and still be effective as leaders if they are functioning in masculinized contexts? What happens when men adopt these "feminist" styles? Is feminist leadership a construction associated with gender? We need to examine the attributions people make of "strong women leaders." Think of the images: "she's a bitch," "what a dragon lady," "she acts like a man," when women behave as strong leaders. What about attributions people make when women "act like women"? Think of the images: "she's maternal," "nurturing," or "persuasion and smiles." Is this intended to convey weakness and ineffectual leadership, that is, form over substance? The answer is empirical but there appears to be lingering bias against women because of an implicit comparison with men and masculinity as superior to women and feminism in leadership.

The Future of Feminist Leadership

Contextual leadership

The process of my presidential initiative on feminist leadership was an enriching one. It spurred us to deconstruct the principles of leadership from a feminist perspective, and to explore the issues about women and leadership as laid out in this book. It has promoted scholarship on feminist leadership, and inquiry about effective leadership styles using a feminist perspective. Currently, women in leadership roles typically lead within masculinized contexts, which are homogenous and do not incorporate the diversity of gender and ethnic differences. Power dynamics, gender role expectations, and added stressors in these masculinized environments are different for women leaders compared to men. This contextual leadership is evolutionary toward the goal of creating gender-equitable environments in which women and men can function as effective leaders. We hope that the dialogue in this book will be transforming in creating new models of leadership which consider the role of gender and differences faced by women as leaders.

Leadership as empowerment

For women leaders and feminist leaders, the objectives of leadership include empowering others through (a) one's stewardship of an organization's resources; (b) creating the vision; (c) social advocacy and change; (d) promoting feminist policy and a feminist agenda (e.g., family-oriented work environments, wage gap between men and women); and (e) changing organizational cultures to create gender-equitable environments. For many women, an effective leadership style is transformational. We see this book as a springboard for how feminist women and women leaders will define effective leadership in the 21st century.

Note

The author was formerly Systemwide Dean of the California School of Professional Psychology at Alliant International University during the preparation of this manuscript.

15

References

Aviolo, B. J. (1994). The alliance of total quality and the full range of leadership. In B. M. Bass & B. J. Aviolo (Eds.), *Improving organizational effectiveness through transformational leadership* (pp. 121–145). Thousand Oaks, CA: Sage.

Bass, B. M. (1990). *Bass & Stogdill's handbook of leadership: Theory, research, and managerial application* (3rd ed.). New York: The Free Press.

Bass, B. M., & Avolio, B. J. (1994). *Improving organizational effectiveness through transformational leadership.* Thousand Oaks, CA: Sage.

Bennis, W. (1984). Transformative power and leadership. In T. J. Sergiovanni & J. E. Corbally (Eds.), *Leadership and organizational culture* (pp. 64–71). Chicago: University of Illinois Press.

Cook, I. (2002). *Ya gotta get'em to wanna: 6 roles of the modern leader.* Washington, DC: Center Collection.

Eagly, A. (1987). *Sex differences in social behavior.* Hillsdale, NJ: Lawrence Erlbaum.

Eagly, A. H., & Johannesen-Schmidt, M. C. (2001). The leadership styles of women and men. *Journal of Social Issues, 57*(4), 781–797.

Eagly, A. H., Johannesen-Schmidt, M. C., & van Engen, M. L. (2003). Transformational, transactional, and laissez-faire leadership styles: A meta-analysis comparing women and men. *Psychological Bulletin, 129*(4), 569–591.

Eagly, A. H., & Johnson, B. T. (1990). Gender and leadership style: A meta-analysis. *Psychological Bulletin, 108*(2), 233–256.

Eagly, A. H., & Karau, S. J. (2002). Role congruity theory of prejudice toward female leaders. *Psychological Review, 109*(3), 573–598.

Eagly, A., Makhijani, M., & Konsky, B. (1992). Gender and the evaluation of leaders: A meta-analysis. *Psychological Bulletin, 117*, 125–145.

Fletcher, J. (2002). *The greatly exaggerated demise of heroic leadership: Gender, power, and the myth of the female advantage.* Retrieved 28 July, 2006 from http://www.ornl.org/adm/cfw/2005/pdf/insights13.pdf

Fletcher, J. (2003, August). *The different faces of feminist leadership.* Paper presented at the Annual Meeting of the American Psychological Association, Toronto, Canada.

Forsyth, Donelson R., Heiney, Michele M., & Wright, Sandra S. (1997). Biases in appraisals of women leaders. *Group Dynamics, 1*(1), 98–103.

Indvik, J. (2004). Women and leadership. In Northouse, P. G. (Ed.), *Leadership: Theory and practice* (pp. 265–299). Thousand Oaks, CA: Sage.

Jacobs, R. L., & McClelland, D. C. (1994). Moving up the corporate ladder. *Consulting Psychology Journal Practice and Research, 46*, 32–41.

Jung, A. (2002). *Asian American wonder women: Executive sweet.* Retrieved May 2003 from http://goldsea.com/WW/Jungandrea/jungandrea.html

Kao, H. S. R., Sinha, D., & Wilpert, B. (1999). *Management and cultural values: The indigenization of organizations in Asia.* Thousand Oaks, CA: Sage.

Karakowsky, L., & Siegel, J. P. (1999). The effects of proportional representation and gender orientation of the task on emergent leadership behavior in mixed-gender work groups. *Journal of Applied Psychology, 84*(4), 620–631.

Kolb, D., & Williams, J. (2000). *Shadow negotiation: How women can master the hidden agendas that determine bargaining success.* New York: Simon & Schuster.

Looman, M. D. (2003). Reflective leadership: Strategic planning from the heart and soul. *Consulting Psychology Journal: Practice & Research, 55*(4), 215–221.

Lord, R. G., DeVader, C. L., & Alliger, G. M. (1986). A meta-analysis of the relation between personality traits and leadership perceptions: An application of the validity generalization procedures. *Journal of Applied Psychology, 71*, 402–410.

McGregor, D. (1960). *The human side of enterprise.* New York: McGraw Hill.

McGrory, M. (2002, November 16). Pelosi's a salve for a wounded party. *Boston Globe*, A12.

Mertz, N. T., & McNeely, S. R. (1997, October). *Exploring the boundaries of gender and role in administrative decision-making.* Paper presented at the annual meeting of the University Council for Educational Administration, Orlando, FL. (ERIC Document Reproduction Service No. ED 412 656).

Motavalli, J. (1994). The voice of our Elders: The outspoken Surgeon General Jocelyn Elders is using her "bully pulpit" to take on the tobacco companies. *E: The Environmental Magazine, 4*, E948.

Northouse, P. G. (2004). *Leadership: Theory and practice.* Thousand Oaks, CA: Sage.

Raelin, J. (2003). *Creating leaderful organizations: How to bring out leadership in everyone.* San Francisco: Berrett-Koehler.

Ragins, B. Townsend, B., & Mattis, M. (1998). Gender gap in the executive suite: CEOs and female executives report on breaking the glass ceiling. *Academy of Management Executive, 12*(1), 28–42.

Rawlings, D. (2000). Collaborative leadership teams: Oxymoron or new paradigm? *Consulting Psychology Journal: Practice & Research, 52*(1), 36–48.

Sergiovanni, T. (1984). Cultural and competing perspectives in administrative theory and practice. In T. J. Sergiovanni & J. E. Corbally (Eds.), *Leadership and organizational culture* (pp. 1–12). Chicago: University of Illinois Press.

Tichy, N., & Devanna, M. A. (1986). *The transformational leader.* New York: Wiley & Sons.

Women may make better managers—study. (1997, April). *Management, 44*(3), 14.

Part I

Models of Leadership and Women: Reconciling the Discourses on Women, Feminism, and Leadership

Introduction

Bernice Lott

In this first section of a book on leadership by women, we are faced with the tasks and challenges of definition and clarification of concepts. My intent here is to introduce some of these conceptual challenges and to examine varying approaches to relevant central constructs. A major objective is to identify common themes as well as differences in discourses on leadership and feminism. I bring to this task my perspective as a feminist social psychologist.

The contributors to this section of the book, that is, the authors of the chapters that follow, as well as the participants in the electronic web discussions, were confronted with a number of "core questions" that I raised to provide a framework for discussion. These were the questions:

- How do we define feminist leadership?
- Are there diverse styles of feminist leadership? How might they be distinguished from one another? How are they similar?
- What special issues need to be considered in feminist leadership?
- How does feminist leadership reflect attention to issues of ethnicity, social class, disability, and sexual orientation? Since recognition of our intersected identities as members of diverse groups is primary in any feminist agenda, multicultural considerations are expected to be a central theme in discussions of feminist leadership.

Among other important questions are the following: How does feminist leadership differ from leadership provided by nonfeminist women? By nonfeminist men? In other words, is feminist leadership primarily related to the leader's gender or to a complex system of values? And once the major features of feminist leadership styles have been identified, we need to consider their probable outcomes. What consequences does feminist leadership have for leaders themselves, for the tasks undertaken, for members of their groups, and for the larger community?

Dominant Approaches to Leadership

The subject of leadership has been studied intensively in psychology as well as in a variety of other disciplines (e.g., business management, educational administration, political science, sociology). Although most contemporary leadership researchers and writers, across disciplines, have gone beyond earlier "great man" theories that stressed special qualities of style or character possessed by only certain individuals, an interest in individual qualities definitely continues. Hogan and Kaiser (2005) favor views of leadership "based on concrete personalities" (p. 170). Research seeking to identify characteristics or personality factors that are correlated with leadership (e.g., Judge, Bono, Ilies, & Gerhardt, 2002) illustrates a perspective focused on leader traits. Some contemporary researchers have been investigating the personal quality of charisma (cf. Greer, 2005), and suggest that "great leaders are a mix of personal charisma, the right situation and devoted followers" (p. 29). Findings from research on charisma as a potential personal attribute, necessary for leadership, suggest that it is constituted of such characteristics as emotional expressiveness, enthusiasm, eloquence, self-confidence, and responsiveness to others. This list is much like the one that Northouse identified from an examination of trait studies—intelligence, self-confidence, determination, integrity, and sociability (cf. Chrisler, Herr, & Murstein, 1998). That these attributes are gender-neutral is suggested by the work of Zichy (2001), who identified shared traits in a group of recognized women leaders that include: self-knowledge, intellectual energy, and sense of mission.

Another influential current perspective focuses not on the individual attributes of leaders but on different styles of leadership. Two styles that figure prominently in the literature are "transactional" and "transformational" (although sometimes called by other names, e.g., aggregative and integrative; Rosenthal, 1998). Kark, Shamir, and Chen (2003, p. 247) describe the transactional style as involving "an exchange of rewards for compliance." They describe the transformational style as motivating others to perform beyond their expectations by setting a personal example of high standards, providing support, and encouraging creativity. These researchers have found transformational leadership to have complex consequences for followers—both empowerment and dependence.

Other descriptions of transformational leadership include: "establishing oneself as a role model . . . ; gaining the trust and confidence of followers; . . . [and] mentoring and empowering their followers" (Eagly, Johannesen-Schmidt, & van Engen, 2003, p. 570). This kind of leadership is said to be similar to an egalitarian or democratic management style (Pines, Dahan-Kalev, & Ronen, 2001). Related, too, are leader behaviors that reflect a "procedural fairness" orientation, expressing respect and a positive social evaluation of group members, and encouraging group-oriented behavior (DeCremer & van Knippenberg, 2002). Raelin (2003) emphasizes similar behaviors: mutual or shared leadership that is concurrent, collective, collaborative, and compassionate. Various forms of transformational leadership have been found to be correlated with higher group effectiveness, that is, with individual productivity as well as greater satisfaction with the work environment (cf. Eagly et al., 2003).

Models of transformational leadership, while not new, are still regarded as distinct departures from earlier approaches. But Fletcher (2003) argues that, while they appear on the surface to incorporate some feminist thinking, they have been developed primarily by nonfeminist men, still present the leader in "heroic" terms, and are focused on individuals rather than groups. These models emphasize the importance of relational skills for effective leadership and management, borrowing from conceptions of what are considered "feminine" skills, that is, stereotypic views of women. Characteristics or behaviors associated with helping people to grow are attributed to women's presumed domestic concerns and experience.

The presumed valuing of so-called feminine-related skills has not led to much of a change in the gender of organizational leaders, supporting Fletcher's (2003) assertion that the rhetoric of transformational leadership is considerably ahead of the practice. Discrimination against women in top positions in industry continues. For example, as noted by McGeehan (2004), White men still dominate Wall Street and "fill the bulk of the most powerful and highest paying jobs." Men are two-thirds of all security industry managers and White men are 80% of those in executive positions. Women are underrepresented in educational leadership as well (Gupton & Slick, 1996), holding only 16% of the CEO positions in colleges and universities, fewer than 5% of all public school superintendent positions, and 20% of all principal jobs in the country (Alston, 2000). In union leadership, only 3 of 35 AFL-CIO Council representatives were women in the 1990s and they are "under-represented as stewards, an influential position that is a traditional pathway to higher office"; minority women are marginalized to an even greater extent (Melcher, Eichstedt, Eriksen, & Clawson, 1992, p. 278).

Attributes of "Feminine" Leadership

Women in Western culture (particularly those who are White and middle class) have been and still are expected to manifest certain qualities in their thinking and action. These are communal qualities, assumed to be hallmarks of femininity, and include friendliness, kindness, and unselfishness. These are distinguished from the agentic qualities assigned to "masculinity" and men, such as assertiveness and instrumental competence (Eagly et al., 2003). Stereotypical beliefs remain strong so that, when working as leaders or managers, women (and men) are expected to behave as our culture defines them on the basis of their gender alone. Thus it is anticipated that a woman leader will be more "relationship centered, nurturing, and sensitive" than a man (Martin, 1993, p. 275).

These beliefs, however, do not match the actual behavior of women and men across situations and contexts. There is predictable variability in within-gender behavior that is related to such factors as age, ethnicity, occupation, income, job status, education, personal experiences, situational demands, and anticipated consequences (Lott, 1990, 1994). I have argued elsewhere that an ideology of gender differences is more a reflection of a political and social status quo than it is of empirical validity (Lott, 1997).

The subject of sex differences in leadership has been well studied. A meta-analysis of 26 such investigations that were reported in the psychological literature in the 1990s (Van Engen & Willemsen, 2004) found only a small difference overall, that was dependent upon context. A more extensive meta-analysis (Eagly, Karau, & Makhijani, 1995) examined 76 studies in which women and men managers, supervisors, officers, department heads, and coaches were compared. This analysis found no significant overall gender difference in judged leader effectiveness. But there was evidence that leadership by women and men was considered more effective when they functioned as leaders in situations thought to be most congenial to the cultural expectations for their gender, as perceived by a sample of college undergraduates. While it is to be expected, as Eagly et al. (1995) suggest, that "gender role expectations spill over onto leadership roles . . . and produce important consequences" (p. 140), these consequences are not simple or easy to predict. LaFrance (2001) argues that there are contradictory expectations for women leaders. On the one hand, they are expected to be "socioemotional" but, as leaders, they are required to be "task-focused" (p. 254). They can do both, LaFrance suggests, by adopting a nonhierarchical and democratic style.

Fletcher (2003) cautions that a leadership style conforming to expectations for women "isn't really good for women." Such behavior will not gain the same recognition as it does for men, since it is considered "natural" for women. Albino (1999, p. 28) notes that the "leadership styles usually associated with women . . . are . . . often employed by effective leaders of either gender." But it is still the gender of the leader that matters to perceivers who filter judgments through the lens of cultural expectations. Applause for the same sensitive and collaborative leadership is more likely to go to a man than a woman. And Kram and Hampton (1998) have discussed the greater scrutiny experienced by women leaders, with small errors more likely to be noticed and criticized.

Feminism: Values and Practice

It is noteworthy that mainstream books on leadership do not include discussions of feminist leadership, even when focused on women. For example, neither Brown and Beverly (1998), in a volume entitled *Women and Leadership*, nor Rosenthal (1998), in one entitled *When Women Lead*, index "feminism." On the other hand, they do index "feminine" and "femininity." Chemers' (1997) book on leadership offers a next-to-last chapter devoted to women. It is only here that gender roles are discussed (as though this is irrelevant to understanding leadership behavior by men).

A leadership style that conforms to the way women are expected to behave, whether attributed to nature, socialization, or gender role, is not the same as a style that is *feminist*. The distinction between "feminine" and "feminist" is a crucially significant one—in both theory and practice.

Situating women's behavior in femininity and gender fails to make salient women's lesser power compared to men, and fails to acknowledge the fact of heterogeneity.

Before turning to the question of feminist leadership, we need to examine what we mean by the concepts of feminist and feminism. Whereas "feminine" is defined by behaviors presumed to characterize women, "feminist" is defined by a set of assumptions and values, and attention to empirically validated historical and contemporary circumstances and power inequities. Farganis (1994) suggests that among feminist theories, despite differences, there are central points of agreement. These are the recognition of gender's central role in people's lives as they interact with one another in both public and private situations, and recognition of "the ways in which women have been thought about, talked about, written about, and ignored" (p. 8). I have elsewhere described the feminist perspective as follows:

> Fundamental to feminism is the value that all persons should be permitted equality of opportunity for full development to the extent that this development does not impede that of others. Since ample historical and contemporary evidence shows that women as a group have experienced significantly fewer opportunities and greater restrictions than men, feminists—who may be either women or men—pay particular attention to women's experiences and circumstances. (Lott, 1994, p. 6)

A feminist analysis of gender inequity and its consequences also proposes remedies, and recognizes that these remedies will reflect the reality of intersections among gender, ethnicity, social class, and sexual orientation (as well as other relevant social categories). Actively working to effect constructive solutions and social change is central to feminism. Feminists recognize and respect multiple communities and diverse circumstances and understand the importance of situational context. Increasingly emphasized is the inclusiveness of feminism in its recognition that "there are multiple differences among men and women based on power relations attendant to race, ethnicity, class, and sexual orientation" (Hallstein, 1999, p. 36), as well as power differentials associated with such categories as age and disability.

Feminist theory seeks to connect knowledge and politics (Farganis, 1994) and, in so doing, connects both to action and to interventions for social change directed against oppression. Central to feminism is recognition of the role of power in affecting people's lives. Power may be understood in terms of access to social and material resources. Thus Martin (1993, p. 276) notes that feminism is primarily a "political orientation." It is aimed at ending the power inequities between women and men, with the social category of woman understood as not unitary—but situated in ethnic, social class, age, and other significant contexts. Thus feminism is concerned with fostering change—political, social, and economic—in the interest of justice and maximizing opportunities for personal growth and well-being. With this as the fundamental objective, feminist practice uses a variety of strategies and tactics to achieve it.

How do feminists work to reach our objectives? Martin (1993) and others suggest that feminist practice illustrates the valuing of mutuality, inclusion, co-operation, nurturance, empowerment, participation, and the devaluing of status differences, competition, and separation. But while community and caring are valued, so also are agency and autonomy (Hallstein, 1999). Knowledge and skills are needed to confidently and competently interact with others in order to achieve acceptable and desired outcomes.

Feminist Leadership

How can managers or leaders translate such values into a "style" of feminist leadership? Fletcher (2003) makes the point that when a feminist manager contributes to the growth of group members, fosters their interactions and connections, this must not be done invisibly, as is expected to be the feminine way, but clearly and openly.

Feminist leadership in community organizations has been described as encouraging the voices of those who are vulnerable and promoting skills needed to effectively question authority and end social injustice. Bond, Belenky, and Weinstock (2000, p. 699), for example, write about "creating an inclusive setting in which all members . . . are heard and engage in growth and development . . . working collaboratively, with reciprocity and mutuality." Empowerment is said to be a primary focus of feminist leadership and group process, with empowerment defined as "those who have been oppressed" learning "to know their strength and recognize themselves as experts about their own lives" (Reinelt, 1994, p. 688).

In other contexts, such as leadership of educational institutions (e.g., Albino, 1999), empowerment is also presented as a key descriptor of feminist leadership in addition to encouraging broad participation, shared decision making, and an appreciation of diverse work styles. Madden (2005) echoes these sentiments. She proposes that effectiveness in higher education administration can reflect the feminist principles articulated by Worell and Johnson (1997) by attending to the sociocultural context and power dynamics within the organization, valuing collaboration, and recognizing that people are active agents. Empowerment was explored in an in-depth interview study of six women leaders (Muller, 1994) who described it in terms of building relationships, valuing others, and sharing decision making and power.

A feminist management or leadership style, according to Martin (1993), encourages competition not between individuals but between work units, promotes open discussion and democratic participation, shares resources, and helps subordinates grow and do their best by empowering, not exploiting, them. A few key descriptors of feminist leadership emerged with great frequency from the electronic messages posted on our feminist leadership website. These were variants of the descriptors proposed by Chin (2003): collaborative, nurturing, empowering, and consensus building. Others suggested visionary, inclusive, addressing difficult issues, encouraging and honoring the contributions of others, valuing growth and development, and being supportive of others' strengths.

I would urge that we move considerably beyond such descriptors. If we are to translate feminist values into the practice of leadership, more is required than positive, collaborative ways of interacting with others. We must insist that feminist leaders also "make waves"—in whatever organization they are situated. A feminist leader must advocate for policies that support child care and family obligations, adequate access to health care, pensions, and other employee-friendly benefits. Such advocacy will certainly be met with arguments about the availability of resources, typically described as "scarce" when perceived as challenging to the status quo. But resources can be reallocated and distributed in accord with feminist values as well as pragmatically geared to improving the environment, satisfaction, and outcomes of work.

Madden (2005) points out that "there will always be institutional inertia, external pressure, and financial constraints" (p. 12) pitted against thrusts for change. But feminist leaders must incorporate into their work attention to the special issues of women and of people who are among the least privileged and typically invisible: ethnic minorities of color, poor and working class, and nonheterosexual. And, when challenging status quo hierarchies and patriarchal structures, feminist leaders must be prepared with relevant knowledge about the consequences of power inequities, and about the effectiveness of strategies for change.

Feminist Leadership: Hope or Possibility?

Difficult issues are confronted when we consider the broad question of whether it is possible for leadership in our current mainstream culture to be practiced in a way that would permit its characterization as feminist. It certainly does not follow, as Chin (2003, p. 2) has observed, that when "women get a seat at the table," feminist principles will "be used to promote a feminist agenda." One issue is consideration of the ends or goals of leadership—that is, in a particular situation, leadership "for what"? In examining feminist leadership, we may focus on the "how" while neglecting the more important question of what the leadership is intended to accomplish.

A study of state legislative leaders (Little, Dunn, & Deen, 2001), for example, reported differences in the legislative agendas of women and men. The former more often reported a concern with family issues, health care and social services. But the presence of women representatives on state legislatures may not influence policy adoption. Tolbert and Steuernagel (2001) found no relationship between the adoption of nine health policies across the 50 states and the presence of a women's caucus, women chairs of committees on health care, and the increase in women's elections to state legislatures. Similarly, a study of upper echelon women in positions of influence within the U.S. Departments of Defense and State (McGlen & Sarkees, 1993) found that gender played no significant role in the vast majority of views on foreign policy issues. Most important was political ideology and organization (State or Defense). The authors concluded that their data "give little evidence that the women already on the inside have a distinctly 'women's perspective' on . . . the major international issues of the day" (p. 302). With respect to style of leadership, the women were as likely as men to be goal-directed, while showing greater concern for the people working for them.

Important in understanding the practice of feminist leadership is the context in which it is taking place: What are the situational demands, constraints, and circumstances; what are the characteristics of the social environment? Feminist leadership may be far more difficult in some environments than in others. For example, Albino (1999), speaking as a leader of an institution of higher education, notes that the most

29

important task in such a position is to protect institutional resources and use them wisely. Would a feminist analysis of the wise use of resources conflict sharply with more status quo assessments? Albino also talks about the need, in certain circumstances, to abandon consensus-building strategies for more directive action. On university campuses, Halpern (in a web-based discussion board, May 16, 2003) notes, groups are frequently in competition for money, space, and tenure lines. Here, leaders intent on "peaceful coexistence" may be "perceived as weak and 'selling out'." Some caution that there are circumstances under which feminist attitudes will give way to the demands of the structural context, which may, as Pines et al. (2001) note, be more important in influencing the behavior of managers.

Always a major consideration is whether and how the leadership confronts issues of power. How can feminist leaders work within and/or challenge the "well-entrenched hierarchies" that characterize bureaucratic organizations (Reinelt, 1994, p. 686)? In a hierarchical structure, it is highly unlikely that there will be much, if any, encouragement for decisions to be made collaboratively or for empowerment to be an objective. Can leaders or managers retain their positions in typical bureaucratic organizations characterized by power inequities while at the same time adhering to a feminist ethic that requires collaboration? When the organization has clearly delineated differentials in power, is there any possible role for a feminist leader (Chin, 2003)? How can feminist leaders practice activism within organizations and advance the "ultimate goal of undoing the oppression of all marginalized peoples" (Steiner, 1997)? Such questions are grappled with in the first section of this book, and reappear throughout the book.

Finally, is the leadership directed at change in the direction of social justice? I would argue that, for leadership to be feminist, the values of feminism must be clearly demonstrated in objectives, practice, and anticipated outcomes. Feminist leaders are likely to face serious ethical dilemmas in carrying out the business of the organization or group where they are employed or voluntarily functioning. Martin (1993) is optimistic in her assessment of change in corporation management. Feminists, she suggests, can challenge and persuade corporations to "include women —and members of other excluded groups—in ways that give them dignity, treat them fairly, and improve their status and opportunities [thereby enhancing] the experience of paid work and family life for majority men as well" (p. 288). This strategy, she argues, is good for corporations because a responsive workplace will increase profits. But is the goal of increasing corporate profits compatible with the feminist value of social justice and equitable access to social resources?

Overview of Chapters in this Part

The chapters that follow tackle some of these difficult questions in a variety of ways. They contain references to relevant research and theory and offer provocative analyses and tentative conclusions. They also set the stage for the chapters in the rest of the book.

After reviewing the prevalent theories of leadership in the mainstream literature, Karen Suyemoto and Mary Ballou propose a bold new conceptualization of feminist leadership. They address issues of race, class, and gender, and note the need for feminist leadership to be directed toward valuing equitable distributions of power and basic human rights. Two case studies of leadership as "coacted harmony" are presented to illustrate their model—one that reduces distinctions between leaders and followers and requires involvement of all in collaboration and continued renegotiation of goals, needs, and skills.

In the chapter by Ann Yabusaki, the participants in her web discussion group speak for themselves as they share ideas about diverse communication styles. A major theme in the discussion was the importance of context in providing added meaning to language. Some spoke of the risks of speaking "truth" as they see it, as well as the dangers of silence. Feminist communication styles are discussed in relation to context, womanism, relationships, power structures, and postcolonialism.

Two feminist leaders present examples from their own experiences: Toy Caldwell-Colbert and Judith Albino, African American and European American respectively, have held important positions in higher administration within colleges and universities. They share views about their objectives in such positions and the challenges and opportunities they have faced. Each presents a personal perspective and then both examine their similarities and differences. They address issues of feminist values, leadership tasks, diversity, and effectiveness within the special context of institutions of higher education. They end with a definition of feminist leadership derived from the intersection of their own experiences with theory and practice.

Ester Shapiro and Jennifer Leigh tackle the complex issues associated with assessing the outcomes of feminist leadership. They review models of evaluation most relevant to assessing culturally competent feminist leadership and then offer their own. They propose an interdisciplinary approach and present a set of guiding principles for generating goals and evaluating desired outcomes. They urge a process that includes determining benchmarks for goal achievement and collaborative feedback on progress toward those goals.

Specifically focused on the corporate world, Karen Korabik and Roya Ayman present a model of leadership that puts gender at the forefront. They explore gender as role, status, cue, and in interaction with situations, and they end their chapter with a discussion of practical implications for corporate women leaders.

Getting Started

Fletcher's (2003) outline of a real feminist leadership paradigm includes challenging the myth of individual achievement and gendered displays of competence and also challenging the power structure. It may well be, however, that we need to regard feminist ethics as aspirational (Steiner, 1997). At the present moment, feminist leadership, with some exceptions, may be more hope than possibility. This makes the explorations in this book even more important and urgent. We talk here of goals and objectives and provide examples of how to achieve them. These goals, not yet fully realized, are hopefully attainable.

References

Albino, J. E. N. (1999). Leading and following in higher education. *The Psychologist-Manager Journal, 3,* 27–40.

Alston, J. A. (2000). Missing from action: Where are the Black female school superintendents? *Urban Education, 35,* 525–531.

Bond, L. A., Belenky, M. F., & Weinstock, J. S. (2000). The Listening Partners program: An initiative toward feminist community psychology in action. *American Journal of Community Psychology, 28,* 697–730.

Brown, G., & Beverly, I. (Eds.) (1998). *Women and leadership: Creating balance in life.* Commack, NY: Nova Science.

Chemers, M. M. (1997). *An integrative theory of leadership.* Mahwah, NJ: Lawrence Erlbaum.

Chin, J. L. (2003, August). *Feminist leadership, feminist visions and diverse voices.* Paper presented at the conference of the American Psychological Association, Toronto, Canada.

Chrisler, J. C., Herr, L., & Murstein, N. K. (1998). Women as faculty leaders. In L. H. Collins, J. C. Chrisler, & K. Quina (Eds.), *Career strategies for women in academe: Arming Athena* (pp. 189–214). Thousand Oaks, CA: Sage.

DeCremer, D., & Van Knippenberg, D. (2002). How do leaders promote cooperation? The effects of charisma and procedural fairness. *Journal of Applied Psychology, 87*, 858–866.

Eagly, A. H., Johannesen-Schmidt, M. C., & van Engen, M. L. (2003). Transformational, transactional, and laissez-faire leadership styles: A meta-analysis comparing women and men. *Psychological Bulletin, 129*, 569–591.

Eagly, A. H., Karau, S. J., & Makhijani, M. G. (1995). Gender and the effectiveness of leaders: A meta-analysis. *Psychological Bulletin, 117*, 125–145.

Farganis, S. (1994). *Situating feminism: From thought to action (Contemporary social theory, vol. 2).* Thousand Oaks, CA: Sage.

Fletcher, J. K. (2003, August). *The different faces of feminist leadership.* Paper presented at the American Psychological Association convention, Toronto.

Greer, M. (2005, January). The science of savoir faire. *Monitor on Psychology, 36*, 28–30.

Gupton, S. L., & Slick, G. A. (1996). *Highly successful women administrators: The inside stories of how they got there.* Thousand Oaks, CA: Corwin Press.

Hallstein, D. L. O. (1999). A postmodern caring: Feminist standpoint theories, revisioned caring, and communication ethics. *Western Journal of Communication, 63*, 32–56.

Judge, T. A., Bono, J. E., Ilies, R., & Gerhardt, M. W. (2002). Personality and leadership: A qualitative and quantitative review. *Journal of Applied Psychology, 87*, 765–780.

Hogan, R., & Kaiser, R. B. (2005). What we know about leadership. *Review of General Psychology, 9*, 169–180.

Kark, R., Shamir, B., & Chen, G. (2003). The two faces of transformational leadership: Empowerment and dependency. *Journal of Applied Psychology, 88*, 246–255.

Kram, K. E., & Hampton, M. M. (1998). When women lead: The visibility–vulnerability spiral. In E. B. Klein, F. G. Gabelnick, & P. Herr (Eds.), *The psychodynamics of leadership* (pp. 193–218). Madison, CT: Psychological Press.

LaFrance, M. (2001). Gender and social interaction. In R. K. Unger (Ed.), *Handbook of the psychology of women and gender* (pp. 245–255). New York: Wiley.

Little, T. H., Dunn, D., & Deen, R. E. (2001). A view from the top: Gender differences in legislative priorities among state legislative leaders. *Women & Politics, 22*, 29–50.

Lott, B. (1990). Dual natures or learned behavior: The challenge to feminist psychology. In R. T. Hare-Mustin, & J. Maracek (Eds.), *Making a difference: Psychology and the construction of gender* (pp. 65–101). New Haven, CT: Yale University Press.

Lott, B. (1994). *Women's lives: Themes and variations in gender learning* (2nd ed.). Pacific Grove, CA: Brooks/Cole.

Lott, B. (1997). The personal and social correlate of a gender difference ideology. *Journal of Social Issues, 53*, 279–298.

Madden, M. (2005). 2004 Division 35 presidential address: Gender and leadership in higher education. *Psychology of Women Quarterly, 29*, 3–14.

Martin, P. Y. (1993). Feminist practice in organizations: Implications for management. In E. A. Fagenson (Ed.), *Women in management* (pp. 274–296). Newbury Park, NJ: Sage.

McGeehan, P. (2004, July 14). *Discrimination on Wall St.? The numbers tell the story.* Retrieved July 15, 2004 from www.nytimes.com/2004/07/14/business/14place.html

McGlen, N. E., & Sarkees, M. R. (1993). *Women in foreign policy: The insiders.* New York: Routledge.

Melcher, D., Eichstedt, J. L., Eriksen, S., & Clawson, D. (1992). Women's participation in local union leadership: The Massachusetts experience. *Industrial and Labor Relations Review, 45*, 267–280.

Muller, L. E. (1994). Toward an understanding of empowerment: A study of six women leaders. *Journal of Humanistic Education and Development, 33*, 75–82.

Pines, A. M., Dahan-Kolev, H., & Ronen, S. (2001). The influence of feminist self-definition on the democratic attitudes of managers. *Social Behavior & Personality, 29*, 607–616.

Raelin, J. A. (2003). *Creating leaderful organizations: How to bring out leadership in everyone.* San Francisco: Berrett-Koehler.

Reinelt, C. (1994). Fostering empowerment: The challenge for state-funded feminist organizations. *Human Relations, 47*, 685–705.

Rosenthal, C. S. (1998). *When women lead: Integrative leadership in state legislatures.* New York: Oxford University Press.

Steiner, L. (1997). A feminist schema for analysis of ethical dilemmas. In F. L. Casmir (Ed.), *Ethics in intercultural and international communication* (pp. 59–88). Mahwah, NJ: Lawrence Erlbaum.

Tolbert, C. J., & Steuernagel, G. A. (2001). Women lawmakers, state mandates, and women's health. *Women & Politics, 22*, 1–39.

Van Engen, M. L., & Willemsen, T. M. (2004). Sex and leadership style: A meta-analysis of research published in the 1990s. *Psychological Reports, 94*, 3–18.

Worell, J., & Johnson, N. G. (1997). *Shaping the future of feminist psychology: Education, research, and practice.* Washington, DC: American Psychological Association.

Zichy, S. (2001). *Women and the leadership Q: The breakthrough system for achieving power and influence.* New York: McGraw-Hill.

Chapter 1

Conducted Monotones to Coacted Harmonies: A Feminist (Re)conceptualization of Leadership Addressing Race, Class, and Gender

Karen L. Suyemoto and Mary B. Ballou[1]

Leadership and related phenomena—such as power, authority and influence—have been the subject of much theorizing, research, and certainly practice. While numerous models of leadership exist, reflecting different disciplines and real world interests, most reveal a somewhat monotone developmental process strongly characterized by a hierarchical model. Our challenge is to listen for the different tones and meld diverse melodies into complicated co-operative harmonies by attending to the ways, views, and qualities of those with varied cultures, histories, social class experiences, ethnicities and races, sexual orientations, and sexes and genders. In this chapter, we focus on the voices of diverse women discussing their own leadership experiences and propose a conceptualization of leadership as an integrative harmony with a feminist foundation.

In accordance with feminist principles of attending to the lived experiences of women, we sought women's experiences as the foundation of our understanding of the meaning of leadership. We are basing our chapter on the discussions we had as part of the Feminist Leadership

Initiative (August 2002 through August 2003). During that time, we facilitated the web discussion on models of diverse feminist leadership which resulted in 11 threads of conversation and 38 responses from a total of 28 people. We also convened two in-person discussions with seven additional discussants. We listened carefully to the voiced experiences. In framing the conversations and in our approach to "analysis," we conceptualized through the lens of feminist principles as articulated by Ballou and Gabalac (1985), Brown and Brodsky (1992), Comas-Díaz (1991), Hill and Ballou (1998), Rave and Larsen (1995), and Worell and Remer (1992) among others. We came to these discussions of feminist leadership with the belief that we were not the experts but rather the reporters and the catalyzers of discussion. We recognize that our own perspectives inevitably shaped these conversations,[2] although we frequently found that the most active discussion topics were those raised by participants themselves or developed in response to particular points made in other "threads" of discussion. Our own perspectives inevitably shaped our "analysis" of these discussions. The themes described here emerged not only from the content of the conversations, but also from our own frameworks and interests and from the dialectical process we developed together. Although we recognize the inevitable impact of our perspectives, we try here to follow the voices of these diverse women, to value their experience as expressed directly in their own voices with their complex interacting experience of oppression and privilege. As in feminist therapy, we see that we hold the power to name, but try to do this largely through recalling others' experiences and encouraging their exploration of it. We aim to build notions of feminist leadership that transform a directed monotone to a coacted complex harmony reflecting women's own self-expressed experiences.

"Liberal" Feminist Leadership: Fitting Harmonies to Dominant Melodies

One group of themes in our conversations addressed leadership experiences in the context of leading within patriarchal structures and coping with patriarchal approaches and measures of success. For decades, there was no alternative structure available and, even now, many women may not have the access or privilege to seek out alternative structures within which to work. We heard repeatedly the belief that, in order to succeed as a leader, women must "play the game," fit in with the goals and methods set by men, and assimilate to the demands of the situation. We heard that women leaders must learn how to "handle" themselves in a male world and meet even higher standards as leaders. And we heard discussion of double standards and beliefs about women's lack of competence. It was clear that women leaders faced multiple challenges and barriers in "moving up" within a male-dominated world. It was also clear that women who considered themselves feminist leaders worked to resist oppression, emphasizing liberal feminist values of fairness, equality, collaboration, and opportunity for all voices to be heard.

New Harmonies Emerging: Considering Diverse Experiences

However, when *theorizing* feminist leadership, we have the freedom to step away from some of the challenges inherent in attempting to enact it within patriarchal structures and consider what might be possible within other structures. A reactive feminist leadership leaves the meaning of success or achievement and the basic concept of leadership unquestioned; feminist values are incorporated into patriarchal structures and contexts. Furthermore, the kinds of experiences attended to are primarily those of more privileged women who can prioritize gender discrimination over other systemic oppressions and have greater choices in both their private and public contexts. Thus a reactive resistance to gender inequality in conceptualizing leadership strongly emphasizes unity in gender and de-emphasizes differences among women related to other systems of oppression. In creating feminist leadership that embraces the diversity of women, we must resist overemphasizing the ways in which we are similarly oppressed (i.e., gender) and underemphasizing the ways in which we may simultaneously be differently privileged (e.g., race, ethnicity, nationality, social class, sexual orientation, ability, etc.). Thus a truly transformational approach to theorizing feminist leadership allows us to question the basic definitions of who is a leader and how leadership is enacted.

While we deeply appreciated the conversational threads that validated styles reflecting liberal feminist values and the ways in which they empowered women to achieve, what most excited us in the conversations were those voices that seemed to break new ground, questioning basic concepts either directly or obliquely, making cultural connections and acting as our stepping stones to new conceptualizations.

Not just gender

> I think it [feminist leadership] should also be inclusive in considering ethnocultural differences in defining feminism so that we don't create a definition of feminist leadership which devalues different understandings of feminism. (Usha Tummala-Narra)

> It is interesting to think about what makes us label certain leadership practices "feminine" and/or "feminist." . . . definitions of feminine differ by culture, yet when we discuss these things we often end up sounding like we all agree on what feminine . . . or feminist . . . principles are. It raises all kinds of questions in trying to describe a type of leadership that is different from the White, Western, Heterosexual, Male model we often accept as the norm . . . (Joyce K. Fletcher)

Such comments point to our need to explore how race, culture, class, and other social systemic differences interact with gender to affect the experience and meaning of feminist leadership. We must attend to the wide range of experiences we have as feminist leaders, the multiple phenomena that affect these experiences, and how these experiences influence leaders' understandings as well as the responses of others.

Women who experience multiple systemic oppressions create meanings and make choices that more privileged women may not need to make. If feminist leadership is defined as primarily prioritizing the advancement of women and the dismantling of gender inequality, then we run the risk of dismissing the complicated intersections of oppressions:

> It is important to note that class has been an integral part of the African American women's club movement. The place where there was more equal opportunity was in the women's organizations within the Black church—especially those churches that attracted a cross-section of the community in terms of social class and education. . . . The complication— are African American women first Black then woman or first woman then Black? This has been a very real issue. I was raised to be a race woman—so my identity is Black first, then woman, without much of a gap!!! Loyalty to the race, i.e., generally defined as Black men in a dominant role, has made it difficult to challenge Black male leadership in some instances. But there are race women as servant leaders who are concerned about the race—now defined as both female and male. These neo-race women will identify patriarchy when that is the issue. Too many Black men continue to be vulnerable in the society. The challenge for Black women as leaders is to balance interests and justice across gender lines. (Jessica Henderson Daniel)

If we do not attend to our differences, we risk excluding those with different cultural meanings and expectations. In one group discussion, Chieh Li explored the meaning of egalitarianism and equal opportunity. She noted that egalitarianism itself may be culturally situated. She described issues of leadership within a Chinese group, with a value on hierarchical authority and deference rather than egalitarianism and democracy. She raised important questions about who had the power to define feminism and leadership. If we define feminist leadership as emphasizing egalitarianism, does this exclude cultures or contexts where the "followers" seem to desire seemingly hierarchical patterns of authority?

Women who experience multiple oppressions are also viewed differently by others. Helen D. Pratt commented: "I do think it is harder for women of color—not because we do not get support but because we are under more scrutiny (my view). Because I am so visible, any absence is always noticed!" As a woman of color, Pratt's leadership experience is different from that of White women not only because of what she brings to the experience, but also because of what others believe about her. Similarly, Toy Caldwell noted in a phone discussion that as an African American woman, she experienced different impacts of gender or ethnicity based on the particular environment. Jean Lau Chin responded that sometimes we have to look at the subtext of a message to understand if race or gender is the cause of a sense of exclusion or isolation. The experiences of women who have relative privilege in relation to nongender statuses (e.g., race, ethnicity, ability, class, sexual orientation, etc.) are also shaped by those statuses, that is, not only by the oppression they experience as women but also by their privilege(s). A theory of feminist leadership must incorporate an understanding of our differences in both experience and privilege:

> These rules ["rules of the game"] are different depending on who you are—Black, female, male, lesbian, heavy, disabled, young, old, a northerner, etc. We must be aware of the fact that the rules are not the same for all of us and don't apply equally to us. We are accorded varied amounts of privilege by others based on our age, race, ability, class, sexual orientation, education, gender and other areas of classification. Some of us are allowed to learn from our mistakes while in other cases, we must perform under high and unforgiving standards. (Penny Sanchez)

Even our discussion of the meaning of feminist leadership reflected our differential privileges, as in this example which addressed language privilege:

I'm african woman from BURKINA FASO. I'm very interressed for the discussion but I speak frensh, so it's very difficult for me. Please help me with translation because it's very impportant for me. Thank you for your comprehension. (Annick Pikbougoum)

Annick's posting is a reminder that even our process of discussing feminist leadership is privileged. To participate in this discussion one must speak English, have web access (or be invited to an in-person discussion), and have the time to devote to this discussion. Furthermore, one must feel that one has something to say. In a phone discussion, Janis Sanchez asked how we could make space for women leaders with multiple identities. Martha Banks responded that it is likely that women with disabilities either never enter the "leadership pipeline" or are quickly squeezed out. She stated that it is almost impossible for women with disabilities to ever establish a critical mass for support outside of an advocacy group.

Clearly, there are voices missing from both the experience of leadership and the discussion of its meaning. Ultimately, we must find a way to include the missing voices directly, both through fostering participation in traditional leadership arenas and learning from the meanings of leadership developed in less privileged, more diverse contexts.

Denying "leadership": leadership as social process

While we cannot conceive of a single model of feminist leadership, given the great diversity of experiences, contexts, and goals discussed by feminist leaders, we were intrigued by discussions that seemed to suggest a different conceptualization of leadership. Many approached the discussion of feminist leadership by denying that they were leaders. In one discussion, Mary Ni talked with us about her experience with Asian Sisters in Action (ASIA). She said "We organized . . ." "We met . . ." "We planned. . . ." What was *not* evident in her discussion was "I led . . ." or even "I. . . ." Other comments were more direct:

> I don't really consider myself a leader, although I always put myself to work in whatever group I am in, which ultimately leads to leadership positions. My goal almost always is to make organizations work better so that they can be enhancing for both the goals of the organization and for the individuals who participate. I do think of myself as a feminist, as I keep a continual focus on empowerment, equality, and collaboration. (Jean Carter)

I do not consider myself to be a feminist leader, as I am not a blatant "flag waver" . . . but I do believe that I am able to positively influence those around me in stimulating thought and action. (Alice F. Chang)

I consider myself to be a leader in some contexts. I have been elected and selected to lead groups since I was in 5th grade. Just thought about that with this question. So I respond in the affirmative due to past experiences. Naming my leadership is another matter. (Jessica Henderson Daniel)

Does intentionality relate to what makes these feminist leaders resist seeing themselves as leaders or naming their leadership? Our discussions explored how some leaders intentionally set out to be leaders, not only setting out to contribute to furthering a cause or reaching a goal, but also intentionally setting out to be "leading" or directing in some way. Frequently, these leaders saw leadership as something that they are skilled in (like trait theories), or they believe that they have a good (possibly better) understanding of what is needed to succeed (like behavior theories).

But some leaders become leaders almost "accidentally" through their contributions. Their intention is to contribute to moving toward the goal, but there may be no inherent desire for "leadership" per se. These leaders may be more likely to see themselves as influencers, collaborators, or contributors. They may place the responsibility for naming and defining their "leadership" on others with whom they are working. They may resist the unspoken assumptions within the language of "leader." In one discussion, Carin Rosenberg, Mizuho Arai, and Dorcas Liriano agreed that it is difficult to conceive of a "leader" without also conceiving of "followers." And once this distinction is made, it is difficult to move away from defining characteristics that *differentiate* leaders and followers, thus contributing to a decontextualized hierarchical approach that resists feminist values. For example, the idea of a "leader" ensuring egalitarian participation is an oxymoron: How can a single person be responsible for ensuring egalitarian participation and have the process itself be egalitarian? Wouldn't everyone need to participate in "leadership" to reflect true egalitarianism?

We do not want to suggest that different people don't have different characteristics, skills, experiences, and so forth that they bring to the process of trying to reach a certain goal. Instead, we are exploring the possibility that, in various contexts, with various people, for various goals, a multitude of characteristics, behaviors, and skills can be "leadership."

41

And furthermore (moving beyond theories of leadership styles and transactional leadership), these different characteristics and skills work best together, so that leadership does not reside within a single person. We are attempting a conceptualization of "leadership" that can encompass the diversity of women's experiences, while simultaneously reflecting the shared goals of feminism. "Leadership" as social process moves away from describing the traits of leaders and even from developing prescriptive descriptions of the interactive process of leading. In order to enact that "model of leadership," leadership must be conceptualized as a constantly changing negotiation of context, goals, and social interactions unfolding within and reflecting shared values. In the next section, we present two in-depth examples to explore and illustrate the idea of leadership as process.

Two Examples of Coacted Harmony

Asian Sisters in Action

Mary Ni described her experience with Asian Sisters in Action (ASIA) during one of the group discussions we facilitated. As we considered the themes that were emerging from the varied discussions and the emerging idea of "leadership" as collaborative process in context, we saw these concepts reflected in Mary's initial descriptions and asked her to expand upon her experience. What follows is an edited, condensed version of her reflection.

In the winter of 1981, the New England Women's Studies Association held a weekend conference on Women and Racism at Simmons College in Boston, MA, with over 1,000 women participating. Of these participants, there appeared to be only 14 women of Asian heritage and the experiences of Asian and Asian American women seemed poorly represented. For example, on the first evening, in an opening panel, presentations were made by a White woman, a Black woman, and a Latina. In the discussion following the panel, one of the Asian women at the conference asked why there was no Asian woman representative on the panel and was applauded by other Asian women present.

Later in the conference, following a discussion period including all the women of color and the Jewish women, Mary suggested that all the Asian women get together for lunch, a suggestion met with great enthusiasm.

The energy was so high in that group, the air almost crackled. It was great to be together and our lunch period ran into the mid-afternoon. The whole group decided they would come to my workshop [the only offering about the experiences of Asian American women] and we ended up staying together throughout the rest of the conference with the decision to continue meeting after the conference ended.

One woman offered mailing supplies and capabilities and another got permission from the Women's Center in Cambridge to use their center for the mailing address.

The group met regularly and welcomed newcomers. Each meeting, whether there were new people or not, began with an introductory circle, making sure that everyone was acknowledged and had a chance to get to know something more about everyone else there. In this way, the women got to know about each other's strengths and values, and the important similarities and differences among them. Beginning as a discussion group, the women soon branched out into more endeavors, including rowing as a team in the Dragon Boat Festivals, running as a team in the Bonne Bell 10K races, developing a speakers' series, and becoming involved in political campaigns and issues. Throughout, the group worked to support each other with cookouts, retreats, writing workshops, and poetry readings. Eventually, the group decided to have a conference and talent showcase related to Asian women and Asian women's issues.

We started to evolve into a real working group as we began to develop our ideas to hold our first ASIA conference in 1982. Everyone's ideas were heard and each person took an area of leadership that she felt most interested in pursuing. Someone took on advertising. Another, finding the locations. A couple of women took on registration issues. One woman was in charge of the talent night. Another, getting the food. Someone else, arranging for workshops and speakers. . . . Everyone co-operated and helped each other out. It was fun, there was a lot of joy involved, and people became friends. . . . Sometimes it seemed our meetings were 2/3 socializing and 1/3 business. . . . We weren't driven, there was a lot of laughter (sometimes tears), and everything got done. . . . In this group, no one was the designated leader, either. We did things through consensus. There wasn't any vying for power and no one tried to take over and be the big cheese. It was definitely a group movement with shared decision making.

ASIA organized a second conference in 1984, incorporated as a non-profit organization, developed an ongoing newsletter and regular offerings of meetings and events which continue to this day (www.asiasisters.org). Mary Ni left in the fall of 1984 to spend a year in China and, upon her return, moved on to other endeavors and groups. Of her time in ASIA, she says:

> I am very grateful for the friendships and consciousness that I developed, and the opportunities I had to bring some of the ideas I had to fruition with a group of women who had similar thoughts and similar hopes. . . . In this group, I felt that my opinions mattered. I felt that people were really listening to what I had to say. . . . I think it was the first place, the first kind of adult forum, where I felt I didn't have to prove myself. . . . I think that kind of environment made me have even more good thoughts and be even more interesting. And, I think we, as a group of women, tried to make everyone feel this way.

Specifically, with respect to "leadership," Mary Ni wrote:

> We were experimenting with each other to see how much we could do. As Asian women, we were also experimenting with voice . . . with making noise, or rather, making music. Some of the reasons I think we were so successful with each other and so able to get things done included: We liked each other. We enjoyed what we were doing. None of us felt that we had to be "the leader." We were open to each other's ideas, criticisms and feedback. We put personal relationships in a primary position to our group goals. We nurtured each other's souls while we worked at public agendas. We focused on issues that were important to us. We took time to play and eat and care about and get to know each other.

An African American leadership dialogue

Marilyn Braithwaite-Hall and her friend and colleague Imani-Sheila Newsome Camara shared with us a transcript of their discussion about leadership experiences as Black women. Leadership as a call to action is one of the first themes that emerged from their conversation. Marilyn and Imani spoke of experiencing a sense of obligation to act, because they are able to and because their development and current experiences are interwoven within the community being benefited. In discussing their joint book project aimed at taking action for dealing with Black women's trauma, Imani and Marilyn stated, "We don't have a choice, this has to be done. Somebody has to do something and we can do it." In responding to a real need in the community for a Black women's theology center, Imani also felt she had no choice—she had to initiate: "I had to fill the gap between two classes of people and that gap wasn't going to be filled by anybody else."

Connected to the obligation to act on behalf of the community, relationships emerged as a primary theme. Relationships with other women, mothers, and multiple aspects of community are imperative. Relationships also extend to generations past and future, and to time, to history, to emotional legacies, and to the continuity and change of family and community.

In the book project and the women's theological center, Marilyn and Imani's "leadership" began by making connections with other women, further building community connections and commitment to the trust extended to them:

> And what happened is that women trusted us, [they] came to the first [book project] event because they knew us and trusted our ability to make a connection with them. And [they] trusted what they already knew about us. Already being leaders or followers or sisters or caretakers.

It is not so much who leads, or even the behaviors necessary for leadership, but rather an issue of representing and collaborating with the community, rising to the occasion, and identifying what must be done together. The community trusted the women not only as leaders, but also as followers, sisters, and caretakers. They trusted Marilyn and Imani to honor the community connections not only in their goals, but in their approach to leadership. The "how" of leadership in these conversations included models and values provided by others in the community, by kin, and by God, who all fostered leadership skills and capabilities in the family and the church.

For Marilyn and Imani, leadership reflects their African American reality that emphasizes relationality with time, with emotion, and with internal knowing. Action is strongly affected by the spiritual experience of "holding the past into the present, any given moment that is past never disappears, it's never past." Marilyn and Imani embraced the knowledge that moving forward requires "looking at where you have been and how that fits with the present moment." This sense that history and relationships are "never past but always consciously with me" affects the emotional motivation and approach to "leadership." The point of past in the present is related by Marilyn and Imani to the trauma experienced by Black women, the need for the African American theology center, the importance of nurturing women leaders in families and in churches, and the strength of connections to women, to mothers, to community. Loss, hurt, grief, and anger are very much within the past *and* within the present. These emotions are actively experienced and channeled into constructive energies that power action: "It was a real conscious decision to process all that and then do what my mother taught me to do when I was younger, sit down and cry and holler, then get up and do something—start moving." Imani and Marilyn discuss continuing to draw mother strength into the present by seeking the support and affirmation of their mothers as grown professional women, drawing too on the skills and person-strength nurtured long ago in their families and church communities where children were identified early on as leader children and given roles that facilitated their capacities and skills for leadership. Past and present into future and past, multiple continuous dimensions of relationality—this is African reality.

Marilyn and Imani also spoke of sometimes choosing not to lead, not to act, and how this was not being passive. There is a right time, and having a sense of readiness is both an internal process and an external moment. It is an external moment in relation to the community's readiness and an internal process in relation to emotion and to experiencing validation and legitimacy. However, this validation is not solicited or expected from external oppressive situations—power comes from elsewhere:

> I think I've always known. I was certainly taught that I had power, internal power, psychological, spiritual power that helped me overcome obstacles. . . . And I knew that I had skills, whether they were recognized in the classroom as being legitimate or not. But they were a set of skills that operated somewhere in the world where I lived, in the family and the church. So nothing was based on the external evaluation—you don't test well enough, you don't read enough, you don't write well enough.

Resistance and internal power is therefore another theme. Marilyn and Imani recognized that there were multiple social messages invalidating them as African American women, and discussed their true sources of validation and internal conviction:

> There was these two parallel institutions, the family and the church, that mitigated any other part of the environment [that said] "you can't lead, you can't function, you can't speak." It's like, "Yes I can, give me a break." Leadership speaks to the whole notion of African American women not

always asking for permission, because permission is not granted. And often the request is not even heard. Right. Explosiveness. The explicit permission or implicit permission is not even there. And so there has to be something internalized for African American women to say, "Yes I can, and I will and actually I didn't even ask you." I already asked, and answered the question for myself. So get out of the way. You know. And if you say, "I can't do it," [I say] "Why not?"

Legitimacy is from self and trusted others, related to being aware of being grown up, of having paid one's dues, a sense of urgency and of decreasing time. Resisting external evaluations and knowing one's skills and psychological/spiritual/intuitive power is central to being called and able to act.

Imani and Marilyn's conversation offers an understanding of power with others and power within. The connection to community and family, the emphasis on trust and community between women to heal from trauma and oppression and to foster one another, the affirmation and support that is felt multigenerationally, and the powerful historical connections known through experience lived in struggle and in trust point toward realities that feminist leadership must seek to articulate. The idea that family and church provide communities that teach young members of racially oppressed groups their power and skills and knowledge, contrary to the negative messages of worth and skill coming from the racist dominant culture, gives leadership training a very different meaning.

Reconceptualizing "Leadership": Coaction

> Difference must not be merely tolerated, but seen as a fund of necessary polarities between which our creativity can spark like a dialectic. Only then does the necessity for interdependency become unthreatening. Only within that interdependency of different strengths, acknowledged and equal, can the power to seek new ways of being in the world generate, as well as the courage and sustenance to act where there are no charters. (Lorde, 1984, p. 111)

In this section, we consider the implications of these discussions for reconceptualizing feminist leadership, accepting difference as the font of creativity, and considering leadership experiences within the contextual complexities of women's lives and differentiated from reactivity to patriarchy. The voices of the women in our discussions made it clear that leadership *is* informed by gender, race, ethnicity, class, and other social systemic phenomena. The influences of these status hierarchies are complex and multilayered; to enact "leadership" that resists the oppression within these systemic hierarchies is particularly challenging. The language of "leadership" itself contributes to constraining the models and meanings, not only representing but also actively creating shared meanings (Gergen, 1985). The language of leadership maintains an individual and hierarchical paradigm affording power to some but not others: "leaders" must have "followers." Furthermore, the language of leadership seems, to us, relatively static. One is a leader or enacts/embodies leadership. But the concept of "leadership" emerging from the discussions focused on people, context, justice, and episodic requirement. We sought language that would reflect and enable our vision: Coaction —literally, acting together—is a process that aims to resist re-enacting oppressive structures while creating collaborative, sociopolitically sensitive, and contextualized movement toward shared goals.

Coaction aims to resist oppression

All approaches to leadership are value-based, even if the values are not explicitly articulated. Coaction is a feminist understanding of "leadership" that aims to integrate intersections of multiple oppressions and resist the effects and enactments of these oppressions. Therefore, coaction must value the experience of relational mutuality and prioritize commitment to creating social change for liberation. These priorities may be evident minimally in the processes of working together and, hopefully, in the shared goals toward which coactors work. Coaction should be evaluated primarily through the development and movement toward shared visions, positive interpersonal relationships, and structural justice, rather than through preset outcomes and profit generation. These fundamental values of relational mutuality and contributing to social justice and resisting oppression largely affect the other characteristics and priorities described below.

Coaction is collaborative

Coaction challenges the hierarchies of status and power embedded in traditional leadership by enacting feminist values of deconstructing power hierarchies, reducing power asymmetries, and establishing more egalitarian relationships. All members working towards the shared goals are coactors and the responsibility for moving forward (in multiple ways) is shared by all. Coaction also recognizes that various cultures, contexts, and individuals may value and define hierarchy and collaboration differently; the possibility exists for the coactors to embrace a seemingly hierarchical structure at some points in some ways in order to organize their collective efforts. Furthermore, coaction does not mean that every person is expected to contribute the same "amount" or in the same ways. Coaction reflects feminist values of pluralism, recognizing that diverse women (and men) bring different skills, abilities, and values that contribute in different ways. Coaction enables each person to offer what they can and bring their own strengths (personal, interpersonal, and group) to the task. Unlike persuading or coercing someone to do a particular behavior, coaction calls for people to self-motivate to act in ways that are appropriate to the people, needs, and the call of the situation.

Because coaction is inherently collaborative, it is also relational and process-oriented. To share responsibility for successfully meeting goals, the shared meaning of the goals and the pathway(s) to reaching them must be collaboratively developed. Thus, sufficient time and energy must be devoted to creating (and, over time, re-creating) these meanings. Coaction requires a greater investment in the process, not just the outcome or reward. In order to work well together and utilize the diverse strengths and skills brought by multiple people, coactors must develop strong relationships, devoting the time and energy to understanding each of the people coacting within a particular context/organization. Part of developing this relational process-oriented approach (Jordan, 1992) is attending not only to thought, behavior, and goal but also to emotional meanings that provide motivation, feelings of investment, and pride in accomplishment. Emotions can be powerful motivators.

Coaction is sociopolitically sensitive: The personal is political (and the political is personal)

To create the collaborative, contextualized experience of coaction that resists the re-enactment of oppressive structures and processes, we must recognize the connections between our personal experiences and interpersonal interactions, and the sociopolitical systems within which we have been socialized and within which we currently interact. These systems shape the goals, organizational structures, and practices of our organizations. While we may need to continue to work within patriarchal structures, we can engage in conscious critique of these structures so that our choices (however constrained) are made with the most awareness possible. And we can, within our own groups, recognize the connections between the personal and the political.

Part of this critique is questioning how we set our goals, what knowledge and approaches are valued, and how the answers to these questions inherently reflect political stances and traditional socialization. The underpinnings of traditional approaches to leadership are positivist and pragmatic without questioning power and profit values. Coaction calls for a different underlying epistemology and allows for expanding ways of knowing and approaching working together to meet the goals. Paula Gunn Allen (1992) in *The Sacred Hoop* discussed the lived knowledge within and among today's Native American women as they connect with traditional ways. She also described the patterns and connections she is energized by as she engages in teaching and scholarship about indigenous peoples. Our positivist Western training makes it difficult to even see these alternative ways of knowing that shape the approaches to "leading."

Many voices in our discussions made it clear that it is not enough to understand ourselves and others as individuals, we must also understand ourselves, others, and the relationships among us in relation to sociopolitical systems of privilege and oppression including gender, race, ethnicity, class, sexual orientation, ability, and so forth. In order to realize shared visions and collaborative action, we must understand the multiple sociostructural meanings and influences on the experiences and perspectives of our coactors and ourselves. Coaction thus requires beginning with (a) a general awareness of oneself (personality, strengths, interpersonal style) and particularly oneself in relation to interpersonal systems of oppression (gender, race, culture, social class); (b) a general awareness of others (e.g., cultural differences, the effects of racism, effects and experiences related to disability, etc.); and (c) a willingness to engage in processes of exploration together in order to maximize the co-operative abilities present in a group of people.

Structures, expectations, and processes that actively open dialogue, make space for voice, and share power are needed for the development of the truly collaborative relationships that recognize the connections between the personal and the political that are necessary for coaction. Creating these structures, expectations, and processes may be challenging because traditional patriarchal values do not emphasize collaboration, relationality, and emotional sensitivity. Understanding the personal–political connection within the abstract level of epistemology may be helpful in deconstructing the challenges to creating structures and processes that enable coaction. At the more personal level, even in more feminist or multicultural organizations, we may find it difficult to create and maintain the structures and processes necessary to create truly collaborative relationships. Those of us with relatively more privilege than others will need to limit some of our privilege in order to build coalitions and allies and enable all coactors to feel connected to the process. The privilege of taking space to speak, for example, may need to be limited in order to actively make space for others whose experiences don't afford them the privilege to "take" space without invitation.

Coaction is contextualized

Coaction is an active process that is unstable and ever-changing. Sensitivity to changing contexts necessitates a constant re-creation of goals and vision and the ways in which the coactors are contributing to these with each other. Changing contexts include a variety of issues that affect the ways in which the coactors interact with each other and the environment, including social-structural changes (e.g., war), organizational changes (e.g., reorganization, new organizational goals), personnel changes, or changes due to the lives of the coactors (e.g., giving birth or adopting a child). Acknowledging change and the associated need for renegotiations reflects the lived experience of women. A strength of coaction is its ability to utilize the multiple contributions of all coactors and thus increase the likelihood of being able to maintain progress towards goals in times of great change when very different "leadership" characteristics may suddenly be in demand.

Conclusion: Coactive Approaches to Developing "Leadership Theory"

We have developed a conceptualization of "feminist leadership" from the many diverse voices participating with us in discussions about leadership, race, culture, and class. Coaction is "leadership" formed by feminist values of social justice, egalitarianism, and recognition of the personal–political intersection. Coaction is collaborative, with people involved not as followers but as co-operative leaders themselves. Coaction is a constant negotiation and renegotiation of personal, organizational, and social-structural goals and needs using varied skills reflecting different personal, social, and cultural backgrounds, operating within (and with attention to) personal, relational, organizational, and social-structural contexts. This negotiation is within the individual, between individuals, and between groups and contexts. As such, it incorporates and prioritizes self-understanding and awareness, knowledge of the contextual and diverse needs of people, and knowledge of the complex relationships among people, all operating at the personal, interpersonal, and structural levels. One understands not only one's personal differences but also the social-structural meanings of those differences given the current and historical systems of power and privilege that shape our experiences. Coaction is indeed a constant renegotiation process, as nothing stays static: The goals, skills, needs, and contexts are constantly changing and shifting.

An obvious question about coaction is whether it is possible to realize this kind of collaborative, process-oriented approach if the context is patriarchal. We don't know. We imagine coaction would be most challenging in an organization valuing profit or numerical productivity. While we recognize the challenges and the possibility that coaction might be limited by patriarchal contexts, we believe that it is still worthwhile to examine what liberating, feminist leadership that is sensitive to diverse voices and experiences might look like. Moving beyond the reactive model helps us to envision alternatives and resist the constraints that make these alternatives difficult to enact.

Attention to the lived experiences of diverse women brought us to the consideration of the difficulties of leading and following in patriarchal environments. This has opened up the *process* of leadership, contributing to the development of one alternative that incorporates feminist values and agendas of social justice: coaction. Coactors step forward to meet particular contextual needs at particular moments through connecting their experiences with the needs of the context, in a considered and collaborative process. Just as we are holding out a process of co-operative, reflective actions as leadership, we clearly need more discussion and interaction about how this works, has worked, and has been and could be enacted. We offer our synthesis of voices, with thanks to the feminists who shared with us, as a beginning to such a discussion.

Notes

1 The authors wish to especially thank Mary Ni, Marilyn Braithwaite-Hall, and Imani-Shelia Newsome Camara. We also wish to thank the following people who contributed to the discussions that shaped this chapter: Judith Albino, "Anonymous," Mizuho Arai, Patricia Arredondo, Siony Austria, Martha Banks, Pati Beaudoin, Mari Bennasar, Toy Caldwell-Colbert, Jean Carter, Alice F. Chang, Jean Lau Chin, Jessica Henderson Daniel, Melanie Domenech-Rodriguez, Joyce K. Fletcher, Rita Dudley Grant, Linda Hartling, Jeanette Hsu, Norine Johnson, Chieh Li, Dorcas Liriano, Bernice Lott, Maggie Madden, Marlene Maheu, Ruth Paige, Elaine Phillips, Annick Pikbougoum, Helen D. Pratt, Joseph Raelin, "Radclyffe Hall," Elaine Rodino, Carin Rosenberg, Janis Sanchez, Penny Sanchez, Willie Sanchez, Ester Shapiro, Steve, Usha Tummala-Narra, Ena Vasquez-Nuttall, Ann Yabusaki. Finally, we thank Sarah Hewes for research assistance.

2 Because of this recognition, we feel it is important to place ourselves in relation to some of the social systems that we found relevant to these discussions:

I (KLS) am a multiracial Japanese American (Sansei—third generation Japanese American—and European American/English, southern Baptist heritage) woman. Although my parents were both from poor families, I grew up with class privilege in my own family. I am monolingual (English), bisexual, and have no major person disabilities.

I (MBB) am a seventh generation Yankee woman of English and French descent. I carry the benefits and burdens of class privilege and I am limited to only the English language although I can manage to read Latin. I have no visible disabilities; my mind works in unusual ways that don't always fit well with linguistic structure. My varied professional and personal lives are engaging and enjoyable mainly.

References

Allen, P. G. (1992). *The sacred hoop*. Boston: Beacon Press.

Ballou, M., & Gabalac, N. (1985). *A feminist position on mental health*. Springfield, IL: Charles Thomas.

Brown, L., & Brodsky, A. (1992). The future of feminist therapy. *Psychotherapy, 2*, 51–57.

Comas-Díaz, L. (1991). Feminism and diversity in psychology: The case of women of color. *Psychology of Women Quarterly, 15*, 597–609.

Gergen, K. J. (1985). The social constructionist movement in modern psychology. *American Psychologist, 40*, 266–275.

Hill, M., & Ballou, M. (1998). Making therapy feminist: A practice survey. *Women and Therapy, 21*, 1–16.

Jordan, J. (1992). *Women's growth in diversity.* New York: Guilford Press.

Lorde, A. (1984). The master's tools will never dismantle the master's house. In *Sister outsider: Essays and speeches by Audre Lorde* (pp. 110–113). Trumansberg, NY: Crossing Press.

Rave, E. J., & Larsen, C. C. (Eds.) (1995). *Ethical decision-making in therapy: Feminist perspectives.* New York: Guilford Press.

Worell, J., & Remer, P. (1992). *Feminist perspectives in therapy: An empowerment model for women.* New York: Wiley.

Chapter 2

Diverse Feminist Communication Styles: Challenges to Women and Leadership

Ann S. Yabusaki[1]

Many years ago during a classroom exercise on counseling, the professor remarked to me, "I didn't realize that you felt so deeply about the subject." I was shocked and remembered thinking, "What an odd comment." I had felt deeply about many issues in this class and I thought I had conveyed them clearly. Had he not noticed my enthusiasm, passion, irritation, or impatience? This incident sparked a lifelong interest in the nuances of communication as influenced by the contexts of culture, power, and gender.

I have learned that I was raised in a high-context culture that values understated or restrained expression and carefully chosen words. This knowledge helped me to understand my struggle of adapting to cultures that valued open and direct communication. I learned that meanings of words and styles of communicating are not universal. Communication is powerfully influenced by contexts, gestures, intonation, pauses, interpersonal space or proxemics, and time. Often, what is not said is far more important than what is. Unfortunately, misunderstandings from limited points of view can lead to the dangerous tendency of judging others harshly.

From September 2002 through April 2003, 11 women shared experiences and thoughts via the internet about how communication styles influence leadership among women. Our discussions were brief but poignant. We shared insights about women, leadership, feminism, and ourselves; we questioned our observations, and considered new points of view.

This chapter attempts to make sense of our conversations; because they occurred via email, there were few, if any, contextual cues. I often felt as if I were speaking in a vacuum. In spite of these limitations, the discussions raised some very interesting questions and viewpoints. By presenting the comments verbatim, I hope to capture the passion and themes from our stories. I invite readers to bring their own experiences to this chapter and to continue the conversation in their own way.

Themes From the Discussion

The influence of cultural context

I (9/20/02) opened the discussion with observations about Asian values and how they might influence communication and leadership styles. I assumed that culture teaches how we interpret and relate to the world, and I wondered what others thought. I wrote:

> Communication . . . for Asians tends to include a moral message . . . I was told by . . . Cambodian and Vietnamese [colleagues] that moral education is part of their education . . . other [aspects] of communication include metaphors, stories directed to the heart, circularity, honors wisdom and hierarchy, and [is] respectful of relationship.

Jean (9/23/02) elaborated that "In Asian cultures, the emphasis on hierarchy influences ways in which leaders and authority figures communicate. Perhaps the expectation of leaders is their wisdom; a corollary then is for leaders to teach or convey a moral message when communicating." She wondered if communication styles among leaders differ across groups or are more effective in different cultural contexts.

Lorene (9/24/02) responded that African American women contend with oppression and power daily. She wrote:

> In discussing possible communication styles of women of African descent . . . we would have to include the context of oppression and power and how they intersect with the everyday lives of women of African descent. . . . our communication styles will vary depending on how

fairly we believe we are treated in an encounter or situation . . . our communication style is very much built on a sense of fairness and trust. . . . great value is placed on family, religion and kinship bonds both blood and extended family member. . . . relationships outside of these structures might be viewed with suspicion until proven to be trusting or they exhibit a sense of fairness.

Following up, Jean (9/24/02) wondered how the context of safety influenced African American women leaders. She asked, "How do they bring this into their leadership, and communicate as leaders?"

Lorene replied (9/27/02):

I believe that African American women throughout history have been able to be effective leaders although living in oppressive and dangerous environments and dealing with power structures . . . that do not always include us or our voice. Depending on the situation, we have had to either speak loud to be heard and not be silenced or to be silent at the risk of being misunderstood. This has meant at times suppressing what we feel and what we have to speak. What I believe African American women have done is to find a middle ground, which is to use our anger as an ally to help us speak what is truth for us in any situation, even though it may be unpopular. Different situations might require communication styles that are direct, indirect, reflective or introspective. . . .

Bernice (11/13/02) wondered whether a feminist communication style existed. She asked, "Are communication styles influenced too heavily by context, power relationships, ethnic custom, etc.?"

Janis (3/5/03) shared an experience of a colleague: "In her . . . experience, it was often women of African descent who spoke up in public arenas to air the concerns of all women." She went on to say that she observed

all too often . . . that the women of African descent were censured for being direct and exposing the problem and a need for a solution while other women benefited without having to participate. What was strange was that my colleague said to me, "you know that's what you always do and always get in trouble for."

Cheryl (3/12/03) suggested that communication should be viewed through circumstances both from the experiences of the person as well as the situation:

Much of the conversation seems to be focused on identifying "who" does what style of communicating. This has led to a focus on difference, especially ethnicity (and) culture. . . . A focus on group differences tends to imply a group [ethnic] homogeneity that does not exist. A useful alternative is to consider what circumstances lead to various communication styles (regardless of whether Asian, Black, or White women engage in them). How do the factors of power, status, alternatives, risks, benefits, and costs shape what anyone might or might not speak of. . . . There is a good deal of variability in the behavior of all women, White, Black, Hispanic, Asian, Jewish. . . . When a Black woman publicly names a problem that White women also experience but are silent about . . . what is the context? What is it about the lives, status, power, fears, and privilege of silent White women that keeps them silent; what is it about the life of the Black woman who speaks up that has fostered this act of courage?

Lorene and Bertha responded that they spoke up because after weighing the risks that they faced as Black women, they felt that they had nothing to lose. Lorene (3/22/03) wrote:

I believe that as a woman of color who is a Black woman, that when I speak out publicly I have nothing to lose and everything to gain in self respect by speaking up even though it may not feel safe in some situations or dialogues. I have learned that when I choose to speak up that this speaking up has to be for me whether anyone else agrees or disagrees with what I am saying. I believe that as a woman of color that I must speak for myself because only I can do this for myself. I also believe that women of color are invisible, not seen or heard by many people when we do speak up, but many do gain from our speaking up even though they may be silent.

Bertha (4/2/03) continued:

I found in many situations the African American woman is the one bold enough to say it exactly as it is . . . It could also mean that because we (African women) are hardly heard that we make use of every opportunity we have to give our voice. I find the style of communication of the African woman refreshing and inspiring. In a leadership position, you know where you stand with her. She communicates in the real sense of the word. Her body tells you when she does not want to be messed about, and when she is emotional and in tune with you. Her direct approach is preferable to those who will smile falsely, or smile and stab you seriously in the back.

At this point, I think we realized that we were on the brink of a vast and significant issue. The contexts of communication included culture, history, and the times and situations in which we lived. We make moment-to-moment decisions on the risks and benefits of acting or speaking, and oftentimes we act out the unspoken privileges of class, status, abilities, sexual orientation, and religion. We asked what were the ingredients of personal courage, and how did they appear in different cultures and forms. We agreed that actions were the result of complex internal processes. Our metaphors and stories seemed to capture the vastness of what we were trying to define and understand.

Styles and forms of communication

I (1/25/03) wondered if our discussion of "style" meant we were speaking of cultural, ethnic, and personal values. "Some cultures and individuals may value collaboration and harmony rather than debate and autonomy."

Lorene (2/2/03) felt that a discussion of feminist leadership styles and leadership by women should also consider the role of race, sexual orientation, and class. Definitions of feminist leadership and communication styles cannot be gleaned from a book. Answers may be found in our dialogue around difficult issues that will not be answered in isolation,

> but in interaction and in relationship with each other. . . . not an academic exercise, but a risk-taking commitment, which includes honest cooperation, communication, collaboration and inclusion. . . . it is through art, culture, our interactions, our experiences, our stories and our histories that we define who we are as women, which may be a foundation for a relationship based feminist leadership style that is open and inclusive to every woman.

Mari (11/05/02) wrote:

> What about art as a means of communication? Not a new concept. I was impressed by a workshop at the Latino Psychology conference . . . on Frida Kahlo's work and Latina women. They use Frida Kahlo's art in outpatient and inpatient group work. It was powerful. It promoted expression, empowerment, recognition. . . . Why Frida Kahlo? Because she is one of the first women in art history to treat with honesty (as well as near-cruelty), themes which almost exclusively affect women: motherhood,

relationships, physical abuse, and family. I wonder what experiences people have had with art in therapy, especially with groups that have been "silenced" for generations. Frida Kahlo was certainly a leader and a powerful woman who expressed her emotions the way she could.

Ester (2/12/03) shared that she had been working with others on the Spanish cultural adaptation of *Our Bodies, Ourselves,* by integrating health and healing as ecological, multisystemic, and context-specific. She said that,

> in adapting the text to a spiritually based family friendly feminism, the group introduced poems at the beginning of many chapters and created an indigenous/women centered healing chapter invoking the sacred healing arts as the heart of an alternative vision of Latina health that rejected male dominated individualistic high technology medicine. I have been speaking to a lot of student groups about Latina health and gender justice and one of my power point slides uses Frida's "Two Fridas" to show the powerful ways she used her Mexican/indigenous cultural identity as an alternative to the upper class White woman who looked good while bleeding to death.

Martha (1/26/03) found dance a powerful and empowering way of communication, similar to Mari's description of Kahlo's art. She wondered if art and dance align more with a feminine continuum rather than a feminist continuum.

> I (11/08/02) shared my experience with art in the therapeutic setting: Kahlo is a powerful figure for women. . . . A few thoughts: her work [reflects] (1) the passionate feelings that stir deeply within, (2) the courage to risk harsh criticism in a world that would rather ignore the cruelty of humankind, (3) and the implications for being an outspoken woman in a culture that would silence women. Difficult messages are sometimes more easily expressed through art, because art speaks in metaphors.

Some Important Issues

The urgency for new leadership styles was voiced recently by Lambrecht (2006). He wrote, "Where trouble and corruption hang in the air, voters around the world are increasingly turning to women to clean up the mess left by bad-old-boy networks." In the article, Kavita

Ramdas, president of Global Fund for Women, noted, "The emergence of a women's political voice is almost directly linked to the exhaustion of alternatives." Lambrecht reports that EMILY's List, which recruits, trains, and finances women candidates who favor abortion rights, claims to have raised three times more money in 2005 than in 2003. Roberta Combs, president of the Christian Coalition, stated:

> By nature, we're [women] compassionate people. Women bear children, and they have that instinct to take care of people. And that kind of spills over to governing. I am an activist as far as women being involved in politics. We deserve that right, and we have paid the price. But we still live in a man's world. (Lambrecht, 2006)

Implied in Lambrecht's article is that if we are to embrace a new style of leadership, perhaps a leadership from the perspective of women's experience, we must embrace a new style of communication as well.

Nuances of communication

Our discussion addressed communication as shaped by culture, the potential for misunderstanding and, by implication, the difficulty of feminist leadership. For example, the act of apology is a highly prized tradition in Japanese culture.

> A person can easily ask forgiveness a dozen times in a day in Japan, using several different phrases. Store clerks will insist to a customer that "there is no excuse" for having made him or her wait a matter of seconds. (Coleman, 2006)

When a U.S. submarine rammed a Japanese training vessel off Hawaii in February 2001, killing nine people (high school students), the commander's initial delay in making a full apology outraged the victims' families. He made a tearful apology a month later, "but the relationship between Japan and the U.S. had been irreparably damaged" (Coleman, 2006). Understanding the importance of the apology in Japanese culture, U.S. officials now are asking Japanese officials for forgiveness immediately.

What relevance do cultural values have for feminist leadership? Studies estimate that only 30–40% of communication is verbal (Sue & Sue, 1990). Tone, gesture, inflection, posture, eye contact, distance between speakers, messages said, avoided, or implied, patterns of interruption, and protocols of interaction, such as beginning and closing conversations, are powerful elements of communication (Hall, 1981). "Communication styles are strongly correlated with race, culture, and ethnicity. Gender has also been found to be a powerful determinant of communication style" (Sue & Sue, 1990, p. 52). Gender roles and values, both culturally defined, become challenges to communication in leadership. Feminist leadership must bridge to the predominant male styles of leadership while maintaining its authentic voice.

In 1995, at the International Women's World Conference in Beijing, China, I attended a panel on organizing protests. Several women from different parts of the world shared their experiences. At the end of the presentations, the moderator, a young woman from New York City, said, "We will now invite questions from the floor. Will the women from North America please step aside so that the women from other countries have a chance to speak. Once they have spoken, you may take the mike." In a few sentences, she graciously acknowledged different styles of communication and made way for everyone to participate. In my experience, it is rare for someone to ask others to wait so that others could participate. I felt welcomed, acknowledged, and grateful for the moderator's sensitivity. This story illustrates feminist leadership.

An aspect of communication we did not consider in our web discussion, but of interest, is the concept of words versus action. Should we believe in the words or the actions of a person? Some cultures focus on words, illustrated by adages that say that one's word is one's honor, while others focus on actions, such as "Actions speak louder than words." How should we understand someone who professes to value relationship and collaboration, but behaves otherwise? Bruner (1990) suggested that more research should focus on understanding how action reveals what one thinks, feels, or believes.

On context

During the discussion on cultural styles, Cheryl (3/12/03) made a very important observation: "A focus on group differences tends to imply group homogeneity that does not exist. A useful alternative is to consider what circumstances lead to various communication styles." She raises the issue of individual action in response to power, status, risks, benefits, costs, and contexts. What fosters acts of courage? What supports or encourages someone to voice her point of view in spite of adversity?

How can one meet the needs of the self and the needs of others? In terms of life span development, the self-defined and individuated woman might be one who has found harmony in meeting her own needs and still participates in the collective struggle for liberation, survival, and well-being. How does a leader maintain her family and community as part of her identity?

A meaning of feminist

At the 1995 International Women's Conference in Beijing, my friends and I attended a forum led by one of the founders—an icon—of the feminist movement in the United States. About 100 women, gathered under makeshift tents, pressed forward to hear her. We discussed the difficulty of moving forward with a feminist agenda and the backlash it may generate.

Shortly into the program, my friend, a Japanese American woman of 75 years, no more than 5 feet tall and 95 pounds, began bending and twisting the program. She shifted in her chair, finally raised her hand, and quickly stood up. In a loud voice she asked, "Where was the feminist movement when Japanese American women were being placed in concentration camps without due process in America? What does the feminist movement have to say about atrocities committed by the government or by the people to women of color?"

A hush fell over the crowd. Another woman stood up. "She's right," she said. "Where are we on issues of social justice for all women including women of color? Lesbian and bisexual women? Women of different religions? Of different abilities? Of different ages?"

After a few seconds of silence, our icon turned and asked the crowd, "Are there any more questions?"

Perhaps the feminist movement cannot represent the experiences of all women. The struggle for equal rights is more complex for women from different cultures. For example, a young woman in traditional Asian culture is expected to respect her elders. She is expected to respect and support men. She is expected to care for her mother-in-law. She must protect her children from racism. These expectations are changing, but to speak out and cultivate a sense of independence is fraught with challenges.

Black women fight for human rights, against racism, and for women's rights. Williams (1994), a womanist theologian, notes that when African American women speak, they confront a society that subordinates all women and a society based on color that considers them inferior. African American women, Williams argues, also confront a culture with certain expectations of women, a culture sometimes of poverty and single parenting, and a culture that worries about the survival of its men, women, and children.

Walker (1983) coined the term *womanist* and, with it, captured the experience of Black feminists in their own words. She says,

> A Womanist is a black feminist or feminist of color. From the black folk expression of mothers to female children, "You acting womanish," i.e., like a woman. . . . A woman who loves other women, sexually and/or nonsexually. Appreciates and prefers women's culture, women's emotional flexibility (values tears as natural counterbalance of laughter), and women's strength. . . . Traditionally universalist, as in: "Mama, why are we brown, pink, and yellow, and our cousins are white, beige, and black?" Ans.: "Well, you know the colored race is just like a flower garden, with every color flower represented." . . . Womanist is to feminist as purple is to lavender. (Walker, 1983, pp. xi–xii)

Williams (1994, p. 1) explains that womanist means, "African-American women's experience has its own integrity and must speak its own truth in its own language expressing its own cultural ideas about women's reality." Perhaps the term feminist was never intended to capture the experiences of all women. Womanist helped us to understand that we need to self-define and encouraged us to use language that encompasses our experiences and represents our deepest cultural selves.

Language power

"Language differentiates and gives meaning to assertive and compliant behavior and teaches us what is socially accepted as normal. Yet language is not monolithic. Dominant meanings can be contested; alternative meanings affirmed" (Weedon, 1987, p. 76). Weedon reminds us of the power in language. Language is an essential tool for socialization and establishing the norms of a society.

Our discussion group tended to agree with Weedon's observation. Black women expressed the belief that they spoke out more often than other women did and then suffered repercussions for doing so. Yet they continued to speak out in spite of the consequences because they had nothing to lose. The Asian women noted that the *how* of speaking was as important as the *act* of speaking. Asian language and thought emphasize the contexts of hierarchy, gender, age, timing, and community harmony. Choosing not to speak is as powerful as speaking out.

Miller (1991, pp. 198–199) defines power as "the ability to augment one's own force, authority or influence as well as to control and limit others." She observes:

> Generally in our culture, and in several others, we have maintained the myth that women do not and should not have power. Usually, without openly talking about it, we women have been most comfortable using our powers if we believe we are using them in the service of others.

Discussion participants did not discuss directly using our power in the service of others, but spoke primarily about the difficulty of claiming our power and leading and speaking from it.

A colonial point of view

"Why should we participate? We are never heard anyway! No one has really written about our experiences except us. So why should we trust you?" This comment, from Pacific Islander women in leadership, is familiar. Colonization and self-determination are dominant themes among people in Hawaii. Furthermore, the women that I approached to join this discussion stated clearly that they could not and would not represent the diverse cultures of women in the Pacific Islands. They also objected to the manner of communication, because communication on matters of the heart occurs face-to-face, not by email.

Two worldviews collide within colonialism: that of the colonizer and the colonized. Individuals and communities continue to struggle to resolve these conflicts many years after initial contact. Over 100 years after Hawaii's queen was forcibly deposed by the United States military, the struggle for independence goes on. Concerns about exploitation and betrayal are always present. The dream of self-determination and self-governance continues.

Ashcroft, Griffiths, and Tiffin (1995, p. 2) observe that "all post-colonial societies are still subject in one way or another to overt or subtle forms of neo-colonial domination." With colonization comes a heightened sensitivity to oppression and suspicion of potential oppressors. One is never free of a protective hypervigilance, and with the strong military presence in Hawaii, one wonders if there ever was a "post-colonial" period.

The Pacific Island women remind us to be sensitive to the ways that language serves the colonizer. They chided me to communicate in culturally respectful ways, treat others as guests, and recognize and respect their distrust of people and ideas from the Continental United States.

Summary

This chapter focused on how communication styles influence leadership among women. Discussions among women via the internet yielded themes with an implicit and intuitive understanding that effective communication is a cornerstone of effective leadership. Our task was to define this important role of communication in leadership and explore what makes it so challenging. The complexity of themes ranging from social justice issues, social and personal contexts, family and cultural values, and personal development reflect the multiplicity of factors through which leadership and leadership styles are influenced by the ways in which we communicate.

We talked about differences and illustrated various communication and leadership styles through ethnicity, culture, art forms, and language. We identified how communication styles needed to be understood within multiple contexts. We spoke at length about the influence of power, marginalization, racism, colonization, and oppression on communication and leadership. Urban and rural experiences, socioeconomic status, ability/disability, gender, sexual orientation, and personal disposition were also identified as major influences on communication and leadership styles. We talked about cultural rules that define how one behaves in the presence of and in the role of authority. We discussed how conveying respect for age, gender, and birth order complicates how messages are delivered and received. Ironically, in spite of our great concern for context, we neglected to address our own struggle to surmount the difficulties of communicating over the internet, a medium with few contextual/nonverbal cues.

The feminist movement, for many women of color, is seen as a White woman's movement. The meaning of feminist was immediately raised in the discussion. How could there be diverse feminist communication styles when the word feminist does not reflect diverse histories or cultures and ethnicities or the experiences of women from different ethnicities, classes, and sexual orientations?

We addressed the struggle of women from nondominant cultures finding their place and voice in leadership. We spoke of the risks and importance of speaking one's truth, albeit different from the dominant worldview. We addressed if, when, and how one should speak up; prohibitions to and risks of speaking up; and how communication style can be misunderstood, misinterpreted, and judged harshly by others. For some, the consequence of not speaking up was tantamount to spiritual death. Often expected to adjust to the dominant culture, women from nondominant cultures were conflicted about their responsibility to their sisters. Should they place themselves at risk for defending another? How does one make that decision? Is defending another an act of leadership?

After our discussion, more questions surfaced. How do women from dominant cultures address issues of power and how do they determine when to speak their truth or remain silent? What are the dynamics of leadership when a leader and others in the group are from different cultures or from similar cultures? Can we distinguish between leadership of those who are advocating for change to the system and those who are leaders within a system and wish to maintain the status quo?

Our discussion seemed to struggle between leadership in context and leadership from the heart. If we focused solely on context, we might override or ignore our hearts. The discussion seemed to center on the challenges of claiming our reality, owning ourselves and self-expression, and speaking from our hearts in ways that are understandable.

Contributors to the discussion seemed to agree that we want leaders who know themselves and appreciate others. We want leaders who speak and act authentically from their experiences. We want leaders who listen, respond to, and act on conviction in spite of adversity. We want leaders to address disparate and controversial points of view in ways that respect and honor the experience of others. The challenge of leadership, it seems, is the art of balancing the heart with the context. Could women's leadership provide this?

I wish to thank all of the discussion participants for their contributions and for making this a provocative and meaningful endeavor. I am deeply grateful for their honesty and courage. I have tried to keep the integrity of their voices, and all omissions and commissions of error and misinterpretations are mine.

Note

1 Discussion participants in alphabetical order: Mari Bennasar, Bertha, Jean Lau Chin, Lorene Garrett-Browder, Bernice Lott, Marlene Maheu, Martha, Janis Sanchez, Ester Shapiro, Cheryl Travis, and Ann S. Yabusaki.

References

Ashcroft, B., Griffiths, G., & Tiffin, H. (Eds.). (1995). *The post-colonial studies reader*. New York: Routledge.

Bruner, J. S. (1990). *Acts of meaning*. Cambridge, MA: Harvard University Press.

Coleman, J. (2006, January 29). U.S. apologies follow Japanese cultural cues. *The Honolulu Advertiser*, p. A6.

Hall, E. (1981). *The silent language*. New York: Doubleday.

Lambrecht, B. (2006, January 22). More women leaders tapped to heal nations' wounds. *The Honolulu Advertiser*, p. A16.

Miller, J. B. (1991). Women and power. In J. V. Jordan, A. G. Kaplan, J. B. Miller, I. P. Stiver, & J. L. Surrey (Eds.), *Women's growth in connection: Writings from the Stone Center* (pp. 197–205). New York: Guilford Press.

Sue, D. W., & Sue, D. (1990). *Counseling the culturally different: Theory and practice* (2nd ed.). New York: John Wiley & Sons, Inc.

Walker, A. (1983). *In search of our mother's gardens: Womanist prose*. San Diego: Harcourt Brace Jovanovich.

Weedon, C. (1987). *Feminist practice and poststructuralist theory*. Maldon, MA: Blackwell Publishers Inc.

Williams, D. (1994, October). African American women develop a new theological vision in the "Ecumenical decade: Churches in solidarity with women." *The Brown Papers*, *1*(1), 1–15.

Chapter 3

Women as Academic Leaders: Living the Experience from Two Perspectives

A. Toy Caldwell-Colbert and Judith E. N. Albino

In this chapter, two senior academic administrators explore and discuss their experiences as feminist leaders in higher education. These perspectives are intended to encourage similar sharing among others.

In a study of women college presidents, Jablonski (2000) noted that the leadership literature as of the early 1990s yielded more than 350 definitions of leadership (p. 243). These definitions, most written by White males, include the following (all cited in Hughes, Ginnett, & Curphy, 1995, pp. 41–2):

- Carlton E. Munson (1981): "The creative and directive force of morale."
- Warren G. Bennis (1959): "The process by which an agent induces a subordinate to behave in a desired manner."
- Edwin Paul Hollander and J. W. Julian (1969): "The presence of a particular influence relationship between two or more persons."
- Fred E. Fiedler (1967): "Directing and coordinating the work of group members."
- Robert K. Merton (1957): "An interpersonal relation in which others comply because they want to, not because they have to."
- C. F. Roach and O. Behling (1984): "The process of influencing an organized group toward accomplishing its goals."

It is not surprising that these definitions use masculine language and sometimes themes of subjugation. Words such as *force*, *induces*, *subordinate*, *directing, influence,* and *comply* suggest power and control and reflect masculine socialization in Western societies.

Rosener noted that women leaders once had no other choice than to model male behavior and to adopt the values and definitions of leadership created by men. But a study sponsored by the International Women's Forum found that some women now define leadership and lead in different ways (Rosener, 1995).

Defining Feminist Leadership

Contributors to a web-based discussion among academic women noted that women not only lead in distinct ways based on their gender socialization, but that some women also are *feminist* leaders. In clarifying the meaning of this term, online team leader Ann Yabusaki quoted Weedon (1987, p. 1): "Feminism is a politics. It is a politics directed at changing existing power relations between men and women in society."

The discussions reflected a strong consensus that feminist leadership is more than leadership style based on female socialization. Feminist leaders are acutely and constantly aware of their parallel roles to serve at the helm as well as to bring about change in power—not only for women, but also for underrepresented racial/ethnic and other oppressed groups. The following descriptions of feminist leaders were offered on the website:

- [She uses] her tremendous energy for connection, coupled with her considerable intelligence and her righteous anger, to support, confront, inspire, and mobilize as the situation warrant[s] (Ester Shapiro, 2/12/03).
- [Is] visionary, inclusive, willing to say things that make others uncomfortable, and willing to tackle and make progress on difficult problems (Janis Sanchez, 2/18/03).
- [Embraces] collaboration and empowerment as two dimensions of [her] leadership [style] (Jean Lau Chin, 10/28/02).
- [Embraces other dimensions,] such as awareness of power relationships and activism. . . . Positive consequences [of feminist leadership] are a combination of effectiveness because of sensitivity to context, awareness of the dynamics of power in groups, and the power of collaboration (Margaret E. Madden, 11/13/02).

The online conversation also included descriptions of incidents in which women, daring to challenge existing male-dominated power structures, were treated as troublemakers or were resented by those whose rights they are seeking to protect. As noted by one of us (Judith Albino, 5/17/03),

> [L]eadership is never without its costs, and the leader who does not eventually pay a price, leads more in form than in substance . . . [T]he risks we take and the prices we pay are proportionate to the public perception of our power.

In addition to discussing the diligence and tenacity required of feminist leaders, contributors to the online conversation raised the issues of culture, race/ethnicity, class, and sexual orientation as contributing to the leadership behaviors of feminist leaders. In the following pages, we reflect on how such demographic characteristics have helped to shape our feminist leadership experiences.

Understanding Feminist Leadership: A Dialogue

Four questions raised by the conveners of the Feminist Visions and Diverse Voices website are explored here through a sharing of two journeys towards and through leadership roles. Those questions are:

1. Do feminist values define certain leadership or management styles?
2. How do we describe the leadership and management tasks that may reflect feminist values, and therefore, feminist styles?
3. Will the expression of feminist management and leadership styles be influenced by factors that define the diversity of feminist leaders? If so, in what ways?
4. How effective are feminist management and leadership styles? Does the context matter?

The scholarship related to feminist leadership is young and characterized by debate about the role of values in defining such leadership. There can be no feminist philosophy without values, but when we move into the real world of management and leadership, values must be operationalized to understand how they influence and drive what happens within organizations.

Toy's perspective

My leadership style grew out of early experiences, including values learned at home and in church, school, and other institutions. Observation and role modeling of others in leadership roles were important, and the context of race, as well as time and place, was salient. I grew up during the civil rights movement in a small, predominantly White community in Kansas, where Brown v. Board of Education framed my thinking about education and leadership. This tumultuous time promised new opportunities and infused in me a sense of optimism and the desire to make a contribution. Phrases such as "separate but equal" and "for Whites only" led me not only to value being treated with dignity, respect, and trust, but also to treating others in the same way. I was often the only African American in the classroom. I wanted to be included and heard, and I also wanted to hear others. My parents were well-respected influential leaders and community change agents, and I wanted to be like them. I valued speaking out on critical issues, confronting injustices head on, and accepting people for what they brought to the situation, regardless of race or socioeconomic status. Worell and Johnson (1997) stated that the sociocultural context in which individuals are located results in differences in their perspectives, based on factors that include cultural and racial ones. My childhood social and cultural experiences laid the foundation for my values as an African American woman.

As a sixth grader, I remember trying to make a difference through the values I embraced. Jason, my White male classmate, was often unfairly treated and excluded by our teacher and classmates. He was seldom called on in class, rarely offered his opinion or responded during discussions, and was always the last one selected as a group participant. We sat close to each other in the back of the classroom, were in the same reading group, and had regular interactions during recess. I found Jason to be a person of many words and ideas, yet our classmates ostracized him and he seemed to lack the self-confidence to fight back. We shared a level of invisibility despite his Whiteness and my being African American.

After discussing this unfair treatment with my parents, I decided that it was my responsibility to make a difference and assumed leadership for creating a more inclusive classroom. When called on in class, I would make a statement, followed by a question posed to Jason—thereby inviting him into the discussion. The teacher finally confronted me and asked what I thought I was trying to do. I very proudly gave her my assessment of the situation, asserting the importance of everyone's contribution, and that Jason was never afforded that opportunity. The teacher separated us, moving Jason's desk closer to hers. She did not support my early attempts to generate social justice in the classroom, but I continued to do what I could. This early experience helped spawn a set of values that reflect my current leadership style, which is consistent with feminist values.

Judith's perspective

Feminist values alone cannot define a leadership or style, but they will contribute to the manifestation of a leader's style. Moreover, the behaviors of feminist leaders are only feminist if they also are imbued with the values and purposes of feminism. For example, feminist leaders may mentor others, or use shared decision-making approaches—yet with different motives. Only the leader who translates the values of feminism into behaviors—and who *also* overtly gives voice and power to those values both publicly and privately—can be considered to have a feminist leadership style.

Giving voice to feminist values is something that I began doing early on, and I learned the price of doing so. More than anything else in my childhood perhaps, I remember my sense of indignation on learning that the world had chosen to set limits on my behavior, experiences, and achievement—simply because I was born female. I was angered by that unfairness. But as a teenager I also experienced the pressure that Matina Horner (1968) later labeled the "need to avoid success." As a young woman in the South, I was taught explicitly that it was important to defer to boys (or men). That presented a dilemma, since I was expected to do well in school—but without competing with or challenging male students.

I recall an incident related to my high school's annual speech contest for senior students. Seniors were required to write a paper, and the authors of the best papers (3 male and 3 female) presented their work and were judged at a public event. As a finalist, I took strong exception when told that the women would be required to wear "long, white formal gowns" for the presentations. I neither owned one nor wanted to, but even more, I did not want to deliver my paper dressed in a way (given the extravagant strapless and bouffant dress style of the day) that would seem to invite attention to my appearance, rather than my oratory. I protested, and I sought unsuccessfully to gain the support of the other women contestants. Ultimately, I was told that I would only be allowed to compete under the prescribed conditions.

From that experience, I learned that I had to choose how I wanted to make my point. I considered boycotting the competition, but decided that it was more important to go on record from a position of strength, and that required me to win the contest. My mother bought me the most beautiful gown she could afford and spent hours coaching me. I was determined to be the best, and I did win. I was disappointed that I had been unable to more publicly make the point that appearance should not be a part of evaluation in an academic setting, but I con-soled myself that I had allowed neither my own perception of my inappropriate dress, nor others' perceptions of my "inappropriate rebelliousness," to be used as an excuse to deny the quality of my per-formance or the legitimacy of my position. Learning to accept the need to choose between conflicting, but equally important, goals—something not uncommon for leaders in higher education—began consciously for me in that competition.

There was another lesson in this situation as well. As a result of my inability to persuade other women to join me in protest, I began to understand that "fairness" may not be everyone's goal in a given situ-ation. While I believed the women contestants were being unfairly pre-sented with an obstacle, they chose not to view themselves as unfairly treated, and I could not deny their right to the values underlying those judgments. This situation is trivial, of course, by comparison with the experiences of oppressed women who dare not speak the truth to power for fear of losing their incomes, their families, or even their own lives, but the mechanics of cultural context are not dissimilar.

Leadership and Management Tasks that Reflect Feminist Values and Style

Margaret Madden pointed out during the online discussion (10/30/02) that leadership is contextual and that it involves identity issues and power relationships. This premise contrasts sharply with the traditional "great man" theory that equates leadership with the personality of the leader. Madden suggested that "[feminist leaders] are active agents who use diverse behaviors and strategies to cope and grow within various environments." To do so requires a consideration of the specific tasks of leadership.

Judith's perspective

"Feminist styles" need to be understood in the context of the particular tasks before the leader. For example, planning, decision making, persuasion, and allocation of resources are tasks through which feminist values can be manifested. There are others as well—for example, goal setting and problem solving, communications, tactical approaches, and the organization of people and tasks.

Often seen as the core skill and task of leadership, decision making is nearly always undertaken for the achievement of goals, and it usually is oriented institutionally, politically, or personally. Furthermore, it is usually informed—either broadly or narrowly—by the views of others. Most feminists would say that consensus decision making is ideal, but when self-interests polarize people, consensus may not be possible. Moreover, if self-interests are strong, voting may only suppress and alienate important minority views and needs. Feminist decision making is inclusive in input, broadly tested for impact, and sustaining of the goals of the organization, those who work for it, and those who are served by it. So feminist leaders may not always choose consensus, but feminist values will always guide their choice.

Today's management theories frequently advocate decision making at the level of implementation, insuring that those who are most affected by a decision make that decision. But flattening the organizational structure by pushing decision making "down" can be complicated. We had great difficulty achieving effective horizontal decision making at a particular university because the elimination of administrative layers was seen as "centralizing" rather than "decentralizing." The same individuals who had complained earlier about unnecessary administrative layers in decision making seemed incapable of addressing decisions that should always have been theirs. When leadership roles were eliminated, they assumed that the approval function had moved "up" instead of "down." In retrospect, the institution needed more collaboration in the development of its new structure than the pressures of time and resources had allowed. Although the basic decision processes had been highly participatory and consistent with feminist values, the meaning of the change and its impact were not well understood or incorporated across the institution.

Problem-based approaches in executive teamwork can be misunderstood. After my first executive cabinet meeting (where all the other university officers were men), the rumor circulated that I didn't know what to do, since "I had to ask their opinions." The executive staff typically used meetings to present reports, but they rarely actually shared perspectives on issues. They were taken aback by my insistence on more interactive decision making and respect for diverse views. Eventually, most came to like the approach and to value the new challenges. Even some feminists with whom I have worked have difficulty with an approach that requires them to think through issues for which they may not be solely responsible, or to listen to others' views of an issue for which they are responsible.

Given some of these complications, we can nonetheless describe what we expect to see in the behaviors of most feminist leaders, who begin by understanding and using the leadership of all the various subgroups within the organization. They recognize that leadership is shared, and they make it clear to other leaders that it is their responsibility to insure that opportunities for meaningful participation are provided. Perhaps most important, they provide the model for doing just that. Meetings are opportunities to use the intellectual resources of all those who are present, not simply times for reporting and pronouncing. Feminist leaders will tend to use problem-solving approaches that engage the interests of others and elicit their most creative thinking. They are not afraid to make suggestions, but they indicate that their ideas are no more important than other ideas. They invite comment and critique, not endorsement. They demonstrate appreciation for the work of others and highlight their contributions. Just like any leaders, feminist leaders ultimately take responsibility for the decisions made within an institution, giving credit for the ideas that others have contributed, and inviting analysis of any aspects of failure. Finally, feminist leaders are outspoken on issues of inclusion and empowerment, and forceful in advocating for diversity and strategies that express, rather than oppress, minority views and opinions.

Toy's perspective

Both subtle and overt experiences with discrimination, stereotyping, racism, and sexism are constants for women of color, and issues of racism and sexism may be hard to differentiate. Maintaining feminist values as an African American leader has helped me to lessen potential feelings of racial oppression, anger, and embitterment and has led to more productive behavior.

One African American woman in the online discussion described herself as a "neo-race woman" and asked, "[A]re African American women first Black then women or first women then Black?" (Jessica Henderson Daniel, 5/23/03; see chapter 1, p. 38, for the rest of this contribution).

According to Heim and Golant (1992), leveling the playing field and flattening the hierarchy are often goals of women in leadership. As a feminist leader, my style is not to wield power, but to share power through collaboration as a strategy for influencing others to assume responsibility for shared goals. But hierarchical structures are common in academic institutions, and individuals tend to participate according to more traditional schema grounded in patriarchal approaches to leadership.

When assuming a new leadership role in a unit traditionally led by men, I found staff members reluctant to make decisions, instead bringing matters to me for input and approval. While institutional culture supported this behavior, by bringing people together to foster shared governance and consensus building, we began to move away from a "go tell daddy" mode of crisis-driven administration, to more unit accountability, where team building, organization of tasks, and shared problem solving were valued.

I also have experienced the collision of my feminist values with the expectations of an organizational culture. As a youngster, I learned to respect people older than me by addressing them by title, a formality common within the African American community. These patterns persist in Black higher education institutions, and it was not until I reached graduate school at a predominantly White institution that I experienced a "leveling of the playing field" whereby graduate students addressed professors by their first names. Moreover, I noticed that staff called the president, vice presidents, and deans by their first names, while at predominantly Black campuses, staff and students referred to administrators by institutional title.

Later, as an African American woman in an HBCU (the customary designation for historically Black colleges and universities) I encouraged a shift to the more informal use of my first name. However, staff viewed this as a sign of disrespect. Expectations for increased responsibility and accountability also heightened their discomfort. Despite being guided by my feminist values and principles, I found that this strategy was not effective within the context of that institution. My goal was to foster trust, but it was too early for that. Others were not comfortable with my giving up the referent power I was fully prepared to yield.

Titles were important in this HBCU setting, and the use of my first name was experienced as disruptive, inappropriate to the culture, and

77

thus disempowering. My perspective, expectations, and level of self-confidence as a woman in leadership were outside the boundaries of the staff members' current confidence levels. The focus needed to be on increasing their preparation, professional development, and self-assurance level, thus leading to their empowerment and ability for accepting more responsibility/accountability. Creating increased levels of trust in leadership style that embraced feminist values and practices was needed, not a shift in referent power to a name. Because of experiences with oppression in society and in organizations, women (and people of color) often need skills for empowering (Chin & Russo, 1997). For African American female leaders, this may mean both demonstrating those skills and demonstrating an understanding of oppression to encourage the development of empowering skills in others.

Diversity in Feminist Leadership

A wide range of factors contributes to diversity in the practice of feminist leadership. There is diversity of style, as well as diversity in the background and approaches of leaders and in the cultures of organizations.

Toy's perspective

Earlier in this chapter, I referenced the dominant influence of male models of leadership, but I do not believe that the traditional male/female dichotomy for characterizing leadership behaviors is useful if we want to understand the influence of values on leadership styles. In other words, feminist leadership styles offer options for how to lead and resonate from a set of values, interpersonal interactions, and processes that a leader chooses to adopt. All leaders do not have the same values and interpersonal skills and do not express ideas, engage in behaviors, or act upon those values in the same way. I concur with Madden's (2002) statement that "feminist principles require the articulation of very clear statements of right and wrong, or acceptable and unacceptable behaviors" (p. 120).

How one chooses to engage as a leader is influenced by the context of the leadership setting. Understanding the organization's politics is critical to successful leadership, and even more so for African American women as feminist leaders. Interacting with a White population versus interacting with other African Americans calls for a different set of leadership behaviors. In HBCU settings, the impact of racial oppression, discrimination, and a civil rights agenda is understood. Within that context, there also is an operating tradition based on a Black patriarchal model of leadership, in which gender and the marginalization of women take on a special meaning. African American women in HBCUs who want to contribute equally as members of a Black campus community may be further oppressed by the Black male privilege and control in that setting. In contrast, experiencing White male hegemony is the more typical context for African American female leaders at predominantly White institutions. At those institutions, issues of feminism are more linked with White female hegemony for African American women leaders (Lewis, 1997). Thus an African American feminist leader in a predominately White setting needs to understand White male and female hegemony and how her leadership as a social change agent is manifested and supported. Who will be the support network(s) for an African American feminist leader—women, other African Americans, or both? How should she exercise leadership that promotes a social justice agenda when the privileges for women and people of color are different, and perceptions are drawn from theories of racial inferiority and deficiency and/or gender discrimination? In a predominantly White setting, an African American woman in leadership is never sure which are most critical—issues of race or of gender. Gender and racial marginalization are equally problematic for African American women.

In predominantly White settings, when I am asked to assume responsibility for issues related to ethnic/racial diversity, there is the presumption that race alone makes one an expert. As an African American, I feel less marginalized when assigned to more general responsibilities, where I am asked to lead to help the group think "out of the box," or as someone who can address diverse points of view or present something different than mainstream thinking. Such assignments present opportunities for feminist leadership at its best. These types of leadership responsibilities were extended and ones I embraced as a feminist leader in a predominantly White setting. What I brought to the situation as an African American woman was personally empowering, and empowering for women of color, as well as other women who were carving out their rightful places as feminist leaders.

Institutional fit provides yet another perspective from which to examine diversity in feminist leadership. As an African American woman at predominantly White institutions, the assessment of fit may be understood within an institutional context based on cultural assimilation. Does she embrace our Eurocentric cultural values or does she have an aggressive racial/civil rights agenda? Will she force issues of affirmative action on us? Of course, one could be hired to meet the institution's affirmative action goals or as a token hire to present a picture of supporting people of color and women. Given these issues, a leader's own assessment of personal values in the context of institutional values is critical to understanding the fit with local politics. This personal assessment is the only way to determine when to remain at an institution or to move on, in seeking leadership opportunities as a feminist leader of color.

Understanding the climate of an HBCU institution, as well as a predominantly White one, requires assessing the institution's perspectives on leadership diversity. The comfort level with traditions of Black patriarchal leadership on an HBCU campus may be even more important than the existence of fewer freedoms for women (Cole & Guy-Sheftall, 2003). As a new hire on an HBCU campus, understanding traditions and embracing the culture were a necessity, yet required a delicate balance for infusing a fresh perspective as a feminist leader. In discussing this inner tension with a male colleague, I had an affirming and empowering experience. His statement to me was, "As a new leader, we are looking for your appreciation and celebration of our culture and traditions, but this also is your opportunity to start new traditions that we can embrace, and I know the campus is poised for this."

Judith's perspective

It is difficult to separate who one is as a person from the leadership style that one demonstrates. We are what we have learned, who has influenced us, and the culture in which we have grown and lived. Even if we wanted to separate ourselves as leaders from those things that have shaped us as human beings, it would be impossible. Others will have perceptions of who we are and how we work, and those will impact us. Those perceptions may, or may not, be accurate; they may be based on ethnicity, on past activities, or on what has been heard from others. If they are flattering perceptions, or if they simply seem to provide a good fit with the way an organization sees itself, style will be described positively and will be seen as effective. On the other hand, if a particular collection of attributes is alien to those interacting with leadership, or if they are not understood, leadership behavior and style will be viewed negatively. Whether or not one is seen as a feminist leader will be a function of many factors, and not just values and behaviors in any objective sense. Leadership style is always multidimensional—quite simply because people are multidimensional.

Throughout my career, I have thought of myself as a leader who is both a scientist and a feminist. The former descriptor has been especially important to me because within an academic community, data are usually respected. But that also depends on the institution. For institutions with a strong research orientation, respect for and identification with science may be extremely important, while at another institution, those same qualities may be threatening to some. I also have learned that data are *never* enough. Absolutely unassailable data supporting a decision or change will not be accepted if those within the organization are not ready or willing to accept that change, or if it is inconsistent with their perceived interests.

Just as I have thought of myself as a scientist-leader, others may think of themselves as teacher-leaders, politician-leaders, organizer-leaders, activist-leaders, and so on. There are leaders who see themselves as Latina, Asian American, or African American leaders, and so on. Others view themselves in terms of a disciplinary orientation—psychologist-leaders, economist-leaders, or historian-leaders. Any of these also may see themselves as feminist leaders, and in all cases, the values brought by the leaders' respective identities can be energizing for an institution.

There is a tendency to believe that there is an "ideal type" of leader, and that by trying to look and think like other leaders, one can be seen as that ideal. Ultimately, however, that ideal has little to do with an individual's performance as a leader. Bennis (1997) listed the traits of good leaders, and I am struck by the fact that he began with the quality of "self-knowledge." He pointed out that the best leaders have worked hard to know and understand themselves and their strengths, what they believe, and what they care about. In thinking about feminist leadership, we need to look at the role of feminist values in our lives as a part of that kind of self-knowledge.

When I was honored by a state women's political caucus some years ago, I was awarded a plaque with the following words by Susan B. Anthony:

> Cautious, careful people, always casting about to preserve their reputation and social standing, never can bring about a reform. Those who are really in earnest must be willing to be anything or nothing in the

world's estimation, and publicly and privately in season and out, avow their sympathies with despised and persecuted ideas and their advocates, and bear the consequences.

Those words remind me that others see my values. I recognize that those values will not be accepted in every situation or institution, and they must not preclude my working with those who may not share them, but they will always give me strength, and they always will influence my leadership.

The choices made by women and the strategies they adopt reflect overlapping as well as unique dimensions of leadership. Both women and men of various racial and ethnic backgrounds use feminist leadership behaviors. Some use them knowingly, with great intentionality, because of a commitment to equity and justice. Others may use them as a more natural outgrowth or response to a situation, yet not necessarily label them as feminist. No one set of words fits all feminist leaders in any and all situations.

I am convinced that the diversity of backgrounds brought by women to the workplace can create and strengthen what we now view as feminist styles of leadership. As a result of social and cultural experiences, women will have different perceptions of what their privileges are, or are not, at work and in other settings. They will have different views of the possible, and of the power of their presence. By observing and supporting one another in our respective roles, leaders can build a broader and stronger repertoire of work behaviors and values that reflect a feminist orientation.

Effectiveness of Feminist Leadership

Virtually no research, and certainly no controlled research, has been carried out on the relative effectiveness of feminist leadership. In keeping with the approach of this chapter, therefore, our answer to this question must be both theoretical and anecdotal.

Judith's perspective

Although feminist leadership can be very effective, gender always matters, and perceptions drive evaluations. In a context where women may be seen by some as indecisive, a style which involves consulting others and seeking broad input may be viewed as weak by virtue of its inclusiveness. Similarly, if the expectations for leadership are that the leader will be forceful in asserting positions, then a feminist leader who listens carefully to the concerns of constituents, who works to empower others, and who is more interested in achievement than in power may be perceived as "not strong enough" for the job. Toy's comparison of leadership perspectives within historically Black and predominantly White higher education institutions underscores the complexity of expectations related to gender roles.

The concept of power, what it is and how it should be used, seems to present one of the most difficult obstacles as we try to assess the effectiveness of feminist leadership. We do not generally talk about power when we talk about women's ways of leading. We talk about empowering others, building consensus, and sharing responsibilities of leadership. I have seen, time and time again, however, that even if I do not accept power, it will be attributed to me as a leader. Even if I do not use it, I will be perceived as using it and, therefore, will have used it.

The concept of power within a feminist context is what Bennis (1997) has described as "value power." This type of power is different from coercive power, the power of expertise, or the power of position. Rather, it is a type of power built on ideas and standards that a constituency can relate to and feel good about. With this type of power, a leader communicates a set of values through words and actions, and works with others to infuse that set of values throughout the system. When value power works, followers are every bit as important as leaders in an organization.

Value power in a feminist tradition nurtures open communication, shared accountability, team leadership, broad participation in consensus-building, and authentic relationships. Achieving this goes beyond what a leader believes and articulates; it requires the development of a high level of trust throughout an organization. In an organization where there is constant blaming, withholding of information, complaining, and even paranoia, value power is not being exercised. Creating this kind of value power starts with the leader, but it cannot reside there exclusively. Effective feminist leadership, then, can be said to support, rather than impose, the development of a sense of trust and shared values. Even when other stakeholder goals are essential to survival, a feminist leader moves the organization towards success through commitment to a set of values that are embraced by the organizational culture. This is a daunting task —more challenging than meeting a bottom line or developing new programs or products. Nonetheless, it is the task for which a feminist leadership approach is most appropriate and will be most effective.

Toy's perspective

In developing my leadership style, I learned from observing leaders with whom I had worked or by whom I was mentored—some highly effective and others less so. Those leaders included women and men, African Americans and Whites, with styles that ran the gamut from autocratic to queen bee, from nurturing and overly empathic to ego-driven and self-serving, from charismatic and bright to aggressive and dictatorial, and from militaristic and micromanaging to mothering and indecisive. I sometimes disagreed with a leader's approach, yet embraced the outcomes of that leadership, and noticed that some change in processes or adoption of new behaviors usually made the difference in outcome.

Effective feminist leadership will nearly always introduce opportunities for re-examining the process by which decisions are reached and implemented through new forms of behavior. Feminist leadership generates new ground rules and shifts the focus to changes in contingencies. This notion is supported by Astin and Astin's (2001) transformational leadership model that uses concepts drawn from feminist values and styles.

Diversity in leadership approaches among women presidents is inevitable. Additionally, I would argue that many of them are influenced by feminist values that promote what are acceptable and unacceptable behaviors for faculty, staff, administrators, and students at various levels of the campus. Recognizing that universities and colleges have more male than female faculty, staff, and administrators, the need to engage men as advocates is vital to ensuring the effectiveness of those leading from a feminist perspective.

Fletcher suggests that gender schemas influence how we filter information, what we see and expect, and how we interpret it. She says:

> gender schemas are powerful . . . and . . . the consequences of practicing new leadership will be different for women and men. While men risk being labeled wimps when they engage in new leadership behaviors, they may have an easier time proclaiming what they do as "new." (Fletcher, 2002, p. 3)

Women, on the other hand, may be negatively characterized and not credited as doing anything new, despite their effectiveness, because they will be labeled as simply doing what women always do as they engage in collaboration, shared decision making, listening, and team work.

Women who are effective feminist leaders are setting the stage for change—by transforming campuses and by influencing others to adopt new attitudes, behaviors, and leadership styles. Feminist leaders empower and influence others to effectively work in more egalitarian climates and to educate students and mentor others, thus preparing future generations of leaders who embrace feminist values. Guy-Sheftall, in writing about transforming the academy says:

> bell hooks . . . makes a compelling argument for the need to transform ourselves into different teachers [leaders/administrators] armed with "radical and subversive" feminist strategies capable of forging a new world desperately in need of emerging: "We must learn from one another, sharing ideas and pedagogical strategies [feminist leadership styles] . . . We must be willing to . . . challenge, change, and create new approaches. We must be willing to restore the spirit of risk—to be fast, wild, to take hold, turn around, transform." (Guy-Sheftall, 1997, p. 123)

Summary and Conclusions

By drawing on the rich content of the online discussion and on our perspectives as an African American and a White feminist leader, we have raised issues of context and values that will differentially affect and influence the behaviors of women leaders. Having shared our personal experiences and observations of the obstacles, the opportunities, and the rewards of feminist leadership, it seems fitting to provide a definition of feminist leadership built on this richness of context. We have combined the elements of feminist leadership described by both of us. Because of that, the definition offered is truly a collaborative one.

Feminist leadership: a collaborative definition

Feminist leadership is, above all, values-driven and forceful in asserting those values. Feminist leadership values people, relationships, absolute fairness and equity, honesty, collaboration, and communal goals and achievements. The behaviors that characterize feminist leadership grow out of, are sustained by, and garner power from these values. They include informed decision making that is participatory and owned by all constituencies of the organization or institution; activities that are aimed at empowering those same constituencies and at maximizing opportunities for personal growth in the workplace; and continual striving for goals that are shared by the community, and directed at creating the best possible outcome for both stakeholders and society.

Note

The authors wish to thank Gloria Thomas and Bettie White from the American Council on Education for the input and edits to earlier draft versions of this chapter. Their candid reflections and written comments helped to clarify differences and capture the essential commonalities of our two diverse experiences. They share our hope that the experiences explored can serve as poignant guides and stepping stones for future feminist leaders.

References

Astin, A., & Astin, H. (January, 2001). Principles of transformative leadership. *AAHE Bulletin, 53*(5) 3–6.

Bennis, W. (1997). *Managing people is like herding cats.* Provo, UT: Executive Excellence Publishing.

Chin, J. L., & Russo, N. F. (1997). Feminist curriculum development: Principles and resources. In J. Worell & N. G. Johnson (Eds.), *Shaping the future of feminist psychology: Education, research, and practice* (pp. 93–120). Washington, DC: American Psychological Association.

Cole, J. B., & Guy-Sheftall, B. (2003). *Gender talk: The struggle for women's equality in African American communities.* Toronto, ON: Random House of Canada.

Fletcher, J. K. (August, 2002). *The greatly exaggerated demise of heroic leadership: Gender, power, and the myth of the female advantage.* CGO Insights, Briefing No. 13. Boston: Center for Gender in Organizations.

Guy-Sheftall, B. (1997). Transforming the academy: A black feminist perspective. In L. Benjamin (Ed.), *Black women in the academy: Promises and perils* (pp. 115–123). Gainesville: University Press of Florida.

Heim, P., & Golant, S. K. (1992). *Hardball for women: Winning at the game of business.* Los Angeles: Lowell House.

Horner, M. S. (1968). *Sex differences in achievement motivation and performance in competitive and non-competitive situations.* Unpublished doctoral dissertation, University of Michigan. University Microfilms, No. 69–12.

Hughes, R. L., Ginnett, R. C., & Curphy, G. J. (1995). What is leadership? In J. T. Wren (Ed.), *The leader's companion* (pp. 39–46). New York: The Free Press.

Jablonski, M. (2000). The leadership challenge for women college presidents. In J. Glazer-Raymo, B. K. Townsend, & B. Ropers-Huilman (Eds.), *Women in higher education: A feminist perspective* (pp. 243–251), ASHE Reader Series (2nd ed.). Boston: Pearson Custom Publishing.

Lewis, S. F. (1997). Africana feminism: An alternative paradigm for black women in the academy. In L. Benjamin (Ed.), *Black women in the academy: Promises and perils* (pp. 41–52). Gainesville: University Press of Florida.

Madden, M. (2002). The transformative leadership of women in higher education administration. In J. DiGeorgio-Lutz (Ed.), *Women in higher education: Empowering change* (pp. 115–180). Westport, CT: Praeger Publishers.

Rosener, J. B. (1995). Ways women lead. In J. T. Wren (Ed.), *The leader's companion* (pp. 149–160). New York: The Free Press.

Weedon, C. (1987). *Feminist practice and post-structuralist theory.* Oxford: Blackwell.

Worell, J., & Johnson, N. G., (Eds.) (1997). *Shaping the future of feminist psychology: Education, research, and practice.* Washington, DC: American Psychological Association.

Chapter 4

Toward Culturally Competent, Gender-Equitable Leadership: Assessing Outcomes of Women's Leadership in Diverse Contexts

Ester R. Shapiro and Jennifer M. Leigh[1]

The Changing Face of Women's Leadership: Opportunities and Resistance

A young African American woman was employed as a mental health worker at a high-prestige teaching hospital and enlisted in the Army Reserve while putting herself through school at an urban public university. She hoped the professional experience would help her meet her goals of attaining a PhD in clinical psychology. The only woman of color on the nursing staff, she was repeatedly assigned back-to-back shifts caring for violent adolescent male inpatients, in violation of hospital rules, because she was the most effective at setting interpersonal limits without requiring patient restraints. When, inevitably, her exhaustion and isolation resulted in an incident of escalation in a young male patient's violent behavior, her shame, fear, and anger coupled with her mistrust of White authority in institutions led her to submit her resignation without offering any explanation, even though her seniority guaranteed her a higher salary than she would receive elsewhere. Her Latina psychology professor and advisor encouraged her to submit a letter of resignation to her unit supervisor, and coached her through a strategic reframing of the events on the unit, placing the violations of procedure and their racialized tone at the forefront of her communication. This intervention helped to restore her self-respect. It also opened the door to an effective conversation with her supervisor about race, equity, and safety on the unit, resulting in more carefully monitored workplace procedures and permitting her to remain in her job.

Another example is that of an Afro-Caribbean counseling psychologist with a master's degree and extensive experience in domestic violence work. Her practicum training and subsequent work experience had all been in teaching hospital settings where her outspoken advocacy for attending to the intersection of race and culture had been used to advertise hospital community relations and commitment to affirmative action. At the same time, she found that she was doing extensive after-hours work while being passed over for promotions. One evening during dinner with her support network of women of color working in domestic violence, a colleague noted that hospitals would inevitably regard her master's degree in counseling as lower in the prestige hierarchy than other degrees. This friend had a senior mentor who had helped her prepare for her current job as executive director of a local domestic violence program, where her experience and credentials as a feminist and woman of color were highly valued. This feedback and support from her mentor and colleagues provided the impetus for sharing her frustrations with her supervisor and generated a change in her job-seeking strategy that resulted in her successful employment as a senior director at a large feminist organization in which her commitment to work in race, ethnicity, and gender is strongly supported.

Both these women used mentor and peer support, institutional analysis, and sociopolitical reframing as resources to successfully confront workplace discrimination and make strategic decisions that advanced their development as emerging leaders who would challenge sexist and racist health care systems. Their experiences illustrate:

- The redefinition of culturally competent, gender-equitable women's leadership as a social developmental process characterizing individuals in relationships and ecologies;
- Culturally competent, gender-equitable leadership as strategic mobilization of personal, relational, and collective resources required to achieve both immediate and long-term goals in specific contexts;

- The need to evaluate skills, resources, and outcomes of culturally competent, gender-equitable women's leadership using complex social developmental and multisystemic assessment frameworks.

Chapter Overview

The goal of creating more diverse workplaces within a more just society offers women leaders extraordinary opportunities and challenges. This chapter presents an interdisciplinary, ecosystemic developmental approach to culturally competent, gender-equitable women's leadership as the effective practice of change promoting equity in diverse contexts. We build from multisystemic approaches to cultural competence, including Chin's approach to cultural competence as a skills-based process (Chin, 2000, 2003); Betancourt, Green, Carrillo, and Ananeh-Firempong's (2003) multilevel analysis of barriers to culturally competent health care; and Dreachslin, Weech-Maldonado, and Dansky's (2004) conceptual framework for reducing racial disparities in health by evaluating the impact of organizational behavior on individual, group, and organizational outcomes. We argue that multisystemic approaches linking personal, organizational, and sociocultural dimensions of cultural competence offer women a collaborative, mutual empowerment approach to leadership development connecting individual, institutional, and collective processes of change. Multisystemic approaches to cultural competence emphasize the critical role of diversity in leadership, the importance of assessing competencies in multiple domains, and results-based accountability. The chapter draws on interdisciplinary work suggesting that culturally competent, gender-equitable leadership requires strategic readings of power in context in order to leverage resources, recognize barriers, and adapt strategies to achieve desired results. Rather than focus on individual leaders, we view leadership as a quality of relationships promoting agency with solidarity and supporting personal and collective action toward mutually desired change.

Using these frameworks, we offer a set of guiding principles for culturally competent, gender-equitable women's leadership as a collaborative practice of empowerment designed to identify and leverage resources in multiple systems supporting achievement of mutually agreed-upon goals. We suggest tools for assessing leadership competencies, evaluating ecosystemic resources and barriers, implementing action to achieve desired goals, and evaluating outcomes of individual and collective leadership. Culturally competent gender-equitable women's leadership is viewed as a shared life journey and work in progress, in which measurement of outcomes toward desired results offers feedback promoting shared learning, helps identify practices promoting equity and opportunity as well as those promoting social inequality, and supports accountability for reaching desired outcomes.

Measurement of individual and collective leadership competencies, ecosystemic resources and barriers, and their impact on desired outcomes requires using multimethod assessment tools specific to the setting and attentive to strategic goals. For example, definitions of "evidence-based practice" that emphasize practitioners, researchers, and patients as partners in determining quality care have been instrumental tools for advocacy in identifying and addressing gender, racial, and ethnic disparities in health and human services (Institute of Medicine, 2001, 2003). In other settings, civil rights or human rights guidelines might offer compelling framings of social justice issues. Multisystemic assessment approaches linking gender and culture can make use of both qualitative and quantitative, reflective and participatory models, as well as causal research models. Selection of process, outcome, and impact evaluations will depend on context and purpose, and are chosen through collaboration (Shapiro, 2005). Research and self-assessment become tools promoting shared development, personal and collective empowerment, advocacy, and progress toward a more just society.

Challenges in Culturally Competent Gender-Equitable Women's Leadership Studies: Complexity, Collaboration, and Accountability in the Practice of Change

The idea of leadership, even more clearly than other social constructs, emerges within a historical and political context and reflects a society's vision for its future, how to best achieve its goals, and who can be empowered to guide these social processes. An earlier academic tradition in leadership studies focused on "great men" in governance, and on a "command and control" view of qualities making these great men effective in leading on a path that others follow. Changes brought about by civil rights and feminist movements, combined with the growing complexity, rapid change, and interdependence of social institutions, have generated substantial shifts in our understanding of who can lead and how effective leadership can best be accomplished. Yet while individuals, social groups, and institutions around the world state a commitment to diversity and equality of opportunity, positions of power in most societies remain primarily in the hands of men belonging to socially dominant groups. Theory and research on gender, culture, citizen participation, and grass-roots leadership in global community development emphasizing "power from below" shows remarkable convergence with literatures on leadership, governance, and the exercise of "power from above" as women and men from nondominant social groups strive to achieve self-determination and access resources necessary for its practice. Equitable access to power requires the mobilization of agency and solidarity at multiple levels of individual, group, institutional, and cultural systems, to counter the multiple redundancies that protect the powerful and preserve the reproduction of privilege.

Recent work in the field of leadership studies suggests a movement away from a hierarchical, "command and control" model toward approaches termed "twenty-first century" leadership (Allen, Bordas, Hickman, Matusak, Sorenson, & Whitmire, 1999), "transformational" (Bass, 1990; Conger, 1999), "collaborative" (Leigh, 2003; Rawlings, 2000), and "bridging." These emerging models view leadership as collaborative, distributed, flexible, contingent and contextualized, responsive to the evolving, dynamic goals of a particular workplace or community (Klenke, 1996). Theories such as family systems (Cobb, 2003; Holvino, 2003), complex adaptive systems (Institute of Medicine, 2001; Wheatley, 1992), feminist ecological approaches (Ballou, Matsumoto, & Wagner, 2002), and learning organizations (Senge, 1990) suggest that effective change in communities and organizations involves dynamic, coconstructive processes linking individual meanings and actions with organizational processes within a wider social context. The ecosystemic levels of individual, relational, organizational, and sociocultural domains contribute potential resources and barriers facilitating or impeding progress toward mutually desired goals.

A number of writers have attempted to operationalize this new model of leadership in terms of leadership principles and practices. Senge (1990) established a set of five tenets that came to be regarded as a landmark in the field of this new leadership paradigm. Senge proposes that in order to change more traditional, hierarchical organizations into organizations that can continually adapt to the challenges posed by a complex society, the members must think and interact in a way consistent with five disciplines:

1. A "systems thinking" approach to understand the role of organizational structure in determining individual action;
2. "Personal mastery" to clarify both what is truly important to them, and to gain a more accurate perception of their relationships and their lives;
3. An awareness of unconscious "mental models" (i.e., our tacit assumptions about how the world works);
4. The ability to build a "shared vision" to foster a climate in which individuals can develop a personal commitment to organizational goals; and
5. An ability to foster "team learning" by being able to listen deeply to others, observe one's own internal reactions, and use this information to guide interventions in a group context.

Kouzes and Posner (1997) have illuminated skills involved in the practice of effective leadership by conducting qualitative research on individual stories of their "personal best" leadership experiences. Kouzes and Posner contend that "leadership" is practiced by every individual at some point in time. For their research, therefore, they interviewed individuals at varying levels within their workplaces, in community groups, and in families. Over the thousands of stories they collected regarding times individuals perceived themselves to have led effectively, Kouzes and Posner were able to distill these five practices common to all:

1. *Challenging the process*—searching for opportunities to improve the organization, being willing to take risks and view disappointments as learning opportunities;
2. *Inspiring a shared vision*—believing that one can make a difference and enlisting others in your dreams;
3. *Enabling others to act*—showing mutual respect and fostering collaboration, and striving to make each person feel capable and powerful;
4. *Modeling the way*—setting an example for others, and setting interim goals for small wins along the way;
5. *Encouraging the heart*—recognizing others for their contributions and celebrating accomplishments. This approach emphasizes that participants at every level of an organization can contribute as leaders, and identifies pragmatic, teachable skills involved in nurturing both personal and collective change within organizations.

Writing about transformational leadership, Conger (1999) identified processes common to this approach: vision, inspiration, role modeling, intellectual stimulation, meaning making, appeals to higher order needs, empowerment, setting of high expectations, and fostering collective identity. Transformational models of leadership emphasize the importance of a leader's vision in giving direction and meaning to others, the communication of high expectations coupled with empowerment of others, nurturance of individual growth in a climate of respect and mutual trust, and de-emphasizing hierarchical control strategies. Consistent with ecosystemic, developmental systems approaches, the nurturing of others becomes the major goal of effective transformational leaders, and these values are incorporated into expectations for and measures of effective leadership. Theories of transformational leadership articulate a systemic, collaborative approach recognizing the interweaving of individual and organizational practices and meanings. Because they often fail to give explicit attention to the roles of gender and ethnicity—or more specifically sexism and racism—as factors in leadership practice, they cannot be directly translated to the real world of power and privilege. Nevertheless, when supplemented with attention to these variables as dimensions of power in which social inequality is reflected in organizational processes, transformational leadership models can be useful.

Approaches to organizational development that focus on race and culture define the truly inclusive organization as one in which diverse participants determine goals and practices at every level of the organization's functioning, contributing to its transformation (Fine, 1995). For example, cultural competence in the health care field requires attention not just to direct health care provider/participant interactions, but to multiple levels of organization starting with the staffing and training of receptionists and culturally competent translators and including senior administrative and board of director diversity (Betancourt et al., 2003; Chin, 2000; Dreachslin & Agho, 2001; Dreachslin et al., 2004). In studying the effectiveness of ethnically diverse health care teams, Dreachslin and colleagues identified an effective "diversity leadership" style directly addressing a team's racial dynamics and validating different perspectives, which made it possible for teams to overcome barriers in worldview, communication differences, and social isolation.

Transformational, collaborative, or complex systems approaches to leadership are highly valued in principle in most contemporary organizations, and have been found to be more effective than hierarchical approaches (Eagly & Carli, 2001; Eagly, Johannesen-Schmidt, & van

Engen, 2003). However, the implementation of such leadership approaches, especially by women and racial or ethnic minorities, has
confronted significant challenges from racist and sexist stereotypes and
other uses and abuses of power to preserve the status quo. While recent
meta-analyses suggest that transformational leadership is more effective than hierarchical leadership, they also suggest that gender, ethnic,
and racial stereotypes substantially impact on how both senior supervisors and subordinates or followers respond to the exercise of power
by members of nondominant groups (Eagly et al., 2003; Eagly, Karau,
& Makhijani, 1995; Fiske, 1998; Fletcher, 1999; Pratto & Espinoza, 2001;
Ridgeway, 2001; Yoder, 2001).

As suggested by contemporary contextual theories of leadership, implementation of collaborative leadership has faced significant challenges
in both work and community settings. For example, Fletcher (1999)
documented that when women practiced "collaborative" and "relational"
skills in the workplace (e.g., allowing room for others to speak), they
were not commended for embodying leaderlike behaviors. Such
behaviors were not particularly noticed because they were expected and
viewed as consistent with women's roles. Some scholars argue that
although organizations are increasingly adopting the language and endors-
ing the skills associated with more collaborative leadership approaches,
individualistic, hierarchical approaches continue to be rewarded
(Fletcher & Kaufer, 2002). Yoder (2001), Eagly et al. (2003), and others
suggest that women are more accepted and more effective as leaders
when they can combine their authority with nurturing, relational qualities that "feminize" their dominant behaviors. While these writers argue
that individual strategies for countering stereotypes may offer greater personal agency and empowerment, only institutional change will create the
contexts that authentically promote greater equity and access to opportunity as well as lasting change in the reward structures of organizations.

For this reason, recent writings on ethnicity, race, gender, and practices of inequality or empowerment have begun to examine the multiple
levels of individual, interpersonal, and institutional beliefs and practices
contributing to specific outcomes in context. In the field of organizational development and diversity, Holvino (2000, 2003) uses a feminist
and postcolonial approach to simultaneous interplays of power, suggesting
that differences play out in organizations at individual, group, organizational, and societal levels. Further, she argues that differences are turned
into inequalities through identifiable processes which she categorizes as
symbolic/discursive, structural, and interactive. Dismantling inequality

in organizations, therefore, requires not just recognition of differences but recognition of the processes contributing to inequality. In the field of public health, Jones (2001) argues that a racial climate is constructed through three levels: institutionalized racism determining distribution of resources and access to power; transactional or personally mediated racism (overt and covert, intentional and unintentional) in direct encounters; and internalized racism in which individuals accept socially and interpersonally communicated limits to their own human possibilities. Effective gender-equitable leadership also requires assessing barriers to change in multiple systems and identifying points of maximum leverage in addressing injustice and promoting change.

Power and the Practice of Leadership: Responding to Inequality While Promoting Change

Culturally competent women leaders need to reflect on their interrelated experiences of personal history, work relationships, organizational processes, and issues in the broader community and culture. Theories of complex systems and participatory ecosystemic approaches to empowerment suggest that innovators must address highly specific local conditions promoting and impeding desired change. Every institution has its own acceptable language for its vision and mission, and its specific practices for protecting the status quo, many of which are mutually reinforcing and operate outside of the official mission statement. Further, our relationship choreographies are quite complex, and social control processes such as subtle cues of inclusion or exclusion or insulting messages about the quality of one's work often operate in subtle ways that are difficult to document. Finally, institutional and interpersonal processes preserving an oppressive status quo count on our co-operation by calling forth deeply internalized messages and self-in-relation schemas in which we deserve reprimand, or preserve polite silence, or focus on our imperfections, or feel deeply shamed by mistakes. These mechanisms for protecting existing rules governing power and privilege operate like a psychological or political double bind, in which the rules of the relationship or the community forbid communication about oppressive practices and beliefs that contradict the "official story" of individual and organizational equity.

Culturally competent women leaders must learn to understand these workings of power by becoming self-reflective about our own histories of internalized oppression, and the ways these vulnerabilities can be exploited by others. However, knowing ourselves, and appreciating our vulnerabilities to cultural messages of our lower value as women or members of a nondominant group, is only a first step in acting as leaders in ways that are safe and effective in promoting change. Awareness of these subjective experiences and their social histories and meanings has to be accompanied by a careful reading of the realistic allocation of resources and privilege as well as the unfair distribution of risks and burdens. It becomes important to identify spaces of safety, connection, and open communication with colleagues who share common goals, whether within the workplace with peers and carefully selected mentors, or supporters outside the workplace.

Hurtado (1996) suggests that we consider the role of privilege as we create a "reflexive theory of subordination" and seek "types of leadership models that lead to strategic action to accomplish particular goals" (p. 159). Sandoval (2000) describes five "technologies" or strategies of differential consciousness used by U.S. third world women of color: reading power; deconstruction; meta-ideologizing, or reflections on ideologies; differential perception; and democratics, which she describes as "the ethical or moral technology that permits the previous four to be driven, mobilized and organized into a singular methodology for emancipation" (p. 24). Sandoval sees these strategies as tools of "prophetic democracy," in which readings of power and careful planning help create "cognitive and emotional maps necessary for guiding internal and collective external action" (p. 24). Moya (2002) argues that U.S. women of color have contributed to a collective project of social change by developing a distinctive border-crossing critical consciousness characterized by the capacity to learn from difference and demonstrating "the viability of, and methods involved in, creating coalitions across difference" (p. 97, n. 39). These strategic methods offer a way of transcending the potentially fragmenting forces of individualistic approaches to "feminisms of difference" or identity politics, using reflective practice to recognize differences while building what Mohanty (2003) calls a "practice of solidarity" to create strategic alliances.

As a reflective methodology, learning from difference to engage conflicts while practicing solidarity to achieve strategic goals requires that we confront not just knowledge generated by our oppressions but also self-protective beliefs and actions controlling destabilizing change and defending positions of privilege. Shapiro (2005) has integrated feminist, critical cultural, participatory, and ecosystemic developmental models of power, agency, and growth to define strategic reflection on valued personal and collective goals. Strategic reflection is a critical, relational practice used to analyze contexts and address barriers while leveraging resources to achieve successful problem solving, enabling individuals to become active agents of their interdependent, contingent development. Strategic reflection permits individuals to monitor their own subjectivity as responsive to relational and organizational messages while conducting readings of power, difference, and conflict in context. These readings of power and its personal impact make it possible to uncover barriers and protect personal vulnerabilities emerging from individual history, positional or emotional and economic investments, as well as to identify, negotiate, and politically utilize contradictions between one's own and others' stated values and actual practices. These reflective strategies make it possible to mobilize existing—and generate new—personal, relational, organizational, and social resources and create more favorable pathways connecting knowledge, solidarity, and action to achieve desired goals.

Assessment of Competencies and Outcomes in Complex Systems: Implications for Culturally Competent, Gender-Equitable Women's Leadership

The above discussion of multisystemic and ecosystemic approaches to culturally competent, gender-equitable women's leadership suggests the need to carefully consider tools for evaluating individual competence. Our methods of evaluating cultural competence in women's leadership must apply multisystemic models of cultural competence (Chin, 2003; Betancourt et al., 2003; Dreachslin & Agho, 2001). Without multisystemic approaches that carefully consider systemic resources and barriers, our evaluation of individual cultural competence might imply that an individual leader alone can change sexist, racist, and ethnocentric institutions and societies. Assessment of outcomes in complex systems does not proceed from the logic of single cause and effect, but rather from the recognition that multiple factors interact to generate desired outcomes.

Two approaches to measurement of effective action in complex systems are useful in evaluating outcomes of culturally competent gender-equitable women's leadership. First, participatory, collaborative, and empowerment approaches in psychotherapy and in program evaluation argue that the articulation and negotiation of mutually desired goals creates the "logic model" or pathway through which outcomes will be operationalized. Wandersman (2003) and colleagues (Wandersman & Florin, 2003; Wandersman, Imm, & Chinman, 2000) describe this approach as "results-based accountability," and describe a community-based participatory process of "Getting to Outcomes" in which research is used to evaluate the capacity of programs to meet mutually determined goals. Leigh (2003) used this kind of participatory approach to generate a quantitative evaluation of an Emerging Leaders Program in the Center for Collaborative Leadership at the University of Massachusetts at Boston. The program's goals of increasing leadership, collaboration, and appreciation of diversity among a cohort nominated for their achievements and potential as diverse corporate and civic leaders were operationalized using valid measures of these constructs available in the published literature. In participatory or empowerment evaluation, the process of reaching consensus on "getting to outcomes" may itself be evaluated through participant observation or interviews with stakeholders. The outcomes themselves may be quantitative or qualitative, depending on what the program is trying to accomplish. Finally, the methods of disseminating research findings emphasize the importance of preparing information so that it is useful and accessible to all participants or stakeholders.

Another approach to evaluation of effective outcomes in complex systems involves systematic case studies of "best practices" in achieving desired outcomes. Best practice approaches often select programs that have documented positive outcomes, and use detailed case studies to communicate program qualities that can be implemented by others. These case studies can be used to pinpoint positive, generative processes associated with desired outcomes, and to specify the local conditions promoting success, making it possible to apply and adapt these principles for success in a different setting. For example, Innes (1999) published a series of case studies evaluating processes associated with reaching consensus, especially in complex systems such as metropolitan development or water resources planning. Kar, Pascual, and Chickering (1999) conducted 40 case studies of effective self-organized women's organizations, most of which were catalyzed by a community leader and created opportunities for collaborative work to achieve women's empowerment across both industrialized and third world communities. Cobb (2003) conducted a case study of widows' organizations in Rwanda, comparing characteristics of an organization that was able to help its members transcend trauma with those unable to resolve conflicts and help members move forward with their lives after brutalizing experiences of personal loss and genocide. In these case studies, we can see the workings of extraordinary resilience, as leaders harnessed collective power of relationships to create organizations mobilizing social change. Case studies of leadership best practice can help identify constraints and barriers to desired outcomes, including communication styles or contradictions in organizational values (Fine, 1995). Wheatley and Kellner-Rogers (1999) argue that appreciating organizations and communities as complex adaptive systems requires shifting from predict and control models of measurement to understanding research as feedback helping co-evolving individuals, groups, and organizations achieve goals of self-determination and innovation in flexible, mutually empowering ways.

Can Leadership be Taught? Lessons from the Field

In keeping with the new focus on transformational leadership, the field of leadership development has become an area of growing concern for corporations and community-based organizations. Although the number of programs has exploded in recent years, the evidence base supporting their effectiveness has been slower in coming. In a recent scan of evaluations in the leadership development field, Reinelt (2002) found mostly process evaluations of participant satisfaction, with some limited evaluations of individual change, typically measured by self-report or with scales of leadership skills development. Reinelt suggests that the new frontier in the evaluation of leadership development requires longitudinal study of the impact of leadership development programs over time, both on participating individuals and on their organizations and communities. Reinelt describes a number of frameworks currently being tested, including EvaluLead (Grove, Kibel, & Haas, 2005), which recognize the ecosystemic complexity and local specificity of any ambitious intervention. These approaches combine qualitative or meaning-making tools such as narrative interviews or journals at the individual level and organizational observations and case studies at the organizational level, using them with quantitative measures of desired outcomes at individual, organizational, and community levels.

Ecosystemic approaches to documenting leadership outcomes as systemic practice of personal and collective empowerment are beginning to be used in the field. Global programs promoting community development and empowerment to correct ever-expanding imbalances of access to opportunity, and to help create sustainable cycles of shared growth, are also calling for multimethod evaluations. Such methods can combine qualitative process indicators of women's empowerment with quantitative measures of women's enhanced income and education or improved health (Earl, Carden, & Smutylo, 2001; Malhotra & Shuler, 2005; Kabeer, 1999).

Concluding Recommendations

This chapter suggests that women's practice of culturally competent, transformational, and collaborative leadership can make an important contribution in addressing entanglements of gender, ethnicity, and racial inequality as they play out in highly specific local contexts. Culturally competent gender-equitable women leaders feel empowered, and empower others, by sharing practical strategies for decoding power in complex, changing systems and leveraging power in multiple domains to achieve innovation with equity. Evaluation of effectiveness in complex systems requires attention to principles associated with mutually respectful, collaborative learning and promoting positive shared development.

Evaluation of outcomes begins with generating mutually agreed-upon goals, and determining benchmarks for their achievement. Feedback on progress toward goals becomes part of a collaborative learning process linking personal, organizational, and social change. As teachers, our student-centered progressive pedagogy can inspire and empower students while helping them decipher rules of power, helping them become leaders in changing health and mental health systems and academic settings. As practitioners, our person-centered practice can help patients receive culturally meaningful services while mobilizing advocacy, helping them become agents of change in health and mental health systems greatly in need of reform. As leaders in institutions and organizations, we can recruit, recognize, support, and mentor women and men from nondominant groups who may not have learned to value their own strengths nor learned rules for power and privilege in organizations. We can share our own stories and strategies for surviving and thriving, lessons learned, often the hard way, about making our way in apparently accessible yet resistant institutions and organizations.

Note

1   We would like to thank Erica Wise, PhD, University of North Carolina, for her contribution to discussions of this chapter.

References

Allen, K., Bordas, J., Hickman, G., Matusak, L., Sorenson, G., & Whitmire, K. (1998). *Leadership in the twenty-first century. Rethinking leadership working papers.* College Park, MD: Academy of Leadership Press.

Ballou, M., Matsumoto, A., & Wagner, M. (2002). Toward a feminist ecological theory of human nature: Theory building in response to real-world dynamics. In L. Brown & M. Ballou (Eds.), *Rethinking mental health and disorders: Feminist perspectives* (pp. 99–141). New York: Guilford Press.

Bass, B. M. (1990). *Bass and Stogdill's handbook of leadership.* New York: The Free Press.

Betancourt, J., Green, A., Carrillo, E., & Ananeh-Firempong, O. (2003). Defining cultural competence: A practical framework for addressing racial/ethnic disparities in health and health care. *Public Health Reports, 118*(4), 293–302.

Chin, J. L. (2000). Culturally competent health care. *Public Health Reports, 115,* 25–33.

Chin, J. L. (2003). Multicultural competencies and managed health care. In D. Pope-Davis (Ed.), *The handbook of multicultural competencies* (pp. 347–364). Thousand Oaks, CA: Sage.

Cobb, S. (2003). Fostering coexistence within identity-based conflicts: Towards a narrative approach. In A. Chayes & M. Minow (Eds.), *Imagine co-existence: Restoring humanity after violent ethnic conflict* (pp. 294–310). San Francisco: Jossey Bass.

Conger, J. A. (1999). Charismatic and transformational leadership in organizations: An insider's perspective on these developing streams of research. *Leadership Quarterly, 10*(2), 145–179.

Dreachslin, J., & Agho, A. (2001). Domains and core competencies for effective evidence-based practice in diversity leadership. *Journal of Health Administration Education, 19*(4), 131–148.

Dreachslin, J., Weech-Maldonado, R., & Dansky, I. (2004). Racial and ethnic diversity and organizational behavior: A focused research agenda for health services management. *Social Science and Medicine, 59,* 961–971.

Eagly, A., & Carli, L. (2001). Gender, hierarchy and leadership [Special Issue]. *Journal of Social Issues, 57*(4).

Eagly, A., Johannesen-Schmidt, M., & van Engen, M. (2003). Transformational, transactional, and laissez-faire leadership styles: A meta-analysis comparing women and men. *Psychological Bulletin, 129*(4), 569–591.

Eagly, A. H., Karau, S. J., & Makhijani, M. G. (1995). Gender and the effectiveness of leaders: A meta-analysis. *Psychological Bulletin, 117*, 125–145.

Earl, S., Carden, F., & Smutylo, T. (2001). *Outcome mapping: Building learning and reflection into development programs*. Ottawa, ON: International Development Research Centre.

Fine, M. G. (1995). *Building successful multicultural organizations: Challenges and opportunities*. Westport, CT: Quorum.

Fiske, S. T. (1998). Stereotyping, prejudice, and discrimination. In D. T. Gilbert, S. T. Fiske, & G. Lindsey (Eds.), *The handbook of social psychology* (4th ed., pp. 357–414). New York: Oxford University Press.

Fletcher, J. K. (1999). *Disappearing acts*. Cambridge, MA: MIT Press.

Fletcher, J. K., & Kaufer, K. (2002). Shared leadership: Paradox and possibility. In C. Pearce & J. Conger (Eds.), *Shared leadership* (pp. 21–47). Thousand Oaks, CA: Sage.

Grove, J., Kibel, B., & Haas, T. (2005). *EvaluLead: A guide for shaping and evaluating leadership development programs*. Oakland, CA: The Public Health Institute.

Holvino, E. (2000). Social diversity in social change organizations: Standpoint learnings for organizational consulting. In R. Carter (Ed.), *Addressing cultural issues in organizations: Beyond the corporate context* (pp. 211–228). Thousand Oaks, CA: Sage.

Holvino, E. (2003). Theories of difference: Changing paradigms for organizations. In D. Plummer (Ed.), *Handbook of diversity management: Beyond awareness to competency-based learning* (pp. 111–132). Lanham, MD: University Press of America.

Hurtado, A. (1996). *The color of privilege: Three blasphemies on race and feminism*. Ann Arbor: University of Michigan Press.

Innes, J. (1999). Evaluating consensus building. In L. Susskind, S. McKearnon, & J. Thomas-Larmer (Eds.) *The consensus building handbook: A comprehensive guide to reaching agreement* (pp. 647–654). Thousand Oaks, CA: Sage.

Institute of Medicine. (2001). *Crossing the quality chasm: Health care for the new century*. Washington, DC: National Academies Press.

Institute of Medicine. (2003). *Unequal treatment: Confronting racial and ethnic disparities in health care*. Washington, DC: National Academies Press.

Jones, C. (2001). Levels of racism. *American Journal of Public Health, 908*, 1212–1215.

Kabeer, N. (1999). Resources, agency, achievements: Reflections on the measurement of women's empowerment. *Development and Change, 30*(3), 435.

Kar, S., Pascual, C., & Chickering, S. (1999). Empowerment of women for health promotion: A meta-analysis. *Social Science and Medicine, 49*(11), 1431–1560.

Klenke, K. (1996). *Women and leadership: A contextual perspective.* New York: Springer.

Kouzes, J. M., & Posner, B. Z. (1997). *Leadership practices inventory [LPI]* (2nd ed.). San Francisco: Jossey-Bass, Pfeiffer.

Leigh, J. (2003). *Outcome assessment of Boston's Emerging Leaders Program: Evaluating effectiveness of training in collaboration and diversity.* Doctoral dissertation, Psychology Department, University of Massachusetts, Boston.

Malhotra, A., & Shuler, S. (2005). Women's empowerment as a variable in international development. In D. Narayan (Ed.), *Measuring empowerment: Cross-disciplinary perspectives* (pp. 71–88). Washington, DC: World Bank, Gender and Development Group.

Mohanty, C. (2003). *Feminism without borders: Decolonizing theory, practicing solidarity.* Chapel Hill, NC: Duke University Press.

Moya, P. L. M. (2002). *Learning from experience: Minority identities, multicultural struggles.* Berkeley and Los Angeles: University of California Press.

Pratto, F., & Espinoza, P. (2001). Gender, ethnicity and power. *Journal of Social Issues, 57*(4), 763–780.

Rawlings, D. (2000). Collaborative leadership teams: Oxymoron or new paradigm? *Consulting Psychology Journal: Practice & Research, 52*(1), 36–48.

Reinelt, C. (2002). *Evaluating outcomes and impacts: A scan of 55 leadership development programs.* W. K. Kellogg Foundation, retrieved February 28, 2006 from http://www.wkkf.org/Pubs/CCT/Leadership/Pub3780.pdf

Ridgeway, C. (2001). Gender, status and leadership. *Journal of Social Issues, 57*(4), 637–656.

Sandoval, C. (2000). *Methodologies of the oppressed.* Minneapolis: University of Minnesota Press.

Senge, P. M. (1990). *The fifth discipline: The art and practice of a learning organization.* New York: Doubleday.

Shapiro, E. (2005). Because words are not enough: Transnational collaborations and Latina revisionings of health promotion for gender justice and social change. *National Women's Studies Association Journal, 17*(1), 141–172.

Wandersman, A. (2003). Community science: Bridging the gap between science and practice with community-centered models. *American Journal of Community Psychology, 31,* 227–242.

Wandersman, A., & Florin, P. (2003). Community interventions and effective prevention. *American Psychologist, 58,* 441–448.

Wandersman, A., Imm, P., & Chinman, M. (2000). Getting to outcomes: A results-based approach to accountability. *Evaluation & Program Planning, 23,* 389–395.

Wheatley, M. J. (1992). *Leadership and the new science: Learning about organizations from an orderly universe.* San Francisco: Berrett-Koehler.

Wheatley, M. J., & Kellner-Rogers, M. (June, 1999). What do we measure and why? Questions about the uses of measurement. *Journal for Strategic Performance Measurement.* Retrieved from http://www.margaretwheatley.com/articles/whymeasure.html

Yoder, J. (2001). Making leadership work more effectively for women. *Journal of Social Issues, 57*(4), 815–829.

Chapter 5

Gender and Leadership in the Corporate World: A Multiperspective Model

Karen Korabik and Roya Ayman

When it comes to gender and leadership, one thing is clear. Women can be successful in leading both private and public sector organizations. In the past, women leaders were tokens. However, with the advent of the new millennium, the range and numbers of women in top positions across fields of endeavor have increased dramatically. Some of the most successful companies in the world are now led by women. For example, Meg Whiteman, the CEO of eBay, is widely recognized as being the secret of eBay's success (Seller, 2004). However, when examining the cases of top women leaders, similar stories do not seem to emerge. Meg's leadership style is reported to be consultative, open, empowering, and visionary (Seller, 2004). By contrast, Carly Fiorina, the past CEO of Hewlett Packard, was said to be focused on her own ideas and alienated her employees and board members (Eunjung Cha, 2005). So, are all women leaders alike? And do women have a special leadership style that makes them different from men? Our research over the past 20 years has been directed at finding out the answers to these questions. In the process, we have developed a multiperspective model of gender and leadership.

Multiperspective Model of Gender and Leadership

The model we present here is based on an extension of our previous thinking (Ayman, 1993; Korabik, 1999). It integrates three perspectives about how gender-related processes impact on leadership. Many people have a very simplistic view of gender, believing it to pertain only to whether someone is a man or a woman. However, the psychological ramifications of being a man or a woman are extremely wide-ranging and affect all aspects of our daily lives (Korabik, 1997). Because of this, social scientists have pointed out that gender is a multidimensional concept that is enacted in a number of different ways. Our model takes three of these perspectives: the intrapsychic, social structural, and interpersonal (Rosen & Reekers and Unger & Crawford, as cited in Korabik, 1999, p. 11) and applies them to leadership.

The first perspective emphasizes gender as an intrapsychic process. Here gender is defined in terms of gender-role orientation, and it encompasses such things as gender schema, gender identity, and gender-role traits, attitudes, and values. Gender-role orientation is considered to be bidimensional, consisting of two orthogonal subdimensions: masculinity (instrumentality or agency) and femininity (expressivity or communion) (Bem and Spence, Helmreich, & Stapp, as cited in Korabik, 1999, pp. 6, 7). It is acquired as a function of gender-role socialization. Technically, it is independent of biological sex, but due to society's continued emphasis on sex-congruent socialization, sex and gender-role orientation are often empirically correlated. According to the intrapsychic leadership perspective (see Figure 5.1), the leader's gender-role orientation (regardless of biological sex) will affect the leader's behavior. This perspective predicts that individuals whose personalities are dominated by masculine or instrumental characteristics (e.g., dominance, assertiveness) will act in a predominantly task-oriented manner, whereas those who have primarily feminine or expressive personality traits (e.g., nurturance, agreeableness) will display predominantly person- or relationship-oriented behaviors. Androgynous persons, who have both instrumental and expressive personality traits, will have both task- and person-oriented behaviors and competencies in their repertoires. However, just because androgynous individuals are able to function in both the task- and person-oriented behavioral domains doesn't mean that they will. Their behavior will depend on situational moderating factors like

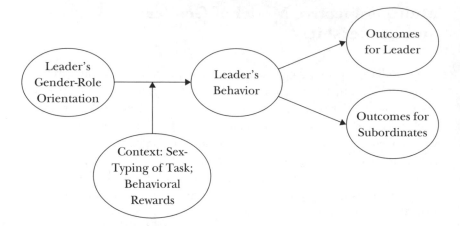

Figure 5.1.   The Intrapsychic Leadership Perspective.

the sex-typing of the task, the environmental context, and what type of behavior is rewarded (Cook, 1985).

Our model also incorporates the social structural perspective. According to this viewpoint, gender is an ascribed status characteristic that influences access to power and resources. A number of theories (e.g., expectation states theory, social role theory, and status characteristics theory) are particularly useful in explicating those aspects of gender dynamics that result from the structural inequality in our society (Ridgeway, 1992). According to the social structural leadership perspective (see Figure 5.2), the most important aspect of gender is the sex of the

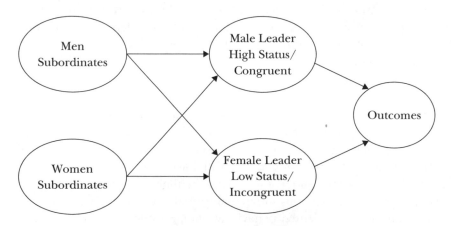

Figure 5.2.   The Social Structural Leadership Perspective.

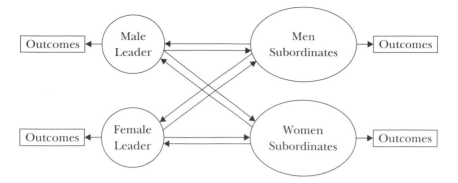

Figure 5.3. The Interpersonal Interaction Leadership Perspective (Leader–Subordinates).

leader, which acts as a stimulus for others' perceptions, observations, and evaluations. According to this perspective, different outcomes will be attained by men leaders (high status individuals in roles congruent with their sex) and women leaders (low status individuals in roles incongruent with their sex). Meta-analytic findings support this by indicating that women leaders are evaluated more negatively than men leaders, particularly when they use a masculine style or are rated by their male subordinates (Eagly, Makhijani, & Klonshy, 1992).

The third perspective focuses on the interpersonal interactions between individuals (Deaux & Major, as cited in Korabik, 1999, p. 12). This approach incorporates aspects of both the intrapsychic and social structural viewpoints because interactions are viewed as a function of gender-related beliefs and expectations both about the self (schemas) and about others (stereotypes). In addition, these processes are influenced by situational cues (e.g., the sex-typed nature of a task; skewed gender ratios in groups) that make gender more or less salient and induce priming. According to the interpersonal interaction leadership perspective (see Figure 5.3), men and women leaders will have different types of social interactions with their men and women supervisors and subordinates and these will influence the outcomes experienced by each party (Ayman, 1993).

Our model is an integration of these three perspectives (see Figure 5.4). We view leadership as a social interaction between leaders and their supervisors and subordinates. The nature of this interaction is influenced by intrapsychic processes (e.g., gender-role orientation) in all of the parties. However, these processes are not as salient and observable

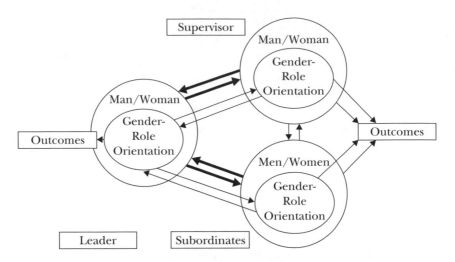

Figure 5.4. Integrative Leadership Process Model.

as is someone's biological sex. Therefore, sex acts as a status characteristic and as a cue that activates stereotypes. These processes are moderated by a variety of contextual cues (e.g., the sex-typing of tasks; skewed
gender ratios in groups).

Our Research Program

During the past 20 years, we have conducted two major research projects
in Canada that have included several independent studies on gender
and various aspects of leadership. Our first sample (Korabik & Ayman,
1987) consisted of 121 men and 126 women middle- to upper-level
managers, matched for position and tenure, from a large public utility
company and two insurance companies, who completed a survey (56%
return rate). We then interviewed 30 women leaders from this sample
(Korabik & Ayman, 1989a). We also asked the survey participants for
their permission to have their supervisors rate their managerial effectiveness. The supervisors of 48 (83%) did so (Korabik & Ayman, 1989b). The
sample for the second project consisted of 155 leaders who responded
to a survey (return rate 53%). The 39 men and 39 women managers
from various business organizations and 38 men and 39 women school
vice-principals were matched for position and organization. With their
permission, we also sent surveys to two men and two women (randomly

selected) who worked for them. Overall, 291 subordinates/teachers responded. The majority of the studies that we refer to in this chapter are related to this data set.

Acculturation issues, skewed sex ratios, and levels of gender-role orientation

Women corporate leaders face a special set of challenges due to the male-dominated nature of these settings. Due to the predominance of men in business and the professions, the norms and culture have developed so as to reflect men's needs and values (Korabik & Ayman, 1990). To understand the experiences of women in these settings, we have adopted Berry's (1983) model of acculturation. According to Berry, newcomers are confronted with the options of either accepting the majority's values and norms or maintaining their own. From the organization's standpoint, both men and women are usually expected to assimilate by adopting the prevailing cultural norms (Powell, 1999). Once, when talking to a White male colleague, the second author remarked, "It will be interesting to see what the workplace will look like in years to come given the increased diversity among workers." He replied, "I don't expect much difference. The newcomers have to accept our way or the highway!" Although this assimilationist mentality is detrimental to men by restricting their choices into stereotypically masculine roles (Powell, 1999), the negative consequences for women are far greater. Because women are members of the lower status minority group, for them assimilation creates problems with cultural adaptation, the inability to maintain a positive sense of identity, feelings of marginalization and isolation, and increased exposure to harassment and other stressors (Korabik, 1997).

Assimilation means that women in male-dominated settings are pressured to behave in a masculine manner. This is because people develop conceptions about who should hold jobs based on the qualities of job incumbents (Perry, Davis-Blake, & Kulik, 1994). Because most leadership positions have been held by men, the stereotype exists that masculine, task-oriented traits are the requisite characteristics for leadership (Powell, 1999). Although recent research shows that this stereotype is held more strongly by men than by women (Schein, 2001), these beliefs have been found to influence both gatekeepers' actions and women's self-identities, resulting in a preponderance of agentic women in management (Powell, 1999). Thus many studies demonstrate that women in

111

the corporate world often fit the masculine stereotype of the ideal manager better than their male colleagues do. And the more experienced women managers are and the higher their positions, the higher in masculinity they are (Korabik, 1992; Powell, 1999). These dynamics, however, are different in different settings. We have found that both the men and the women in our (traditionally male-dominated) corporate subsample were more masculine compared to both the men and the women in our (traditionally more gender-balanced) educational subsample, who were more androgynous (Korabik, 1992).

Unfortunately, once established, these business cultures are highly resistant to change and they create a vicious cycle that keeps women in a disadvantaged position relative to men. This dynamic has been costly to companies. For example, we have been witness to the flight of many highly competent women from major corporations to either start their own businesses or to work for companies with more hospitable cultures. Over the last few decades, however, major changes have started to occur. Organizations have begun to include a more diverse workforce and have become more pluralistic (Cox, 1993). This has been partially due to the pressures of affirmative action. But organizations have also realized that it is not enough to increase the numbers of diverse employees and that the only way to move forward is by changing culture. This can best be accomplished by promoting a norm of integration, whereby both the majority and the newcomers (e.g., women and minority groups) come to accept some of each others' values and norms (Korabik & Ayman, 1990; Cox, 1993).

The Trait Approach to Leadership

One of the oldest approaches to leadership is the trait approach (Bass, 1990). Research indicates that several psychological traits are associated with effective leadership. Among these is self-monitoring (Snyder & Gangestad, 1986), a trait that differentiates between those whose actions are guided by their internal values (low self-monitors) and those whose actions are guided by cues from the external social environment (high self-monitors). Meta-analytic results (Day, Scheicher, Unckless, & Hiller, 2002) have demonstrated that although women were more likely than men to be low self-monitors, for women there was a strong association between being high on self-monitors and emerging as a leader.

The Behavioral Approach to Leadership

Task-oriented vs. person-oriented leadership behavior

One of the most investigated areas in the leadership literature has been task- versus person-oriented leadership behavior. Much research has supported a dual model that views both task-oriented (i.e., initiating structure) and person-oriented (i.e., consideration) behavior as necessary for effective leadership (Ayman, 1993, 2004). Most previous research on gender and task- versus person-oriented leadership has looked at sex differences. Here meta-analysis has shown that there are no differences in the behavior displayed by men and women in leadership positions (Eagly & Johnson, 1990).

Intrapsychic processes.   We were among the first researchers to examine whether intrapsychic processes affected task- and person-oriented leadership behavior. The intrapsychic perspective on gender and leadership predicts that gender-role orientation will be a better predictor of self-reported leadership behavior than will biological sex. Moreover, according to this perspective, those who have instrumental or masculine gender-role traits should report the use of task-oriented or initiating structure leadership behavior, whereas those who have expressive or feminine personality traits should report the use of person-oriented or consideration leadership behavior. We have found support for all of these contentions throughout our research program—with all samples of participants and using both quantitative survey and qualitative interview methodologies (Korabik, 1996; Korabik & Ayman, 1987, 1989a). Our findings have never shown any significant main effects for sex. Moreover, gender-role orientation was always significantly related to self-reported leadership style in the manner predicted (i.e., instrumentality predicted initiating structure, whereas expressivity predicted consideration, with androgyny being related to both structure and consideration). These findings are also consistent with those from a number of studies where the leadership behavior of psychology students who differed in gender-role orientation was observed (studies by Korabik as cited in Korabik, 1996; Korabik, 1990; Zugec & Korabik, 2003). What's more, these latter studies have demonstrated that androgynous individuals not only have the ability to display both task- and person-oriented leadership behaviors, but also that they are able to switch roles in a flexible, adaptive manner to take on whatever leadership function is lacking in a group.

113

Interpersonal processes. We have found, however, that in addition to intra-psychic processes, interpersonal processes also affect perceptions about task- versus person-oriented leadership behaviors. To demonstrate this we looked at the degree to which men and women leaders' perceptions of their own behaviors coincided with those of their men and women subordinates (Becker, Ayman, & Korabik, 2002). The interpersonal inter-action leadership perspective predicts that differential effects will occur as a function of the gender of the leader and/or subordinate and that these will be moderated by the nature of the context and the type of task. In support of this, we found that in corporate settings, compared to educational settings, there were greater discrepancies between women leaders' ratings of the extent to which they engaged in both task- and person-oriented leadership behaviors and their subordinates' ratings of the extent to which the women used these behaviors.

Moreover, the greatest disagreements between self-perceptions and subordinate perceptions occurred for high self-monitoring women leaders in corporate settings on ratings of initiating structure behaviors. It is probable that the masculine stereotyped nature of the leadership behavior coupled with the male-dominated environment served to prime the stereotypes and schemas of the leaders and/or subordinates. High self-monitoring women leaders would have been more sensitive than low self-monitoring women leaders to these contextual cues. In contrast to previous research (Day et al., 2002), we did not find that the women in our sample were lower in self-monitoring than the men. But we did find that self-monitoring, a trait that has been associated with effective leadership, did not appear to work for women in the same way as it did for men. Moreover, the results of this study indicated that the context of the work setting acted as a moderator that affected the perceptions of women leaders more than those of men.

The issue of whether leaders' self-perceptions are in tune with those of their subordinates is important, because of the increasing use of mul-tirater assessment that contributes to approaches such as 360 degree feedback for leadership development and evaluation (Atwater & Yammarino, 1992). On a daily basis, leaders have access only to their own perceptions of their behavior and if they are not aware of the potential discrepancy between how they view themselves and how their subordinates view them, they may operate under false pretenses. Moreover, when the leaders are in environments that are unfamiliar to them, their assumptions about their behavior may become even more inaccurate.

Transformational leadership behavior

Transformational leadership is a well-recognized leadership behavior, which has been shown to have a strong relationship with valued organizational outcomes such as leadership effectiveness, employee satisfaction, organizational commitment, and extra effort (Judge & Piccolo, 2004). Transformational leadership includes four subdimensions: intellectual stimulation, individualized consideration, idealized influence, and inspirational motivation. A recent meta-analysis of transformational leadership behavior in men and women (Eagly, Johannesen-Schmidt, & van Engen, 2003) demonstrated that women leaders are slightly more transformational than men leaders.

Intrapsychic processes. According to the intrapsychic leadership process theory, gender-role orientation, and not biological sex, should be related to self-perceptions of transformational leadership behavior. When we (Korabik, Ayman, & Purc-Stephenson, 2001) investigated the relationship between gender-role orientation and self-reported transformational leadership, we found no significant effects for biological sex. However, gender-role instrumentality was significantly predictive of higher self-ratings on all four of the subdimensions of transformational leadership. Gender role expressivity was significantly predictive of higher self-ratings on idealized influence, individualized consideration, and inspirational motivation. In corporate settings, masculine individuals reported higher use of intellectual stimulation, whereas in educational settings feminine and androgynous individuals reported greater use of intellectual stimulation. In general, being androgynous (i.e., having high instrumentality and expressivity) was related to high transformational leadership. Additionally, the more leaders reported being androgynous and transformational, the more both they themselves and their subordinates reported lower job stress and higher job satisfaction.

Social structural processes. We have also found evidence for the impact of social structural processes on transformational leadership behavior. We examined how the gender composition of leader–subordinate dyads influenced the relationship between a leader's self-perceived transformational leadership and subordinates' evaluations of the leader's effectiveness (Ayman, Korabik, & Morris, 2006). We found that, regardless of organization type, there was a significant difference in the way that men and women subordinates reacted to those women leaders who reported greater transformational leadership. In particular, the higher

115

women's transformational behavior was in terms of intellectual stimulation and individualized consideration, the less effective their men, but not their women, subordinates thought they were as leaders.

This is one of the first studies to examine how the gender composition of leader–subordinate pairs affects the relationship between leadership behavior and organizational outcomes. It is alarming that transformational leadership behavior, a behavior which is hailed in the literature as being almost universally effective and one at which women seem to be slightly better at performing than men, does not yield similar results for men and women leaders. It is possible that because this study only included leaders' self-reports of their behavior, the men subordinates did not see the women leaders as being as transformational as the women leaders perceived themselves to be.

A more viable explanation, however, is that, as predicted by the social structural leadership perspective, men subordinates devalued the women leaders who reported using more of these types of behavior. The low social status that men subordinates ascribed to women leaders could partially account for this lack of appreciation. More specifically, based on role incongruence theory (Eagly & Carli, 2001), for a person of low social status (a woman) to ask men subordinates (who view themselves as higher status individuals) to provide a rationale for their actions or ideas (an aspect of intellectual stimulation) could be construed by these men as overly controlling and inappropriate. Moreover, when a woman (perceived as a low status individual) displays a feminine stereotyped behavior like individualized consideration, her men subordinates may view her as weak and ineffective.

The Relational Approach to Leadership: Leader–Member Exchange

Leader–member exchange (LMX) is a paradigm in which leadership is conceptualized as an interpersonal relationship between leaders and their followers (Graen & Uhl-Bein, 1995). Gerstner and Day's (1997) meta-analysis indicated that LMX is strongly related to various organizational outcomes such as job satisfaction, organizational commitment, and organizational citizenship. Some previous research has examined the relationship between the gender composition of the leader–subordinate dyads and the quality of the leadership relationship as measured by LMX, but the results have been unclear. Notably, most research has demonstrated that similar gender dyads have a stronger LMX. However, the possibility that there could be an asymmetrical effect in the types of relationships men and women leaders form with their men versus women subordinates has not been considered.

Interpersonal processes

In our study of interpersonal processes and LMX (Ayman, Rinchiuso, & Korabik, 2004), we included one man or one woman subordinate for each man or women leader. Our initial analysis did not show any gender effects on LMX either within or between dyads. We then examined the moderating effect of the gender composition of leader–subordinate dyads on the relationship between the LMX and the subordinate's satisfaction with the leader. Our findings supported the interpersonal interaction leadership perspective. We found an asymmetrical relationship, such that dyads in which the parties were similar in gender differed from those of opposite gender. When there was a moderate quality LMX relationship, the subordinates in dissimilar gender dyads (women subordinates with a man leader and men subordinates with a woman leader) were more dissatisfied than were the subordinates who were similar in gender to their leaders. In addition, this dissatisfaction was significantly more pronounced for men leaders with women subordinates. This may mean that the women subordinates of men leaders are more concerned with the quality of the leadership relationship than their male peers. But, relationship quality was not unimportant for men. The results showed that the men subordinates of women leaders were significantly more satisfied with their leader when their relationship was of high quality than when their relationship was moderate in quality.

Leadership Competencies

Organizations are very interested in assessing leadership competencies for both performance appraisal and leadership development purposes. In most of these assessments, raters evaluate the leaders on competencies that demonstrate a desired behavior or outcome. Overall, research on leadership competencies has shown support for the influence of intrapsychic, interpersonal, and social structural gender-related processes. For example, men and women in actual leadership positions have not been found to be different on leadership effectiveness (Eagly, Karau, &

117

Makhijani, 1995). Despite this, much research has shown that task-oriented competencies have come to be associated with leadership success, whereas expressive, person-oriented qualities are generally given low weight in the determination of leadership (Korabik, 1990). These beliefs appear to be held by men more than by women. Atwater, Brett, Waldman, DiMare, & Hayden (2004) found that men were more likely than women to consider most of the competencies on a well-respected management competency tool to be masculine. Moreover, across outcomes, women are viewed as slightly less effective when in more masculine roles or in work settings that are male-dominated (Eagly et al., 1995).

Intrapsychic processes

We examined the relationship between gender-role orientation and self-reports of leadership competencies. The intrapsychic leadership perspective predicts that gender-role orientation should be a better predictor of self-reported leadership competencies than biological sex. Moreover, instrumentality should be related to having task-oriented competencies, whereas expressivity should be related to having person-oriented competencies. According to this perspective, androgynous individuals, who would have both task- and person-oriented competencies, would make the most effective leaders. Overall, our research offers strong support for these contentions.

When we interviewed the women leaders from our first sample (Korabik & Ayman, 1989a), the masculine women reported that task-oriented competencies like planning and decision making were their strengths, but that they had problems managing interpersonal relationships with their subordinates. By contrast, the feminine women said that promoting a co-operative and harmonious work atmosphere was their strong point. But they said that their lack of assertiveness, problems delegating work and conveying negative feedback, and poor organizational skills hindered their effectiveness. Androgynous women leaders spoke about the need to balance the task- and people-oriented demands of their jobs and they felt that they were skillful at doing both.

The survey data from our first sample indicated that there were no significant effects of biological sex on self-ratings of leadership competencies. However, leadership effectiveness (over all competencies) was a function of gender-role orientation. Androgynous leaders perceived themselves to be significantly more effective than either masculine or feminine leaders did (Korabik & Ayman, 1989b). Moreover, their supervisors rated androgynous managers as being the most effective (Korabik & Ayman, 1989b). Supervisors rated androgynous managers of both sexes as being more effective than feminine leaders. And they saw androgynous women leaders as more effective than masculine and feminine men.

When it came to self-perceptions of leadership competencies, the data from our second sample (Korabik & Ayman, 1994; Stephens, 2004) also supported the intrapsychic leadership perspective. Based on factor analysis we divided the 18 competencies on our leadership effectiveness measure into: (a) task-oriented competencies (e.g., problem solving, decision making, planning and organizing, time management), (b) person-oriented competencies (e.g., listening and interpersonal skills), and (c) neutral competencies (e.g., ability to conceptualize, learning). The leader's biological sex did not account for any variance in leader or subordinate ratings of the leaders' competencies. Androgynous leaders rated themselves as significantly higher in task-oriented competencies than masculine leaders who saw themselves as significantly higher than feminine leaders. Androgynous leaders also perceived themselves to be significantly higher in person-oriented competencies than both masculine and feminine leaders and significantly higher in neutral competencies than feminine leaders. When it came to subordinates' evaluations of their leaders, subordinates perceived masculine and androgynous leaders to be significantly higher in task-oriented and neutral competencies than feminine leaders. By contrast, subordinates perceived feminine and androgynous leaders to be significantly higher in person-oriented competencies than masculine leaders.

Interpersonal processes

To assess interpersonal processes, we (Speron, Ayman, & Korabik, 2000) examined the agreement between self and subordinate ratings of task-oriented, person-oriented, and neutral competencies. The results showed that the leader's gender and level of self-monitoring and the type of organization interacted to predict leader–subordinate agreement about the leader's person-oriented competencies. More specifically, high self-monitoring women leaders in corporate settings had the lowest agreement with their subordinates regarding their effectiveness on person-oriented competencies. By contrast, low self-monitoring corporate women were almost in agreement with their subordinates about these functions.

Conclusions and Practical Implications for Women Leaders

Our model has the advantage of integrating three divergent perspectives on gender and leadership. Our research provides convincing evidence for our model by demonstrating that leadership is a function of all three types of gender-related processes. In terms of intrapsychic processes we have found that leaders' gender-role orientation, but not their biological sex, affects their self-perceptions of their behavior, competencies, effectiveness, and organizationally related outcomes, as well as their supervisors' and subordinates' evaluations of them. However, we have also found that social structural and interpersonal processes are important in those instances where others (supervisors and subordinates) were evaluating a leader's behavior, competencies, or effectiveness based upon their perceptions of their relationship with them. In particular, we found differential effects when men and women leaders had men versus women subordinates. In addition, we found that environmental cues often acted as primes so that women leaders who were in male-dominated corporate settings or who were being evaluated on masculine-stereotyped behaviors and competencies were placed at a disadvantage. High self-monitoring women leaders, who were more sensitive to masculine organizational norms than low self-monitoring women, appeared to fare the worst. Thus we have shown that the impact of gender on leadership varies depending upon the situational context, the aspect of leadership and the particular outcomes investigated. Hopefully, our findings should help to dispel several persistent myths, namely that: (a) men and women differ in their leadership style or effectiveness, (b) task-oriented qualities are the only necessary prerequisites for effective leadership, and (c) women have a special leadership advantage due to their "feminine" style.

To bring about change, both women leaders and their organizations need to engage in plans of action. Women leaders need to develop a better understanding of the impact of organizational culture and gender stereotyping in the workplace. Not only do they need to educate themselves, but they need to educate their colleagues as well. They also need to support other women by making sure that they are not judged in a stereotyped manner. In terms of their own leadership behavior, increasing their self-awareness will give women leaders knowledge of their potential blind spots and will make them more conscious of how they are perceived as leaders. Women leaders need to be particularly attentive to their interpersonal relationships when they are operating in male-dominated settings, when they are performing masculine stereotyped behaviors, and when they are interacting with men. Through training programs and coaching processes, women leaders can learn new behaviors and when to use them. This will broaden their behavioral repertoires and enhance their ability to be flexible and responsive to the needs of the situation. Overall, we feel that androgyny is particularly advantageous for women leaders. By being androgynous and balancing task- with person-orientation, women can avoid being judged according to stereotypes and be perceived as more effective leaders.

On the other hand, organizations also need to do their part. By recognizing that the diversity of skills and perspectives among their employees is an asset, organizations can develop programs to welcome newcomers and reduce potential systematic structural discrimination. This necessitates that organizations promote a norm of integration, which respects both masculine and feminine perspectives, and places emphasis on competencies that are relevant to organizational effectiveness. In order to do so, organizations must better identify their objectives and relevant criteria for the assessment of effectiveness. Such clarity of objectives will reduce the extent to which judgments of men and women leaders are based on stereotypes or on past tradition. Job analysis and competency modeling can provide a systematic foundation upon which organizations can train their employees and their leaders. Thus an appreciation of how intrapsychic, social structural, and interpersonal gender-related processes affect leadership will allow both individuals and organizations to improve their effectiveness.

References

Atwater, L. E., Brett, J. F., Waldman, D., DiMare, L., & Hayden, M. V. (2004). Men's and women's perceptions of gender typing of management subroles. *Sex Roles, 50*, 191–199.

Atwater, L. E., & Yammarino, F. J. (1992). Does self–other agreement on leadership perceptions moderate the validity of leadership and performance predictions? *Personnel Psychology, 45*, 141–164.

Ayman, R. (1993). Leadership perception: The role of gender and culture. In M. M. Chemers & R. Ayman (Eds.), *Leadership theory and research: Perspectives and directions* (pp. 137–166). New York: Academic Press.

Ayman, R. (2004). Situational and contingency approaches to leadership. In J. Antonakis, A. T. Cianciolo, & R. J. Sternberg (Eds.), *The nature of leadership* (pp. 148–170). Thousand Oaks, CA: Sage.

Ayman, R., Korabik, K., & Morris, S. (2006). *The gender composition of the leader–subordinate dyad as a moderator of the relationship between the leader's transformational leadership, contingency reward and performance.* Manuscript submitted for publication.

Ayman, R., Rinchiuso, M., & Korabik, K. (2004, August). *LMX, satisfaction, and organizational commitment in Canadian organizations: The moderating effect of dyad gender composition.* Paper presented at the 28th International Congress of Psychology, Beijing, People's Republic of China.

Bass, B. M. (1990). *Bass & Stogdill's handbook of leadership* (3rd ed.). New York: The Free Press.

Becker, J., Ayman, R., & Korabik, K. (2002). Discrepancies in self/subordinates' perceptions of leadership behaviors: Leader's gender, organizational context, and leader's self-monitoring. *Group and Organization Management, 27,* 226–244.

Berry, J. W. (1983). Acculturation: A comparative analysis of alternative forms. In R. J. Samuda & A. L. Woods (Eds.), *Perspectives on immigrant and minority education* (pp. 66–77). Lanham, MD: University Press of America.

Cook, E. P. (1985). *Psychological androgyny.* New York: Pergamon.

Cox, T. Jr. (1993). *Cultural diversity in organizations: Theory, research and practice.* San Francisco: Berrett-Koehler.

Day, D., Scheicher, D. J., Unckless, A. L., & Hiller, N. J. (2002). Self-monitoring personality at work: A meta-analytic investigation of construct validity. *Journal of Applied Psychology, 87,* 390–401.

Eagly, A., & Carli, L. (2003). The female leader advantage: An evaluation of the evidence. *The Leadership Quarterly, 14,* 807–834.

Eagly, A., Johannesen-Schmidt, M. C., & van Engen, M. L. (2003). Transformational, transactional, and laissez-faire leadership styles: A meta-analysis comparing women and men. *Psychological Bulletin, 129,* 569–591.

Eagly, A. H., & Johnson, B. T. (1990). Gender and leadership style: A meta-analysis. *Psychological Bulletin, 108*(2), 233–256.

Eagly, A. H., Karau, S. J., & Makhijani, M. G. (1995). Gender and the effectiveness of leaders: A meta-analysis. *Psychological Bulletin, 117,* 125–145.

Eagly, A. H., Makhijani, M. G., & Klonsky, B. G. (1992). Gender and the evaluation of leaders: A meta-analysis. *Psychological Bulletin, 111,* 3–22.

Eunjung Cha, A. (February, 2005). Hewlett-Packard forces celebrity CEO to quit. *Washington Post.* Retrieved August 2, 2006 from http://www.washingtonpost.com/wp-dyn/articles/A10295-2005Feb9.html

Gerstner, C. R., & Day, D. (1997). Meta-analytic review of leader member exchange theory: Correlate and construct issues. *Journal of Applied Psychology, 82,* 827–844.

Graen, G. B., & Uhl-Bien, M. (1995). Relationship-based approach to leadership: Development of leader–member exchange (LMX) theory of leadership over 25 years: Applying a multilevel multi-domain perspective. *Leadership Quarterly, 6,* 219–247.

Judge, T. A., & Piccolo, R. F. (2004). Transformational and transactional leadership: A meta-analytic test of their relative validity. *Journal of Applied Psychology, 89,* 755–768.

Korabik, K. (1990). Androgyny and leadership style. *Journal of Business Ethics, 9,* 9–18.

Korabik, K. (1992, June). *The masculinization of women managers.* Paper presented at the annual meeting of the Canadian Psychological Association, Quebec City, Quebec.

Korabik, K. (1996). Gender, leadership style, and managerial effectiveness. *Proceedings of the International Association of Management.* Toronto, ON.

Korabik, K. (1997). Applied gender issues. In S. W. Sadava & D. R. Mc Creary (Eds.), *Applied social psychology* (pp. 292–302). Upper Saddle River, NJ: Prentice-Hall.

Korabik, K. (1999). Sex and gender in the new millennium. In G. N. Powell (Ed.), *Handbook of gender in organizations* (pp. 3–16). Thousand Oaks, CA: Sage.

Korabik, K., & Ayman, R. (1987, August). *Androgyny and leadership style: A conceptual synthesis.* New York: American Psychological Association (ERIC Document Reproduction Service ED291-032).

Korabik, K., & Ayman, R. (1989a). Should women managers have to act like men? *Journal of Management Development, 8,* 23–32.

Korabik, K., & Ayman, R. (1989b). Androgyny and managerial effectiveness. In J. McGuire (Ed.), *Proceedings of the Administrative Sciences Association of Canada Annual Conference: Women in management* (pp. 1–9). Montreal, QC.

Korabik, K., & Ayman, R. (1990, July). *Gender and leadership: An acculturation model.* 22nd International Congress of Applied Psychology, Kyoto, Japan.

Korabik, K., & Ayman, R. (1994, July). *Sex-role orientation and self-perception of managerial ability.* 23rd International Congress of Applied Psychology, Madrid, Spain.

Korabik, K., Ayman, R., & Purc-Stephenson, R. (2001, June). *Gender-role orientation and transformational leadership.* Paper presented at Conference on Gender, Work, and Organizations, Keele University, UK.

Perry, E. L., Davis-Blake, A., & Kulik, C. T. (1994). Explaining gender-based selection decisions: A synthesis of contextual and cognitive approaches. *Academy of Management Review, 19,* 786–820.

Powell, G. N. (Ed.) (1999). *Handbook of gender and work.* Thousand Oaks, CA: Sage.

Ridgeway, C. L. (Ed.) (1992). *Gender, interaction, and inequality.* New York: Springer-Verlag.

Schein, V. E. (2001). A global look at psychological barrier to women's progress in management. *Journal of Social Issues, 57,* 675–688.

Seller, P. (October, 2004). eBay's secret. *Fortune*, 160–178.

Snyder, M., & Gangestad, S. (1986). On the nature of self-monitoring: Matters of assessment, matters of validity. *Journal of Personality and Social Psychology*, *51*(1), 125–139.

Speron, E., Ayman, R., & Korabik, K. (2000, April). *Self and subordinate agreement on leader performance: Leader's gender, organizational type, and leader's self-monitoring*. Paper presented at 15th annual meeting of the Society for Industrial/Organizational Psychology, New Orleans, LA.

Stephens, H. E. (2004). *Gender-role orientation and leadership effectiveness*. Unpublished Master's Thesis, University of Guelph, Guelph, ON.

Zugec, L., & Korabik, K. (2003, June). *Multiple intelligences, leadership, and androgyny*. Paper presented at the annual meeting of the Canadian Psychological Association, Hamilton, ON.

Part II

Collaboration and Leadership

Introduction

Joy K. Rice

Gender, Collaboration, and Leadership

Feminist psychology has long appreciated and recognized the importance of collaboration as a means of changing social structures, organizations, and policies (Astin & Astin, 2000). Collaboration and/or
collaborative decision making are often seen as the hallmark and the
fundamental tenet of a feminist leadership style (Chin, 2004; Eagly, Karu,
Miner, & Johnston, 1994). Collaboration can be defined as working jointly
with others, especially in an intellectual endeavor, to co-operate with,
to network with, to harmoniously share (Singley & Sweeney, 1998),
and to build coalitions while appreciating diversity of opinions and
ideas (Brunner, 1999). Collaborative behaviors that are "feminist" are
generally intentional and constructed through conscious choices that
affirm feminist principles of inclusion, egalitarianism, and sharing of
power (Cafferty & Clausen, 1998).

From a feminist perspective, however, collaboration takes on other
meanings beyond co-operation, networking, or sharing. Feminist
collaboration between individuals or organizations involves working
together effectively in an egalitarian manner that also enables and
empowers women (Fletcher, 1999). Collaboration is sometimes seen as
compatible with women using nurturance and emotional sensitivity in
communication with others and as a way to share power and build consensus in groups. The shared leader model embraces collaborative and
egalitarian processes as the leader engages the participants in setting

goals and outcomes while simultaneously alternating between leader and follower and teacher and student roles. A common expectation in management as well as other groups is that women will demonstrate greater warmth and collaboration in their leadership styles while men are expected to be more task-oriented on the job and to rely on the privilege of the individual leader in their leadership style (Carli & Eagly, 1999; Fletcher, 2002).

Is collaboration then seen as a more feminine style of leadership, and correspondingly, a "softer" style of leadership? As Chin notes in the Overview to this book, the first phases of psychological studies about leadership theory attempted to analyze the critical variables that contribute to a charismatic leader and strong leadership with scant attention to the factor of gender. More recently, however, theories of leadership have focused less on the individual and more on the dimensions of team leadership, which has given the construct of collaboration a far more central role in what is considered effective leadership irrespective of gender. With an increasing awareness of a global economy, more recent attention has also been given to analyzing the interaction of complex, multicultural factors in leadership and to examining the validity of generalizing leadership and management practices cross-nationally and cross-culturally. The importation of Western business and leadership practices and strategic management theories is increasingly questioned by non-Western economies and businesses who may utilize some elements of Western theory while incorporating and retaining key indigenous factors related to their particular culture and country (Kao, Sinha, & Wilpert, 1999).

If modern theory and practice in management styles and leadership effectiveness now is more likely to embrace a collaborative style of leadership as both desirable and effective, we might ask what is there that is different or unique about a "feminist" style of collaborative leadership? How can we deconstruct collaboration as a feminist process, and what is critical in differentiating the kind of and meaning of collaboration in leadership when gender is included as a key variable? The chapters in this part provide some insights into the special aspects of a feminist style of collaboration. As we read across the chapters, certain themes reappear again and again, but perhaps the most recurrent one and the one that is central to a discussion of what is feminist takes us back to the advent of the feminist movement and the adage that "the personal is the political." Thus any process that is feminist must by definition attend to an analysis of the underlying power structures that define an organizational structure or an individual or group communication. This analysis includes an appreciation and keen understanding of both the historical and patriarchal hegemony underlying societal institutions including the family, church, education, work and business, and how women have been systematically excluded from the higher echelons of power and decision making. A collaborative management practice may seek to include workers and participants in decision making. If it does not also attend to the factor of gender and the place of women in the power structure, and embody change strategies that increase and empower their participation and their leadership, it is not feminist nor a feminist collaborative leadership style.

Furthermore, as feminism enters a second phase of growth and development, we have come to appreciate that analyzing gender by itself is not sufficient in understanding discrimination or effective in implementing systemic social change. We now know that the task of deconstructing one's "social location," a construct that embraces gender, race, and social class as well as the elements of historical place, time, and culture in which the individual lives (or in which the organization is embedded), is a far more difficult task, but likely a more valid and profitable way of approaching research and theory on feminist process. Thus a feminist collaborative style of leadership is based on the understanding that gender interacts with a multitude of other factors. The feminist leader who employs a collaborative style of leadership attends to multiple and systemic forms of oppression and privilege and the complex interactions of gender, race, and other aspects of "social location" that impact on participants' responses, contributions, and perspectives. Thus for example, while Raelin (2003) promulgates the "Four Cs" of modern leadership practice (see Chin, Overview), that is, leadership styles in this century must be concurrent, collective, collaborative, and compassionate, nowhere is there a mention of the importance of gender, or for that matter, of social location, in the analysis and implementation of these constructs, nor of feminism as the framework for understanding historical power relations.

Perspectives from Women Leaders on Collaboration and Feminist Leadership

The four chapters in this section contribute to our understanding of what is feminist collaborative leadership and whether collaboration by

129

itself is necessary and sufficient for feminist leadership. What is unique about this part of our book are the many interesting applications and actual examples of feminist collaborative leadership and its characteristics, processes, advantages, and challenges from which readers can glean insights and suggestions for implementation in their own work. While many of the examples come from leadership within academia and the American Psychological Association (since the contributors are psychologists), the experiences, insights, and processes described also apply to other disciplines and settings in the nonprofit and corporate worlds.

Chapter 6 engages four former women APA presidents and one APA executive director in a discussion of what is feminist policy, what are the basic principles that underlie feminist policy, and how can we promote the development of feminist policy. As a basis for deciding what is a feminist process, Worell and Johnson (1997) describe seven feminist behaviors: (a) structure for diversity of participants and diversity of viewpoints, formats, and procedures; (b) shared leadership; (c) shared responsibility; (d) valuing of all voices; (e) honoring personal experience; (f) deciding through consensus; and (g) promoting social change.

Feminist leadership as a construct and action has yet to be fully developed. Nonetheless, we can apply the above factors to help us discern unique aspects of feminist collaborative leadership. Besides fostering a sharing of power and decision making among their constituents, APA women presidents strove to promote equity, empowerment, and the improvement of women's lives. They also embraced a multicultural perspective in policy making and process. Florence Denmark notes the difference between power "to" and power "over," and that a model of "power to" can mean sharing power and working towards equal access to power. Being inclusive, furthermore, means including those with less power as students and committee members as well as people who traditionally have had less power as women of color. Dorothy Cantor and Diane Halpern both emphasize that collaborative leadership includes collaborating with men, not just women, and inspiring men to appreciate that implementing feminist policies and initiatives is in their own best interest (e.g., the wide availability of quality child care would support and help both men and women). Halpern emphasizes that we must change the metaphor from achieving a balance of power to achieving a synthesis which is win–win rather than win–lose. One does not avoid politics, but uses the political process as a way of effecting positive social change for equity. To get buy-in from men as well as women, the feminist leader articulates shared purposes, joint goals, and respectful disagreement. This is then another aspect of feminist collaboration and leadership which we might call transformational in that it seeks to transform relationships between men and women by including men in the vision of a changed society and a synthesis of power that is advantageous to both sexes.

While collaboration is believed to be the cornerstone of feminist process, it may also be tedious, time-consuming, and frustrating, especially when the goals are at odds with those in power. Gwen Keita ends this chapter by offering us some cogent observations on the advantages and challenges of a collaborative process. Collaboration can utilize the diverse strengths of all participants and the most effective use of resources. Real collaboration, however, requires active listening, negotiating, and compromising that may not be easy to achieve. Getting buy-in to consensus involves giving up a degree of control and some concessions to further the overall goal. For example, she discusses a situation in which in order to ensure the passage of a resolution on violence against women, language was changed which implied the mandating of APA activities rather than the encouragement or enabling of staff activities.

Deciding which compromises can be made without jeopardizing the overall feminist goals or violating feminist principles and process is not easy, but it is critical and probably a hallmark of the successful, experienced feminist leader. To gain the co-operation of the participants who are "not in the choir," one must do the groundwork of raising awareness and education before lobbying, negotiating, and compromising. This clearly is an area of controversy, and some feminists may assert that they would never compromise, but this posture is more easily taken when working outside a system than within.

Interorganizational, Interdisciplinary, and International Feminist Collaboration

Chapter 7, by Joy Rice and Asuncion Miteria Austria, introduces concepts of interorganizational feminist collaboration. The examples of interorganizational feminist collaboration from the Society for the Psychology of Women (SPW), the Institute for Women's Policy Research (IWPR), and the National Council of Research on Women (NCRW) offer inspiring examples and models of how feminist collaborative leadership implicitly involves the goal of social advocacy. This behavioral goal builds upon and implements the tenet that feminist collaboration seeks to empower women and strives to work towards an egalitarian society and world in which men and women and people of all cultures harmoniously share responsibilities, privileges, and benefits. Thus a common theme in all the examples in the chapter is the social advocacy goal of the collaborative process.

The case study presented of the Society for the Psychology of Women is given to illustrate that in order to work effectively and collaboratively with other feminist organizations to promote a common advocacy agenda, the organization must broaden its vision to include an interdisciplinary and international focus. A key step for SPW in this process included changing its name to reflect a broader scope and identity and building liaisons not only with other divisions in APA, as it had historically, but with other psychological organizations, women's organizations from other disciplines, social policy institutes and coalitions, and international organizations. The transformative process described involved:

- establishing a vision and systematically communicating it to the membership through the efforts of key leaders who embraced a broader vision and goal for the organization;
- encountering initial resistance to change by old leaders and people who had worked hard to achieve the secure place and recognition of the division within the parent organization;
- building coalitions among other leaders and members and overcoming resistance to change through patient, long-term education, information sharing, and exemplary and successful collaborative projects with other interdisciplinary, international organizations;
- working through more resistance as competing agendas, resources, and priorities were discussed and debated;
- achieving consensus to broaden the mission and aims of the group and to implement this by working collaboratively with other interdisciplinary, national, and international organizations.

While feminist collaboration with other women leaders on an individual level can facilitate women's resistance to oppression (Singley & Sweeney, 1998), an important advantage with a larger group like SPW is that working collaboratively with other women's organizations enhances the impact of the advocacy effort and the potential for positive change. It does so not only because more people and resources are involved, but because the strategies, projects, and policies involved may cut across professions, disciplines, and nations in scope and impact. When SPW collaborated with key partners within APA and also with outside organizations who represented a wide variety of disciplines from sociology, economics, political science, and public policy, the product, a position paper on women, work, and welfare policy, was richer, of greater depth, and ultimately had broader social impact in influencing legislation and social policy for low income women than an individual effort of feminist research might have had (Rice, Wyche, & Lott, 1997).

This kind of interdisciplinary and interorganizational collaboration makes possible products and policies that can extend far beyond one's limited constituency in one's country or region as embodied, for example, in working collaboratively with other feminist organizations and groups to develop international guidelines for psychological practice and nonsexist research. A whole set of new challenges applies when one tries to operationalize a feminist collaborative model for interdisciplinary organizations and their individual representatives. Thus you have a culture within the organization as well as a culture within the discipline that is being represented. The contributions of Elizabeth Horton and Barbara Gault to this chapter underscore how important it is that the "group spirit" extend beyond the individuals to the organizations or disciplines represented in the group collaboration.

The benefits of leadership in collaborating among diverse constituencies in research and advocacy projects such as those undertaken by the IWPR and NCRW include shared expertise, contacts, communication abilities, and most importantly, a strong collective voice. For example, the involvement of European women parliamentarians and media leaders significantly enhanced the cross-cultural exchange of models for improving gender equity. The challenges to such collaboration among many diverse groups and constituencies are many. They include resolving the tensions inherent in building coalitions with diverse groups; having a clear, equitable division of labor and available resources and funding; reaching consensus over agendas, priorities, turf, and decision making; overcoming geographical barriers of working with participants at different sites; and giving appropriate credit and recognition. While inclusion is a key tenet of a feminist collaborative

133

leadership style, Gault perceptively notes that many of the tensions are directly related to issues of inclusion: who defines the priorities, the agenda, who should be at the table and how diversity issues of race and sexual orientation as well as generation and discipline are bridged. Who gets included in funding? Who gets to determine the message and form of the final project or policy?

When collaborating internationally, you have the additional challenges of bridging different cultures, traditions, and languages as well as differing methods of research and what is considered appropriate in terms of psychological assessment, intervention, and methodology as it intersects with culture. Another is the problem of deciding what strategies to use in communicating effectively with feminist colleagues from other cultures and nations to foster similar aims and advocacy projects. The point to be made, however, is that when one does successfully meet these challenges and bridge those tensions, you get a richer product and outcome that reflects the multiperspectives and expertise of many individuals and diverse organizations that speak across the borders of race, generation, culture, and nation.

Marlene Fine in chapter 8 adds yet another dimension to our question about what is feminist collaborative leadership. She offers an ethics-based model of women's leadership that leads to social change and advocacy. Fine notes that the principal leadership theories are fundamentally rooted in the experiences of men and fail to account for ethical considerations. She identifies key concepts from the literature on women and leadership that provide a unique ethics-based model of leadership grounded in feminist principles of collaboration and inclusiveness with the aims of social change and improving the lives and welfare of women. She reviews studies that suggest that women perform leadership roles in ways that are distinct from men, and that their performance is likely to include more collaborative, nurturing, and egalitarian strategies that emphasize communication. This "ethic of care" includes responsiveness, sensitivity to others, acceptance, relatedness, and collaboration (O'Brien Hallstein, 1999). Her exploratory research found that women's stories revealed a narrative of moral behavior shaped not by the demands or cultures of particular organizations or situations, but by the women's own ethical principles. The narratives suggested that the women discursively constructed leadership through a *moral discourse of leadership* that emphasized leading in order to make a positive contribution in the world, collaboration, open communication, and honesty in relationships.

Feminist Collaboration in Strategic Planning

An ethics-based model of leadership grounded in feminist principles can also be characterized as "transformative leadership," a key term also used by other authors in this book. Transformative leadership is purposeful, value-based, and seeks to change institutions and organizations (Astin & Astin, 2000). Thus the leader becomes a change agent within a collective process that fosters strategic planning for the future. In chapter 9, Margaret Madden states that this viewpoint is consistent with a feminist approach to leadership and strategic planning. This approach is also consistent with a view of feminist collaborative leadership that embodies a vision of social change and advocacy as it inherently seeks positive change rather than preserving the status quo.

A feminist view then requires an examination of the context and control in which the strategic planning occurs, and of the role of gender norms. Masculine norms of controlled, rational processes, instrumentalism, careerism, and competition may privilege men, and assumptions about gender roles and values may pervade documents and contracts that provide the structure of organizations (Acker, 1998). There may be corresponding devaluation in stereotypic expectations of women as leaders. Women may also be expected to demonstrate an even greater degree of capability, knowledge, and competence than a man to be considered an effective leader (Ridgeway, 2001). Women may adopt leaderships styles that reflect and take advantage of the gendered expectations about co-operation and emotional sensitivity and nurturance that others have for them. Madden notes that while these gendered styles represent a realistic coping strategy for the barriers imposed by stereotypes and discrimination, a feminist analysis helps women and men better understand and change the constraints imposed on their leadership behaviors from gendered contexts and stereotyped expectations.

While there is positive rhetoric about the important role of collaboration in meeting the demands of a global economy and information age, the actual implementation is often unrealized, for organizations still rely on autonomous individual achievement and status and control images in considering what good leadership means. Thus merely hiring better hierarchical managers who demonstrate some emotional intelligence does not change the leadership paradigm nor work to transform the organization or its processes towards gender neutrality or gender equity (Fletcher, 2002). Again, a process that is feminist includes a contextual

135

analysis of gender power relationships and a view towards transformation that goes beyond mere stating of stylistic gender differences in leadership or strategic planning behaviors and preferences.

Because feminist collaborative leadership implies social action that seeks to change assumptions about women and men and to transform the very nature of leadership or at the least to challenge patriarchal ideas about women and leadership, the goals may be perceived as threatening to traditional hierarchical male leadership and the maintenance of the status quo in terms of power relations within the organization or institution. Thus the social justice motive is sometimes couched in less threatening terms as an obligation to give back to the community or to mentor the less privileged and experienced.

Madden ends her chapter by asking what characteristics of strategic planning might make it consistent with feminist principles. The answer that she offers includes sensitivity to context, appreciation of diverse perspectives, analysis of hierarchical imbalances of power, empowering individuals, fostering mentoring, and respectful, caring, and authentic interactions (Madden, 2004).

Lessons Learned

It is useful to end this introduction with a brief summary of the "lessons learned" from these five chapters and the experiences and insights they give us about feminist leadership, collaboration as a centerpiece of feminist leadership, and the challenges and opportunities of employing a model of feminist process in collaborations among individuals and organizations. What might we take away?

1   First, collaboration in feminist leadership is both a feminist principle and feminist practice (see chapter 7). It embodies feminist tenets of inclusion, power sharing, and egalitarian aims, but it also implicitly expects that the process of feminist leadership will demonstrate those aims in distributive leadership and in the empowerment and advancement of women leaders.

2   The personal is the political. For example, so-called "feminist" therapy is differentiated from "nonsexist" therapy in that it not only embraces and respects differences, but it also recognizes systemic disenfranchisement within society and the fact that psychotherapy as an

institution is a mirror of society. So feminist leadership would go beyond shared leadership or even collaborative leadership, beyond a simple respect of differences and inclusion, to recognizing how women have been disenfranchised; how power, politics, and gender interact; and how to translate those societal dynamics at the macro and micro levels into more equitable outcomes. Thus feminist collaborative leadership implicitly is based on a philosophy of gender equity and transforming women's role and position in society.

3   Feminist collaboration in its broadest meaning includes an appreciation of social location, cultural difference, world perspective, and discipline bias. All interact in the collaboration process and offer not only challenges, but opportunities for greater inclusion, scope, and ultimately impact of product, policy, or project.

4   Feminist collaborative leadership does not mean the embodiment of traditional feminine qualities of service, nurturance, and selflessness. While authoritarian means are eschewed and emotional sensitivity and respect for diverse voices are celebrated, effective feminist leaders are not afraid to use the power of their authority and office in decisive ways to empower others, nor to face controversy in building consensus and coalitions, nor to be flexible in forging equitable compromises without violating the tenets of feminism.

5   Feminist collaborative leadership builds partnerships between women and men and seeks to increase the mutual understandings of shared goals, aims, and benefits in an egalitarian society and world. A collaborative feminist model of leadership enhances the mutual ownership of egalitarian aims and outcomes and is rooted in an ethics of care that includes responsiveness, relatedness, and sensitivity and acceptance of others.

6   A feminist model of collaborative leadership can be described as nonhierarchical, collective, inclusive, egalitarian, flexible, co-operative, participatory, appreciative of multiple perspectives, transformational, and activist. This is in contrast to a model that is hierarchical, dualistic, power-based, ego-based, authoritarian, dogmatic, exclusive and individualistic, and seeks to preserve the status quo.

7   Feminist leaders who wish to employ a feminist collaborative leadership style in working with individuals and organizations:

- are able to challenge traditional hierarchical ideas about power relations;

- are comfortable with ambiguity, change, and value collaboration;
- are willing to work for the good of others rather than the promotion of self;
- are able to relate well interpersonally and honestly, building trust among participants (Brady, Dentith, & Hammett, in press);
- are experts in bringing the right people to the table ensuring breadth, depth, and diversity of the collaboration;
- develop shared goals, values, and trust among diverse constituencies to build a shared agenda and aims;
- mentor, share, and empower others in the process of leadership;
- promote an action agenda that includes social advocacy and activism.

A tall order? Perhaps it is, but to fulfill the kind of vision and transformation that we as women leaders have for society, for our earth, and for our children and their future, feminist women and men must seek to learn the meaning of collaboration in its fullest sense of societal transformation and to act on that vision through engagement, long experience, and lifetimes of collaboration. The fulfillment of this vision will take a different kind of leadership, one that is changing, collective, and courageous.

References

Acker, J. (1998). Hierarchies, jobs, and bodies: A theory of gendered organizations. In K. A. Myers, C. D. Anderson, & B. Risman (Eds.), *Feminist foundations: Towards transforming sociology* (pp. 299–317). Thousand Oaks, CA: Sage.

Astin, A. W., & Astin, H. S. (2000). *Leadership reconsidered: Engaging higher education in social change.* Battle Creek, MI: W. K. Kellogg Foundation.

Brady, J., Dentith, A., & Hammett, R. (in press). Feminism and theories of leadership. In F. English (Ed.), *Sage encyclopedia of educational leadership and administration.* Thousand Oaks, CA: Sage.

Brunner, C. C. (Ed.). (1999). *Sacred dreams: Women and the superintendency.* Albany, NY: State University of New York Press.

Cafferty, H., & Clausen, J. (1998). What's feminist about it? Reflection on collaboration in editing and writing. In E. G. Peck & J. S. Mink (Eds.), *Common ground: Feminist collaboration in the academy* (pp. 81–98). Albany, NY: State University of New York Press.

Carli, L. L., & Eagly, A. H. (1999). Gender effects on social influence and emergent leadership. In G. N. Powell (Ed.), *Handbook of women and work* (pp. 203–222). Thousand Oaks, CA: Sage.

Chin, J. L. (2004). Feminist leadership: Feminist visions and diverse voices. *Psychology of Women Quarterly, 28*(1), 1–8.

Eagly, A. H., Karu, S. J., Miner, J. B., & Johnston, B. T. (1994). Gender and motivation to manage in hierarchic organizations: A meta-analysis. *Leadership Quarterly, 5*(2), 135–159.

Fletcher, J. (2002, August). *The greatly exaggerated demise of heroic leadership: Gender, power, and the myth of the female advantage.* CGO Insight, Briefing No. 13. Boston: Simmons College Center for Gender in Organizations.

Fletcher, J. K. (1999). *Disappearing acts: Gender, power and relational practice at work.* Cambridge, MA: MIT Press.

Kao, H. S. R., Sinha, D., & Wilpert, B. (1999). *Management and cultural values: The indigenization of organizations in Asia.* Thousand Oaks, CA: Sage.

Madden, M. E. (2004). Can strategic planning be feminist? *The Feminist Psychologist: Newsletter of the Society for the Psychology of Women, 31*(1), 1–2.

O'Brien Hallstein, D. L. (1999). A postmodern caring: Feminist standpoint theories, revisioned caring, and communication ethics. *Western Journal of Communication, 63*(1), 32–56.

Raelin, J. (2003). *Creating leaderful organizations: How to bring out leadership in everyone.* San Francisco: Berrett-Koehler.

Rice, J. K., Wyche, K., & Lott, B. (1997). *Implementing welfare policy to insure long-term independence and well-being.* Washington, DC: American Psychological Association.

Ridgeway, C. (2001). Gender, status and leadership. *Journal of Social Issues, 57*(4), 637–656.

Singley, C. J., & Sweeney, S. E. (1998). In league with each other: The theory and practice of feminist collaboration. In E. G. Peck & J. S. Mink (Eds.), *Common ground: Feminist collaboration in the academy* (pp. 63–80). Albany, NY: State University of New York Press.

Worell, J., & Johnson, N. G. (1997). Introduction: Creating the future: Process and promise in feminist practice. In J. Worell & N. Johnson (Eds.), *Shaping the future of feminist psychology: Education, research & practice.* Washington, DC: American Psychological Association.

Chapter 6

Leadership through Policy Development: Collaboration, Equity, Empowerment, and Multiculturalism

Norine G. Johnson, Florence L. Denmark, Dorothy W. Cantor, Diane F. Halpern, and Gwendolyn Puryear Keita

Five psychology feminist leaders were posed the following three questions: *What is feminist policy? What are the basic principles that underlie feminist policy? And how can we promote the development of feminist policy?* Regardless of the individual character or personality of the feminist leader or the setting in which she attempts to enact policy, a picture emerged from the answers that highlights the inseparability of content, process, and enactment for feminist policy makers.

Four contributors to this chapter, Denmark, Cantor, Johnson, and Halpern, represent almost 50% of the women former presidents of the American Psychological Association and bring perspectives of women in academia and women in professional practice. The fifth contributor, Gwendolyn Keita, is the Executive Director of APA's Public Interest Directorate, and brings extensive experience in formulating public policy on women's issues and initiatives. The women used their leadership positions within psychology to promote policy changes that impact social change and improve women's lives, that is, expanding the inclusion of women and women's issues in textbooks (Denmark); focusing national attention on adolescent girls' strengths and diversity through books and the media (Cantor); advocating for health care for diverse constituencies (Johnson); exploring the interface between work and family including poverty and childcare (Halpern); and fostering the enactment of health policies that included race, culture, gender, and social class (Keita). Through their stories, which are included in this chapter, they described how they worked as leaders in psychology and APA, and how certain attributes of feminist process consistently emerged, that is, fostering collaboration among participants; promoting equity, empowerment, and the improvement of women's lives; and embracing a multicultural perspective in policy making and process.

Feminist Leadership and Collaboration: Florence L. Denmark

Collaborative leadership and feminist policy

A policy is a definite course of action or procedure adopted and pursued in order to influence and determine decisions, actions, and other matters. In order to promote feminist policies, that is, policies advancing the social, political, and economic equality of women with men, we have to be activists and speak up as feminists for the principles in which we believe. As a long-time feminist before the current Woman's Movement, my working collaboratively as an activist to effect change did not begin until the 1970s, when I was elected to positions of leadership in various organizations. Leadership can be defined in many ways. It can be inspiring, transformative, or instrumental. To me, leadership is the ability to influence and work with others to achieve shared feminist goals. "Others" include students as well as those already established in the field. Sustainable changes take place through nonhierarchical collective approaches. As APA President, I believed it was important to initiate a long-term impact and to advocate for change within APA as well as for social change. As an elected leader, I was able to influence publishers' policies through presentations and papers in my role as President. I examined numerous introductory psychology texts and found a surprising lack of material about women despite the existence of APA Division 35, the Society for the Psychology of Women, for 10 years, and of several feminist journal publications (e.g., *Psychology of Women Quarterly, Sex Roles*). Publishers in the audience listened to my recommendations and took action. Many introductory texts now include

141

separate chapters on women (or gender) or material on women infused throughout the text.

Promoting feminist policy through collaboration

In my experience, women leaders working collectively can be powerful catalysts for change and can use their positions of leadership to set policy. As the influence of feminism gets stronger, so does the resistance to it. I have found that change is frightening to many people, and change threatens the existing power structure. Consequently, we need to address such fears, not ignore them. Power is a word that repels many feminists; however, we do not want to be powerless and, as other feminists have pointed out, we can think of power as "power to," not "power over."

In our professional organizations or in larger political arenas, we must support candidates committed to women's issues as a top priority. We must be heard through organizational work as well as through our votes. To call attention to feminist issues, more militant actions such as demonstrations may sometimes be necessary. We must go beyond our places of work and professional activity and recognize that it is important to effect changes in many aspects of life and society and to give voice to our convictions. Having long been known as a feminist, I would have lost all credibility during my APA presidency if I didn't make my position clear and speak up for what I (and those who voted for me) believed in. It was also important to work with those who had different concerns and views, and this necessitated a certain amount of give and take; however, I made my position clear and never compromised on feminism. I may have had a "soft" style, but I "stuck to my guns."

To promote feminist policy it is important for women leaders to work in a collaborative relationship with other women. I supported and participated in developing many feminist policies as a leader of APA, all in close collaboration with other women, for example, having childcare at conventions, refusing to meet in sites not supported by the Equal Rights Amendment (ERA), and increasing the representation of ethnic minority women and men into governance positions and in the publication process. The issues may change, but the underlying theme of feminist collaboration does not. Successful feminist leaders embrace women's causes, encourage and help other women, and bond with other women to bring about the greatest gains. Positive change will continue to come about as women create bonds with one another, and those of us in positions of leadership must serve as feminist role models and mentors, imparting both knowledge and political momentum.

Implementing Feminist Policy as an APA President: Dorothy W. Cantor

In 1996, I served as the eighth woman president in the 105-year history of the American Psychological Association. Earlier, a good friend and colleague and I had published *Women in Power: The Secrets of Leadership*, a study of 25 women in high elected office in the United States (Cantor & Bernay, 1992). We wondered what was different about their leadership style and approach to office from that of their male colleagues. We formulated "The Leadership Equation": Leadership = a Competent Self + Creative Aggression + WomanPower. A Competent Self was defined as the positive, indelible self-concept that isn't erased by challenge, confrontation, or even failure. Creative Aggression is aggression in the service of life and growth, which allows a woman to set goals, take initiative, lead others, and speak out for what she believes in. "WomanPower" is power that includes the ability to hear others, respond to their needs, and integrate others' ideas into the agenda.

Feminist leadership includes both content and process levels. I would define feminist process as including a structure for diversity, distributed leadership, distributed responsibility, valuing all voices, honoring personal experience, deciding through consensus, and promoting social change. These ideas and ideals are congruent with what we learned from the women in politics whom we studied, women who were putting feminist policy into action. Those women served as role models to me, from the time I was first encouraged and asked to run for the APA presidency by Norine Johnson, one of my successors in the job. I replied that I was ambivalent. She said, "That's not the answer I wanted from *my* candidate." I thought about her comment and recalled that so many of the women in politics said that they never really planned their career paths; they needed a push to get them going. Norine had provided me the push that I needed.

When I learned of my election, I thought about how I would use the opportunity psychology had given me to best advance women. I had already, as a member of the Board of Directors, organized a Task Force on the Changing Gender Composition of Psychology because of the growing number of women in graduate programs and the belief that when women enter a profession, it loses prestige, status, and earning power. I believe that the most significant thing we learned from this task force was that women's domination of a field is the result of, rather than the cause of, the shift in prestige, status, and earning power. That knowledge presented a goal to all of us as women: as women grew in the ranks of psychology, we need to maintain the high reputation and admiration of psychology as a discipline and profession in spite of trends to the contrary. It became a challenge for us to work even harder.

Feminist leadership and collaboration in the kitchen cabinet

Just before assuming my seat on the Board of Directors as President-elect, I called a meeting of 40 women leaders from all parts of the Association to decide together what important area could be addressed through Presidential Initiatives money available to me. We brainstormed for nearly two hours. Consensus emerged that we should focus on adolescent girls, a group then being described in the literature as dysfunctional, that is, pregnant, drug-abusing, and eating-disordered. To change that perception, therefore, we charged the task force to focus on the strengths and resiliencies of teenage girls. The outcome of that task force resulted in the edited volume, *Beyond Appearances: A New Look at Adolescent Girls* (Johnson, Roberts, & Worell, 1999), and an extremely useful book for adolescent girls and their parents, *The Inside Story on Teen Girls* (Rubenstein & Zager, 2002).

The whole experience of my "kitchen cabinet" serves as an example of feminist leadership. The decision to form the task force was made, not singularly, but by a diverse group of women using a style of leadership that was distributed and collaborative. The fact that it was my presidential task force did not translate into my need to chair it; rather, I entrusted the leadership to two distinguished colleagues, who in turn, shared the responsibility with the members of the task force. The "kitchen cabinet" recommended these members and included a man to ensure that male voices would be heard. The feminist goal of the task force was to promote social change by changing the perception of adolescent girls and promoting the image of their emotional health and normal development.

Collaboration among coalitions

I had yet another opportunity to apply feminist principles during my presidency. In 1996 a key problem for practitioners was the managed care system encroachment on practitioner judgment and treatment of patients. I brought together the presidents of all of the national associations of mental health professionals, including psychiatry, social work, nursing, and counseling, to develop a document called "Your Mental Health Rights," which was widely distributed to national and state legislators and to our respective memberships. In honoring the feminist ideal of collaborative leadership, we were successful in effecting change. I cochaired the summit meeting with the president of the American Psychiatric Association which looked beyond the issues that divided our professions to the issues that brought us together, another hallmark of feminist process.

The challenge to transforming leadership is how to bring men into the system as feminist leaders. They do not instinctively operate using a collaborative process, as many women do. As a personal example, Dr. Bernay and I began to use the concept "EmpathyPower" in our leadership talks because so many of our male colleagues and clients were uncomfortable with the first word, "WomanPower," that we had crafted. I look to how we can find a way to describe feminist leadership and policy so that it is not gender-bound and will lead to better leadership outcomes for everyone.

You Have the Power to Convene:
Norine G. Johnson

What is feminist policy?

An early feminist might have defined feminist policy as policy that affected women. Certainly the XIX Amendment to the United States Constitution, giving women the right to vote, is an example of feminist policy. Later feminists began to question if feminist policy should be expanded to include other issues beside those focused on women, for example, how the policy was enacted and issues of process that were important to the discussion. Worell and Johnson (1997) articulated a framework of seven feminist processes used at the first National Conference on Education and Training in Feminist Practice in 1993. The conference provided an opportunity to understand how feminist *process* influenced the formulating of policy *content* that is consistent with feminist principles (Eagly & Johnson, 1990; Yoder, 1999).

Today we have moved a giant step further from the 1990s. Feminist theory is enriched by considering the interactions of race, ethnicity, sex, gender, class, sexual preferences, and physical abilities (Caraway, 1996; O'Leary & Flanagan, 2001). For feminist policy to be multicultural in scope and process, the policy must use a multicultural lens; must not be limited in scope to one element, such as gender; and the policy must result from the inclusion of diverse voices and participation in the process.

Initiating collaborative policy towards positive social change

As the ninth woman President of the American Psychological Association in 107 years, I experienced men as more likely to emerge as leaders (Matlin, 2004, p. 199) in mixed-gender groups (such as the APA). The leadership of APA and the membership appeared to welcome me as a woman leader, but I was also challenged by both women and men. For example, some wanted me to be more nurturing. Male colleagues were also burdened by gender stereotypes. Whereas some men behaved as feminist leaders, other men experienced the style as a weakness, resulting in their increasing verbal challenges to such styles.

My first priority as APA President was to focus the Association on psychology as a health discipline and to propose that we espouse a biopsychosocial-cultural model of health (Johnson, 2001). Health policy is a feminist issue (Johnson, 2002). The biopsychosocial model (Engel, 1977) currently in vogue in national health policy must be expanded to include culture consistent with a biopsychosocial-cultural model of health (Johnson, 2003). Feminist process was used to advance this policy decision during my presidential year. Diverse constituencies within psychology designed and implemented two initiatives: *Psychology Builds a Healthy World* and *Expanding Opportunities in Psychology Science and Practice* (Rozensky, Johnson, Goodheart, & Hammond, 2004). The outcomes reflected the values of multiculturalism. In May of 2001 the membership of APA voted an association bylaw change, to amend its mission statement to include the word health: "The objects of the American Psychological Association shall be to advance psychology as a science and profession and as a means of promoting *health*, education, and human welfare" (American Psychological Association, 2001). The outcome was an affirmation by APA that psychology was a key to a healthy society with even broader policy implications to come in the future.

Another key event during my presidency was the terrorist attack on the United States on September 11, 2001, which killed thousands of

U.S. citizens; this led to opportunities for leadership from our association. As the United States called on psychology for help, psychology responded. As APA's President, I was asked to be one of the spokespersons in our effort. In the months afterwards, I spoke on several television shows including two nationwide segments on CNN of the psychological effects of terrorism. In addition, for the next 18 months I crisscrossed the United States speaking at universities and colleges, and State Psychological Association meetings. I sought to acknowledge the efforts of psychologists who were leaders in the recovery effort by giving them presidential citations. I believe that my feminist leadership style and use of a feminist process was helpful during this difficult time by empowering others, stressing culturally appropriate interventions, and fostering policy decisions so that the diverse strengths of psychology were used to meet this national crisis.

What is feminist policy and how can we promote it?

I have no certain answer to the questions "What is feminist policy?" or "What is collaborative feminist policy?" Often when we raise such questions, it raises other questions more readily than it yields an answer. For instance, I would ascertain that a policy enacted to benefit women is not a feminist policy if it is enacted through autocratic leadership or if it privileges some while disadvantaging others. I believe that policy, process, and enactment cannot be separated in feminist policy making. I will assert that feminist policy, in addition to having content that is feminist, will be enacted through a feminist process that would: (a) incorporate a structure for diversity of participants, of viewpoints, formats, and procedures; (b) distribute leadership; (c) distribute responsibility; (d) value *all* voices; (e) honor personal experience; (f) decide through consensus; and (g) promote social change (Worell & Johnson, 1997).

As women leaders in positions of influence and power, we can promote the development of feminist policy by initiatives which provide multiple forums for discussion, and thereby educate and illuminate the complexity of feminist policy. We can look at the outcomes of current policies within our institutions and associations to discern patterns of effective policies that carry feminist values. During my term as President of the American Psychological Association and during the preceding four years on the APA Board of Directors, I found both men and women engaging in feminist leadership and feminist policy enactment. Leadership brings the power to convene. Feminist leaders have the power to convene with the purpose of enacting feminist policy. We may not be able to define what feminist policy is yet, but as with good art, we know it when we see it.

Feminist Policies: Mainstreaming, Budgeting, and Building Alliances: Diane F. Halpern

As 2004 president of the American Psychological Association, I did not have the luxury of looking back through the dusty haze of memory or the softening perspective of time to think about answers to these questions about feminist leadership. I grappled with those definitions as I worked my way through endless meetings and agenda books that could double for weights at the gym. I think of feminist policy as feminist thought and philosophy put into action—making feminist principles happen.

Feminist policies have three essential components: mainstreaming, budgeting, and building alliances. The *mainstreaming* component refers to having the policy goal become the concern of everyone—not just women or feminists. Consider poverty or childcare. These are not "women's issues," but they continually end up on "women's agendas" because a disproportionate number of people who live in poverty are caretaking women and their dependent children.

Making feminist policy everyone's issue

A feminist policy concerning poverty or childcare would be written to become everyone's issues. How? A larger portion of the budget would be devoted to reducing poverty and improving childcare. A budget is a policy document. It is a way of "putting a group's money where its mouth is." If we really care about children, for example, then universal early childhood education programs and health care need to be funded at levels that demonstrate that concern.

Budget allocations for feminist political issues are known as "gender economics." We need to ensure that our dollars follow our values, and our allies don't become quiet when their crucial voices are needed during budget "fights." The best way to avoid budget fighting is by building alliances with other groups. Feminist policies have commonalities with minority group policies, and despite the misleading language, the minority group designation is often used for the majority world. The use of the word "minority" is one way of hiding that the nonwhite population is a sizeable majority in many places where they are described as minority groups (where they do have minority status in power).

Promoting feminist policies: collaboration and self-interest

The best way to promote feminist policies may be to get all parties to see the advantages in the feminist policies that would accrue for themselves. Self-interest is a strong incentive to "do the right thing." Often a feminist policy is framed as giving something up by one group so that another group can gain, and almost always there are other ways to think about the same issues. For example, I am coeditor of a book that is changing the metaphor in the work–family conflict literature from "balance," which literally means taking from one side to add to the other, to "interaction" or "synthesis," which allows for win–win or mutual returns-on-investments (Halpern & Murphy, 2005). To successfully promote feminist policies, there needs to be shared goals with real collaboration and respectful disagreement. To get "buy-in," everyone will need to want the policy feminists are selling.

Leadership to promote feminist policies

Although at the time I was not consciously thinking about feminist policies, I believe that the initiatives I selected for my presidential term are feminist and action-oriented with a goal of improving women's lives. My main initiative uses social science research to make data-based recommendations for working families, employers, public policies, and communities and schools that can realign the world of work with the realities of working families (Halpern, 2004). The conflict between work and family and the far too pervasive feeling of being "squeezed for time" is not a woman's issue any more than caring for children is, but it is a greater problem for women because they feel greater pressure to maintain traditional care responsibilities while increasing their hours of paid work. This stressor cuts across socioeconomic status. Low wage earners have the additional stress of making ends meet and even the wealthy often work long hours combined with the stress of high pressure jobs and little time with family. The recommendations in my APA Presidential Taskforce Report call for changes in policies that will make work and family life more compatible.

Closing thoughts on not winning a popularity contest

I recently read an empirical study of sentencing by women and men judges (Steffensmeier & Hebert, 1999). Overall, the women sentenced repeat offenders more harshly and paid more attention to contextual factors, but there was also considerable overlap in sentencing patterns. The authors concluded that "in many respects women and men judges have similar sentencing practices . . . however, we also find an important gender difference in sentence decision making (i.e., greater contextualization among women judges)" (p. 1186). I conclude with these remarks because they are relevant to feminist politics and policies. I do not know if women presidents of large professional organizations like APA select different initiatives or lead in different ways or, on average, select similar topics or act the same as presidents who are men; there have been too few women in this top leadership position and most have been elected in recent years. Regardless of the differences, feminist policies are for everyone. It takes a great deal of old-fashioned strength to propose unpopular policies or to buck the crowd, and feminist policies are often unpopular, and the job of real leadership sometimes means not being afraid to take a stand or even to stand alone. I hope the job will be easier for those who follow in future years.

Feminist Collaboration in Developing Policy and Social Change: Gwendolyn Keita

Like most of the other contributors to this chapter, I found Worell and Johnson's definition of feminist process very useful as a framework (1997, p. 8). They stress the importance of collaboration, which is viewed as the basis of feminist process. Important goals of this process are consensus that is developed by negotiating decisions through mutuality with no winners or losers in decision making rather than through competition, and mediation through discussion and compromise rather than through power assertions. As a feminist, I have also attempted to make collaboration a cornerstone in developing and moving social policy that improves women's lives. Collaboration has proven effective and rewarding, especially when it leads to a positive outcome for all those involved. The process can become particularly challenging when one's position is at odds with that of those in power or those with strong opposing views.

Collaboration at APA

The success of the collaborative process is often determined by who the players are and who or what they represent. At the APA Women's Programs Office (WPO) we have used collaborative leadership in working with many other organizations, coalitions, and federal agencies to effect social change and to move social policy forward. Feminist collaboration on policy issues within the APA occurs through the co-operative work of several offices and committees devoted to women's issues and additional collaborations within APA and in the larger professional, policy, and governmental community. Feminist collaboration on policy issues begins by prioritizing issues that aim to improve women's lives. The process of prioritizing issues and allocating resources toward those issues can be difficult given limited resources of time and funds. We focus foremost on the empowerment of women and the structural changes necessary to realize this empowerment. In recent years, depression, poverty, issues of work and stress, women's health, women's advancement in academe, women's leadership, reproductive rights, and violence against women have been some of the important women's issues addressed by WPO.

Cross-collaboration on a critical women's issue

Collaboration between the various parts of a professional membership organization such as APA draws upon the diverse strengths of many members, uses resources effectively and requires listening, negotiating, and compromising. The development of the Resolution on Male Violence Against Women and its approval by the APA Council of Representatives in February, 1999, is a good example of this type of cross-collaboration. In 1991, APA established the Task Force on Male Violence Against Women, which proposed a number of research, education and training, and policy recommendations in its final report, *No Safe Haven: Male Violence Against Women at Home, at Work, and in the Community*. WPO agreed it was important to implement these recommendations, yet the process of gaining recognition and influencing policy was unclear. After consideration and consultation, it was concluded that a formal APA resolution on male violence against women would give the larger organization an effective tool to advocate at the state and federal level for legislation combating violence against women, and the need to improve the training of psychologists to better recognize and treat victims of violence. Consequently,

WPO, the APA Committee on Women in Psychology (CWP), and the Task Force on Male Violence Against Women collaborated to develop the resolution, with input from the APA Public Policy Office.

After the resolution was drafted, and in the first step of the APA consensus-building process, WPO submitted the draft resolution to all APA boards and committees for comment. Based on feedback, some changes were made to the document; in keeping with the feminist collaborative model, we responded to each board and/or committee with a complete explanation for the incorporation or rejection of the suggestion. For example, we chose not to include an extensive addition by the Committee on Disability Issues in Psychology (CDIP), feeling that it might broaden the original focus of the resolution beyond its original intent, and informed CDIP of this decision and rationale. Other groups had concerns that the title should be "Violence Against Women," rather than "Male Violence Against Women," as violence also exists between partners in lesbian couples. Because the Task Force and CWP felt it most critical to address the most frequent and serious kind of partner violence, neither the focus nor wording was changed based on this recommendation.

CWP and WPO also made concessions in order to advance the overall goal. One of the APA boards indicated that they could not approve the resolution as it was and requested "rephrasing the resolution with language that *enables* staff activity rather than language that appears to *mandate* activities." A negative response from a board could lead to a major conflict on the floor of Council, or possibly result in failure to get the resolution passed during a time of tight fiscal constraints. CWP and WPO thus decided to change the wording to: "Therefore, be it resolved that the American Psychological Association: . . . *support* legislative efforts . . ." instead of "*advocate* for legislative efforts," and "*explore* avenues to improve training of psychologists . . ." instead of "*develop* avenues to improve . . .".

The goal was for the APA to have a policy on male violence against women that would give guidance and authority to our public policy staff for advocacy on Capitol Hill, that would increase psychologists' awareness of the extent of and consequences of male violence in women's lives, and that could be used in improving training of psychologists to address the needs of this population. These goals could be met while changing the language as requested.

All comments received from boards and committees, along with responses regarding those comments, were included with the resolution and sent to the APA Board of Directors for approval and then to the

Council of Representatives, the official policy arm of the organization, for adoption as formal APA policy. As part of Council, Women's Caucus then became another critical collaborator in moving items/issues through this final stage. The Caucus led the discussion in support of the resolution on the floor of the Council. Other key collaborators that were also instrumental in supporting and advocating were the Ethnic Minority and Public Interest Caucuses. The Resolution on Male Violence Against Women was passed as formal APA policy, and the APA Public Policy Office (PPO) was then able to use it as a framework for its policy efforts in this area.

The resolution was disseminated by PPO among coalition partners and members of Congress and was used to support passage of the Violence Against Women Act of 1994, its subsequent reauthorizations, and increased funding. PPO staff, led by Lori Valencia Greene, participated in a policy briefing organized by New York Democrat Senator Charles Schumer on violence against women and drafted legislation, "Expanding Research for Women in Trauma Act of 2003," that was introduced by North Carolina Democrat Senator John Edwards. The legislation sought to establish initiatives to increase research on the psychological risk of and sequelae of violence against women and adolescents. Unfortunately, some coalition partners had concerns about the legislation because of their reluctance to support anything that might take resources away from supporting shelters and other direct services. Clearly, APA policy strategy must include educating coalition partners and members of Congress on the role of psychology on issues impacting women and their families before the organization engages in direct lobbying, in addition to recognizing and responding to important competing interests.

This example of extended cross-collaboration on a critical issue for women's health and welfare illustrates the complexities, advantages, and compromises of feminist collaboration as a leadership vehicle to effect social change. Our experience may offer some guidance for other volunteer organizations working with diverse constituencies desiring to effect important social change through feminist leadership and collaboration.

Summary

Women's leadership to promote feminist policy emerges in this chapter as containing four major attributes: (a) collaboration as a key process,

(b) improving women's lives as a key goal, (c) empowerment and equality as key outcomes, and (d) multiculturalism as both a key process and goal. The chapter highlights how feminist policy interweaves the policy content, process, and enactment, and that all three elements must receive equal attention.

Collaboration may take several forms. Bringing together individuals holding diverse viewpoints, forming alliances of representatives from key organizations, and forming partnerships with organizations whose policy you hope to change illustrate a few examples of the multiplicity of possible collaborating forms. Specific examples of successful collaborations included building alliances, assembling a kitchen cabinet, working with important partners (e.g., publishers), involving the women who would be affected by the policy change, and forming coalitions across constituency groups.

The enactment of feminist policies requires prioritizing. Feminist leaders must learn to focus their efforts in order to be successful. The examples in this chapter suggest that prioritizing requires several steps for the woman leader who seeks to impact policy and social change. She decides her primary goals. Then she evaluates the range of possibilities of enactment and the time span necessary to complete the work, including the fiscal implications and budgeting. Both steps are frequently done in collaboration with others. She knows how to build alliances and the importance of forging collaborative partnerships with diverse constituencies. At some point, the feminist leader must decide where the primary goal(s) and focus will be.

Improving women's lives as a key goal inspires women leaders. Feminist women leaders are inspired and energized by the opportunities to enact policy that enhances the lives of women, girls, and people oppressed by conditions such as race, ethnicity, and class. The difficult journey toward feminist policy goal strengthens the conviction of feminist leaders to persist. For example, Keita discussed her persistence through obstacles and across time to enact national policy on the prevention of violence toward women.

Empowerment and equality are key outcomes in feminist policies and directly related to the goal of improving women's lives. Women leaders look to enact policies that will improve women's lives by empowering women and giving them equal opportunity. Empowering women may be threatening those in power who seek to keep the power. As Denmark states, "Any kind of significant change is frightening to many people."

Multiculturalism emerges in current feminist leaders as an integral component of feminist policy and feminist process. Cantor's work on adolescent girls took the values of diversity and strength to empower adolescent girls in today's society. Denmark challenged the publishers of introductory psychology texts to be inclusive. Halpern put the spotlight on "gender economics." Johnson proposed expanded health policies to include race, ethnicity, class, and gender, in addition to biopsycho factors.

What emerges in reading this chapter is the joy each feminist leader experienced in promoting change that impacted the lives of women. Reading between the lines, one sees how women leaders might occasionally wish for more autocratic power as each comments on how developing and moving to enacting feminist policy through a collaborative feminist process is hard work. Nonetheless, they find the promotion of feminist policy to be enduring and satisfying and look forward to the leadership of the next generation, while hoping, as stated here by Halpern, that ". . . the job will be easier for those who follow."

References

American Psychological Association. (2001, February). Council of Representatives. February, 23–25, 2001. *Draft minutes.* Washington, DC: Author.

Cantor, D. W., & Bernay, T. (1992). *Women in power: The secrets of leadership.* Boston: Houghton-Mifflin.

Caraway, N. E. (1996). The riddle of consciousness: Racism and identity in feminist theory. In L. L. Duke (Ed.), *Women in politics: Outsiders or insiders?* (pp. 17–29). Englewood Cliffs, NJ: Prentice Hall.

Eagly, A. H., & Johnson, B. T. (1990). Gender and leadership style: A meta-analysis. *Psychological Bulletin, 108*, 233–256.

Engel, G. L. (1977). The need for a new medical model: A challenge for biomedicine. *Science, 196*, 29–136.

Halpern, D. F. (2004). *Public policy, work and families: The report of the APA presidential initiative on work and families.* Washington, DC: American Psychological Association.

Halpern, D. F., & Murphy, S. E. (Eds.). (2005). *From work–family balance to work–family interaction: Changing the metaphor.* Mahwah, NJ: Lawrence Erlbaum Associates.

Johnson, N. G. (2001, December). President's column: Women leadership: in health and in war. *APA Monitor, 32*, 11.

Johnson, N. G. (2002, August). President's Report. Special Issue: 2001 Annual Report of the American Psychological Association: Psychology Builds a Healthy World. *American Psychologist, 57*(8), 502–504.

Johnson, N. G. (2003). Psychology and health: Research, practice, and policy. *American Psychologist, 58*, 670–677.

Johnson, N. G., Roberts, M. C., & Worell, J. (Eds.). (1999). *Beyond appearances: A new look at adolescent girls.* Washington, DC: American Psychological Association.

Matlin, M. W. (2004). *The psychology of women* (5th ed.). Belmont, CA: Wadsworth/Thomson Learning.

O'Leary, V. E., & Flanagan, E. H. (2001). Leadership. In J. Worell (Ed.), *Encyclopedia of women and gender* (pp. 245–257). San Diego, CA: Academic Press.

Rozensky, R., Johnson, N. G., Goodheart, C., & Hammond, W. R. (Eds.). (2004). *Psychology builds a healthy world: Opportunities in research and practice.* Washington, DC: American Psychological Association.

Rubenstein, A., & Zager, K. (2002). *The inside story on teenage girls.* Washington, DC: American Psychological Association.

Steffensmeier, D., & Hebert, C. (1999). Women and men policymakers: Does the judge's gender affect the sentencing of criminal defendants? *Social Forces, 77*, 1163–1196.

Worell, J., & Johnson, N. G. (1997). Introduction: Creating the future: Process and promise in feminist practice. In J. Worell & N. Johnson (Eds.), *Shaping the future of feminist psychology: Education, research, and practice* (pp. 1–14). Washington, DC: American Psychological Association.

Yoder, J. D. (1999). *Women and gender: Transforming psychology.* Upper Saddle River, NJ: Prentice Hall.

Chapter 7

Collaborative Leadership and Social Advocacy Among Women's Organizations

Joy K. Rice and Asuncion Miteria Austria

Collaboration has been said to be a hallmark of a feminist process. This chapter will first briefly define feminist collaboration and its components as a feminist principle and practice. The advantages and difficulties of feminist collaboration, and how it is used by feminist leaders as a tool to promote an advocacy agenda, will also be discussed. The primary focus of the chapter, however, is to provide readers with in-depth examples that they can draw upon in their own work, highlighting how various national and international feminist organizations have successfully operationalized a feminist collaborative process to achieve their mission and goals and to further their research and advocacy agendas. Also presented is an interesting discussion of the recent history of our own professional organization, the Society for the Psychology of Women (SPW) of the American Psychological Association (APA), and how it evolved and struggled to attain an identity and organizational structure with the capacity to form feminist collaborative leadership projects and to influence social policy on the national level. While the primary focus of this book and examples given in this chapter come from feminist collaboration in academic institutions and organizations, many of the principles involved and the processes described could apply as well to other settings where women work and advocate for change.

What Is Feminist Collaboration?

According to Singley and Sweeney (1998), to collaborate means "to work jointly with others, especially in an intellectual endeavour, to cooperate with . . ." (p. 63). From a feminist perspective, collaboration between individuals or organizations means working together effectively in an egalitarian manner. In contrast to a traditional hierarchical model of collaboration in which most of the tasks are assumed or delegated by the committee chair to others, feminist collaboration is characterized as egalitarian. In feminist collaboration, work is often presumed to be shared equally and women are more likely to use styles involving completion of tasks and interpersonal competencies with subordinates (Statham, 1987). Feminist collaboration is often viewed as a cornerstone of a feminist process (Worell & Johnson, 1997). It is identified with the practices of "sharing information, coalition building, shaping direction, and appreciating diversity of opinions and ideas" (Brunner, 1999, p. 203).

The collaboration process is essentially a continuing communication in which each member contributes and listens to all perspectives and diverse voices (Janis Sanchez, personal communication, June 23, 2003). All views are considered, and while there could be disagreements, they are discussed and differences are resolved through compromise or consensus. Differences in feminist collaboration are complementary rather than divisive. Kaplan and Rose (1993) said that, "sisterhood is powerful, the personal is political, women do not trash women . . ." (pp. 552–53). The goals in feminist collaborative undertakings are to enable and empower others (Fletcher, 1999).

Feminist collaboration is egalitarian

As will be discussed in the exemplary projects in the following sections, feminist collaboration between the representative members of organizations requires sensitivity to the differing perspectives, values, and goals of the organizations as well as to the individuals involved. Both emotional and cognitive feedback is involved, and an awareness and acknowledgment of members' feelings are important to team success and effectiveness. Psychological theory suggests that individuals who feel understood and accepted are more likely to be accepting of others (Fletcher, 1999). Mutual trust is developed, and an increased willingness to see another person's point of view takes place. This openness to the perspectives of others evolves to a sense of group commitment and group spirit that is characterized by increased energy, desire for interaction, connection, and collective achievement (Fletcher, 1999). Such a process is particularly important in collaboration between organizations where the "group spirit" needs to extend beyond the individuals to the organizations or disciplines represented in the group collaboration. According to Cafferty and Clausen (1998), feminist collaboration does not "just happen" or is an "accidental act of grace" (p. 83). They believe that their own collaboration was constructed with "varying success through conscious and unconscious choices affirming feminist politics of inclusion, power sharing, egalitarianism, consensus, and trust in the context of shared feminist commitments" (p. 83).

Other factors necessary for successful collaborative leadership are effective communication skills, conflict management strategies, and group role assignment procedures (O'Meara & Mackenzie, 1998). In addition, other writers have noted the importance of high levels of support; consistent helpfulness, concern, and responsiveness to others; appreciation and valuing of the feelings, needs, and opinions of others; high level of participation and involvement in decisions; strength of purpose; and equitable leadership opportunities provided to participants (Bennis, 2003; Thompson, 2000).

Feminist collaboration is empowerment and advocacy

Collaboration is both a feminist principle and a feminist practice. It empowers women who might otherwise remain isolated, silent, and fearful. In a social system that encourages female passivity, it brings women together to change the circumstances of their lives. It also reflects their socialization as people whose identities depend on relations to others (Singley & Sweeney, 1998). Interorganizational and interdisciplinary collaboration enhances power and energy to accomplish the common goal of advancing knowledge about women and improving their status in academia and the workplace. Such collaboration is also about advocacy and acting to change society to improve and transform the lives of women, especially disadvantaged women, as will be described in detail in the sections to follow.

Challenges to the feminist collaborative process

When successful, collaborative feminist leadership promotes egalitarian, empowering relationships among women, and advocacy and change

159

to help women; however, feminist collaborative relationships within and between organizations and disciplines are not without complications and challenges. In general, one of the major problems encountered by most collaborators is limited time, energy, and resources. For example, women in academia who work collaboratively may also carry a full load of teaching credits along with advising and service obligations to the university and the community, leaving little leeway to take on the extra time demands of working with collaborators, especially long-distance collaborators.

Problems in finding common themes to pursue, personality differences, and lack of enthusiasm have also been cited as barriers to effective collaboration (Cafferty & Clausen, 1998). Later in this chapter, Barbara Gault and Elizabeth Horton discuss the tensions within a collaborative process that involve differences in communication styles, disciplines, and perspectives; competing agendas, priorities, and goals; and different timetables. Conflicting role pressures and simultaneous role demands on women both to be caregivers and as leaders may present additional sources of stress in the collaborative process.

Furthermore, despite the many advantages that accrue in collaborative enterprises, many organizational settings are not structurally or philosophically conducive to the collaborative process. Certainly, academia discourages collaboration. Colleges and universities "neglect or underutilize group rewards for group performances in evaluating scholarship and research for tenure, promotion, and merit raises" (Kaplan & Rose, 1993, p. 558). Some administrators divide the credit for publications by the number of collaborators. Similarly in industry and in the corporate world, individual achievement is valued while collaborative contributions "disappear" (Fletcher, 1999).

Feminist collaboration is transformational and inclusive

A challenge in feminist collaborative leadership is the idea of cross-cultural and cross-racial collaboration that becomes transformational and inclusive. Nesbitt and Thomas (1998) argue that "scholarship from a European American focus cannot be transformative without the experience of scholars of color." They added, "Writing from a singular perspective or European American point of view is similar to men being the sole writers of history" (p. 40). The prevalence of monocentric and Eurocentric collaboration favors the dominant paradigm; thus the doors of collaborative enterprise have not been easily accessible to people of color. Some women leaders may not have had training or opportunities to work with women of color. At the same time, many women leaders of color may be hesitant to work with White women leaders. Trust, which is an important ingredient in a collaborative relationship, may be attenuated in a cross-racial collaboration, as the woman of color may have to deal with the issue of the possible imposition of Western standards and values.

In light of the rapid transformation of our society, it is crucial for European and American scholars to actively address cross-racial, cross-cultural, and cross-national collaboration. In order to achieve authentic feminist collaboration, there is a need to move forward to a broader multicultural paradigm. We need to nurture multicultural collaboration, for we all benefit from a broader paradigm and collaboration that includes the voices of women of color.

Exemplary Feminist Collaboration

In this section, we present some examples and models of how women leaders in large nonprofit organizations and institutions have utilized the process of feminist collaboration in research, advocacy, and networking efforts to improve the welfare of women. The examples attest to the tenets of feminist collaborative leadership described above that embody inclusive, collaborative leadership with goals of social advocacy and change. Our own work in this area has evolved within SPW and will be discussed first. The final contributions present the collaborative work of the Institute for Women's Policy Research in Washington, DC, and The National Council for Research on Women in New York.

The Society for the Psychology of Women: Expanding Our Identity

In 1994, Division 35 of APA was known as The Psychology of Women. Like many special interest groups within the larger umbrella of a professional organization, Division 35 had established and appointed liaison representatives to many of the over 50 other divisions within the APA that shared common concerns and goals. There was, however, no liaison representative to other women's groups outside of APA, nor was there any significant interdisciplinary or international focus. Although the division was one of the largest in APA, with over 2,000 members at the time, it only took a handful of concerned members who wanted to broaden the perspectives and vision of the division to make a difference and to change the course of the division. A feminist collaborative process was the foundation for these efforts. A key first step was asking the current president to appoint a liaison to national and international women's organizations, a post the first author continues to serve. With a formal liaison in place, the division was then able to correspond with other women's organizations, maintain a current directory of women's organizations and centers, exchange news and information with these groups, and publish periodic profiles in the quarterly newsletter about the efforts and projects of these groups in such areas as education, aging, violence, poverty, and diversity.

Collaboration to achieve a social justice agenda

As divisional liaison to women's organizations, the first author had written a report for our newsletter on research on women and welfare by many women's policy centers across the US. This came at a time when our divisional membership, the fourth largest in APA, was deeply concerned about the major impact and possible negative effects of the federal 1996 "Personal Responsibility and Work Opportunity Reconciliation Act of 1996" (PRWORA) and the states' welfare reform legislation on the lives and futures of low income women and their families. A Task Force on Women, Poverty, and Public Assistance was appointed, which included a dozen women leaders involved in research, teaching, and advocacy for low income women and children. From the inception, its focus was interdisciplinary and collaborative, as the women psychologists all realized that their work on the lives of low income women and women of color was intimately related to the work of their colleagues in sociology, law, economics, public policy, and social welfare.

The first goal was to study and research the effects of welfare policy on poor women and children in several key subareas: health, education, job training, child care, low-cost housing and homelessness, delivery systems, resiliency, domestic violence, substance abuse, media images, and the politics of welfare. There was cultural and racial diversity among the task force members, and the process of choosing topics, recommendations, and follow-up action exemplified a feminist collaborating style in which diverse participants sought consensus and strove for open communication and respect of differences. The resulting position paper included the voices of low income minority women, emphasized key supportive structures that needed to be in place for poor women to succeed in the work world, and discussed alternative strategies, policies, and programs that could work better than the current punitive legislation (Rice et al., 1997).

The second focus of the leadership task force was one of social advocacy, with the mission of educating the more than 50,000 members of the home professional organization, APA, about women and public assistance issues and also helping and influencing legislators and policy makers who were to implement the welfare reform bill in the upcoming months. Thus the task force members closely collaborated with and sought information and resources from APA's Women's Program's Office, Public Policy Directorate, and Committee on Women as well as other key organizations doing work on women and welfare such as the Institute for Women's Policy Research, the Center for Women's Policy Studies, the Coalition on Women and Job Training, the Child Exclusion Task Force, the Children's Defense Fund, and the Center for Law and Social Policy.

Making Welfare to Work Really Work was attractively packaged and published by APA (1998) and disseminated to nearly a thousand legislators on Capitol Hill, including all Congressional representatives, State Medicaid Directors, and State Health Service Directors. The task force also took a leadership role in developing and collaborating with a network of 25 psychologist representatives recruited from APA, SPW, and a Listserv of active women psychologists. These helpful people personally gave the paper to their state representatives, asking them to make amendments and changes in welfare reform legislation and to implement other initiatives that address the more important problem, eliminating poverty. The executive summary was used by Senator Paul Wellstone and others to advocate for positive changes to welfare law that would enable women on welfare to receive more postsecondary training and education, a critical item for poor women in low paying entry jobs who cannot break out of the revolving door of welfare to work to welfare. As a result of these collaborative efforts and hundreds like it across the county, Congress amended PRWORA and most states acted to increase funds for supportive services for low income women on welfare, especially for child care. In 1998 when the House proposed further restrictions on education and training for welfare recipients, our task force collaborated with the Institute of Women's Policy Research and the Center for Women's Policy Studies, sending repeated faxes and emails to key Senate staff members that presented compelling evidence

163

on the effects of training and education. We were gratified that the Senate did ultimately reject those short-sighted measures. New members of the task force went on to write a resolution on women and poverty that was passed and endorsed by the APA in 2000. All these efforts involved collaboration with colleagues in other disciplines and organizations.

Changing a name to promote leadership and collaboration

The time seemed right in 1999, after all the above outreach work, to think about changing the name of the division to a name that would evoke a larger scope and awareness of leadership and collaboration with others in and outside of the greater organizations. Many divisions within APA had become "societies," and after some debate by the Board and reluctance on the part of some members who wanted to retain a primarily "divisional" APA affiliated name and image, Division 35 members were given a referendum on a name change, and an overwhelming majority voted to change our name to the "Society for the Psychology of Women." This important change has enabled activists and members working internationally and in public policy to make contacts and initiate projects with other organizations as representatives of an organization of repute in its own right. Establishing this identity then, was another key step in laying the groundwork for broadening the mission, goals, and efforts of the organization to become a leader in collaboration with other women's organizations.

Establishing reciprocal relationships to promote change

At the same time the visionary president of the Society, Jan Yoder, began the first partnership with another women's psychological organization, the Section on Women and Psychology (SWAP) of the Canadian Psychological Association (CPA). The interdivisional liaison position was again used as an extremely effective model for interorganizational collaboration. Today a very large number of such liaison positions exist, providing links with units within APA (e.g., the Committee on Women, other divisions, etc.) as well as independent associations (e.g., SWAP of CPA).

Perhaps the most compelling illustration of the value of this organizational model is the development of joint initiatives or collaborative ventures. One such collaborative effort between SWAP and SPW was the beginning of the SWAP Institute, a highly successful full day preconvention workshop featuring presentations by both SPW and SWAP members. Another example of a key successful collaborative initiative was the development and implementation of a reciprocal dues arrangement involving the two organizations. Under the terms of the agreement, members of one of the associations can join the other organization at a reduced rate and also receive its journal and newsletter.

Collaboration as a centerpiece to feminist leadership

The evolution of all these efforts culminated in 2002, a year devoted to leadership and collaboration by SPW's new president, Jean Lau Chin. This book stemmed from that initiative which is described in greater detail in the Overview to this volume. Viewing collaboration as a cornerstone to feminist process and leadership, Jean asked many SPW leaders to be part of the initiative and book. It represented a wonderful opportunity to build on the foundation of a decade's work to raise awareness among SPW members and the Executive Board about the need to foster feminist interdisciplinary and international collaboration. With some special funding, SPW sponsored a special kickoff luncheon panel at the 2002 APA Convention in Chicago on "Feminist Leadership and Collaboration," chaired by Joy Rice (Rice, 2002). The aim was to explore how we, as a leading volunteer professional women's organization, could develop some areas and advocacy projects for collaboration to achieve feminist aims of advancing our knowledge about women and improving their status and welfare. The six panelists represented an interdisciplinary and international group of women leaders, all presidents or chairs of various women's organizations in psychology, sociology, business, and international and minority psychology. They spoke of their outreach projects, task forces, and collaborative research in key areas of concerns for women within their organization, and then SPW members met in four groups led by the panelists. The objective was to discuss and explore how we could begin to develop some collaborative efforts in a wide variety of arenas including the workplace.

Follow-up to the very successful feminist leadership and collaboration panel and work groups was then begun immediately with plans for joint symposia at APA in Toronto in 2003. Knowing we could accomplish only a small fraction of the excellent ideas of the 2002 group, our aim was to foster partnerships with women's organizations that not only have similar feminist aims, but also help us to work in interdisciplinary mutual endeavors utilizing the readily available means of the annual conference and opportunities for joint symposia. Thus as representatives of SWP, Rice and Austria partnered with representatives of SWAP, the International Council of Psychologists (ICP), Sociologists for Women in Society (SWS), and the APA Women's Office to present four well publicized and attended programs at the next APA Annual Conference in Toronto. Because many psychologists appear ill prepared to lobby effectively on behalf of women's issues, a roundtable conference on "Psychologists as Advocates for Women's Issues," chaired by Austria, was also held at the 2004 APA Convention in Honolulu. The conference theme itself highlighted the importance of feminist leadership in policy change affecting women. Indeed, these different collaborative enterprises promoted interactions and friendships to accomplish social system change.

International collaboration to foster a global perspective

The collaborative efforts of SPW blossomed in parallel with the effort to bring an international focus to the division. Whether there are social justice concerns, as in the aftermath of apartheid, or ethnic civil wars or economic concerns, as in the proliferation of new markets and multinational corporations, international events are becoming increasingly relevant not only to psychology's interests and involvement (Viney & King, 2002), but to all fields and disciplines. The formation of a Global Issues Committee, a standing committee of SPW, was accomplished a few years earlier thanks to the efforts of Corann Okorodudu, an SPW leader. She repeatedly framed the need for a global perspective to SPW members, began an international Listserv, and distributed reports on UN liaison work and opportunities for international networking. These international efforts led to collaborative research and advocacy projects and to the development of APA symposia with a focus on international women's issues. SPW's Global Issues Committee also began a partnership and collaboration with the International Committee for Women (ICFW) of Division 52, International Psychology. Annual meetings are now held together; mutual cross-listed symposia and poster sessions are offered at the annual convention; and advocacy projects to help needy women and children in Pakistan, Afghanistan, and China have been accomplished. One participant, Dr. Roswith Roth, former President of the ICP, notes that:

> international collaboration helps one to initiate research in various areas that one would never have looked at if one's perspective had only

been national. Personally, international collaboration broadens my mind, lets me have a look at what "equality" means in different counties, and helps me meet interesting people, especially wonderful women, and make friends all over the world.

This discussion has presented a case study of a decade of work by many women psychologists within a large professional organization who are striving to break parochial traditions of narrow scholarship and disciplinary self-interest and to transform their professional organization into a place of interdisciplinary and inclusive national and international collaboration. The process is only begun, and as outlined in the beginning of this chapter, there are many challenges and barriers to the actual implementation of good ideas and a vision of change, but the story of SPW offers women leaders in other volunteer organizations inspiration and optimism. Other national examples of women's organizations striving to implement feminist collaborative leadership to achieve social advocacy and change follow.

Think Tank Collaboration: The Institute for Women's Policy Research

As noted in the above experiences of the Society for the Psychology of Women, feminist leadership often involves advocacy and social justice issues compared to masculine leadership that is based in power and status recognition. Many national women's organizations focus on social justice and equity and embrace a collaborative model to achieve these aims. The Institute for Women's Policy Research (IWPR), a feminist think tank based in Washington, DC, has extensive experience collaborating with a range of organizations, and has seen both the rewards of collaboration and the challenges. The benefits of collaboration are clear, in terms of shared expertise, contacts, communications, abilities, and collective voice. Challenges include being clear about dividing labor and available resources, reaching consensus on messages communicated to the public, resolving conflicts, negotiating timelines, working with others who are not at the same site, and applying credit appropriately.

IWPR has collaborated in the form of research/advocacy partnerships, in which these two functions are divided between two groups, funded by the same foundation, and on joint research projects. Other work includes joint congressional briefings, either as a part of a series or as single events, in collaboration with a university, other nonprofit research organizations, and with national women's advocacy organizations. The IWPR biannual conference involves active cosponsorship from a set of affiliated groups, and the Status of Women in the States projects involves state-based committees that review, disseminate, and write sections of state-level reports, and contribute financially to report publication. Expert advisory committees help design and review research and are sometimes compensated for their efforts.

Dr. Barbara Gault, Director of Research for IWPR, believes that collaborations can enhance the quality and impact of projects in planned and in unanticipated ways. For example, involvement by the Friedrich Ebert foundation in the IWPR biannual conference brought European women parliamentarians and media leaders to the sessions and enhanced the cross-cultural exchange of models for improving gender equity. Collaboration also brings diversity and expertise that may be difficult to secure otherwise, as when Native American women leaders of IWPR's Status of Women in the States advisory committee helped to interpret data on Native American women from the decennial census. Collaboration with university-based labor economists helped develop a new model for estimating the costs of proposed state family leave policies. Status of Women in the States advisory committees built new legislative agendas, carried out far-reaching educational campaigns, and leveraged funding for new state institutional resources such as Commissions on the Status of Women.

IWPR participates actively in the National Council of Women's Organizations (NCWO), an umbrella group of more than one hundred women's organizations that fosters and facilitates co-operation among groups in the form of joint actions, educational efforts, and policy statements. Watching the members of NCWO in action is to witness an assembly of primarily second wave feminist leaders who are master collaborators and adept at achieving consensus in the face of debate and dissent. In that context the effects of policy experience on the ability to collaborate are readily apparent.

Not surprisingly, the scarcity of foundation dollars available for work on women's issues seems to be at the root of most collaboration challenges. Many women's organizations see themselves as competing for a very limited pool of money, which can make it difficult to share billing and credit with other groups that may be applying for the same, as is also the case among the constituent member centers of The National Council for Research on Women discussed below.

Research Collaboration: The National Council for Research on Women

Collaboration is central to the mission, history, and structure of the NCRW. Dr. Elizabeth Horton, Deputy Director of NCRW, believes that the basic strengths and challenges of the organization directly reflect the tensions that arise in collaborative relationships. She notes that in 2002 and 2003, as part of a strategic business plan, the NCRW Board and staff looked hard at NCRW's effectiveness as an organization and highlighted the notable absence of women's voices in public life and policy. Central to this plan was NCRW's identity as a collaborative network. An intensive self-analysis of the complexity of women leaders working in network collaboration led to a new initiative and vision named "The Chamberlain Initiative." In order to implement this vision, the historical, structural, and personal tensions within the NCRW network had to be addressed and resolved, but the leaders also knew that some of these tensions might not be able to be bridged.

A collaborative model brings many challenges when your constituencies are numerous and diverse in their missions, philosophies, size, institutional resources, constituencies, structures, and geographic reach. Founded in 1981, NCRW is a large independent nonprofit membership organization whose mission is to use research on and by women and girls to improve their lives and the lives of their families and communities. It is made up of over a hundred national and international research and policy centers with 28 member centers, mostly on college or university campuses. The Council also increasingly incorporates other constituencies, including activists and advocates, international researchers, the corporate sector, policy makers, and others.

Fostering collaborative work among diverse constituencies

NCRW undertakes collaboration in a variety of ways and on a variety of levels with various constituencies. As the nexus, it plays a leadership role in convening and staffing work, amplifying the work of member centers, facilitating collaboration among them and our other constituencies, and catalyzing research and analysis. Collaboration within the Council occurs in membership programming, but has historically involved projects that draw on the expertise of member centers like our *Girls Report* or *Balancing the Equation: Where are Women and Girls in Science,*

Engineering, and Technology. Other projects are cosponsored by NCRW and one or more member centers, yet others occur between member centers without direct participation by the central office like the Institute for Women's Policy Research's (IWPR's) *Status of Women in the States* series.

When successful, these collaborative processes have provided opportunities to strengthen feminist research and institutions by building new and stronger working relationships among organizations and individuals. Through its projects and membership activities, NCRW helps expand and shape the research and action agenda for the whole network, for example, by emphasizing global perspectives and including a stronger focus on generational, class, and racial differences at annual conferences. Furthermore, because of collaborative projects, the work of all the member centers is amplified—some local organizations have received national attention, and national organizations have become more familiar to people in local settings.

Tensions within the collaborative relationships

Even in the most successful collaborations, the tensions within the collaborative relationship have been variously evident—tensions over resources, philosophies, and turf, and between the centers and the central office, and with the Council's other constituencies. Tensions are also apparent between the diverse centers themselves: the small versus large well-funded centers, the academic versus nonacademic centers, and the research versus policy centers and associations. Some of the tensions are related to funding issues: who gets funding, how is it distributed, who pays the substantial expenses incurred in building the partnership, and who ultimately determines what is funded and what is not. Other tensions are related to inclusivity: who defines the agenda; who should be at the table; how are differences of race, sexuality, generation, discipline, and so forth bridged; and who determines the message, form, and quality of the final product. Yet other tensions reflect those within the centers themselves as well as the larger women's movement: succession issues and racial and generational differences.

These tensions have challenged all participants, but when these challenges have been successfully met, they also underlay the success of the projects. The work of negotiating differences in approach, discipline, and perspective results in particularly rich products and outcomes. For example, *The Girls Report* encompasses the work of researchers studying the social/psychological/developmental problems of adolescent girls and cultural forces that victimize them, and that of other researchers and service providers whose focus is on empowering girls, listening to their voices, incorporating their aspirations, and providing space for them to shape their own destinies and that of their communities.

Lessons learned

Building fruitful and positive collaborations is hard work, even within feminism, whose theory and values are based on collaboration, consensus building, and an interdisciplinary approach that includes diverse perspectives and experiences. A network can pay lip service to the value of collaboration, but actually undertaking and succeeding at collaboration takes more than lip service. One of the overarching lessons of NCRW's history is that board leadership that brings independent resources and commitment is necessary to bring people together. Even when much of the content of the work was done by the collaborating institutions, board leadership helped to negotiate the many differences and tensions among constituents, including final control over the project, and board involvement brings necessary independent funding and staffing.

For NCRW, there have been a host of necessary strategies to create and sustain collaborative projects. These strategies are fairly obvious, but not always easy to implement. They are:

1. *Bring the right people to the table.* To ensure the breadth, depth, and diversity of the collaborative, NCRW expanded its network of member centers to include research, policy, and activist organizations as well as membership associations, created new constituency circles like the Corporate Circle, and worked on the particular challenges of including global voices as well as those speaking across borders of race, generation, and sexuality.
2. *Encourage participation.* NCRW has also worked to build alliances with respected and/or charismatic leaders in the field.
3. *Develop and give voice to shared goals/values.* NCRW's history, its membership and board structures, provide the foundation for a shared agenda. Activities such as the Annual Conference test its legitimacy and its power to bring the network together as well as help build consensus among the diverse membership. Projects where NCRW can "regrant" or provide resources to collaborators help create

171

stakeholders in the collaborative work. Collaborative programming, when framed in terms of a shared agenda, also provides opportunities for diverse individuals and organizations to reaffirm their commitment to their underlying shared values and goals.

4. *Build trust.* To the extent NCRW has been able to sustain participants' trust and good will in working through conflicts, NCRW has succeeded in forging collaborative action based on the shared goals and values. Sustaining trust demands a high level of transparency in terms of process and decision making, paired with real sensitivity to differences in points of view. Personal interaction, whether at conferences, regional, or one-on-one meetings seems to be essential to building trust and identifying the causes for lack of trust. This element may limit the size of successful coalitions. Working to keep the focus on the issues and shared goals, and to expand the total resources available, is essential, as is addressing and isolating specific conflicts.

5. *Maintain general leadership that's relatively stable and serves as a communication loop to the members.* NCRW has been fortunate in having stable, continuous leadership. This has guaranteed a number of key people who can speak with legitimacy to build consensus or address specific issues.

6. *Shape collaborative activities.* Coalitions work best when everyone has something to gain from an activity and when each organization contributes and, to some extent, controls the area where they have the strongest expertise and resources. Activities that specifically benefit some or all of the membership, for example, prominent links to centers' webpages, can help, although in some cases unrealistic expectations for added visibility on the part of members can undercut the positive effect. Flexibility in implementing collaborative plans is often necessary. For example, when partners are not ready to move forward together on a project, it can often be phased in or undertaken with fewer partners, with some early first successes encouraging wider commitment to the larger undertaking.

7. *Develop funding specifically for building collaboration.* Most funders want results and do not invest in process. Yet the process of coalition building is expensive, demanding time of high level staff as well as travel, meeting, and other expenditures. This work must therefore be funded by unrestricted core funding, or through projects where the network building activities are framed within an overall project goal.

The verdict is not yet in on the success of the Chamberlain Initiative in giving new force and focus to this 23-year-old coalition. The current political climate and the successes of many of the socially conservative coalitions, whose agendas are often viewed as antiwomen by the women's research community, have served to underscore the importance of coming together and finding ways to collaborate meaningfully.

The issue of resources is central to meeting this challenge, but even more important is the question of leadership. What does it mean to lead a collaborative organization? How can we act together when leadership is diffused? How can agendas be negotiated among independent institutions, and responsibility, resources, and credit shared? What are the personal and professional traits of effective collaborative leaders? What are the institutional structures that must be in place for such leadership? How must the collaborative view leadership? What expectations can we have for leaders to move collaboratives successfully? Where are the limits to leadership in a coalition, and what are the mechanisms for moving beyond those limits? Finally one must address the key question of how to ensure the emergence of new and many collaborative leaders—board members, member center directors, or staff leadership—moving to the fore and asserting leadership at different moments and in different spaces.

Parting Thoughts

Feminist collaboration extols egalitarianism, inclusion, power sharing, consensus building, and mutual support. Participation in decision making becomes more egalitarian and consensual because of incorporation and implementation of the feminist principles of equitable power distributions and involvement. Individuals who work in feminist collaborative relationships work with rather than against their differences. To illustrate the complex nature of feminist collaboration, we drew upon the writings and experiences of feminist leaders in actual projects and organizations whose missions are to serve and enhance the status of women. We also drew upon our own experiences as collaborators with national and international women and organizations. The exemplary projects and feminist interorganizational collaborations presented in this chapter hopefully have demonstrated the positive outcomes of the feminist collaborative process on organization process and achievement of feminist goals as well as personal and professional benefits.

Our national and international collaborative relationships, however, were complicated by challenges that were not easy to dismiss; for example, we found that collaboration could be draining, time-consuming, and not easy to achieve. Our schedules had to be reconciled with our job demands, professional obligations, and family responsibilities. Limited funding for travel and the lack of resources or staff to assist in collaborative research projects presented major challenges. Grant monies from the collaborating organizations to help defray the expenses related to travel and staff resources would be of great help to women leaders attempting international collaboration.

Collaborating internationally also involves a lot of attention to cultural nuances, cultural differences, and communication issues as well as language barriers. All present major challenges to successful communication cross-culturally and cross-nationally. Differences in communication styles may be triggered by certain stereotypes or beliefs one may have about others, underscoring the importance of both how and what one communicates to others (Sue & Sue, 2003). There is also a need to train leaders in multicultural sensitivities and understandings as they attempt to work collaboratively on an international or cross-cultural basis. In terms of research, encouragement should be given to European and American scholars to actively invite ethnic minority women to collaborate on research and advocacy projects as equal partners. Such positive initiation and inclusion may help overcome possible feelings of alienation and help them to find a voice and increase their influence on research and advocacy agendas. Feminist intercultural and international collaborations can benefit organizations and stem from a view that is also interdisciplinary as well as global. Most importantly, such collaborations help us to find creative solutions to social and psychological problems that benefit multicultural societies and women and men in a shrinking world. Moreover, as this book illustrates and the several narratives in this chapter reinforce, feminist collaboration has helped transform women's lives personally as well as professionally.

Note

The authors are grateful for the help, contributions, and thoughts of Dr. Sandra Pike, Canadian Psychological Association, Section on Women and Psychology; Dr. Roswith Roth, University of Graz and Past President, International Council of Psychologists; Dr. Barbara Gault, Director of Research, The

Institute for Women's Policy Research; and Dr. Elizabeth Horton, Deputy Director, The National Council for Research on Women.

References

American Psychological Association. (1998). *Making welfare to work really work.* Washington, DC: Author.

Bennis, W. (2003). Leading through tough times and beyond. *The 2003 Linkage Excellence in Management & Leadership Series* (pp. 17–39). Burlington, MA: Linkage, Inc.

Brunner, C. C. (Ed.). (1999). *Sacred dreams: Women and the superintendency.* Albany, NY: State University of New York Press.

Cafferty, H., & Clausen, J. (1998). What's feminist about it? Reflection on collaboration in editing and writing. In E. G. Peck & J. S. Mink (Eds.), *Common ground: Feminist collaboration in the academy* (pp. 81–98). Albany, NY: State University of New York Press.

Fletcher, J. K. (1999). *Disappearing acts: Gender, power, and relational practice at work.* Cambridge, MA: The MIT Press.

Kaplan, C., & Rose, E. C. (1993). Strange bedfellows: Feminist collaboration. *Signs: Journal of Women in Culture and Society, 18*(3), 547–561.

Nesbitt, P. D., & Thomas, L. (1998). Beyond feminism: An intercultural challenge for transforming the academy. In E. G. Peck & J. S. Mink (Eds.), *Common ground: Feminist collaboration in the academy* (pp. 31–49). Albany, NY: State University of New York Press.

O'Meara, A., & Mackenzie, N. R. (1998). Reflection on scholarly collaboration. In E. G. Peck & J. S. Mink (Eds.), *Common ground: Feminist collaboration in the academy* (pp. 209–225). Albany, NY: State University of New York Press.

Peck, E. G., & Mink, J. S. (Eds.). (1998). *Common ground: Feminist collaboration in the academy.* Albany, NY: State University of New York Press.

Rice, J. K. (2002, August). Chair, *Feminist leadership and collaboration.* Panel presented at the Annual Meeting of the American Psychological Association, Chicago, IL.

Rice, J. K., Wyche, K., Lott, B., Bullock, H., Sanchez-Hucles, J., Riger, S. et al. (1997). *Implementing welfare policy to insure long term independence and well-being.* Washington, DC: American Psychological Association.

Singley, C. J., & Sweeney, S. E. (1998). In league with each other: The theory and practice of feminist collaboration. In E. G. Peck & J. S. Mink (Eds.), *Common ground: Feminist collaboration in the academy* (pp. 63–80). Albany, NY: State University of New York Press.

Statham, A. (1987). The gender model revisited: Differences in the management styles of men and women. *Sex Roles, 16,* 409–429.

175

Sue, D. W., & Sue, D. (2003). *Counseling the culturally diverse: Theory and practice* (4th ed.). New York: John Wiley & Sons.

Thompson, M. D. (2000). Gender, leadership orientation, and effectiveness: Testing the theoretical models of Bolman & Deal and Quinn. *Sex Roles, 42*(11, 12), 969–992.

Viney, W., & King, D. B. (2002). *A history of psychology: Ideas and context* (3rd ed.). Boston: Allyn & Bacon.

Worell, J., & Johnson, N. G. (Eds.). (1997). *Shaping the future of feminist psychology: Education, research, and practice.* Washington, DC: American Psychological Association.

Chapter 8

Women, Collaboration, and Social Change: An Ethics-Based Model of Leadership

Marlene G. Fine

Public discourse about leadership over the last decade has been dominated by discussions about ethical leadership, particularly the lack of ethical leadership in public life. The list of public figures and organizations accused of ethical breaches at times seems endless. The popular press decries the loss of public faith and the absence of ethical leadership, but current leadership theories offer little direction for developing theories of ethical leadership (Rubenstein, 2003).

Although there are numerous books and articles on ethics and leadership, no coherent theory of leadership that is grounded in ethics has emerged. In this chapter I review the predominant leadership theories, which are based on the experiences of men; discuss how they fail to attend to ethical considerations; and then identify key concepts from the literature on women and leadership that provide a foundation for an ethics-based model of leadership. This model is based on women's discursive representations of their leadership experiences and is grounded in ethics. It represents feminist principles of collaboration and inclusiveness with the aims of social change and gender equity. The last section details the implications of the model for both leadership theory and practice, and explains how the model is consistent with feminist principles and practice.

Theories of Leadership

Theories of leadership can be grouped according to their focus on different aspects of leadership: the leader, the situation or organizational context, or the relationship between leaders and followers (i.e., the process of leading).

Leaders

Trait, skills, and *style* approaches each focus primarily on characteristics of the leader. The *trait* approach identifies the personality characteristics that make leaders unique from their followers (Kirkpatrick & Locke, 1991; Stogdill, 1948; Zaleznick, 1977). Although integrity appears on the list of most-often cited characteristics, it is not defined as any more important than any other characteristic. More importantly, the *trait* approach looks only at the integrity of the leader, not the larger ethical context in which leadership is practiced. Transformational or "charismatic" leadership, a more recent manifestation of the trait approach, looks at how leaders inspire followers to accomplish great things (Bass & Avolio, 1994; Bryman, 1992). Ethics is sometimes considered a part of transformational leadership, but is not the central focus. Nor is ethics a necessary component of charismatic leadership; numerous despots in history were charismatic leaders, but lacked an ethical base.

The *skills* approach focuses on teachable skills sets and identifies problem-solving and social judgment skills and knowledge that leaders need to solve organizational problems (Mumford, Zaccaro, Harding, Jacobs, & Fleischman, 2000). The *style* approach identifies two predominant constellations of leadership behaviors—concern for people and concern for results—and provides a typology of leadership based on the amount of emphasis a leader places on each (Blake & Mouton, 1964, 1978, 1985). Both skills and styles approaches define leadership through the actions of leaders and relate those actions directly to organizational outcomes without particular regard for their ethics. From the perspective of these leadership approaches, the most important question is whether organizational outcomes are achieved.

Situations

Situation-based leadership theories expand the focus of leadership theory to the situation in which leadership is exercised. Depending on the competence and commitment of subordinates, leaders should emphasize either directive or supportive behaviors (Hersey & Blanchard, 1969). Contingency theories also focus on the leadership situation. Rather than having a leader adapt to particular situations, however, contingency theorists argue that organizations need to select leaders who fit the needs of the organization (Fiedler, 1967; Strube & Garcia, 1981). Path-goal theory is a particular contingency approach that looks for the best fit between the behaviors of a leader and the characteristics of followers and the task (Evans, 1996; House, 1971). Both contingency and path-goal approaches view the situation as ethically neutral; moral codes of conduct play no role in either approach and the vocabularies of each are relatively devoid of moral terms.

Relationship between leaders and followers

Leader–member exchange (LMX) theory broadens the focus of leadership theory beyond the leader and situation to defining leadership as a process that happens between leaders and followers, making the focal point the dyadic relationship between them (Dansereau, Graen, & Haga, 1975; Graen & Cashman, 1975; Graen, 1976). LMX theory posits that high quality exchanges between leaders and subordinates produce positive organizational outcomes for everyone, for example, less employee turnover, greater organizational commitment, and more promotions (Graen & Uhl-Bien, 1995). A strength of LMX theory is that it draws attention to the importance of communication in leadership (Northouse, 2004), but its focus on individual dyads makes it more suitable to managerial theory than leadership theory *per se*. Furthermore, although a set of ethical behaviors can be inferred from the characteristics of high quality exchanges (e.g., mutual trust, respect, and obligations), the vocabulary of LMX does not feature moral terms.

Although current theories of leadership do not encompass an ethics-based leadership model, the literature on women and leadership offers direction for developing such a model.

Literature on Women and Leadership

The literature on women and leadership comprises two strands. The first examines the gendered nature of organizations and reveals a masculine bias in leadership practice that devalues women's ways of leading. The second strand focuses on identifying differences in how women and men lead and suggests that there is a unique women's leadership style.

Gendered nature of organizational leadership

The research on how leadership is conceptualized and valued within organizations asserts that organizations both represent and reproduce the gender and power relations that exist in the larger society. Beginning with Kanter's (1977) *Men and Women of the Corporation*, numerous writers have identified the ways in which organizations are gendered (Acker, 1990, 1992; Buzzanell, 1994; Court, 1997; Ferguson, 1984; Fondas, 1997; Mills & Tancred, 1992). These authors describe how organizational structures, policies, and practices feature men and marginalize women, and valorize "male modes of thinking, feeling, acting, and forming identities while devaluing their female counterparts" (Fine & Buzzanell, 2000, p. 130).

Researchers suggest that male modes of leadership are more valued and rewarded in organizations (Chin, 2004). In the United States and other Western cultures, leaders are believed to have stereotypic masculine qualities; leaders are direct, assertive, commanding, and powerful (Fine & Buzzanell, 2000). Although masculinity is a social construction that differs across cultures, it appears to be correlated with leadership regardless of the cultural context (Izraeli & Adler, 1994). Schein (2001) concluded that to "'think manager—think male' is a global phenomenon, especially among males" (p. 682).

The fact that few women hold senior leadership positions in the US is not surprising given that leadership and masculinity are seen as synonymous. There are only nine female CEOs in the top 500 corporations in the US, and women comprise only 5% of the top earners, 16% of corporate officers, and 13.6% of board members (Brady, 2005). Equating leadership and masculinity, however, also has consequences for theorizing about leadership. Women's voices and experiences are generally absent from the academic discourse on leadership, and that absence has profoundly affected theorizing about leadership.

Collaboration and sharing power: ways women lead

Numerous studies lay claim to a unique women's leadership style. Across studies, in comparison to male leaders, women leaders use more nurturing, inclusive, and collaborative strategies that encourage participation and create egalitarian environments (Adler, 2005; Chin, 2004; Eagly & Johannesen-Schmidt, 2001; Rosener, 1990), and they more often use transformational leadership styles, in which leaders motivate employees to look beyond their own narrow interests to the good of the group (Burke & Collins, 2001; Rosener, 1990). In addition, research indicates that women are more motivated than men to help others, are more likely to choose careers in the helping professions, and use more caring, personal styles (Wood, 1994). Taken as a whole, these studies suggest that women's leadership styles are distinct from men's, and that they are likely to use more collaborative, nurturing, and egalitarian strategies that emphasize communication.

In her work on the moral development of women, Gilligan (1982) found that women expressed greater care for relationships than desire for individual autonomy in making moral choices. This "ethic of care" included responsiveness, sensitivity to others, acceptance, relatedness, and collaboration (O'Brien Hallstein, 1999). Some feminist ethicists criticized Gilligan's work for valuing emotion over reasoning. O'Brien Hallstein (1999) offers a revisioned care perspective, which incorporates empathy and reasoning. Both the original and the revised ethic of care, however, feature the need to attend to and care for others through collaboration and communication.

In addition to examining how women lead, researchers have also looked at women's professional motives. Women teachers indicate that they view teaching as a mission or calling (Whatley, 1998) and frame it as a political act through which they can address social inequality and injustice (Smulyan, 2004). This desire to make a difference in the world is consistent with the career choices of highly motivated women, who tend to favor teaching, social work, medicine, and human services rather than higher status careers (Bridges, 1989).

This discussion of the research on women's leadership styles and professional motives is not intended to essentialize women, that is, reduce all women to a particular set of characteristics. All women do not lead in the same way. In fact, meta-analyses of research on women's leadership styles suggest that there are few behavioral differences between women and men (Eagly & Johnson, 1990). The research on women's leadership styles, which is based primarily on self-report data, does, however, point to a vision of leadership held by some women. The circumstances under which women lead may constrain their ability to act in a way that is consonant with their ethics-based vision of leaders and leadership. Regardless of the possible disparity between belief and behavior, the values expressed in the research on women and leadership suggest new ways of theorizing about leadership.

Values in women's leadership: an ethic of care and social change

The literature on women and leadership tends to focus on how women lead. The characteristics of women's leadership that are identified, for example, collaboration, participation, communication, nurturance, are viewed in terms of their agency or their use as a means of reaching organizational ends. That focus can be shifted, however, to the underlying *values* expressed in those means. Collaboration, participation, communication, and nurturance all imply care for other people. The ethics underlying the "means" or "agency" of leadership are consistent with the ethic of care revealed in women's career choices and their desire to help others.

I recently completed a study that looked specifically at women's discursive representations of leadership as a means to develop a new approach to leadership theory (Fine, 2005). I analyzed narrative interviews with 15 senior women from a range of private, nonprofit, and government organizations. The women were asked to tell how and why they became leaders and to describe times when they were successful and unsuccessful in exercising leadership. The stories revealed a narrative of moral behavior shaped not by the demands or cultures of particular organizations or situations, but by the women's own ethical principles. The narratives suggested that the women discursively constructed leadership through a *moral discourse of leadership* that emphasized four main principles: leading in order to make a positive contribution in the world, collaboration, open communication, and honesty in relationships.

1   *Making a positive contribution.* In describing how they became leaders, the women emphasized the influence of early role models and mentors who instilled lessons of citizenship and community involvement. A key lesson was the importance of giving back to their communities: "I am a child of the 60s and was raised by Irish parents and grandparents that came here from Ireland. You're going to volunteer, give back to your community, and give back as a citizen." The women learned that leadership and success are about more than self-interest or corporate interests: "It's okay to be profitable, but you've got to make a difference where you're at—whether it's your local community or your global community."

2   *Collaboration.* The women repeatedly described the importance to leadership of building a team, seeking consensus, and getting all points of view. Leaders listen to and rely on people, and they reach out to people and make them believe that they have a role to play in accomplishing the group's purpose or work.

3   *Open communication.* Open communication was a powerful theme. One woman said that it is up to the leader "to create an environment where people feel heard and feel safe to raise issues in order to make things better." The women emphasized the reciprocal nature of open communication: "The more information you share, the more you communicate with them [employees], the more you get back from them. The more they know about the business, the more they contribute to the business."

4   *Honesty in relationships.* Several women reported that their major mistakes involved getting blindsided by office and/or corporate politics, and each advised other women to watch their backs in organizations. They described their encounters as a loss of innocence and personal trust. The founder and executive director of a major nonprofit organization described her disillusionment when her long-time codirector split with her over the direction of the organization and took many members of the Board of Directors with him: "I trusted totally and didn't have the ability to stand back and see it coming. . . . It has to do with not understanding people's Machiavellian interests."

Whether describing how parents and other early role models impressed upon them the importance of "doing good" for others and "giving back" to their communities, or telling tales of being "done in" by people they trusted in organizations, or offering advice on the value of listening, open communication, and caring for employees, the women selected narratives that featured ethical behavior. They described a world in which leaders, followers, and organizations shared a code of conduct based on a clear moral order. The narratives create a moral discourse of leadership that places ethics at the center of leadership, a contrast to the most prevalent approaches to leadership described earlier.

Ethics, as defined by these women, is not situational (which is not to say that ethical decisions don't take context into account). "Doing good" as the bottom line, believing that relationships are defined by trust, and assuming that other people want to do good also are core values that the participants brought with them into organizational life, regardless of the particular organizational cultures in which they worked. Although these women were disappointed when people's actions or events contradicted their core values, they did not give up their values or even modify them. They sought out organizations that allowed them to behave in ways that were consistent with their beliefs and work and that gave them meaningful opportunities to "give back."

Taken together with the literature on women's leadership styles, the moral discourse of leadership found in these narratives offers a way to re-vision women's leadership specifically and leadership theory more generally. The next section describes an ethics-based model of leadership that emerges out of the literature.

The Ethics-Based Model

This model (see figure 8.1) is constructed from terms provided by Kenneth Burke in *A Grammar of Motives* (1969). Burke, a literary theorist and philosopher, believed that people use symbols to create social reality. In Burkeian terms, social interaction is a form of drama, which we can understand through five elements of narratives: act (what happens), scene (the background or situation in which the act happens), agency (the means), agent (the kind of person), and purpose. These five elements are called the pentad. Burke posits that how the terms of the pentad are featured within any particular discourse provides a way of understanding human motives.

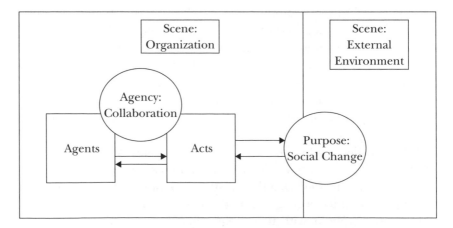

Figure 8.1. Ethics-Based Model of Leadership.

The pentad is particularly appropriate to creating a model of leadership for two reasons. First, the model I am developing here is based on women's narratives of their own leadership stories and on research findings from women's self-reports of their leadership styles. These narratives and self-reports constitute a symbolic construction of leadership that is appropriately understood through a dramatistic lens such as the pentad. Second, leadership is constituted through performance. Although we talk about leadership as if it were a concrete object, it is, instead, a process enacted by people. Leaders do not pre-exist. They are constituted through their performance and interaction with others and a dramatistic approach is helpful to understanding the performance of leadership.

Some feminists may find it odd to use Burke to re-vision leadership as Burke is also known for his belief that hierarchy is fundamental to human nature, a belief that is at odds with some feminist theories. As I explain below, however, the model I am proposing does not feature or privilege one part over the other in creating order or coherence in the performance of leadership. The parts of the pentad are considered equal and interdependent.

The literature on women and leadership suggests that women imbue *each* element of the pentad with a moral dimension, suggesting a moral discourse of leadership, which differs substantively from the dominant discourses in current leadership theory. Theories of leadership that focus on the qualities of leaders or the relationship between leaders and followers do not provide an all-encompassing discourse of morality, nor do situational and contingency approaches to leadership. Although situational and contingency approaches focus on context, they do so with the caveat that the context is unchangeable. These approaches ask leaders to adjust their behavior to situations and/or to pick organizations that "fit" their leadership style.

The ethics-based model of leadership says that *each of these elements has a moral dimension.* Good leadership must meet the ethical demands of each. Thus the purpose of ethical leadership is social change, to make a positive contribution in the world. People take on leadership roles because they have a duty and responsibility to do good for others, both inside the organization and in the larger external environment. Ethical leadership requires ethical leaders (agents), that is, people whose actions are governed by a set of moral precepts that define right and wrong. Ethical leaders use collaborative, democratic, and inclusive means and strategies; build consensus among constituents; and communicate openly and honestly. Act and agency are often difficult to separate. Open

185

communication is both an act and a means through which one acts. Regardless, both the act and its means must meet the ethical imperative of the model. Finally, ethical leadership demands that organizations, as the containers in which ethical leadership takes place, be ethical. As Burke (1969) says, the scene must be a "fit" container for both the agent and the act.

Implications of the Model

The ethics-based model of leadership that I am proposing here adds value to the existing models of leadership in five ways. First, and perhaps most importantly, it places ethics at the center of our understanding of leadership. Leadership, as it is performed, is fraught with moral choices. How much information should I share? What goals should we establish? How will we accomplish our work? What value will we place on the work that people do? Every leader confronts these questions and the moral choices they imply. A theory of leadership must provide a way to make sense of those choices.

Second, the model provides a framework for integrating the research on women and leadership into leadership theory. Most of the research in this area has focused on either comparing how men and women lead or defining a unique women's leadership style, whether "feminine" or "feminist." The debate over differences can be resolved by shifting how we interpret and apply the results of the research. The research on women and leadership views women's leadership as a set of strategies for achieving organizational goals. This focus on instrumentality is not surprising given the masculine nature of traditional leadership theory. The ethics-based model of leadership shifts the focus from the instrumentality of leadership practices to the underlying values expressed in those practices. We move from seeing women leaders choosing collaboration as a means to an end, to seeing collaboration as the performance of leadership that creates and maintains trusting and nurturing relationships among people and leads to positive organizational and social change. The means become the ends and both are consistent within a feminist ethical framework.

The third way that this model enriches the literature is that it provides a method for interrogating and evaluating leadership. Each of the five elements of the pentad becomes a site for interrogation. We can look at the act, actor, agency, scene, and purpose to ensure that each is ethical. Is the purpose to make a positive contribution to the organization and the world outside of the organization? Is the organization itself ethical? Are people in the organization engaged in ethical relationships with the leader(s) and with each other? The model ensures that we question each element. Further, it tells us to look for consistency among the elements. The means and ends should be consistent. "Doing good" through unethical means is not ethical leadership. Ethical leaders achieve good through ethical means, and they perform leadership within ethical organizations.

A fourth value of the model is that it offers a perspective for redesigning leadership training programs. Traditional programs focus on individuals and their personal characteristics or styles. Two of the most popular assessment tools used in leadership training programs are Blake and McCanse's (1991) leadership grid, which assesses the degree to which an individual is either task- or people-directed, and the Myers–Brigg Type Indicator, which assesses an individual's personality type. The ethics-based model suggests expanding the domain of leadership development to other dimensions of ethical leadership: means/ends consistency, questioning organizational goals, and working to ensure organizations act ethically. We need to develop an approach to leadership development that looks not just at individuals and their attributes, behaviors, and skills, but also the organizations in which those individuals work and the values and norms that structure them. To develop tomorrow's leaders, we need to focus on developing organizational cultures in which ethical behavior, including ethical leadership, is appreciated and nourished.

Finally, the ethics-based model of leadership directly links leadership with social action. The model values leaders who work for organizational and social changes that better the lives of employees and all citizens rather than leaders who use their resources to achieve ends that only further the status quo. This emphasis on social change is consistent with both the research on women and leadership and feminist principles generally. Second-wave feminists defined feminism as revolutionary because its goal is freedom from subordination for all women, which presupposes sweeping social changes (Eisenstein, 1983; Gordon, 1979). In an earlier essay, I named this feminist imperative for social change "revolutionary pragmatism" (Fine, 1993). Young third-wave feminists make this same commitment to revolutionary pragmatism, but expand the scope of their social action to have "compassion for all, including the heads of heinous multinational corporations and the executives at the IMF. . . ." (Labaton & Martin, 2004, p. xviii).

187

It is important to note, however, that the ethics-based model of leadership is based primarily on the fixed, historical standpoint of White women in the US, yet many of the underlying values in the feminist ethics embodied in the model are consonant with the cultural values of women of color, suggesting that the model has broader applicability. African Americans are deeply committed to community service (Fine, 1995). The leadership discourse of African American women reveals an emphasis on interactive leadership based on listening, open communication, collaborative debate, and participative decision making (Parker, 2001). The centrality of relationships in Asian cultures (Fine, 1995) and in Latinas' roles in family, work, and leadership (Lazzari, Ford, & Haughey, 1996) also suggests some degree of consonance with the model for these women.

A commitment to social change through collaboration that is grounded in a feminist ethic of care provides a new vision of leadership for women and men. The ethics-based model of leadership offers a heuristic for both deconstructing and understanding the leadership vacuum in our culture today, while simultaneously providing an imperative for leaders to do better.

References

Acker, J. (1990). Hierarchies, jobs, bodies: A theory of gendered organizations. *Gender & Society*, *4*, 139–158.

Acker, J. (1992). Gendering organizational theory. In A. Mills & P. Tancred (Eds.), *Gendering organizational analysis* (pp. 248–260). Newbury Park, CA: Sage.

Adler, N. (2005). Leadership journeys: The courage to enrich the world. In L. Coughlin, E. Wingard, & K. Hollihan (Eds.), *Enlightened power: How women are transforming the path to leadership* (pp. 3–13). San Francisco, CA: Jossey Bass.

Bass, B. M., & Avolio, B. J. (1994). *Improving organizational effectiveness through transformational leadership*. Thousand Oaks, CA: Sage.

Blake, R. R., & McCanse, A. A. (1991). *Leadership dilemmas—grid solutions*. Houston, TX: Gulf.

Blake, R. R., & Mouton, J. S. (1964). *The managerial grid*. Houston, TX: Gulf.

Blake, R. R., & Mouton, J. S. (1978). *The new managerial grid*. Houston, TX: Gulf.

Blake, R. R., & Mouton, J. S. (1985). *The managerial grid III*. Houston, TX: Gulf.

Brady, D. (2005, March 28). The glass ceiling's iron girders. *BusinessWeek online*. Retrieved August 8, 2006 from http://www.businessweek.com/bwdaily/dnflash/mar2005/nf20050325_1553_db042.htm?chan=search

Bridges, J. S. (1989). Sex differences in occupational values. *Sex Roles, 20,* 205–211.

Bryman, A. (1992). *Charisma and leadership in organizations.* London: Sage.

Burke, K. (1969). *A grammar of motives.* Berkeley, CA: University of California Press.

Burke, S., & Collins, K. M. (2001). Gender differences in leadership styles and management skills. *Women in Management Review, 16*(5/6), 244–256.

Buzzanell, P. M. (1994). Gaining a voice: Feminist perspectives in organizational communication. *Management Communication Quarterly, 7,* 339–383.

Chin, J. L. (2004). Feminist leadership: Feminist visions and diverse voices. *Psychology of Women Quarterly, 28,* 1–8.

Court, M. (1997). Removing macho management: Lessons from the field of education. In D. Dunn (Ed.), *Workplace/women's place: An anthology* (pp. 198–219). Los Angeles: Roxbury.

Dansereau, F., Graen, G. B., & Haga, W. (1975). A vertical dyad linkage approach to leadership in formal organizations. *Organizational Behavior and Human Performance, 13,* 46–78.

Eagly, A. H., & Johannesen-Schmidt, M. C. (2001). The leadership styles of women and men. *Journal of Social Issues, 57,* 781–797.

Eagly, A., & Johnson, B. (1990). Gender and the emergence of leaders: A meta-analysis. *Psychological Bulletin, 108,* 233–256.

Eisenstein, H. (1983). *Contemporary feminist thought.* Boston: G. K. Hall.

Evans, M. G. (1996). R. J. House's "A path-goal theory of leader effectiveness." *Leadership Quarterly, 7*(3), 305–309.

Ferguson, K. (1984). *The feminist case against bureaucracy.* Philadelphia: Temple University Press.

Fiedler, F. E. (1967). *A theory of leadership effectiveness.* New York: McGraw-Hill.

Fine, M. G. (1993). New voices in organizational communication: A feminist commentary and critique. In S. P. Bowen & N. Wyatt (Eds.), *Transforming visions: Feminist critiques in communication studies* (pp. 125–166). Cresskill, NJ: Hampton Press.

Fine, M. G. (1995). *Building successful multicultural organizations: Challenges and opportunities.* Westport, CT: Quorum Books.

Fine, M. G. (2005, October). *Women leaders: Developing an ethics-based theory of leadership.* Paper presented at the Organization for the Study of Communication, Language, and Gender Conference, Reno, NV.

Fine, M. G., & Buzzanell, P. M. (2000). Walking the high wire: Leadership theorizing, daily acts, and tensions. In P. M. Buzzanell (Ed.), *Rethinking organizational and managerial communication from feminist perspectives* (pp. 128–156). Thousand Oaks, CA: Sage.

Fondas, N. (1997). Feminization unveiled: Management qualities in contemporary writings. *Academy of Management Review, 22,* 257–282.

Gilligan, C. (1982). *In a different voice: Psychological theory and women's development.* Cambridge, MA: Harvard University Press.

189

Gordon, L. (1979). The struggle for reproductive freedom: Three stages of feminism. In Z. Eisenstein (Ed.), *Capitalist patriarchy and the case for socialist feminism* (pp. 107–132). New York: Monthly Review Press.

Graen, G. B. (1976). Role-making processes within complex organizations. In M. D. Dunnette (Ed.), *Handbook of industrial and organizational psychology* (pp. 1202–1245). Chicago: Rand McNally.

Graen, G. B., & Cashman, J. (1975). A role-making model of leadership in formal organizations: A developmental approach. In J. G. Hunt & L. L. Larson (Eds.), *Leadership frontiers* (pp. 143–166). Kent, OH: Kent State University Press.

Graen, G. B., & Uhl-Bien, M. (1995). Relationship-based approach to leadership: Development of leader–member exchange (LMX) theory of leadership over 25 years: Applying a multi-level, multi-domain perspective. *Leadership Quarterly, 6*(2), 219–247.

Hersey, P., & Blanchard, K. H. (1969). Life-cycle theory of leadership. *Training and Development Journal, 23*, 26–34.

House, R. J. (1971). A path-goal theory of leader effectiveness. *Administrative Science Quarterly, 16*, 321–328.

Izraeli, D. N., & Adler, N. (1994). Competitive frontiers: Women managers in a global economy. In N. Adler & D. N. Izraeli (Eds.), *Competitive frontiers: Women managers in a global economy* (pp. 3–21). Cambridge, MA: Blackwell.

Kanter, R. M. (1977). *Men and women of the corporation.* New York: Basic Books.

Kirkpatrick, S. A., & Locke, E. A. (1991). Leadership: Do traits matter? *The Executive, 5*(2), 48–60.

Labaton, V., & Martin, D. L. (Eds.) (2004). *The fire this time: Young activists and the new feminism.* New York: Anchor Books.

Lazzari, M. M., Ford, H. R., & Haughey, K. J. (1996). Making a difference: Women of action in the community. *Social Work, 41*(2), 197–205.

Mills, A. J., & Tancred, P. (Eds.) (1992). *Gendering organizational analysis.* Newbury Park, CA: Sage.

Mumford, M. D., Zaccaro, S. J., Harding, F. D., Jacobs, T. O., & Fleishman, E. A. (2000). Leadership skills for a changing world: Solving complex social problems. *Leadership Quarterly, 11*(1), 11–35.

Northouse, P. G. (2004). *Leadership: Theory and practice* (3rd ed.). Thousand Oaks, CA: Sage.

O'Brien Hallstein, D. L. (1999). A postmodern caring: Feminist standpoint theories, revisioned caring, and communication ethics. *Western Journal of Communication, 63*(1), 32–56.

Parker, P. S. (2001). African American women executives' leadership communication within dominant-culture organizations. *Management Communication Quarterly, 15*(1), 42–82.

Rosener, J. B. (1990). Ways women lead. *Harvard Business Review, 68*(6), 119–129.

Rubenstein, H. (2003, Feb. 5). Ethical leadership. *Conservative Monitor*. Retrieved September 27, 2005, from http://www.conservativemonitor.com/opinion03/28.shtml

Schein, V. E. (2001). A global look at psychological barriers to women's progress in management. *Journal of Social Issues, 57*(4), 675–688.

Smulyan, L. (2004). Choosing to teach: Reflections on gender and social change. *Teachers College Record, 106*(3), 513–543.

Stogdill, R. M. (1948). Personal factors associated with leadership: A survey of the literature. *Journal of Psychology, 25*, 35–71.

Strube, M. J., & Garcia, J. E. (1981). A meta-analytic investigation of Fiedler's contingency model of leadership effectiveness. *Psychological Bulletin, 90*, 307–321.

Whatley, A. (1998). Gifted women and teaching: A compatible choice? *Roeper Review, 21*(2), 117–124.

Wood, J. T. (1994). *Gendered lives: Communication, gender, and culture*. Belmont, CA: Wadsworth.

Zaleznik, A. (1977, May/June). Managers and leaders: Are they different? *Harvard Business Review, 55*, 67–78.

Chapter 9

Strategic Planning: Gender, Collaborative Leadership, and Organizational Change

Margaret E. Madden

This chapter will first apply a feminist analysis to traditional strategic planning theory and practice and attempt to articulate hallmarks that distinguish feminist strategic planning. *Collaboration* is the most prominent theme in feminist leadership and management, as is evident from the other chapters in this book. Other components of strategic planning based on feminist principles include sociocultural context, empowerment, agency, and multiple perspectives.

Traditional Strategic Planning Definitions

Strategic planning is "a disciplined effort to produce fundamental decisions and actions that shape and guide what an organization is, what it does, and why it does" (Bryson, 1988, p. 5). Strategic planning concepts gained popularity in corporations during the 1960s and 1970s (Dooris, 2003), and were soon applied to public and nonprofit service organizations (Bryson, 2000). In the 1980s, higher education got on the strategic planning bandwagon, with models utilizing concepts such as strategic niche, competitive position, shareholder values, and strength and opportunity analyses. By the 1990s, other management trends, like total quality management, re-engineering, and learning organizations, gained popularity (Dooris, 2003).

There are numerous models of strategic planning with varied advantages and disadvantages (Bryson, 2000). Some are process models, proposing a system for *doing* planning. The parent of process models, the Harvard Policy Model, has evolved at the Harvard Business School since the 1920s. Focusing on finding the best fit between the organization and its environment, it relies upon the "SWOT" analyses of internal *s*trengths and *w*eaknesses of the organization, and external *o*pportunities and *t*hreats. Other process models have emerged over the years, including total quality management, which focuses on motivating personnel to provide quality products or services; logical incrementalism, which allows units below the corporate level to handle decisions incrementally; and innovation planning, which focuses on an entrepreneurial culture of innovation. By design, process models do not focus on the content of strategic issues, but require that decision makers can achieve some consensus on general values and goals. They vary in the degree to which they suggest methods to develop those strategies.

Content models focus on prescribing answers to substantive questions. One content approach is the Portfolio Model, which proposes managing a business portfolio like an investment portfolio to help businesses gain market share and reduce unit cost. In general, strategic planning addresses the need for organizations to face discontinuities proactively rather than simply reacting to changes (Andrade, 1999; Dooris, 2003), but strategic planning is not a single concept or procedure. Bryson (2000) argues that administrators need to be familiar with a range of strategic planning activities to tailor hybrids to fit specific situations, as well as having political and technical skills to adapt to their situations.

Facility with strategic planning is prevalent in almost all characterizations of good leaders in contemporary work environments (Rowley & Sherman, 2001). Writing about higher education, Astin and Astin (2000) outline principles of "transformative leadership," leadership that transforms institutions. They define leadership as fostering change, "a purposive process which is inherently value-based" (p. 8). Therefore, a leader is a "change agent" who involves others in a collective process. Astin and Astin's monograph outlines strategies for implementing change through transformative leadership, a vision of leadership as fostering strategic planning that is consistent with a feminist approach to leadership and strategic planning.

Feminist Analysis of Strategic Planning Concepts

A feminist analysis of strategic planning concepts includes an understanding of their masculinized context and assumptions, how context acts to influence control and power, and how management styles have borrowed aspects of feminist relational thinking without truly transforming organizational processes.

Masculinized context

Understanding the masculine assumptions in organizations, and the difficulties those pose for women leaders, lays the foundation for an analysis of gender and strategic management. Examining strategic planning and management through the lens of feminism, Albino (1992) remarks that the very word "strategy" invokes masculine imagery, but women in leadership positions need to understand the environment of their institution, behave in ways compatible with that setting, act more like some men some of the time, and avoid perceiving strategy as shady.

In an analysis of strategic management in the financial services industry in Britain, Kerfoot and Knights (1993) use feminist concepts to discuss assumptions implicit in common practices. Strategic management began to enter financial services in the 1970s in response to a change in the competitive climate in the banking and insurance industries, with the goal of increasing corporate control of internal and external business practices and enhancing competitiveness. By promoting a façade of masculine invulnerability, management practices can silence or displace expressions of weakness, fears, and uncertainties. Hence, gender is an organizing principle in the managerial workplace.

Because normative aspects of masculinity shift over time, at any given point in history particular forms of masculinity are sustained, reproduced, and privileged by particular management practices. When one aspect of the "real man" involves having and managing money, financial services can contribute greatly to maintaining masculinity, by contrasting it with femininity or homosexuality. Even when normative masculinity accommodates the sensitive and caring "new male," masculinity is maintained by encouraging only certain kinds of nurturing, for example, appropriating the most rewarding aspects of childcare.

The masculinist nature of management is rooted in the paternalism of philanthropy and religion of 19th century industrialists, which simulates patriarchal, family-like relations, exerting power for the good of workers and promoting compliant and predictable employees. Kerfoot and Knights argue that strategic management displaced paternalism after World War II because of competitive shifts in the balance of supply and demand, but retained paternalist assumptions. Strategic management emphasizes qualifying, examining, and grading people and events. The engagement of staff at various levels of decision making demands that all members of an organization be concerned with the success of business initiatives and overall strength of the enterprise, creating an illusion of trust through the pretence of equality.

Strategic management emphasizes power and status differently by putting managerial control at the heart of the workgroup, shifting responsibility and accountability lower, encouraging collective loyalty and corporate identity. It reflects concepts of masculinity in that everything becomes subject to controlled and rational processes, sustaining a hierarchy founded upon instrumentalism, competition, productivity, and risk-taking. It privileges men, ranks some men above others, and supports dominant forms of masculinity (Kerfoot & Knights, 1993). While Kerfoot and Knights are speaking of one industry, their detailed analysis provides a substantive example of the ramifications of embedded masculinism for strategic management.

Context and control

A feminist analysis of strategic planning requires an examination of the context in which planning occurs. Many years ago, Kanter (1977) noted that organizations are gendered, but Acker (1998) contends that most feminists writing about organizations assume that structure is gender-neutral. In fact, assumptions about gender pervade documents and contracts that provide the structure of organizations. Gender segregation in paid and unpaid work and gender inequality in the status of jobs and income are mechanisms for control. Ignoring the implications of gender for organizational goals mystifies bureaucracy while maintaining class and gender hierarchies. Contemporary notions of strategic planning, therefore, are founded on organizational principles that are inherently masculine.

Examining education in Australia, Blackmore (1999) makes similar points about management, arguing that education as a career has become feminized, casualized, and deprofessionalized. Bureaucratization in education is based on normative gender dichotomies, for example, "hard" finance and administration versus "soft" curriculum and pedagogy. "Hegemonic heterosexual masculinity" (p. 10) in education management assumes the need for toughness. Strategic management that flattens the hierarchy relocates managerial control to the work group, creating competition or "strategic masculinity."

As others in this volume have noted, there is substantial evidence that people devalue the work of female managers (Carli & Eagly, 2001). Because the perceived power and strengths of men evoke strategy-related competencies, men may more readily be viewed as likely to be successful at strategic management. Yet research ranging from case studies of women entrepreneurs (Chaganti, 1986) to thorough and sophisticated meta-analyses (Eagly, Karau, Miner, & Johnson, 1994) does not show large differences in strategic management techniques. Eagly et al. (1994) found modest gender differences in that men displayed greater motivation to manage than women, but the authors suggest that this may be because managerial style is defined in masculine terms. Another study of perceptions of behaviors found that women were regarded as less likely to have key leader behaviors, especially by male raters (Martell & DeSmet, 2001). While the effect was small in statistical terms, other studies show that small biases can compound over time to disadvantage career mobility. Stereotypic expectations of women seem incompatible with the leadership characteristics desirable for strategic planning; however, actual behavior is less gendered than stereotypes suggest, and it is not clear that women are less effective planners.

Borrowing relational theory

Despite the rhetoric about changing managerial practices that might be more compatible with women's preferences in leadership behavior, writers have argued that in reality, women are still at a disadvantage. Blackmore (1999) contends that women are viewed as change agents only when it serves organizational goals. Fletcher (2002) says that leadership that is now called "postheroic" is a "more relational approach . . . intended to transform stodgy, top-down organizational structures into flexible, knowledge-based entities able to meet the demands of the information age and global economy" (p. 1). However, organizations have difficulty implementing it because of underlying assumptions that support autonomous, status-enhancing, and control behavior. Envisioning leadership as collaboration and valuing relational or emotional intelligence significantly shifts what it means to be a good leader, yet management has neither adjusted its definition of leadership nor redefined planning in gender-neutral terms. Although the stated goal may be to facilitate collective learning, managers rarely get promotions for this. The result, then, is simply hiring better hierarchical leaders who have emotional intelligence, and using the same approaches to strategic planning, rather than truly transforming organizational processes (Fletcher, 2002).

Speaking about higher education leadership, Bensimon (1995) uses post-structuralist concepts to analyze the strategic management process Total Quality Management (TQM). TQM dictates how quality is defined, improved, and controlled. Translated to education, university constituencies are defined as customers, and a university's "product" is equated with goods and services. TQM defines quality as lack of variation, dichotomizing sameness versus variation. Relying on benchmarking to measure success assumes that quantitative measures can be used to define performance improvement or production. Controlling quality means eliminating variations or nonconformance. Restricting admission practices, focusing recruitment on high schools with strong quality, and rewarding students who are good at passive learning serve to reduce variation and diversity. The aversion to difference in TQM strengthens an argument against multiculturalism, for multicultural scholarship then represents inessential knowledge valued only for improving relations, not knowledge legitimate by its own merit. For the same reason, discouraging difference supports gender dichotomy; scholarly conformity, based on masculine values, becomes the norm. While the complexity of institutions does not lend itself to statistical forms of quality control, the language of TQM makes the university appear more rational to corporate executives on boards of trustees, encouraging inappropriate attempts to impose ineffective or inaccurate measures of performance (Bensimon, 1995).

In another domain, urban or community planning, a feminist post-structuralist framework illustrates how gendered power relations undermine participatory planning (Lennie, 1999; Roy, 2001). Mainstream planners tend to use adversarial models of consultation and paternalistic techniques such as using experts to overpower community members, which can be alienating to women. An analysis emphasizing empowering community members disrupts the dichotomy between scientific experts and nonexpert community members. Postmodernism and feminism add a number of dimensions to the critique of planning, such as awareness of difference, identity, and forms of power; challenge of dichotomous construction and recognition that dualisms are often deeply gendered; and concern with procedural equity, not just outcome. Feminism recognizes issues as dilemmas in contexts of interdependence and intersubjectivity.

Alternative Models of Strategic Management

Alternative planning models have been suggested in a number of varied contexts. An alternative strategy seeks to change power relations in a community and to challenge patriarchal planning processes (Lennie, 1999). A planning strategy based on feminist values assumes that local contextual knowledge and experience are as valuable as experts' knowledge, which can be exclusionary; contradictions and paradoxes are inevitable; and social, economic, and environmental issues of particular concern to women are valid. The planning method is trans-disciplinary, assuming that gendered power relations are always present, and values the diversity of women and their subjective experiences. Planning is assumed to be socially constructed and empowering for women, taking everyday lives into account, facilitating local self-reliance, and using communication techniques accessible to women. If one substitutes the word "organization" for "community" in these assumptions, they provide a useful starting point for constructing a feminist strategic planning process.

Descriptions of management in social work administration describe skills and values needed for planning. A feminist professional development program helps women become competent in process and task skills for managing people and information; addresses responses to sexism and discrimination; and covers models of organizational structures and cultures, appropriate managerial styles for organizations, and organizational change processes (Halseth, 1993). In other words, this proposes a curriculum of strategic planning with feminist values.

The workplace in which planning is fostered is structured for worker control, autonomy, and empowerment (Arches & Schneider, 1994). For example, there might be flexible teams, mutual planning and problem solving, consensual decision making and process, rotating leadership based on specific expertise, and nonhierarchical staff relations. Members have a chance to become co-ordinators as they develop expertise in a specialty or program area and tasks are rotated among program co-ordinators to avoid hierarchical power relationships.

In in-depth qualitative interviews with women administrators, Arches and Schneider report that power emerged as a pervasive theme; however, in contrast to many models, power was seen as the ability to influence rather than to dominate, and viewed as infinite and something to be shared. Other themes included women's need for support and empowerment in their various roles, equality, staff connectedness, and mutual planning and decision making. Hence agencies with feminist values tended to redefine power relationships by eliminating hierarchical structure, reducing the division of labor and specialization, sharing programmatic decision making, and focusing on empowering both workers and clients.

Implementing strategic planning in organizations that are not explicitly feminist requires a deeper and more radical analysis. Blackmore (1999) argues that feminists have not confronted the investment men have in existing gender relations, and women are often discouraged from changing organizational rules to eliminate gendered procedures or structures. Blackmore's respondents, higher education administrators, frequently reported that they found their environments disempowering, with resistance taking on subtler forms as they moved up in organizations. Attempts to alter strategic management practices frequently elicit responses that undermine women's growing influence, through denigration of women who do things well, or derogatory comments meant to bait them. Changes are deflected by using "strategic masculinity" to appropriate analyses of gender and portray men as equally imprisoned by gender roles.

Thus these analyses of strategic management identify the gendered nature of management and planning strategies and examine how feminist theories can illuminate underlying assumptions that must be addressed to change organizations, rather than focusing on molding women to conform to masculine definitions of leadership.

Feminist Psychology and Management

Principles from feminist psychology can further expand our understanding of the gendered nature of strategic management. Madden (2005) discusses leadership in higher education within a framework of five principles of feminist psychology adapted from Worell and Johnson's (1997) *Shaping the Future of Feminist Psychology*. The principles are:

1. Sociocultural context influences leadership situations. Context includes differences in perspectives based on gender, culture, ethnicity, and other dimensions.
2. Power dynamics are present in all sociocultural structures.
3. People are active agents who use diverse strategies to cope and grow as individuals and to change their environments.
4. Multiple perspectives are more useful than dichotomous ones, which are both ineffective and unrealistic.
5. As a strategy to change organizations, collaboration is both effective and desirable.

Echoing themes found in the feminist management literature, these concepts can also be used to articulate components of a feminist paradigm for strategic planning.

Sociocultural context

The notion that human behavior and perception are embedded in contexts is a common theme in feminist thought. Context includes characteristics of the organizational climate, such as past history, the presence of gender discrimination and stereotyping, hierarchical structures, masculinization of process and structure, and the extent of interconnection of gender and status. Context also includes the influence of differences in perspectives based on gender, culture, ethnicity, and other identity dimensions of participants.

Feminist analyses of organizations and strategic management usually mention context, as in the previously mentioned articles proposing that the gendered nature of work itself underlies constructs in organizations (Acker, 1998). Strategic management creates competition-based organizations that might be called "strategic masculinity" (Blackmore, 1999), while modes of interaction encourage masculine norms (Kerfoot & Knights, 1993). Implicit assumptions of rationality, gendered work language, and orderliness are prevalent even in descriptions of new management forms that appear more compatible with female gender roles (Hatcher, 2003).

Psychological literature further elucidates when and how context impacts women's management strategies. Considerable research examines the dynamics of gender discrimination and stereotyping from a feminist perspective. Incongruity between leadership roles and female gender roles (prescriptive expectations for women's behavior) leads to

200

prejudicial judgments and actions (Eagly & Karau, 2002). Because people more easily perceive men as highly competent, men are more likely to be considered leaders, given opportunities, and emerge as leaders than women. Behavioral preferences may vary by gender, as well. Women engage in more positive social behavior and agreement. Direct language, disagreement, and autocratic and dominating leadership are less well received from women than from men. Thus, as Carli and Eagly note, "women are more constrained than men in the kinds of behaviors that they can engage in and still be influential" (1999, p. 215).

A complete model of strategic planning must recognize and respond to the gendered expectations regarding women's management skills; however, as in most behavioral gender differences, there is a great deal of overlap in women's and men's behavior and much more variability within each gender than between them (Eagly & Johnson, 1990). A feminist analysis is useful only if it helps women and men understand and respond to constraints on their behavior from gendered expectations and contexts, not if it perpetuates false stereotypes about women's leadership style. A thorough contextual analysis is necessary to avoid essentialization from focus on simplistic questions about whether women and men have similar or different leadership styles or strategic planning preferences (Eagly & Johannesen-Schmidt, 2001).

Power and empowerment

Feminist theory assumes that power dynamics are present in all sociocultural structures. In addition to noting the impact of context on power relations, feminist approaches redefine power as the power to achieve goals, rather than power over others (Yoder, 2001). Empowerment of others, therefore, becomes a major leadership strategy for enhancing the effectiveness of organizations. Feminist authors also always cite power dynamics in organizations. Strategic management is designed to control workers, to maintain the status quo of gender inequality in most aspects of work (Acker, 1998; Bensimon, 1995), and resistance to women managers occurs because it disrupts power relations in organizations and therefore reduces the privilege of the powerful few, mainly men (Blackmore, 1999). Fletcher (2002) points out that leadership is defined in terms of status and command-and-control images—having power over others—even when it does lip service to collaborative strategies.

In a social psychological analysis of sources of interpersonal power, Carli (1999) used meta-analysis to examine gender differences. Men are perceived as having traits reflecting competency, or *expert power*. Even when the behavior of men and women is identical, men are viewed as more competent. Men also have more *legitimate power*, power conferred by one's status, simply by virtue of being male. In contrast, women use more relationship-based, or *referent power*. Differences in power types are correlated with the influence strategies used by women and men. Therefore, women have greater difficulty exerting influence, particularly when influence relies upon competence and authority. Feminist strategic planning processes must be highly attuned to gender-laden power dynamics inevitable in any organization.

Agency and leadership

Feminist psychology views people as active agents who use diverse strategies to cope and grow as individuals and to change their environments. In this vein, gendered leadership styles may be seen as necessary mechanisms to survive as a leader in a context imposing prescriptive gendered definitions of good leadership. To create feminist strategic planning, one must understand how women have exerted influence on their environments despite low status. Because of the context in which they are employed, women adopt leadership styles that take advantage of gendered expectations others have for them and perhaps they have for themselves (Carli & Eagly, 1999; Eagly & Johannesen-Schmidt, 2001). Thus gendered styles represent active and realistic coping with constraints imposed by stereotyped notions of leadership and discriminatory opportunities for gaining experience.

Some women invoke alternative cultural interpretations of women's roles as sources of strength. Lips found that Puerto Rican women reported no conflict between concepts of power and femininity because in the concept of *hembrismo* "femaleness connotes strength, perseverance, flexibility, and ability for survival" (2001, p. 810). Likewise, matriarchal traditions of many non-European ethnic groups are sources of strength for women of color (Valverde, 2003). The importance of a strong sense of one's own values, beliefs, and abilities; finding professional and spiritual role models; and using family support are also important (Dillard, 2000; Valverde, 2003). Planning processes should value and exploit these coping mechanisms.

Social action

In addition, a commitment to social action and the pursuit of equity often pervade feminist views of leadership. Fortunately, women's leadership styles do tend to have characteristics consistent with transformational leadership, relying on motivating followers, optimism, and excitement for the future (Eagly et al., 1994; Eagly & Johannesen-Schmidt, 2001). Other qualitative studies interviewing women in leadership positions confirm the prevalence of social justice motives. Sometimes the social action theme is couched in an obligation to give back to the community and mentor others (Miller & Vaughn, 1997). Sometimes the focus is on transforming the very nature of leadership: transforming the culture of one's organization by confronting masculinist styles directly (Valverde, 2003; Yoder, 2001), or by transforming societal notions of leadership (Blackmore, 1999; Bryans & Mavin, 2003; Dillard, 2000; Moultrie & de la Rey, 2003; Valverde, 2003). Other times the focus is more explicitly on transforming society through work against racism, violence, and heterosexism (Strachan, 1999). Feminist strategic planning must acknowledge that participants' goals may go beyond immediate organizational goals to focus on transforming society.

Multiple perspectives

Feminism highlights tendencies toward false dualism, recognizing that multiple perspectives are more useful than dichotomous ones. Utilizing interdisciplinary problem-solving approaches and encouraging multiple voices in decision making are ways to avoid simplistic analyses of problems and their solutions. Because dualisms are often deeply gendered, they promote simplistic analyses of complex problems (Roy, 2001). Women of color, such as black women in South Africa (Moultrie & de la Rey, 2003) and American Indian women (Warner, 1994), often discuss conflicts between their cultural backgrounds and institutional norms and resistance of those institutions to planning processes incorporating assumptions from other cultures. Interdisciplinarity is an important tenet of feminist theory. Multicultural and feminist pedagogies encourage students to examine complex problems from multiple perspectives and think critically about their own experiences (Grumet & McCoy, 1997; Madden & Russo, 1997). Feminist strategic planning should do the same for an organization.

Collaboration

The value of collaboration is one of the most common themes in the feminist strategic management literature, and is perhaps the most prominent feature distinguishing feminist leadership from masculine styles (Eagly et al., 1994; Kerfoot & Knights, 1993). Masculine styles rely on individual competency and privilege of individual leaders (Fletcher, 2002; Kerfoot & Knights, 1993). Feminists discuss not only collaboration among leaders, but also with clients or students or rotation among team members based on emerging expertise and needs (Arches & Schneider, 1994; Roy, 2001; Halseth, 1993). Psychological literature demonstrates that collaboration effectively promotes strategic change (Astin & Astin, 2000). Collaboration works because participatory and consensus-based decision making is more satisfying for participants and produces plans that people buy into readily. Articulating reasons for collaborative leadership as part of a shared value system can clarify tactics for participants or skeptical colleagues accustomed to authoritarian modes of leadership.

The difficulties in implementing collaboration cited elsewhere in this volume reduce women's effectiveness when they attempt this kind of leadership, even when business rhetoric seems to value them. Eagly and Carli (2003) evaluated the assertion by trade books and journalists that women have leadership advantages. While contemporary approaches to leadership may seem to create advantages for women in their focus on coaching, teaching, and facilitating, the popular literature ignores still powerful biases against women. Despite these difficulties, collaboration must be a fundamental component of strategic planning based on feminist principles, along with the other components outlined in this section: context, power, agency, and multiple perspectives.

Therefore, feminist psychology is consistent with the observations of writers on management and planning, but also informs the interpersonal principles that underlie the dynamics and challenges of attempting to plan in a feminist way. Analyses focus on both the process of strategic planning, such as collaboration, empowerment, agency, and interdisciplinarity; and the content, emphasizing factors such as gendered context, language, tasks, and power hierarchies.

Feminist Strategic Planning Questions

Principles from feminist psychology and organizational literature can provide a useful organizational framework for thinking about strategic planning. One way to assess consistency with these principles is to ask a series of questions reflecting them:

1. What is the context in which the planning will occur? How masculinized is the organization in structure, tasks, gender ratio of staff and clients, or corporate language? What is done to facilitate the expression of diverse perspectives, for example, from various cultural, ethnic, sexual orientation, ability, and age groups?
2. What are the power dynamics in the organization and the environment in which it exists? How can planning be structured to minimize disparate status of participants and to provide widespread access to resources that bring power?
3. How can planning facilitate the growth of organization participants and promote activism to change the environments of the institution or broader community?
4. How are multiple perspectives encouraged and simplistic or dualistic solutions avoided?
5. How is collaboration encouraged? Are the parameters for collaboration and decision making explicitly stated for participants? Are aspects of the planning process in which collaboration is inappropriate or ineffective clearly specified?

Because most organizations are not feminist in their values, developing a shared commitment to these principles may be challenging, yet, even in a highly masculinized environment, attempting to invoke them by asking questions like these may push the organization, inch by inch, towards becoming more empowering for women. By articulating the issues, feminists may become more intentional and committed to achieving more equitable work situations.

References

Acker, J. (1998). Hierarchies, jobs, and bodies: A theory of gendered organizations. In K. A. Myers, C. D. Anderson, & B. J. Risman (Eds.), *Feminist foundations: Towards transforming sociology* (pp. 299–317). Thousand Oaks, CA: Sage.

Albino, J. E. (1992). Women as leaders: The dirty work they must learn. *The Education Digest, 58*(3), 33–35.

Andrade, S. J. (1999). How to institutionalize strategic planning. *Planning for Higher Education, 27*(2), 40–54.

Arches, J. L., & Schneider, P. (1994). Analyzing administrative experiences: Feminist, labor, and organizational culture perspectives. *Journal of Sociology and Social Work, 21*(4), 147–162.

Astin, A. W., & Astin, H. S. (2000). *Leadership reconsidered: Engaging higher education in social change.* Battle Creek, MI: W. K. Kellogg Foundation.

Bensimon, E. M. (1995). Total quality management in the academy: A rebellious reading. *Harvard Educational Review, 65*(4), 593–611.

Blackmore, J. (1999). *Troubling women: Feminism, leadership and educational change.* Buckingham, UK: Open University Press.

Bryans, P. & Mavin, S. (2003). Women learning to become managers: Learning to fit in or to play a different game? *Management Learning, 34*(1), 111–134.

Bryson, J. M. (1988). *Strategic planning for public and nonprofit organizations.* San Francisco: Jossey-Bass.

Bryson, J. M. (2000). Strategic planning. In J. M. Shafritz (Ed.), *Defining public administration* (pp. 208–229). Boulder: CO: Westview Press.

Carli, L. (1999). Gender, interpersonal power, and social influence. *Journal of Social Issues, 55*(1), 81–99.

Carli, L. L., & Eagly, A. H. (1999). Gender effects on social influence and emergent leadership. In G. N. Powell (Ed.), *Handbook of women and work* (pp. 203–222). Thousand Oaks, CA: Sage.

Carli, L. L., & Eagly, A. H. (2001). Gender, hierarchy, and leadership: An introduction. *Journal of Social Issues, 57*(4), 629–636.

Chaganti, R. (1986). Management in women-owned enterprises. *Journal of Small Business Management, 24*(4), 18–30.

Dillard, C. B. (2000). The substance of things hoped for, the evidence of things not seen: Examining an endarkened feminist epistemology in educational research and leadership. *Qualitative Studies in Education, 16*(6), 661–681.

Dooris, M. J. (2003). Two decades of strategic planning. *Planning for Higher Education, 31*(2), 26–43.

Eagly, A. H., & Carli, L. L. (2003). The female leadership advantage: An evaluation of the evidence. *Leadership Quarterly, 14*, 807–834.

Eagly, A. H., & Johannesen-Schmidt, M. C. (2001). The leadership styles of women and men. *Journal of Social Issues, 57*(4), 781–797.

Eagly, A. H., & Johnson, B. T. (1990). Gender and leadership style: A meta-analysis. *Psychological Bulletin, 108*, 233–256.

Eagly, A. H., & Karau, S. J. (2002). Role congruity theory of prejudice toward female leaders. *Psychological Review, 109*(3), 573–598.

Eagly, A. H., Karau, S. J., Miner, J. B., & Johnson, B. T. (1994). Gender and motivation to manage in hierarchic organizations: A meta-analysis. *Leadership Quarterly*, *5*(2), 135–159.

Fletcher, J. (2002, August). *The greatly exaggerated demise of heroic leadership: Gender, power, and the myth of the female advantage.* CGO Insight, Briefing No. 13. Boston: Simmons College Center for Gender in Organizations.

Grumet, M., & McCoy, K. (1997). *Education: Discipline analysis.* Baltimore, MD: Towson State University National Center for Curriculum Transformation Resources on Women.

Halseth, J. (1993). Infusing a feminist analysis into education for policy, planning, and administration. In T. Mizrahi & J. Morrison (Eds.), *Community organization and social administration* (pp. 225–241). New York: Haworth.

Hatcher, C. (2003). Refashioning a passionate manager: Gender at work. *Gender, Work, and Organization*, *10*(4), 391–412.

Kanter, R. M. (1977). *Men and women in the organization.* New York: Basic Books.

Kerfoot, D., & Knights, D. (1993). Management, masculinity and manipulation: From paternalism to corporate strategy in financial services in Britain. *Journal of Management Studies*, *30*(4), 659–677.

Lennie, J. (1999). Deconstructing gendered power relations in participatory planning: Towards an empowering feminist framework of participation and action. *Women's Studies International Forum*, *22*(1), 97–112.

Lips, H. M. (2001). Envisioning positions of leadership: The expectations of university students in Virginia and Puerto Rico. *Journal of Social Issues*, *57*(4), 799–813.

Madden, M. E. (2004). Can strategic planning be feminist? *The Feminist Psychologist: Newsletter of the Society for the Psychology of Women*, *31*(1), 1–2.

Madden, M. E. (2005). Gender and leadership in higher education. *Psychology of Women Quarterly*, *29*(1), 3–14.

Madden, M. E., & Russo, N. F. (1997). *Psychology: Discipline analysis.* Baltimore, MD: Towson State University National Center for Curriculum Transformation Resources on Women.

Martell, R. F., & DeSmet, A. L. (2001). A diagnostic-ratio approach to measuring beliefs about the leadership abilities of male and female managers. *Journal of Applied Psychology*, *86*(6), 1223–1231.

Miller, J. R., & Vaughn, G. G. (1997). African American women executives. In L. Benjamin (Ed.), *Black women in the academy: Promises and perils* (pp. 179–188). Gainesville, FL: University Press of Florida.

Moultrie, A., & de la Rey, C. (2003). South African women leaders in higher education: Professional development needs in a changing context. *McGill Journal of Education*, *38*(3), 407–420.

Rowley, D. J., & Sherman, H. (2001). *From strategy to change: Implementing the plan in higher education.* San Francisco: Jossey-Bass.

Roy, A. (2001). A "public" muse on planning convictions and feminist connections. *Journal of Planning Education and Research, 21*, 109–126.

Strachan, J. (1999). Feminist educational leadership: Locating the concepts of practice. *Gender and education, 11*(3), 309–322.

Valverde, L. A. (2003). *Leaders of color in higher education.* New York: Alta Mira.

Warner, L. Sue (1994). A study of American Indian females in higher education administration. *Initiatives, 56*(4), 11–17.

Worell, J., & Johnson, N. G. (1997). *Shaping the future of feminist psychology: Education, research, and practice.* Washington, DC: American Psychological Association.

Yoder, J. D. (2001). Making leadership work more effectively for women. *Journal of Social Issues, 57*(4), 815–828.

Part III

From Margin to Center: The Voices of Diverse Feminist Leaders

Introduction

Janis Sanchez-Hucles and Penny Sanchez

Feminist leaders are found across racial, ethnic, sexual orientation, socioeconomic, and ability statuses. Leaders in these groups, however, have historically been ignored, marginalized, and unacknowledged. When Jean Lau Chin began her Presidential Initiative to investigate feminist leadership, she explicitly included the leadership experiences of women who have often been overlooked by subtitling her project "feminist visions and diverse voices."

Part of the reason that issues of race, ethnicity, class, ability status, and sexual orientation are often not discussed is because of the complexity they add to the areas of leadership and collaboration for women. First, issues of diversity mediate how women choose to be leaders, how they collaborate with others, and how diverse women leaders are perceived by themselves and others. Complexity is also added as we examine how issues of diversity are handled within groups of different women. How sensitive are Euro-American women to issues of racial and ethnic diversity? How attuned are racial ethnic minority women to issues of sexual orientation, disability, and the experiences of racial ethnic women who are different from them? Finally, a major issue that has recently been discussed in the literature is the intersection of identities. There is a growing recognition that many women do not identify along a singular dimension such as gender but instead identify in accord with multiple identities without prioritizing one over others. For example, an Asian woman leader who is bisexual and has disabilities

should be able to draw on her experiences from her multiple iden-
tifications versus highlighting only one.

This part on diverse feminist groups highlights the voices of diverse
women and helps to broaden our understanding of different models of
effective leadership. The authors of these chapters note that diverse
leaders are often subject to different expectations, evaluations, barriers,
and reinforcements as compared to Euro-American men and women. The
chapters in this part explore how culture and dimensions of diversity can
change the context and dynamics of leadership. Addressing the following
questions shaped the discussions of diverse feminist leadership:

- How do diverse women leaders lead?
- How can feminist leadership be defined for each group?
- How does feminism affect their leadership?
- How are diverse leadership styles different from other leadership styles?
- What challenges exist?
- What needs to be done to promote more feminist leaders within
  these groups?
- How can information on diverse feminist leaders expand our
  knowledge of effective feminist leadership?

Overview

In our introduction to this part on diverse feminist leadership, the discussion of diverse feminist leadership will be augmented by the voices
of women who participated via a conference call on this topic and those
who contributed by joining our website-based discussion.[1] Given the
paucity of literature on diverse feminist leadership, one of the first goals
for this group was to begin to develop a shared understanding of the
central elements of diverse feminist leadership. This process began on
a conference call that was led by the two authors. Penny Sanchez with
her background in national corporate leadership, and based on her reading of the literature, proposed that effective leadership for diverse feminist leaders should include three essential components:

1. Using a style of leadership that is reflective of who you are and
   what you believe;
2. Recognition of the different demand characteristics of context and
   different environments;
3. Understanding and addressing the rules of one's organization.

Styles of Leadership

Using a style of leadership that is reflective of who you are and what you believe will ultimately allow individuals to achieve their greatest good and/or best performance. Accordingly, feminist theorists realized that they needed to move away from patriarchal and gender-stratification analyses and move towards more person-centered, feminist, and constructionist approaches (Lykes & Stewart, 1986). In a similar fashion, diverse women leaders have found that their styles of leadership may overlap to some degree with those of Euro-American men and women, but their individual and cultural experiences have shaped them to have unique views on leadership. These diverse women leaders believe that there is still pressure for them to do more than men and Euro-American women to earn, sustain, and prove their competence in leadership roles. Moreover, positive elements of their leadership styles need to be incorporated into the style of all leaders.

Double binds

Diverse women leaders encounter an immediate conflict because theories of leadership are modeled along "great man" theories, with effective leadership associated with stereotypically masculine characteristics. Despite the fact that more recent research has validated the need for effective leadership to incorporate stereotypically feminine interpersonal qualities such as co-operation and collaboration, women still risk appearing too soft or too strong (Jamieson, 1995). This narrow range of appropriate behavior is seen in research that shows that when women leaders adopt more stereotypically masculine behaviors they are rated as less effective, especially by men, but those with more feminine styles are not perceived to be effective leaders either (Eagly, Makhijani, & Klonsky, 1992).

An example that diverse women leaders frequently cite is that if they speak up strongly to make a point, they are viewed as too strident. When these leaders try to speak up in quieter and less assertive ways they are viewed as too passive. As noted by Carli and Eagly (2001), women are more limited in the behaviors that they can employ and still be perceived as influential. Diverse women leaders are very vulnerable to being limited in what is deemed to be acceptable leadership behavior.

One diverse woman leader wondered how to address the possible contradiction of being yourself and following the rules for leadership when the rules were developed for the advancement of White men. In patriarchal settings, women face a double bind because, despite an acknowledgment that effective leadership can be masculine or feminine, stereotypes still paint women as less able than men (Appelbaum, Audet, & Miller, 2003).

The lack of clarity on this issue can also be seen in the comments of Carly Fiorina, then chair and CEO of Hewitt Packard, who first denied that there was a glass ceiling for women as long as they played by male rules. Fiorina later amended her statement to say that she knows that there are barriers that she and other women have faced but she prefers not to focus on these barriers (Wilson, 2004, p. 2). This double bind has been expanded to a "feminine-competency bind" (Jamieson, 1995) because whereas acting feminine can still be perceived negatively, acting competently is associated with acting masculine, which leads a woman to believe that she can only be perceived as competent if she is unfeminine.

Ideas of what is feminine and what is not become more complex for diverse women, given cultural stereotypes that define "feminine" based on Euro-American standards and then regard women of color, lesbian and bisexual women, and women with disabilities as somehow not conforming to the feminine stereotype. Diverse women leaders are often accused of being too much or too little on the masculine–feminine continuum. If there is a conflict between integrity to self and rules, they must first honor who they are. If necessary, they must find support in some sectors of their work or outside the work world that allow them to sustain their identities and values.

Similarities across diverse leaders

The chapters that follow show that diverse women leaders continue to be perceived as "marginal" and "other" as opposed to Euro-American male leaders. The chapter on diverse women leaders in corporate America in this part speaks to many of these challenges. It is interesting to note that Presbyterian pastor Patricia Kitchen argues that precisely what is needed in the United States at this time is "otherism." Kitchen asserts that in contrast to male leadership that focuses on self-centered and self-preservation perspectives, women are more inclined to embrace a leadership style in family as well as national venues that focus not on self but on others (Wilson, 2004, p. 5).

In the chapters that follow, the authors describe an array of diverse leadership styles that seem to embrace some core values. Natalie Porter and Jessica Henderson Daniel outline several models that make transformational, multicultural, and feminist models of leadership unique. First, these models endorse inclusiveness. Diverse styles of leadership address the needs of all individuals who suffer from oppression and move beyond women to include men and children. This is analogous to the findings of Sally Helgesen (1995) in her book *The Female Advantage*. Helgesen believes that her research shows that women's skill in relationships fosters a special ability to weave networks of inclusion that are better for business than traditional systems that keep power in the realm of just a few. Women's inclusive leadership styles also entail a broader vision of society that can include the family, education, the environment, and even world peace. This desire to change not just their organizations but the world reflects transformational leadership and sound management (Wilson, 2004).

Second, diverse women leaders strive to avoid the creation of hierarchies of oppression. These styles of leadership address the reality that many individuals have multiple identities, and advocate for using interactive identities rather than trying to make individuals prioritize single identities. Insight into the perspectives afforded by embracing the power of difference has been modeled on the experiences of women of color and others with multiple identities. Being at the intersection of interlocking indices of oppression can allow a unique view as to how dimensions like race, class, gender, ability, and sexuality operate as loci of power in society. Paula Moya (2001) calls this special insight "epistemic privilege."

Challenges to the idea that leadership must be hierarchical, relating to the public and not the private domain, and focused on dominance, authority, and control over others comes from work on Black women leaders. According to Reid-Merritt (1996), "phenomenal" Black women leaders are creating a new leadership model that incorporates new perceptions of power, decision making via consensus, hard work, tenacity, and a willingness to break rules.

Third, these leaders, by virtue of not being fully included in mainstream organizations, have used their marginal status to critique feminism and be creative about problem solving, and have found ways to support and empower one another. This is an example of "positive marginality" (Mayo, 1982).

These findings of core values in diverse women leaders are in accord with the work of Patricia Darlington and Becky Mulvaney (2003). As part of their attempt to construct reality and to validate and endorse a new style of leadership and power they have developed the concept of *reciprocal empowerment*. This describes a leadership style of reciprocal respect, equality, and personal authority that is characterized by concepts such as mutuality, compassion, collectivity, engagement, and a consensus to enhance oneself and others.

A subtle similarity seen to some degree in diverse women leaders is the tension between their ability to exercise the type of expertise and legitimate power often associated with men versus referent power which is based on interpersonal skill building in relationships (Carli, 1999). Many of these leaders appear to be uncomfortable identifying themselves as leaders because of negative associations with individual use of dominance and hierarchy. Frequently, the leaders cited describe their leadership activities by using terms such as serving, caretaking, community activism, sharing information and resources, and empowering. These terms are aligned with ideas of "servant leadership" but also reflect in part their lack of access to traditional masculine sources of power (Gilkes, 1983). Unfortunately, this tendency of diverse women leaders to avoid masculinized versions of power may lead to men and other women minimizing the import and effectiveness of their leadership endeavors. Typically, individuals who lack power are often forced to use collaborative styles of leadership that involve coalitions, networking, mentoring, and seeking support from others (Madden, 2005).

A final shared similarity found in the following chapters' descriptions of diverse leaders involves the vulnerability to stereotype threat (Aronson, Quinn, & Spencer, 1998) which is a process of heightened anxiety and low performance when placed in situations where individuals fear conforming to negative stereotypes about their group. In addition to fielding the stereotypes and perceptions of others, diverse women leaders must be aware of their own self-perceptions. Diverse leaders may experience stereotype threat when challenged to fill difficult tasks, in evaluative situations, and when their work is subject to stereotyping. Fears of stereotype threat can make diverse women leaders unwilling to risk leadership lest they confirm negative stereotypes and self-perceptions.

Differences among diverse women leaders

There are also many differences among the experiences of these diverse feminist leaders. It is readily apparent that there is little discussion of feminist women leaders with disabilities, which led to a chapter that was focused on what questions need to be addressed to promote more growth in this area. The unique barriers that leaders with disabilities face include the small numbers of women with access to adding to the literature, the perception that these women can only be leaders within limited areas such as disability advocacy, limitations due to disability accommodations, the stigma associated with visible and invisible dis abilities, and problems associated with either minimizing or pathologizing disabilities. Another potential area of difference is that for women with disabilities, and for lesbian, transgendered, and bisexual women, these statuses can be invisible to others.

It is apparent, however, that despite a shared commitment to inclusion among ethnic minority groups, Native American women leaders believe that they have an egalitarian relationship with Native American men with respect to fighting the different types of oppression that they encounter. Researchers have also noted the highest levels of collectivism, complementarity, and gender equality among Native American men and women (Darlington & Mulvaney, 2003). The chapters that follow reveal the variations as to how power is shared among ethnic minority men and women within their respective ethnic groups.

Several theorists have also noted the distinct experiences of African American women. These women have a long tradition of talking about their oppression and resistance through what Collins (1990) refers to as "breaking the silence" or "coming to voice." Because these women were forced to work outside of the home due to slavery and subsequent economic pressures, their interactions allowed them access to the hidden knowledge and tools of power and leadership that these women then leveraged in their own communities and eventually outside of their communities as they entered political arenas. An example of the leadership experiences of Black women is described as "sister power" by Reid-Merritt (1996). This power and leadership stems from understanding history, being moved by the spirit, social consciousness, principled leadership, and a commitment to carry a dedication to social change throughout all arenas from local neighborhoods to national political arenas.

Asian American, Native American, and Latina women have been stereotyped by the larger society as being passive, submissive, and preferring the private domain of home to public leadership roles. Hence, many of these women have to actively fight this stereotype by being visible, outspoken, and persistent in exposing others to recognizing power in different people (Wilson, 2004).

217

Context

Historically, leadership research focused on distinctive personality traits. However, recent research contends that effective leadership also relates strongly to context and the relationship between the characteristics of leaders and the perceived needs, goals, and circumstances of the followers (Klenke, 1996). As Deborah Rhode (2003) has noted in her edited book *The Difference "Difference" Makes*, there is no agreement as to what a difference gender, race, class, ethnicity, age, and sexual orientation can make in leadership with different groups in different contexts.

Further, the implicit masculinized context of organizations can be overlooked even by feminist leaders (Acker, 1998). Masculine gender values in organizations mediate social interactions, styles of logic, rules, contracts, directives, evaluations, and gender analyses of work tasks (Madden, 2005). The "old boys' network" is also alive and well in many institutions, and diverse women leaders are not typically members of this club. All-male networks and male-dominant contexts lead to diverse women leaders being viewed as outsiders, different, and problematic.

Diverse women leaders must immediately address the salience of their identity vis-à-vis their environment. For example, a nationally esteemed African American woman explained that when she experiences a disconnect in her work setting she must evaluate whether the issue relates to her gender, race, or both. In settings where the other participants are of the same race, she has sometimes encountered a type of "old-fashioned" sexism that she does not encounter in majority groups. An Asian American participant commented that as diverse women with multiple identities, we must examine the subtexts of messages in order to determine whether a sense of isolation or exclusion is due to our race, gender, or some other dimension of our identity.

Being the "first" or "only"

Even when diverse women strive to be attentive to the subtle clues and dynamics of subtextual messages, it is difficult for them to be objective about their experiences, particularly when they are "the only one" in the group. Many women leaders have had the experience of being dismissed, ignored, or treated paternalistically, but when they turn to male colleagues to validate their concerns about these behaviors, the men may genuinely respond that they did not notice this treatment, or the women were told that they were "being too sensitive."

The clarity that diverse women leaders have about discrimination and oppression is developed because of their lack of privilege. Those who are privileged seem to be oblivious to the experiences of diverse women leaders or, as Simone Weil stated, "someone who does not see a pane of glass does not know that she does not see it" (cited in Young, 1990, p. 39).

Moreover, individuals often subscribe to a "just world" philosophy that asserts that people generally get what they deserve and deserve what they get. So if there is a scarcity of diverse women leaders, or if they face extra barriers, a psychologically convenient rationale is that these women are not as qualified as other leaders or are lacking in their commitment (Rhode, 2003). As a result, the problems posed by minority status are frequently minimized or overlooked.

Extra challenges and stressors

Many of the diverse leaders have attributed the "little things" and micro-aggressions that they experience to a variety of factors. Although there are laws to prevent, minimize, and address blatant racism, majority members are often unaware that they operate from assumptions of similarity and shared culture, level playing fields, the "fiction of equality," and the belief that the best practice is to be "color blind." There are several results to these misguided strategies. These expose diverse women leaders to extra challenges and stress, unequal footing with peers, having to defend one's perceptions of different or negative treatment, and minimization of the contributions that they make. Worrying about the possibility that one will have to contend with these types of distortions, fictions, and misunderstandings can foster a condition that Livers and Caver (2003) have termed "miasma." This wariness, defensiveness, and alertness taxes energy, time, productivity, and creativity. It promotes the double burden of contending with increased scrutiny by others while being vigilant in attending to the possible landmines in the environment that could threaten one's status.

Diverse women may have to develop a network of trusted associates to use as a sounding board to assess and validate concerns and perceptions and to defend against miasma. In addition, individuals and organizations need to be better prepared to support, mentor, and value the differences that diverse leaders bring. The misunderstandings precipitated by different styles of leadership can result in reduced trust, overpreparing to prove one's competence, and increased guardedness

(Livers & Caver, 2003). These women often also feel the added burden of tokenism and are mindful that if they stumble, the road for others like them may become even more challenging. Muzette Hill (2003) references Jacob Herring's observation that the rules for men and women are still different with respect to how they are evaluated. For men, successes are group successes and their failures are individual failures. Hence, men are not burdened with being examples of their gender in the ways that women and diverse leaders are.

Often, diverse women leaders are so isolated that there are not enough of them to form a "critical mass" that offers support, mentoring, and reality checks on what they are experiencing. Hill (2003) notes that men have leaders to spare but in the case of diverse women leaders, any negative publicity is used against the next leader to come along. Progress will be made when one diverse woman's challenges will not set the leadership of others back. Hill argues that to move to a point where there are leadership opportunities to spare: (a) we must educate others to appreciate the value of our differences, (b) we must mentor other women and men as well so that they will be comfortable with women in leadership roles, and (c) every "first" must make it her business to guarantee that there will be a second.

When diverse women leaders are "the first" or "the only" in their groups, they have frequent experiences when colleagues give them compliments that are actually insults. Several women who were the first ethnic member or first ethnic chair in their departments were "complimented" about how articulate they were, how well they spoke, and what good English they used. One diverse leader was praised for her colloquium because she was told that she spoke so well that no one would have known that she was African American!

These are compliments that are not typically addressed to majority members. Interestingly, if women leaders comment on these slights, both majority members and their own minority group may accuse them of being overly sensitive or even paranoid. It appears that many minority members use denial and minimization to avoid dealing with these types of discrimination. The rationale appears to be that these types of insults are minor and that minorities should save their energy to address major battles only. But these "1000 points of slight" (Fassinger, 2002) are exhausting and divert the time and energy that women want to use to focus on their work responsibilities. These "slights" can also build up inside an individual and manifest themselves subsequently with health challenges.

How to Handle Discrimination or Different Treatment

Diverse women participants have noted that even if they are able to identify a particular form of discrimination, they must then address the decision point of what to do. Do they address content, process, both, or neither? There seemed to be a consensus that it was easier to address content issues in a group setting than process issues. When process issues relating to exclusion emerge, they require time, care, preparation, and perhaps meeting with individuals on a one-to-one basis in order to enact clarification, support, or perhaps remediation.

Networks and support systems

One of our diverse women leaders who has held several highly visible leadership positions acknowledged that being a diverse leader is made more difficult by solitary status. An effective strategy that this leader has developed is that when she becomes aware of some type of discriminatory treatment, she alerts her colleagues to what is happening by citing specific and concrete examples of incidents and behaviors that were challenges to her leadership or personhood. This has often led to the group taking the responsibility for addressing issues with the individuals involved rather than having the leader fulfill this function. This involvement of others has produced positive outcomes with the group and not just the minority person becoming responsible for protocol, civility, and inclusiveness. Another strategy that diverse women leaders sometimes employ is the use of humor to deflect an attack. Although this can be effective, women often feel so ambushed and unprepared for the attack that they are unable to render any response, humorous or otherwise.

Some diverse women leaders stressed the need to have a support system on an ongoing basis to deal with their feelings of isolation and invalidation. Diverse women leaders sometimes find collegiality from support staff, women in other work areas, friends, family, or in non-work organizations such as civic or religious groups, sororities, or book clubs where they can at times discuss work issues in a safe and confidential space where they are provided with peer leadership support. One leader commented that it can be very draining to be a diverse feminist leader. We need people in our lives who understand the demands that we face and activities that provide healthy distraction.

221

We also need people of various ethnic and diverse backgrounds who can mentor and/or coach these diverse women leaders outside of the work environment.

Balance

It is challenging to face all the demands of being a diverse woman leader while balancing the demands of partners, children, and self-nurturance. One participant stated that she finds that caring for herself spiritually is critical to ensuring that she is centered so that when she faces challenges she can remain balanced rather than reactive. Several women have noted the importance of reading inspirational materials, exercising, meditating, and reserving time for reflection and self-care. These leaders indicated that having a supportive partner is critical to balancing their multiple and competing demands. Couples often have to be creative in solving dual-career, long-distance, and commuter relationships.

The Intersection of Identities

Identity can comprise a variety of factors. It is also a process in which there is an interaction between how we think of ourselves and how others perceive us. Many diverse women leaders have multiple identities that are interlocking rather than additive, and each decides what components of identity are most relevant at a particular time and in a specific place. Parts of our identity may be easily seen by others. Some diverse women leaders are easily recognized by the salience of their skin color or by an obvious physical disability. Lesbian and bisexual women, and women with disabilities that are not obvious, are not necessarily recognized as diverse women leaders unless they self-identify to others. Even when women are open about having multiple diverse identities, they may feel pressured by others to prioritize only one or to assimilate to the dominant culture.

Diverse women leaders worry about how much of their identity they can reveal to others without risking censure or rejection. Issues of accents in speaking, styles of dress and hairstyles, the decision to bring a same-sex or different-race partner to a social event, or even the choices of food for meetings, are issues of identity that can be areas of criticism for diverse women leaders. Diverse women are constantly assessed against an implied norm based on majority standards, and differences in how they express their identities are commented upon and brought up for discussion. These women have acknowledged that much of their life is devoted to code-switching, which is going back and forth between the cultures of their identity and majority culture. This coping strategy can backfire if overused, however, because the tension of constantly switching on and off repeatedly can also lead to harm.

In addition, diverse women leaders often are caught in a catch-22 where they must conform to some of the standards of the majority culture, while contending with pressures from others who share aspects of their identity to challenge the status quo. Because of their leadership role, diverse women leaders are often expected (by both the majority and minority populations) to support the needs of underrepresented groups and to advocate strongly for diversity. They are challenged to fit in with the mainstream culture in order to have power and clout but not so well that they "sell out." Marie Wilson (2004) has observed that we need more diverse women leaders so that the current few are not expected to speak for an entire race or gender and carry the burden for all of us: "It is a fact that the more people like *you* in a working group, the more likely *you* are to be yourself" (p. xiii).

One nationally known leader pointed out that it is very difficult for women with disabilities to be able to balance this area of identity with others because these women lack a critical mass that allows them to reach or remain in leadership positions outside of the disability advocacy arena. This comment led to the recognition that we must find ways to support other women leaders whose areas of diversity differ from our own. In addition, we must continue to use the gifts of comfort and strength that can stem from our healthy sense of multiple identities.

Because diverse women leaders are often so isolated, we must search more actively for ways to support one another. This may require us to look within to examine our internalized homophobia, racism, sexism, ageism, and prejudices towards individuals with disabilities and majority as well as ethnic minority members. Just because we may embody one dimension of difference does not mean that we are immune to practicing subtle or blatant intolerance or bias towards other diverse leaders.

Burnout

The isolation and costs of being a diverse leader can become so demanding that many of these women feel like giving up their leadership

223

positions, and many women observing will be unwilling to step up to leadership roles. The constant challenges may lead women to feel that they are not making any progress, and their disillusionment and lack of support can lead to feelings of hopelessness and disempowerment. There was a strong sense among diverse women leaders that when an environment becomes too toxic or dysfunctional, it is definitely time to move on. One leader who has held the highest levels of executive leadership cautioned other women that it was important to give ourselves permission to step back from leadership roles when the need arose and to perhaps return after a period of revitalization.

Another suggestion for when we are feeling overtaxed is to seek input from trusted advisors, mentors, or colleagues to gain a greater sense of perspective about leaving or remaining in a leadership position. This is a key step because, when we are feeling overwhelmed and focused on the pain of our leadership role, we are not able to evaluate our situations objectively. Securing other perspectives is necessary prior to making a major decision.

Part of the solution to the sense of burnout and isolation can come from involving others. We need to channel more women into leadership opportunities by using natural training experiences that can be found in sororities, civic and social organizations, and faith communities. We can decrease the stress that current diverse leaders experience by offering them support and encouragement. Diverse leaders might also receive help in sharing the leadership load by inviting other women into positions of responsibility. There are many strong and competent potential leaders who do not feel comfortable about volunteering themselves for leadership roles and do not self-identify as leaders but are happy to serve if asked. Each diverse women leader must continually identify potential leaders and help mentor them with an "each one, teach one" philosophy.

Understanding and Addressing the "Rules" of One's Organization

Every organization has its own unique culture and way of operating. It is important for all individuals to know the "rules of the game" for their respective organizations. Although it is clear that successful leaders must know and conform to the rules of their organization, this is not necessarily a straightforward task, especially in the case of diverse feminist leaders. Rules vary across organizations so successful strategies in one environment may not transfer well to a new setting. In addition, difficulty in adhering to the rules stems from the fact that many of the most important rules in organizations are unwritten and unspoken. You will not find these rules in a manual or policy document.

The first dilemma diverse women leaders face is finding out what these loosely documented rules are. In this discussion, we are not implying that you need to adopt these rules or follow them. But what is important is that you are aware of them so that you will be able to make a conscious decision on whether you choose to follow the rules or not. This may help diverse women leaders to be able to better predict how they will be received, and minimize surprises.

One example that was discussed was that in some organizations making "authoritarian" decisions is part of the accepted management practice, which makes it one of the "rules." But among diverse women leaders, there is a tendency for many of us to operate more collaboratively. Understanding the rules will enable you to modify your style, yet still accomplish your goals using your preferred leadership style. You will need to be conscious of how to do this. In this example, in order to be seen as a credible and authoritative leader, you might still collaborate in getting the facts, but ensure that the leaders in the organization know that "you" made the final decision.

Another point to note is that many times just when you think you know the rules of the game, they change or they are not applied consistently or fairly because of your gender, race, sexual orientation, or ability status. The rules can change at any time, especially when there is a change in leadership. Finally, we need to realize that these rules are not shared openly, so it is up to diverse women leaders to find creative ways to understand these rules so that they will be able to minimize the time they spend on this type of "political" activity, and spend more time meeting and exceeding the objectives of the organization.

Conclusions

Given the many challenges of being a diverse women leader, the chapters that follow and the conference call point to the fact that these leadership roles are not for the faint of heart. In order to facilitate the growth and retention of diverse feminist leaders we must collaborate with each other, men, and majority women to change the rules and transform organizations to make them more congruent for diverse women. As Fannie Lou Hamer so eloquently stated:

> Whether you have a Ph.D. or no D, we're in this bag together. And whether you're from Morehouse or no house, we're still in this bag together. Not to fight to try to liberate ourselves from the men—this is another trick to get us fighting among ourselves—but to work together ... then we will have a better chance to just act as human beings, and to be treated as human beings ... (Price & Markham, 1994, p. 431)

Note

1 Contributors: Asuncion Miteria Austria, Martha Banks, Lorene Garrett-Browder, Jean Lau Chin, Toy Caldwell-Colbert, Jessica Henderson Daniel, Jeanette Hsu, Norine Johnson, Marlene Maheu, Ann Yabusaki.

References

Acker, J. (1998). Hierarchies, jobs and bodies: A theory of gendered organizations. In K. A. Myers, C. D. Anderson, & B. J. Risman (Eds.), *Feminist foundations: Towards transforming sociology* (pp. 299–317). Thousand Oaks, CA: Sage.

Appelbaum, S. H., Audet, L., & Miller, J. C. (2003). Gender and leadership? Leadership and gender? A journey through the landscape of theories. *Leadership and Organization Development Journal, 24*(1), 43–51.

Aronson, J., Quinn, D. M., & Spencer, S. J. (1998). Stereotype threat and the academic underperformance of minorities and women. In J. K. Swim & C. Stangor (Eds.), *Prejudice: The target's perspective* (pp. 83–103). San Diego, CA: Academic Press.

Carli, L. L. (1999). Gender, interpersonal power, and social influence. *Journal of Social Issues, 55*(1), 81–99.

Carli, L. L., & Eagly, A. H. (2001). Gender, hierarchy, and leadership: An introduction. *Journal of Social Issues, 57*(4), 629–636.

Collins, P. H. (1990). *Black feminist thought: Knowledge, consciousness, and the power of empowerment.* Boston, MA: Unwin Hyman.

Darlington, P. S. E., & Mulvaney, B. M. (2003). *Women, power, and ethnicity: Working toward reciprocal empowerment.* New York: The Haworth Press.

Eagly, A., Makhijani, M., & Klonsky, B. (1992). Gender and the evaluation of leaders: A meta-analysis. *Psychological Bulletin, 117,* 125–145.

Fassinger, R. (2002, January). *When familiarity breeds content: The management of similarity in women's relationships.* Paper presented at the Kaleidoscope of

Women's Lives: Complexities and Challenges of Psychotherapy with Women, Midwinter Conference for APA divisions 17, 35, 45, 49. Austin, TX.

Gilkes, C. T. (1983). Going up for the oppressed: The career mobility of black women community workers. *Journal of Social Issues, 39*(3), 115–139.

Helgesen, S. (1995). *The female advantage: Women's ways of leadership.* New York: Doubleday.

Hill, M. (2003). Where have all the sisters gone? In D. Rhodes (Ed.), *The difference "difference" makes: Women and leadership* (pp. 98–101). Stanford, CA.

Jamieson, K. H. (1995). *Beyond the double bind: Women and leadership.* New York: Oxford University Press.

Klenke, K. (1996). *Women and leadership: A contextual perspective.* New York: Springer Publishing Co.

Livers, A., & Caver, K. (2003). *Leading in black and white: Working across the racial divide in corporate America.* San Francisco: Jossey-Bass.

Lykes, M. B., & Stewart, A. J. (1986). Evaluating the feminist challenge to research in personality and social psychology. *Psychology of Women Quarterly, 10*, 393–412.

Madden, M. (2005). Gender and leadership in higher education. *Psychology of Women Quarterly, 29*(1), 3–14.

Mayo, C. (1982). Training for positive marginality. In C. L. Bickman (Ed.), *Applied Social Psychology Annual, 3* (pp. 57–73). Beverly Hills, CA: Sage.

Moya, P. M. L. (2001). Chicana feminism and post-modernist theory. *Signs: Journal of Women in Culture and Society, 26*(2), 441–483.

Price, B., & Markham, A. P. (1994). Fannie Lou Townsend Hamer. In K. K. Campbell (Ed.), *Women public speakers in the United States, 1925–1993: A biographical sourcebook* (pp. 424–435). Westport, CT: Greenwood Press.

Reid-Merritt, P. (1996). *Sisterpower: How phenomenal black women are rising to the top.* New York: John Wiley and Sons.

Rhode, D. (2003). The difference "difference" makes. In D. Rhodes (Ed.), *The difference "difference" makes: Women and leadership* (pp. 3–50). Stanford, CA: Stanford University Press.

Wilson, M. C. (2004). *Closing the leadership gap.* New York: Viking Penguin.

Young, I. M. (1990). *Justice and the politics of difference.* Princeton, NJ: Princeton University Press.

Chapter 10

Increasing Diverse Women Leadership in Corporate America: Climbing Concrete Walls and Shattering Glass Ceilings!

Penny Sanchez, Phillip Hucles,
Janis Sanchez-Hucles, and Sanjay C. Mehta

In this chapter, we discuss many of the problems facing corporate America in its quest to transcend traditional norms and improve leadership opportunities for diverse women. There has been progress in the growth of diverse women leaders. One manager of color has noted: "we are what they said we could not become" (Livers & Caver, 2003, p. ix). Yet there are still major barriers to overcome. A 2002 study showed that only 163 or 1.6% of 13,673 corporate officers were women of color compared to 15.7% or 2,140 White women (Catalyst, 2002). These results do not conform to the demographic representation of these women in the workforce. Further, they do not reflect the intentions of diverse women, as 85% of women of color versus 70% of White women aspire to leadership and 53% versus 45% want to be in the top leadership positions (Catalyst, 1999).

Research indicates that diverse women leaders must contend with double or multiple marginalization produced by the intersection of gender, race, and other dimensions of identity. The experiences of diverse women leaders have some similarity to those of majority women and minority men but they also face unique obstacles that have been ignored until recently due to their "double outsider" or "double token" status of race and gender. Women of color have noted that it is impossible for them to compartmentalize their experiences as due to race, gender, or work–family issues as these challenges interact and lead to different consequences for them than other workers.

Over the last 20 years, research has finally been conducted on and among diverse women in corporate America and findings indicate that these women show slower rates of advancement which appears related to more limited mentoring, networking, and role models as compared to other workers (Catalyst, 1999). The equality movement has led to "whitewashing," that is, more benefits for White women such as faster promotions and higher salaries than for women of color, and has led to different experiences, consequences, and perceptions (Bell & Nkomo, 2001; Betters-Reed & Moore, 1995).

The sexism experienced by majority women has been described as a "glass ceiling." However, diverse women in corporate America encounter a "concrete wall" or "sticky floor" that they must first overcome before they can contend with the sexism of the glass ceiling. Bell and Nkomo (2001) suggest that the racialized sexism that women of color encounter can be visualized as a two-dimensional concrete wall topped by a glass ceiling. This concrete barrier precludes a vision of the glass ceiling and is denser and more difficult to penetrate as it is constructed of the following obstacles: racism, higher standards, over-scrutiny, stereotypes, double outsider status, invisibility and hypervisibility, exclusion from information networks, challenges to authority and credibility, lack of "fit" in the workplace, work–family conflict, and weak or nonexistent commitment to the advancement of diverse individuals (Bell & Nkomo, 2001; Catalyst, 2001).

In this chapter we explore the history of diversification in the workplace as it applies to diverse women leaders in corporate America. We examine the models that have been used to increase the representation of diverse leaders. We offer an overview of the experiences of these women with respect to barriers and challenges. Finally, we make recommendations for increasing the numbers of diverse women leaders in corporate America through greater inclusion. To date, corporate America has allowed greater access without addressing more complex issues that must be restructured to ensure continued promotions and retention. Current policies that view diversity as a business initiative to promote profits and as a way to reflect the demographics and increase communication fail to address the historical and structural use of power in organizations and the resistance to social justice and the sharing of power and privilege (Giscombe & Mattis, 2002). It is clear that proactive strategies and new paradigms are required in order to help diverse women leaders shatter glass and concrete ceilings.

Although there is an extensive literature on gender and leadership, there is a paucity of information on the intersection of leadership and gender with various additional dimensions of diversity such as race, sexual orientation, ability status, and culture. Hence, this review will focus primarily on racial diversity as this is the area that has been most extensively explored.

History of Diverse Women Leadership in Corporate America

Affirmative action, diversity initiatives, and caucuses

In 1961, President Kennedy announced Executive Order 10925 calling for affirmative action to ensure that applicants are treated equally without regard to race, color, religion, sex, or national origin. This was the start of a prodigious legal and social battle that was designed to help alleviate years of discrimination. Legislation was passed and amended to ensure that diversification occurred in the workplace because it was shown that diversification benefited companies. After President Kennedy, President Johnson mandated that affirmative action be used to expand jobs for minorities in his Executive Order 11246, and a year later amended it to include women.

While the use of affirmative action led to important advances for women and minorities, it has also stimulated a backlash of opposition with opponents who claimed that it discriminates against nonminorities. Women and minorities were often hired but then faced problems of both overt and covert racial and gender discrimination. Women and minorities found themselves excluded from informal networks of support, information, and mentoring that other sales and managerial staff enjoyed (Pearse & Zrebiec, 1997). In response to this lack of inclusion at the Xerox corporation, seven black caucus groups were formed around the United States. These organizations functioned as self-help groups to prepare Black employees for promotions and as pressure groups to push for policy changes within the corporate structure (Pearse & Zrebiec, 1997).

In another example of how companies responded to the need to diversify, in the late 1990s, Georgia Power put together a diversity program that specifically targeted affinity groups of ethnic minorities and women. The major focus of these groups was mentoring, sharing survival tactics and career strategies, diversity training, and supervisor accountability. The results reflected a 50% increase in the hiring of women and minorities and an increase from 0 to 10% in women executives (Potwora, 2006).

Minority status and identity.   Unfortunately, progress has been uneven since the initiation of caucuses. Although racial and gender caucuses made significant strides to help improve the chances of success within corporate America, they were not prepared to address the complexities of multiple and intersecting identities across race, gender, sexual orientation, and disability and the impact of these dimensions on leadership. Basic gender and racial stereotypes were still employed but operated differently across diverse dimensions of identity. Corporate America opened its doors a few inches to minorities and women but guarded the keys to the penthouse suites.

Diverse women leaders faced multiple stereotypes from racism, sexism, and discrimination because they simply did not "fit in." When these women chose to reflect their cultural identities at work, they risked emphasizing their difference and lack of fit with majority norms and ideals. Diverse women also did not completely resonate with White women's groups. This was because White women shared White racial privilege with White males and used this status to their advantage. They appealed to the senior White male leaders by reminding them that they represented their sisters and daughters. Finally it was noted that White females were not complete newcomers to the corporate world because of the historical access afforded to them through their relationships with White men. It was evident that White females fit in more comfortably than did diverse women as they claimed key positions and began to move up the ladder within the corporation. Despite the widespread perception that diverse women represented a "two for one" advantaged status in hiring and promotion, it was actually White females who became the minority of choice.

Work experiences in different racial/ethnic groups

According to recent data, women of color participation in management, professional, and related occupations is at the following levels: African American, 2,483,000 or 5% of managerial and professional positions;

231

Asian Americans, 1,285,000 or 2.6 %; Latinas, 1,632,000 or 3.3%; Native American data are unavailable (Bureau of Labor Statistics, 2005).

Because these women are deemed nontraditional, they are vulnerable to unique pressures, challenges, and misunderstandings as they strive to understand their role in difficult interactions versus the responsibilities of others. This constant sense of vigilance and unease has been called "miasma" and may lead to reduced trust, a belief that these women must work twice as hard, and the perception that they must be careful and guarded in their interactions with others (Livers & Caver, 2003). Meanwhile, majority members may be unaware of the different work experiences that women of color face but may only be aware of strain and awkwardness in interactions. These diverse women leaders may also feel a significant degree of isolation as the majority of these women are exposed to racial and gender jokes that offend them, but majority members seem not to notice these slights and White females seem less sensitive to gender bias (Bell & Nkomo, 2001).

African American women. In a 2004 study by Catalyst, African American women managers continue to face challenges different from other majority and minority men and women. More than half of these women managers had graduate educations, their promotion experiences were similar to Latinas and higher than for Asian American managers, but overall these women saw their opportunities to move to higher leadership positions eroding despite corporate diversity initiatives. Lighter skinned African American managers reported more satisfaction with their pay and opportunities for promotions than did their darker skinned cohorts. Across skin color these women believed that they faced intransigent negative stereotypes and questioning of their authority and credibility, they had more conflicting relationships with White females than with other women of color, and they had to contend with inconsistent support from their companies. All of these dynamics lead these women to be guarded and sensitive about discussing race and personal issues. In addition, the historical legacy of slavery has made it difficult for African American women to seek out and be accepted for mentoring by White males (Bell & Nkomo, 2001).

In contrast, the unique experiences of African American women have also facilitated areas of strength and resiliency. They have the insight and behavior afforded by being bicultural; they build positive relationships with others; and they use their "outsider within" status to communicate directly, detect subtle nuances, and to challenge rules and norms (Catalyst, 2004a).

232

Asian American women.   Although Asian American managers have higher educational attainment than other women of color, they are less likely to be born in the United States and they are less likely to obtain high level supervisory or line jobs. Barriers to their advancement include lack of key relationships with managers and others who facilitate career advancement, fewer informal networks, more family and elder care responsibilities, and they are less likely to have a mentor. Cultural factors also appear to mediate the experience of Asian women. Specifically, values of humility, respect for authority, and a strong work ethic that minimizes social interactions may run counter to accepted corporate tactics of assertiveness, self-promotion, and networking. These pressures can be especially acute for less acculturated women (Catalyst, 2003a).

Latinas.   Latina managers, like Asian American women managers, vary greatly in their levels of acculturation and whether they were born in the United States. What they share in common with other diverse women leaders are challenges in developing role models, sponsors, mentors, and informal networks. Most Latinas have a strong allegiance to family and frequently cite family commitments as impediments to their advancement. Because 20% report that they care for elderly relatives, company policies that decrease work/family pressure are important. About one third of these managers have a graduate education (Catalyst, 2003b).

American Indian women.   In one of the few empirical studies of American Indian managers, Helen Muller (1998) notes that the "living in two worlds" phenomenon that is often experienced by diverse leaders is even more profound for these women. To be a female leader in a business can violate traditional tribal gender expectations, and to work in corporate America can risk the retraumatization of the cultural assaults that these women have historically endured. Because American Indian women come from a collectivist versus an individualist culture, they face many disconnects in assuming leadership including discomfort and unfamiliarity with Anglo values of assertiveness and competition, linear orientation to time, taking pride in work and academic achievements, prioritizing work motivation over community and family activities, using communication differently to show dominance rather than mutuality, and they must contend with discrimination and stereotyping. Because American Indian women come from a tradition that values female leadership more so than the majority culture, gender bias is difficult for these women to accept. These differences lead many American Indian women to seek leadership in tribal communities rather than in corporate America. Those women who choose to work in corporate organizations adapt by code-switching, that is, altering their behaviors in accord to their locations and their tribal and work cultures. These women balance their two worlds by choosing work environments where these different values can coexist. The ability to achieve this balance appears to be a sign of their managerial skill and leadership.

Balanced workforce strategy

In the mid-1980s a "balanced workforce" strategy (Tucker & Thompson, 1990) became the model used by human resource departments. This new model was deemed superior to affirmative action. Most companies at this time were seeking a balance in their hiring and wanted the corporation to reflect the representation of women, men, and people of color within their communities. An example of this is seen at IBM, where human resource personnel report to its board of directors on the status of their "global workforce diversity." After setting the goals, progress is reviewed annually to determine if the goals have been achieved (Catalyst, 2004b). As a result of the balanced workforce approach, all groups of employees were now considered when reviewing the company's success with hiring and promoting employees, and minority females were now in a separate category, no longer part of the overall "female" category.

Backlash and complacency

During the 1970s and 1980s the focus was on creating a diverse workforce with the belief that competitive advantage was linked with the diversification of U.S. citizenry. But as we left the 1990s and went into the 2000s, most corporations became complacent about diversity. They felt that they had made enough progress and they became more focused on "business survival." Any inquiries about a decline in the commitment to diversity was answered to the effect that diversity was still a key business priority and that they had hired a diversity manager.

The virulent backlash against affirmative action also led companies to halt their diversity initiatives. White males believed that affirmative action policies hindered their employment and advancement. The stereotype developed that any time women or minorities were hired into top level positions, they were affirmative action hires and more qualified people were denied the position because they were not women or minorities. As with other stereotypes, once entered into mainstream popular culture, it became another obstacle for diverse women to overcome in order to land top leadership positions and convince their followers that they were capable of leading.

Multiculturalism and diversity as a business initiative

Committing to multiculturalism means ensuring that your senior leadership team and board of directors reflect the diversity of your workforce and your customers. Using this focus allows the corporation to attain the highest levels of success. Evidence suggests that this is true. One study by Catalyst showed that "companies with the most women executives had a 34 percent higher return to shareholders" (Potwora, 2006).

Factual data supporting the link between gender diversity and corporate performance can be found. A Catalyst study conducted in 2004 found a positive correlation between the gender diversity of top management teams and the financial performance of companies. These findings confirmed Catalyst's overall belief in the business impact of gender diversity. As stated in the study, "In companies that focus on diversity—developing and leveraging women's talent—the relationship to the bottom line is remarkable" (Catalyst, 2004b, p. 2).

Fletcher, Bolinger, and Williams (2002) assert that business leaders see the handwriting on the wall, and are moving in the direction of using diversity programs to develop more human capital within minority and women's communities. These authors note that presently diversity initiatives exist mainly in employment opportunities within the corporation, and not yet on corporate boards. Statistics reinforce this perspective as diverse women leaders are still encountering a cement wall at the place where leadership and change should originate—the board level. Women of color are the most underrepresented group as they comprised only 2% of 11,500 Fortune 1000 board seats in 2002 out of a total of 986 or 13.7% of seats held by women (Floyd, 2003). Women of color represent 18% of women board members, with 74% African American, 17% Latinas, and 8.4% Asian Pacific Islanders. With the onset of recent scandals, megabankruptcies, retirements, stricter rules for accountability by board members, and the public's questioning of various policies and procedures, changes are taking place on corporate boards. These changes will hopefully lead to more opportunities for diverse women leaders to serve.

235

Diverse Female Leaders and Leadership Theories

Corporate America has learned that in order to train their future leaders, they must provide leadership models. However, many of these models do not fit the needs of a diverse corporate America. For the most part, many of the leadership models focus on the leaders themselves rather than the corporation as a whole (Rost, 1993). If leaders do not know how to stimulate the needs of a diverse workforce, then they will never be able to positively impact their corporation. Similarly, a diverse female leader will not be able to learn how to lead her corporation through such models. Some companies have tried to focus on simple trait and behavioral theories in order to show their future leaders the themes that great leaders have shown, but these theories fail to account for individual differences in perspective, customs, and culture.

Another historical approach to understanding leadership involves behavior models which focus on the actions of leaders rather than their traits. However, these behavior theories have not proven to be necessary and sufficient to include the creation and acceptance of a diverse group of female leaders.

In addition to the numerous difficulties diverse women face which put them at a disadvantage in gaining positions of leadership within the corporate world, they also must contend with the reality that White male leaders fail to see the benefits of managerial styles and personal qualities of these women because their leadership styles differ from their own.

Vilkinas and Cartan (1997) looked at perceptions of male and female managers from all levels of various public and private companies. Peers, subordinate staff, and even female managers themselves all rated women higher than men on anywhere from two to five of eight managerial roles. However, the male supervisors of the managers in question did not perceive any significant differences between these male and female managers. The authors point out that these findings suggest a marginalization of the abilities that women possess as managers. Another alarming trend within the study was the fact that female managers were continually rated as less superior by supervisors as they climbed the hierarchy of the corporate ladder. Subordinates rated women higher on five of the managerial roles but supervisors rated no difference between the sexes. This suggests a lack of recognition for the contributions of female managers by supervisors due to not valuing qualities different from their own or simply marginalizing the ability of women to lead.

It might seem that a simple solution to gaining support for diverse women leaders would be to adopt masculine styles of leadership. Yoder (2001) points to previous research that suggests that it does not aid women if they adopt masculine forms of leadership and it can in fact hurt their efforts to be viewed as competent leaders. For example, high levels of assertiveness are not looked upon as being as positive within female individuals as within male individuals (Carli, 1999). Instead of valuing only one style of leadership that is based on White male leadership styles, organizations could benefit from multiple leadership styles that are complementary to each other, with each contributing its own strengths and weaknesses to the situation. Several studies suggest that one of the key ways to ensure that women are taken more seriously in managerial positions is for companies to recognize the unique benefits of having diverse forms of leadership represented within the company, which would allow them to cope effectively with the largest variety of problems.

Thus, while many companies and managers are actively trying not to practice discrimination openly based on membership in a minority group, they need to be educated on the role that other forms of leadership can play in their companies, and made to understand that the qualities that White males possess are not the only ones which make a successful leader. While it is difficult to get individuals to realize that a different set of qualities may be equally or more helpful in certain managerial situations (particularly if the current group of managers is not familiar or comfortable with these traits), it is the only way to stop innate prejudices over the qualities a person subjectively feels makes a valuable leader. Without this realization on the part of corporations, diverse women leaders will continue to face difficulty obtaining corporate leadership positions, becoming prisoners to their own diverse and unique backgrounds.

Parker and Ogilvie (1996) observe that the leadership literature recognizes both a male and a female model based on middle-class White Americans. They assert that these models are inadequate for understanding other culturally distinct groups because gender does not operate similarly across racial/gender groups and that these models ignore the unique socialization of other cultural groups by assuming that racism and sexism are parallel processes. These authors propose a culturally distinct model of leadership for African American women based on their styles, traits, behaviors, and their unique social location within dominant culture organizations. We need more theories along these lines that help us understand the diversity of culturally distinct leadership styles exemplified by diverse women leaders.

What are the Barriers to Diverse Women Ascending to Top Leadership Positions?

Stereotypes

Although we have made progress in corporate America, the numbers of female and diverse female CEOs in large corporations are still relatively low. There are many reasons for this low number including lack of line experience, inadequate career opportunities, gender differences in speech and socialization, gender-based stereotypes, old boy networks, and tokenism (Oakley, 2000).

However, according to a Catalyst study (2005), women leaders cite stereotypes as the top barrier to their advancement. For diverse women leaders, stereotypes can be quite complex. Madden (2005), in a summary of the intersection of ethnicity with leadership, reports that ethnic stereotypes for women can lead to status differences; that racial stereotypes can be more pervasive than those based on gender; that many women of color must contend with sexual stereotypes; and that token status may lead to inaccurate assessment of work productivity and unrealistic expectations that can promote burnout, fatigue, and unwillingness to seek high level positions.

It is also important to recognize that stereotypes can affect diverse women leaders not only through the perceptions of others but through their own self-perceptions. Working in hostile environments, challenges to authority and credibility, feeling the need to work twice as hard and still struggle to gain recognition can erode even the most resilient self-esteem over time and can lead to diminished performance, health concerns, burnout, and work separations.

Many people studying leadership argue that one of the biggest stereotypes is the word "leader" because many associate the word with men. This is one of the first stereotypes that women leaders have to overcome. A 2005 Catalyst study found that gender stereotypes tend to portray women as lacking the very qualities that people typically associate with effective leadership. As a result, they often create inaccurate perceptions that women leaders just don't measure up to men. Traditional definitions and stereotypes of leadership are often too narrow to include diverse women. Leadership models based on White males put pressure on diverse women leaders to abandon their unique cultural identities and conform to the majority culture. Not being true to their cultural identities puts undue strain on these leaders and may lead to feelings of psychological emptiness or invisibility. Ella Bell and Stella Nkomo (2001) have noted that diverse women leaders may encounter a unique dilemma. They are often very visible due to their race, gender, or other diverse status but are expected to obscure their cultural identities and experiences. We must find ways to redefine leadership to include diverse women and eliminate stereotypes that suggest that women cannot be effective leaders.

Glass ceilings versus concrete walls

Approximately 75% of Fortune 500 companies have a formal diversity program (Catalyst, 2004b). However, most diverse women leaders feel that diversity policies are not effective in helping to create inclusive work environments or in addressing racism. Specifically, 66% of African American women and 55% of Latinas felt that subtle biases were not addressed by diversity policies at their companies and only 9% of Asian women felt they have benefited from the diversity programs at their companies (Potwora, 2006).

A recent Catalyst study suggested that well-run diversity programs should look at human resource data and analyze it to determine if women of color are actually benefiting from their diversity initiatives. In addition, these programs should deal with resistance to diversity initiatives (backlash), encourage open dialogue on the benefits of these initiatives, make available informal and formal mentor programs, and establish diversity councils, diversity task forces, and employee networks. They should use these groups to help discover real solutions that will have lasting impact on companies (Potwora, 2006).

Mentoring

One of the interesting enablers for diverse women leaders has been seeking out and utilizing mentors. Since this group of leaders has been excluded from informal networks, mentors help them learn the rules of the game and offer needed support.

In a 2004 Catalyst study that examined the advancement of diverse women, 38% of African American women, 33% of Latinas, and 27% of Asian women indicated that they had a mentor. In a 1990 study by

Thomas, he examined 487 mentor–protégé relationships in the WRL Corporation (a major public utility company in the Northeast), which is 10% Black and 30% female. Although White men formed the majority of mentors for all races and genders, and disproportionately for White males and females, only Black females had a relatively even distribution of mentors by race and gender. Thomas concludes that these data indicate that Black women are able to transcend gender and race boundaries to create resourceful mentoring relationships. An alternative explanation that is of concern is to note that Black women were *least likely* to be mentored by those individuals with typically the most power and stature in the organization, that is, White males. These are the individuals who can assign them to highly visible projects and who make decisions about promotions to line versus staff positions that are more beneficial to advancement. It is also significant that in Thomas's study he found that psychosocial support was most evident in same-race versus cross-race mentoring. More research is needed to facilitate the understanding of how diverse women leaders can receive the most effective mentoring.

The old boy's network

In addition to the major barriers of stereotyping and mentoring there is an additional concern that the current corporate leaders and CEOs don't want to "share their power." According to Judith Oakley (2000), the "old boy's network" is alive and well. Most research focuses on the challenge that newcomers pose as a threat to the ever-increasing salaries and perks of the selective males at the top of the club (Gordon, 1995). It is important to note that what is at stake is even more basic than financial rewards; it is the unwillingness of those with power to share it. The "old boy's network" is a solid barrier to diverse women leaders because it filters out those who they believe can lead and those who they believe should not be allowed to lead.

Barriers summarized

Based on these facts, it is clear what areas we need to improve if we expect to see a major increase in diverse female CEOs in the future. These females have stated it quite clearly with many supporting studies:

1. Eliminate stereotyping and preconceptions of roles and abilities;
2. End the "old boy's network";
3. Connect with influential sponsors;

4. Increase informal networks of communication;
5. Increase diverse women role models;
6. Develop mandatory diversity programs that decrease racism, increase career development, and that hold managers accountable for results;
7. Increase line experience and highly visible and challenging assignments;
8. Allow for flexibility in meeting personal and family responsibilities (Catalyst, 1999, 2001).

Taking these steps signals to diverse women leaders that senior leadership in corporations are committed to diversity and to creating a work environment that is supportive, inclusive, and respectful of their cultural identities (Mattis, 2001).

Redefining leadership

In addition to taking proactive steps, we need to help redefine leadership. In most studies that have looked at leadership differences between men and women, stereotypes rather than major differences stood out. The old leadership model of command and control, and top-down leadership, is truly a male-dominated model that is outdated. David Gergen, former Director of the Center for Public Leadership, asserted that a new leadership approach is evolving, called "the influence model of leadership." This model persuades, empowers, collaborates, and partners for success. If he is right, diverse women leaders will finally become part of the definition of leadership (Gogoi, 2006). We must also strive to develop more culturally distinctive leadership theories that recognize the unique experiences of diverse women.

Summary and Conclusions

The economics of corporate America indicate that it will need qualified workers in the years to come. If they do not address current barriers for diverse women leaders, vast reservoirs of talent will be lost as these future leaders for corporate America will elect to start their own businesses rather than fight the battles in corporate America. Currently, women of color are opening business ventures at twice the rate of all women-owned businesses (Potwora, 2006).

241

In order for men to continue to enjoy the benefits of corporate America, they must change their strategies. Rather than keeping the door to their exclusive club closed, they must learn to permit greater access and share the power in order for their profits to continue. Diversity programs can be used to improve the work cultures for all employees, and companies will need to be "proactive" to retain diverse women leaders at their companies—because the competition for the skilled leader will be greatly enhanced over the next five years.

It is imperative that corporations understand that diversity training is more than a program of minimizing racism and that commitment to diversity means sharing power, not just adding to profits. Corporations must train and hold all employees accountable, from the CEO to the entry-level employee, for understanding and implementing inclusion, respect for difference, eliminating stereotyping and the old boy's network, and learning new strategies to share power. Workshops and e-learning can be major resources to reach many employees while not hindering corporations' ability to achieve a profit.

As diverse women leaders continue to rise to power in major corporations, they will need to be the leaders of not only their company, but of a new era of equality for underrepresented leaders in the workplace. While many changes have been made in the past 40 years, more will be needed. We believe that a "new revolution" is needed to significantly increase diverse female leaders in corporate America, even if progress comprises many small victories.

This revolution will need to come from the corporations' leadership and also from "grass roots" initiatives. We need to learn from the past, but execute change using today's technology and today's tactics to be effective. We will need a few very strong corporate leaders to "lead by example" and support diverse women leaders in many different roles, but especially in the top positions. Boardroom Bound highlights that the "first movers" will be able to benefit from the large population of talented women and minorities to create better balance in the boardrooms (Fletcher et al., 2002).

As dismal as this picture might look today, we are optimistic that it will eventually change. Corporations will need diverse women workers more than ever in the near future, because the U.S. Dept. of Labor predicts a labor shortage by 2010 (Tischler, 2004, p. 52). Stanford economist Edward Lazear asserts that companies will create new work environments to prevent the attrition of women from corporate America. He forecasts that 20% of CEOs will be women in 15 to 20 years (Tischler,

2004, p. 53). We believe that by educating corporate America today on these issues, we will be able to move that timeline up. As we always want to do in corporate America—let's overachieve that goal. Let's get to that 20% number much faster than in 15–20 years!

References

Bell, E. L. J., & Nkomo, S. (2001). *Our separate ways: Black and white women and the struggles for professional identity*. Boston, MA: Harvard Business School Press.

Betters-Reed, B., & Moore, L. (1995). Shifting the management and development paradigm for women. *Journal of Management Development, 14*, 24–38.

Bureau of Labor Statistics. (2005). Current Population Survey, Table 1. Employed and experienced unemployed persons by detailed occupation, sex, race, and Hispanic or Latin ethnicity, Annual Average 2005. Unpublished data.

Carli, L. L. (1999). Gender, interpersonal power, and social influence. *Journal of Social Issues, 55*, 991–994.

Catalyst (1999). *Women of color in corporate management: Opportunities and barriers*. New York: Catalyst.

Catalyst (2001). *Women of color executives: Their voices, their journeys*. Catalyst Publication code D48, ISBN#0-89584-216-5. Retrieved August 9, 2006 from http://www.catalystwomen.org/files/full/Women%20of%20Color%20Executives%20-%20Their%20Voices,%20Their%20Journeys.pdf

Catalyst (2002). *Catalyst census of women corporate officers and top earners in the Fortune 500*. Retrieved September 4, 2006 from www.Catalystwomen.org/files/COTE%20Factsheet%202002updated.pdf

Catalyst (2003a). *Advancing Asian women in the workplace: What managers need to know*. New York: Catalyst.

Catalyst (2003b). *Advancing Latinas in the workplace: What managers need to know*. Retrieved August 9, 2006 from http://www.catalystwomen.org/files/fact/WOC%20Latina%20Factsheet.pdf

Catalyst (2004a). *Advancing African-American Women in the workforce: What managers need to know*. New York: Catalyst.

Catalyst (2004b). *The bottom line: Connecting corporate performance and gender diversity*. Catalyst Publication code D58, ISBN #0-89584-244-0. Retrieved August 9, 2006 from http://www.catalystwomen.org/files/full/financialperformancereport.pdf

Catalyst (2005). *Women "take care", men "take charge": Stereotyping of US business leaders exposed*. Catalyst Publication D62, ISBN #0-89584-252-1. Retrieved August 9, 2006 from http://www.rochester.edu/SBA/100years/PDFs/Women%20Take%20Care%20Men%20Take%20Charge.pdf

Fletcher, A., Bollinger, L., & Williams III, S. (2002). *The next frontier*. Retrieved September 4, 2006 from www.boardroombound.biz/research.html

Floyd, K. (2003, September). Women of color and the corporate boardroom: Breaking through the "cement ceiling." *Interfaith Center on Corporate Responsibility: The Corporate Examiner.* Retrieved May 15, 2006 from www.iccr.org/publications/examiner_pastarticles/examiner_Cementceiling.php

Giscombe, K., & Mattis, M. C. (2002). Leveling the playing field for women of color in corporate management: Is the business case enough? *Journal of Business Ethics, 37,* 103–119.

Gogoi, P. (2006). Heading for the top then and now. *Pink Magazine, 4,* 69–71.

Gordon, A. (1995). The work of corporate culture: Diversity management. *Social Text, 44,* 3–30.

Livers, A. B., & Caver, K. A. (2003). *Leading in black and white: Working across the racial divide in Corporate America.* San Francisco: Jossey Bass.

Madden, M. (2005). Gender and leadership in higher education. *Psychology of Women Quarterly,* 29(1), 3–14.

Mattis, M. C. (2001). Advancing women in business organizations: Key leadership roles and behaviors of senior leaders and middle managers. *Journal of Management Development, 20,* pp. 371–388.

Muller, H. J. (1998). American Indian women managers: Living in two worlds. *Journal of Management Inquiry,* 7(1), 4–28.

Oakley, J. G. (2000). Gender-based barriers to senior management positions: Understanding the scarcity of female CEOs. *Journal of Business Ethics,* 27(4), 321–334.

Parker, P. S., & Ogilvie, D. T. (1996). Gender, culture and leadership: Toward a culturally distinct model of African-American women executives' leadership strategies. *Leadership Quarterly,* 7(2), 189–214.

Pearse, R. F., & Zrebiec, D. A. (1997). A diversity management in the total quality organization. *Compensation and Benefits Management,* 13(2), 43–49.

Potwora, J. (2006, Feb/March). Concrete ceilings. *Pink Magazine,* 1(5), 63–66.

Rost, J. C. (1993). *Leadership for the twenty-first century.* Westport, CT: Praeger.

Thomas, D. A. (1990). The impact of race on managers' experiences of developmental relationships: An intra-organizational study. *Journal of Organizational Behavior, 11,* 479–492.

Tischler, L. (2004, February). Where are the women? *Fast Company Magazine, 79,* 52.

Tucker, S. H., & Thompson, K. D. (1990, November). Will diversity = opportunity + advancement for blacks? *Black Enterprise Magazine.* Retrieved April 30, 2006 from aad.english.ucsb.edu/docs/BE-11-90.html

Vilkinas, T., & Cartan, G. (1997). How different are the roles displayed by female and male managers? *Women in Management Review,* 12(4), 129–135.

Yoder, J. D. (2001). Making leadership work more effectively for women. *Journal of Social Issues,* 57(4), 815–882.

Chapter 11

Developing Transformational Leaders: Theory to Practice

Natalie Porter and Jessica Henderson Daniel

Developing transformational leaders within a feminist, multicultural framework is essential for 21st century corporate, civic, educational, and philanthropic institutions. We are two psychologists who have spent much of our professional lives both as educators and in academic, civic, and professional leadership roles. We have witnessed firsthand the critical need for both women and men to participate in achieving a more equitable and just society. In this chapter, we approach the topic of developing transformational leaders pragmatically. Our primary goal is to articulate the values, theories, and approaches we have used to (a) develop and hone our own leadership abilities throughout our professional careers, and (b) engender leadership interest and ability in others from a perspective that is multicultural, feminist, and inclusive of other diversities.

Key Components in Developing Feminist, Multicultural Leaders

Becoming a successful leader is a lifelong process that unfolds and evolves through the roles we assume in our professional and personal lives. In this chapter we outline the aspects of leadership theory and processes that we consider important in learning to be effective feminist-oriented leaders and in facilitating the development of leadership in others. As "leaders in process" we are continually refining our definitions of leadership and studying leaders who embody feminist and multicultural values in order to understand how they have achieved their goals. One of our goals is to encourage women to see the potential of leadership in their own lives.

We have focused in this chapter on identifying the elements crucial to effective leadership and to continuous learning and development via self-reflection, mentoring, supervising, and peer learning. These elements are: (a) understanding the theory and practice of transformational leadership within a social change and diversity framework; (b) establishing a clear working definition of feminist, multicultural leadership that incorporates values and vision; (c) learning and sharpening implementation strategies and tactics that effectively promote the leader's values, vision, and the organization's well-being; (d) learning key lessons from the examples of transformational leaders; (e) placing leadership within a social constructivist and contextual model and learning leadership behaviors that emphasize inclusion and collaboration; (f) fostering a service leadership paradigm; and (g) incorporating self-reflection and lifelong learning.

Transformational Leadership

Profiles in transformational leadership

Ruth Simmons. Ruth Simmons is the 18th President of Brown University, and the first African American appointed president of any Ivy League university. Prior to her position at Brown, which began in 2001, Simmons had served as President of Smith College and Provost of Spelman College and Princeton University. Simmons was presented to the trustees and fellows of Brown by Chancellor Stephen Robert as an "extraordinary leader, a person of character, of integrity and depth" (Robert, 2000). As President of Smith College, Simmons had been named by *Time Magazine* as America's best college president, because "Like university presidents of an earlier era, Ruth Simmons is the moral compass of the school she governs" (Morse, 2001). A farewell tribute from Smith colleagues to Simmons extolled, "We have been truly blessed by her strength and courage, her warmth and ability to listen, and most especially by her willingness to act on those things in which she believes" (NewsSmith, 2001).

Dr. Simmons, who was the 12th child born to sharecropper parents in East Texas, was educated in public schools after her family moved to Houston, where her father worked in a factory and her mother worked as a maid. Simmons reported learning the dignity of doing one's best work by watching her mother who completed each monotonous task with perfection. Simmons's desire to understand how her own society could countenance racial cruelty and legally enforced segregation led her to a lifelong interest in the humanities and in other cultures (Simmons, 1998). At Brown, Simmons has not only set the most ambitious fundraising goal in the university's history, a one billion-plus capital campaign, she has also instituted need-blind admissions, expanded financial aid awards, and appointed a Slavery and Justice Task Force, the first such endeavor in any university (Jordan, 2005).

Wangari Maathai. Dr. Maathai, Kenyan environmentalist and deputy minister of the environment, is the 2004 recipient of the Nobel Peace Prize. She is the first African woman to be awarded this honor, bestowed for her contributions to sustainable development, democracy, and peace. Dr. Maathai founded the Green Belt Movement almost 30 years ago. More than 30 million trees have been planted, and Kenya's public lands have been sustained and restored, as a result of her efforts. Maathai's work in Kenya has led to a global green belt movement, and she has spoken out for environmental sustainability globally (Beaubien, 2004).

Dr. Maathai, a biologist, was the first women to receive a Ph.D. in east and central Africa and the first pioneer woman in several academic posts in Kenya. She has been the cochair of the Jubilee 2000 Committee, which attempted to seek cancellation of backlog debts of poor African nations. She has endured beatings, arrests, and public censure for her activism over the last 30 years (Lewis, 2004). A vocal feminist, she was censured for undermining Kenyan culture by subverting the roles of women after she was divorced from her husband in the early 1980s. In the 1990s the police clubbed her into unconsciousness when she organized a fight to prevent the government's seizure of Nairobi's Uhuru (freedom) Park in order to build a 66-story high-rise. Various news accounts have described Dr. Maathai as the Iron Lady of Kenya and as one of the greatest environmental activists of all times. Her leadership has been described as inspirational for all Kenyans and particularly for women and girls.

Examples of exceptional values and exceptional commitment. The commonalities between Simmons and Maathai are notable. Both leaders articulate strong value positions that inform their actions. Both women are repeatedly described as committed, determined, and courageous.

Both of them recognize that they cannot meet their goals alone and have forged strong alliances. They both appear to possess the resilience needed to remain true to their values and goals in spite of social pressure and criticism. Their goals are related not to their own needs for power or status but from their visions of a better society. The status and power they have attained seem to be the result of successfully pursuing goals that are service-oriented. They pay attention to detail. Their visionary, larger-than-life strategic goals are accomplished by attending to day-to-day tasks that frequently are more tedious than glamorous, more similar to the monotonous "housekeeping" tasks described by Simmons as performed "perfectly" by her mother (Simmons, 1998).

Social and personal transformations occur, as exemplified by Maathai, one tree at a time. Demystifying leadership by examining its more ordinary forms shows us that leadership is possible in our own lives. Understanding this process compels us to assume leadership roles. As feminists we are committed to empowerment and social change, outcomes that begin with the exercise of leadership in our daily lives. Maria Otero, CEO of the nonprofit Acción International, understood that leadership is in the daily details. When she sought ways to empower women globally, she joined an organization that financed small work ventures as a way to make them "leaders in their own lives" (Kantrowitz, Peterson, & Wingert, 2005).

Understanding transformational leadership. Leadership has historically been considered the province of men operating in stereotypically masculine, and even heroic, fashion in primarily hierarchical and patriarchal structures. However, the demands of contemporary society and organizations have highlighted the need for alternative models of leadership based on collaboration, empowerment, and inclusion (Eagly, Johannesen-Schmidt, & van Engen, 2003). Successful future-oriented organizational structures require effective teamwork, functioning within a higher ethical and moral plane, and the co-operation of an increasingly diverse and global constituency (Conger & Kanungo, 1998). Otero of Acción International has expanded on the need for feminist models of leadership:

> Being a woman makes me a better manager. We reinforce each other. In some ways, being able to develop a management-leadership style that is based on forming a team is very much in line with the way I interact with my sisters or other women. We're all in it together. (Kantrowitz, Peterson, & Wingert, 2005)

Many of the qualities required for leadership of any effective organization in the current climate are those commonly associated with transformational leadership (Bass, 1985, 1998; Burns, 1978; Chia-Chen, 2004) and with women leaders (Applebaum, Audet, & Miller, 2002; Eagly & Johnson, 1990; Eagly, Karau, Miner, & Johnson, 1994; Yoder, 2001). Four components identified as comprising transformational leadership (Kark, Shamir, & Chen, 2003) are related to both effective leaders (Lowe, Kroeck, & Sivasubramaniam, 1996) and effective organizations (Dvir, Eden, Davolio, & Shamir, 2002):

1. Inspirational motivation—stirring others to action by communicating one's vision vividly, with optimism and enthusiasm.
2. Idealized influence—modeling behaviors that place the group's good over one's personal needs and reflect high ethical standards.
3. Individualized consideration—supporting, coaching, and encouraging constituents.
4. Intellectual stimulation—problem solving with constituents in collaborative and innovative ways (Kark et al., 2003).

By definition, feminism is a transformational ideology, with the aim of improving the social conditions for all members of society (hooks, 1981; Moraga, 1983; Smith, 1981). Effective feminist leadership requires the conscious incorporation of all four aspects described above.

Learning to Lead: From Definition to Execution of Feminist Leadership

Definition of feminist leadership

Multiple definitions of feminist leadership have been provided throughout this book, and attention has been paid to the research supporting these definitions. We have adopted the following working definition of feminist leadership as the foundation for our educational and training endeavors.

Feminist leadership is transformational in nature, seeking to empower and enhance the effectiveness of one's team members while striving to improve the lives and social conditions of all stakeholders including those indirectly affected, such as consumers and other members of society. A feminist leader:

- Is informed by social context, both as it relates to her own social location and privilege, to the group members' individual and social contexts, and to the paths for their empowerment and effectiveness;
- Pays attention to social context, which requires flexibility, reflexivity, and the ability to understand multiple perspectives rather than engage in dichotomous thinking;
- Assumes responsibility for her actions and requires accountability of herself and others characterized by mutual respect, clear communication, and the promotion of ethical action;
- Fosters inclusion of diverse groups within organizational structures that encourage diverse perspectives and experiences and eliminates discrimination of people of color, gays/lesbians, people with disabilities, elders, and poor people;
- Attends to power and boundary issues as well as the relationship of language to the social construction of gender, race, class, ethnicity, sexual orientation, and disability;
- Facilitates ongoing self-examination, learning, and professional development in herself and others.

This definition contains the elements central to educating feminist, culturally competent leaders. *Values* make up the heart of feminist leadership. With "values" as the foundation, the other elements are:

- *V*ision that is transforming, effectively communicated, and courageously executed;
- *A*ction that is collaborative, community-focused, and respectful;
- *L*earning that is empowering, reflexive, and lifelong;
- *U*nderstanding of power and boundaries issues that strive to empower;
- *E*thical practices that promote inclusiveness, integrity, and responsibility;
- *S*ocial constructivism that informs one's practice of leadership.

Moving from definition to execution: key educational issues

Values. One question often raised about organizations is whether they should promote values or remain "value-free." Tichy (1997), in *The Leadership Engine*, argued that values form the core of effective organizations. Effective leaders not only bring their values into the organizations, they articulate them clearly and use them to shape organizational missions. Simmons's and Maathai's remarkable long-term accomplishments were grounded in the daily execution of their beliefs and values. Simmons was motivated by her conviction that higher education was crucial to improving the lives of people of color and that elite institutions of higher education had to assume greater responsibility for educating the poor. Maathai was determined to ensure that the next generation of Africans would have their environmental legacy.

Simmons (2001) contended that institutions always communicate values, whether intentionally or not. Universities, for example,

> teach values in the way they hire and treat employees; they teach values in the way they admit students; they teach values in the way they set curricula and requirements. Thus, universities teach values even when they do not set out to do so.

She continued that how an institution addresses the issues of individual responsibility, community involvement, or diversity reveals its values around these issues.

A crucial educational issue for feminists is the balance between fighting for one's principles versus compromising or backing down on some issues in order to achieve others. When are we "selling out" and when are we being realistic about how long it takes for change to occur? How do we evaluate whether we are moving forward or merely capitulating? How do we educate leaders to evaluate how their values influence their actions?

Values in practice: a case study. The history of Elizabeth Odio Benito, an esteemed judge on the International Criminal Court in The Hague, highlights these questions. Dr. Odio Benito previously served as Attorney General, the Minister of Justice, and the Second Vice President of the Republic of Costa Rica. She also sat on the International Criminal Tribunal for the former Yugoslavia (ICTY) from 1993 to 1998. Her professional history reflects the struggle of achieving parity for women (International Criminal Court, 2004). As a judge on the tribunal, Dr. Odio Benito heard many criminal cases that involved rape, torture, and extermination by Serbians in Croatia, Bosnia, and Herzegovina. During the proceedings, Odio Benito and Gabrielle Kirk McDonald, a judge from the United States, introduced into the Rules of Procedure and Evidence, Rule 96, evidence in cases of sexual assault. This rule was groundbreaking for the tribunal, which

> established new jurisprudence in international criminal law and international human rights by interpreting the rape of two Serbian women

... in [a] detention camp as a form of torture and cruel treatment, that is, a grave breach of the law or customs of war in accordance with the ICTY Statute and the Geneva Conventions. (International Criminal Court, 2002, p. 193)

Subsequently, sexual attacks against women in the course of armed conflict became war crimes through the inclusion of articles 7 and 8 in the Rome Statute of the International Criminal Court. Prior to these statutes, few if any consequences accompanied the raping of women during war (International Criminal Court, 2004).

Previously, while campaigning for Vice President of Costa Rica, Odio Benito had to refrain from campaigning on her position favoring abortion, even when the mother's life was in jeopardy, because the Catholic Archbishop publicly opposed it. Conventional wisdom dictated that she would be unable to win against the Catholic Church; hence she did not highlight the abortion issue (Ellyn Kaschak, personal communication, November 12, 2004). Benito's actions illustrate the dilemma that all leaders face, particularly those with social justice or human rights agendas. One is not able to accomplish all goals commensurate with one's values. Unlike Benito, many women eschew politics and leadership roles in order not to compromise their positions. For others, the political process is viewed over the long term, with progress occurring incrementally and slowly.

Vision. An effective leader needs not only to have a compelling vision and plan for the organization but an effective way to communicate this vision. Too often, leaders think of this vision only as the blueprint for where the organization is going. Transformational leaders motivate their constituents to work for the good of the organization by effectively communicating a collective vision (Burns, 1978). For a leader with broader social values, the vision must provide a clear view of what the organization *is*, or *will be*, and how it will behave.

Action that is collaborative, community-focused, and respectful. Working in conjunction with others for a socially healthier and inclusive community, whether in an organizational, civic, or social community, are hallmarks of feminist and multicultural movements. They are also hallmarks of good leaders. Carly Fiorina, former CEO of Hewlett Packard, implored corporate leaders to use their leadership to improve the lives of people worldwide, for collaboration with communities globally, and to recognize the importance of corporate character and citizenship

(Fiorina, 2004). For these efforts, she was awarded the 2002 Appeal of Conscience Award and the 2003 Concern Worldwide "Seeds of Hope" Award (Hewlett Packard, 2004).

Leadership education must address effective collaboration and consensus building on the one hand and staying on course and moving forward on the other. A leader often has to balance the mission and health of the organization, which is the leader's primary responsibility, with the aims and interests of its individual constituents. Collaboration has to serve the organization over the needs of individuals or subgroups. Learning to possess and exhibit the resilience and confidence that it takes to accomplish significant goals in the face of disparate groups with conflicting interests is a challenge faced by all leaders. Fiorina of Hewlett Packard (HP) is a case in point. She has both been lauded and vilified for moving forward with a corporate merger in spite of disagreement by HP's long-time employees. *Businessweek* (Burrows & Elstrom, 1999) lauded her ability to stick to her vision and move forward in spite of the controversy. When the new venture was not immediately successful, she was removed by the corporation's Board of Directors. Jack Welch, former CEO of General Electric, has described this removal as premature and as inappropriate micromanaging by a board (McGinn, 2005).

A common tenet of feminist and culturally responsive philosophies is that broader social change, and not just "local" (organizational) or individual change, is necessary. Leaders of organizations recognize that at times the larger context must be changed in order to effect organizational change. An effective leader also recognizes when "local" actions will have broader social consequences.

For example, when one of the authors (Daniel), as chair of the Massachusetts Board of Registration of Psychologists, sought to change state licensing requirements to include both instruction and training about persons of color, she was cognizant that others potentially could have proposed less controversial educational requirements. She proposed the amendment at the end of her four-year tenure as chair. During that period, her leadership style had been collaborative and respectful as she reorganized and streamlined the functioning of the board. Everyone, including herself, was held to the same performance standards. Consequently, the board was seen as more effective and responsive to licensees, applicants, and consumers. The board members voted unanimously in support of the proposed additional requirements. Such a change has been the impetus for other state licensing boards to consider ways to include diversity requirements for both licensure and continuing education.

Learning that is empowering, reflexive, and lifelong. The feminist literature advocates each person's empowerment, self-determination, and self-sufficiency. A feminist leader, regardless of setting, empowers others by fostering autonomy, personal responsibility, and problem-solving and decision-making skills. Feminist thinkers have historically promoted ongoing development of themselves and others. Contemporary organizational theorists increasingly view these qualities as crucial for all leaders of effective organizations. Tichy (1997) contended that effective organizations are learning organizations, and great leaders are great teachers who teach their constituents to be leaders, not followers. He further asserted that effective leaders accomplish their goals through the people they teach. Eagly and her colleagues (2003) pointed out that mentoring is a transformational behavior that serves women leaders well; it allows women leaders to deal constructively with the lesser authority often granted to them by their constituents while creating a participative learning environment that increases everyone's effectiveness. Leaders must also attend to their own ongoing development and self-evaluation. Leaders need to engage in personal and professional reflection as well as foster these actions in others.

Feminist leadership not only involves stances against repressive social or organizational practices, but also proactive practices that foster greater inclusiveness and social justice. Explicit and ongoing diversity training and visible support for these issues by the leader are keys to furthering these goals within an organization. Because many sources that outline effective training are available, this chapter does not describe them. For each leader, lifelong learning, self-reflection, and self-monitoring around attitudes and behaviors pertaining to racism, ethnocentrism, sexism, classism, homophobia, disability, and so forth, are essential. Feminist leaders may fall along a continuum in understanding or embracing these issues, particularly those that are outside of one's own experience. Although these issues may not all be salient in every action or decision a leader makes, they should be salient in a feminist leader's overall vision and in one's ongoing self-evaluation and learning.

One of the authors (Porter) was dean of a clinical psychology program where the faculty was attempting to increase its responsiveness to students of color. Faculty identified the need to work collectively to improve their own awareness and sensitivity, expand their commitment, and develop more culturally responsive pedagogies. Porter wanted this endeavor to succeed and found ways to provide course release time for all faculty members for them to engage in weekly and monthly multicultural development activities ranging from learning to be more effective in difficult dialogues, to engaging in group and self-reflection, to updating course content. The faculty spent more than a year in intense self-examination.

Understanding of power and boundaries issues and striving to empower. As in other feminist or culturally responsive practices, a leader strives to understand how to use power in the service of others rather than to exploit them. Feminist leaders understand the responsibilities that accompany power and avoid abusing their power in either the treatment of individuals or the operation of an organization. However, a leader must keep the mission and health of the organization at the forefront, which may be quite different than attending to the needs of the individuals of the organization. Empowerment must occur in the context of the specific organization. The feminist literature addresses boundary violations and exploitation, a literature that is essential in educating leaders. Greenleaf's (1970) concept of servant leader is consistent with the high priority placed on meeting others' needs rather than those of the leader. Qualitative life changes, as well as the increased likelihood that those who are being led will become servant leaders, are two major criteria of success. For those most vulnerable, the servant leader seeks to improve their lives or at the least not to cause more harm.

An anecdote about Ruth Simmons aired on the CBS news program *60 Minutes* illustrated that great accomplishments may result when one adopts a servant leader role. While Provost at Princeton, Simmons recruited Toni Morrison to the faculty. Morrison accepted the invitation but declined to send a curriculum vitae, noting that the public documentation of her accomplishments should be sufficient. The trustees would not approve the appointment without Morrison going through the usual faculty personnel "hoops." Dr. Simmons, unable to convince either party to change their positions, ended up preparing the curriculum vitae herself. She was not going to lose this unique opportunity for Princeton, its students, or for Morrison. Neither the board nor Toni Morrison realized for many years that their standoff was solved by a pragmatic and humble leader focused on the needs of the organization rather than by the "other side" having capitulated.

255

Ethical practice that promotes inclusiveness, integrity, and responsibility. Ethical principles play a key role in the values set forth by the leader. Transformational leadership has been linked to Rokeach's (cited in Hood, 2003) four types of values—personal, social, competency-based, and morality-based values in business leaders. Transformational leaders tended to hold all four types of ethical values, and their organizations tended to reflect these values in their ethical practices (Hood, 2003).

A feminist leader views inclusiveness as an ethical mandate and promotes diversity throughout an organization and in the broader society. A feminist leader strives to incorporate people from diverse backgrounds at all levels of an organization and crafts a mission and vision with inclusion as a central theme. Inclusion of multiple perspectives is also central to a feminist vision, and feminist leaders avoid rigid or dichotomous positions. Again, this value is more complex in execution than in theory and requires lifelong self-examination and self-monitoring, elements which are essential to emphasize in any leadership development format.

Social constructivism that informs one's practice of leadership. A culturally responsive or feminist leader attends to the social construction of race, class, gender, disability, sexual orientation, and so forth, and how language defines social roles and perceptions of performance. The feminist leader is aware of the literature on women and people of color in leadership roles that unequivocally shows they are subjected to different expectations, evaluations, and rewards, and attempts to address these issues, when feasible, in order to mitigate their impact.

A key educational issue is: How does one lead "cross-culturally"? How does a leader effectively lead a group comprised of culturally diverse individuals, who may hold different expectations of leadership? How does one become a leader for all people? Can the traits required for one group conflict with those that will be effective with another? Individuals with certain cultural expectations may expect more traditional and "paternal" actions from their leaders, whereas others may want more latitude for decision making and growth. Some may not even believe that women should or could be leaders.

If one cannot lead from many cultural standpoints at the same time, how does one ensure, at the very least, that members from differing groups feel respected and valued through the actions of the leader? In addition to educating about diversity, leadership education can also help leaders remain open to the types of feedback that allow them to evaluate their performance on these dimensions. This is particularly necessary for European American leaders who may not be able to differentiate when their goals and actions are being shaped by their dominant culture position and privileged perspectives and have neglected the objectives or values of women of color. On the Division 35 Feminist Leadership website, one participant, BraVada Garrett-Akinsanya, summarized this issue for women of color in the following way:

> I realized that my power as a Black woman was surely connected to the empowerment of my white sisters. The problem has been, however, that when they have gotten power, it has been difficult for them to share because the barriers of race have been overlooked in our discussions of feminism. I think that any viable model of teaching about feminism must involve the dynamics of "abuses of power" and models of "shared power." Any model must involve the discussion of race. . . .

Many women of color have played leadership roles in their respective racial and ethnic cultural communities. Unfortunately, too often it has been seen as "women's work" and consequently devalued. While stereotypes of women of color vary across the racial and ethnic groups, the dominance of paternalism decreases both the likelihood that women will assume or be appointed to leader roles and the respect that they may be accorded.

Cultural context includes the leader and those who are being led. Demographics matter. Groups of people can be homogeneous in one way and very heterogeneous in other ways. Sometimes the leader matches the group; other times there are distinct differences. Leading in cultural context, regardless of perceptions of match or mismatch, can be challenging. It entails welcoming communications and a flexibility to change courses when necessary.

Promoting Feminist Leadership with Women of Color: A Model

Persons of color constitute approximately 6% of all psychologists. Despite this small representation, the Society for the Psychology of Women (Division 35) within the American Psychological Association has had four presidents who were women of color since it was founded in 1973. With the exception of the Society of the Psychological Study of Ethnic

Minority Issues (Division 45), this constitutes the largest group of women of color (WOC) division presidents in over 50 APA divisions.

One of the authors (Daniel) initiated a "Women of Color Leadership Training Program" within Division 35 of the American Psychological Association. She invited two of the WOC Division 35 past presidents, one Latina and one Asian American, to join her in identifying junior women from their respective racial/ethnic groups who were seen as potential leaders in psychology. The philosophy behind the identification of younger women is consistent with the National Council of Negro Women's mantra "Lift as you climb." Despite repeated efforts, the program was unsuccessful in recruiting American Indian junior women.

The Black, Latina, and Asian American junior women saw the legacy of WOC leadership as exemplified by the presence of the three current and former presidents of SPW. The senior women shared personal histories that affirmed the skills and accomplishments of various women leaders in their families and communities. Then the junior women's narrations about familial and personal stories of courage and persistence that involved women as leaders confirmed that their being leaders would be the continuation of a family and community legacy of leadership. WOC are often confronted directly and indirectly by stereotypes that can undermine their self-confidence and others' perceptions of them as leaders. Open discussions about the different stereotypes across the racial and ethnic groups can lessen the power of these stereotypes as well as provide strategies for managing comments and behaviors that reflect stereotyping. The senior women shared experiences and responses to stereotyping, that is, they modeled coping strategies.

The junior women were encouraged to consider how their racial and ethnic identity might influence their leadership. Messages from the senior women indicated that having strong racial and ethnic identities could be sources of strength rather than obstacles in interacting with a diverse group of people. Pressures associated with acculturation and assimilation can be constants for WOC. The total abandonment of one's racial and ethnic heritage can mean entering majority situations feeling empty and vulnerable. In contrast, the acknowledgment of the contributions of kin and others through sharing histories facilitates entering such contexts with a recognized legacy of skills, strengths, and successes.

The WOC Leadership Program incorporated the components of feminist leadership identified above. All the senior women are committed to leadership from a social justice perspective. The group was intentionally multicultural to stress the importance of cultural flexibility and understanding. The three senior women demonstrated mutual respect as they shared different ideas; consensus was neither expected nor desired.

Values: The junior women were on different career paths in psychology and consequently were directing their energies in several directions. The senior women's narratives about their decision making while in leadership positions reflected values and clearly communicated that, regardless of the track, personal integrity was important.

Action: Collaboration was the core of the initiative as the author (an African America woman) acknowledged that she needed the assistance of other WOC women to develop a successful leadership program. The senior women's career paths were not similar, yet each had a community focus, with "community" ranging in size and scope.

Learning: The junior women were provided with two types of reading materials: leadership literature and WOC leaders' biographies. Both were meant to be empowering and thought-provoking. The senior women expressed their love of learning and how each leadership position has led them to acquire new skills and to expand their perspectives.

Understanding of power: One philosophical perspective shared with the women was the concept of "servant leader." It is an honor to serve; one serves to empower others and not oneself. This does not mean that one is reticent in the leadership role, but it does call for a responsible leadership style.

Ethics: Personal integrity is integral to effective leadership. Managing diversity in its many manifestations can be challenging. Personal accountability and fairness can contribute to success as a leader.

Social constructiveness: The WOC commented on feeling as though they were under a microscope at times, that is, high scrutiny. Their perceived margin of error seems to be slim or nonexistent. The data suggests that persons of color are included based on track record while majority persons are included on the basis of potential. WOC leaders may need to guard against repeating this unjust practice and to help others change these inconsistent practices.

The program was so constructed to provide mentors on both vertical and horizontal bases. When persons are from their communal cultures, connections are empowering and familiar. Inclusion in the program made the participants feel special and encouraged them to pursue leadership positions.

Leadership Involves Lifelong Learning

One of the authors (Daniel) is embarking on a new leadership role. It is one of those "first and only" (F & O) positions, that is, she is the first and only African American woman in the role. Preparation is critical. The "F & O" status often means being under a microscope and feeling that one has a slim margin of error. But it does not necessarily mean isolation. One of the first tasks is to talk to both men and women about their experiences of serving in the leadership role in order to determine the nature and content of the mentoring that will be needed. Mentors can serve as guides and advisers in new contexts. The gender and racial differences between the new leader and those who have served do not preclude seeking perspectives about the culture of the organizational unit and the various roles that leaders have played. Learning includes reading documents, talking to other leaders, following the series of emails on a given topic, and observing the meetings. It is fortunate that the new leader has worked with many of the leaders who will be serving at the same time. While it is the same general organization, the leadership is at a different level.

The vision held by a candidate may change after being able to view the organization from another perspective. It may need to be revised or even discarded. Regardless of the fate of the vision, action will require building coalitions with other leaders. Relationships are neither instant nor static. They require time and attention. In the process of establishing and nurturing relationships, the new leader will learn about power in the organization as well as the existence of boundaries. Personal integrity will be a guiding value as people, interactions, and issues are considered in order to decide on a course of action or nonaction.

Each new leadership experience is an opportunity for personal growth that can entail cognitive and affective challenges. It can result in the acquisition of skills and strategies that can be generalized to other "leader" experiences. It is both a privilege and a responsibility to be in position to "make a difference."

Summary and Conclusions

This chapter has explored feminist leadership, diversity, and training from theory to practice. The reader has met women who exemplify feminist leadership in different contexts. Feminist leadership has been deconstructed for those who seek to understand and teach the components of this leadership style. By definition it is a dynamic leadership style that requires openness to learning, being responsive, and understanding the importance of values. Values stated and assumed are the guiding forces in an organization. Being a leader means participating in the articulation and implementation of the values.

The rewards of empowering others can be gratifying as one sees people growing as a result of being empowered. Feminist leadership is legacy leadership, with the potential of creating more caring and responsive leaders who are leader-healers-empowerers.

Fiorina (2004) has characterized it in this way:

I think [the charge of this generation] is to use the capabilities of this age to uplift the character of this age; to use the greatest [media] tools the world has ever seen not just to entertain, but to educate, to inform, to inspire, to uplift; and in the process, to make all of us believe a little bit more that we can solve the challenges of this age—to remind us that we can make the world a better place. That will do a lot more than define greatness for a new age. It will help strengthen ties between people; promote understanding and compassion; and act as a bridge between cultures.

References

Appelbaum, S. H., Audet, L., & Miller, J. C. (2002). Gender and leadership? Leadership and gender? A journey through the landscape of theories. *Leadership and Organizational Development Journal, 24,* 43–51.

Bass, B. M. (1985). *Leadership and performance beyond expectations.* New York: The Free Press.

Bass, B. M. (1998). *Transformational leadership: Industry, military, and educational impact.* Mahwah, NJ: Erlbaum.

Beaubien, J. (2004). Kenyan activist wins Nobel Prize for Peace. *All things considered,* National Public Radio, 8 October. Retrieved August 10, 2006 from http://www.npr.org/templates/story/story.php?storyId=4077230

Burns, J. M. (1978). *Leadership.* New York: Harper & Row.

Burrows, P., & Elstrom, P. (August 2, 1999). HP's Carly Fiorina: The Boss. *Businessweek.* Retrieved February 19, 2006 from http://www.businessweek.com/1999/99_31/b3640001.htm

Chia-Chen, K. (2004). Research on team impacts of leadership effectiveness on team leadership. *Journal of American Academy of Leadership, 5,* 266.

Conger, J. A., & Kanungo, R. N. (1998). *Charismatic leadership in organizations.* Thousand Oaks, CA: Sage.

Dvir, T., Eden, D., Avolio, B. J., & Shamir, B. (2002). Impact of transformational leadership on follower development and performance: A field experiment. *Academy of Management Journal, 45,* 735–744.

Eagly, A. H., Johannesen-Schmidt, M. C., & van Engen, M. L. (2003). *Psychological Bulletin, 129,* 569–591.

Eagly, A. H., & Johnson, B. T. (1990). Gender and leadership style: A meta-analysis. *Psychological Bulletin, 108,* 233–256.

Eagly, A. H., Karau, S. J., Miner, J. B., & Johnson, B. T. (1994). Gender and motivation to manage in hierarchic organizations: A meta-analysis. *Leadership Quarterly, 5,* 135–159.

Fiorina, C. (2004). *Keynote address.* National Association of Broadcasters, Las Vegas, NE, April 19, 2004. Retrieved November 1, 2004 from http://www.hp.com/hpinfo/execteam/speeches/fiorina/nab04.html

Greenleaf, R. (1970). *What is servant leadership?* Greenleaf Center for Servant Leadership. Retrieved December 10, 2004 from http://www.greenleaf.org/leadership/servant-leadership/What-is-Servant-Leadership.html

Hewlett Packard. (2004). *Carly Fiorina. Biographies of HP's executive council.* Retrieved November 1, 2004 from www.hp.com/hpinfo/execteam/bios/fiorina/html

Hood, J. N. (2003). The relationship of leadership style and CEO values to ethical practices in organizations. *Journal of Business Ethics, 43,* 263–273.

hooks, b. (1981). *Ain't I a woman?* Cambridge, MA: South End Press.

International Criminal Court. (2002). Judges: Statements of qualifications and resumes (ICC-ASP/1/4/Add.1). (December 12, 2002). Documents related to first election of judges, CV Digest. International Criminal Court, pp. 190–196. Retrieved August 11, 2004 from http://www.iccnow.org/documents/CVDigest200212Eng.pdf

Jordan, J. (2005, May). Ruth Simmons. *Projo.com.* Retrieved October 15, 2005 from http://www.projo.com/news/content/projo_20050529_ruth29x.2266685.html

Kantrowitz, B., Peterson, H., & Wingert, P. (2005). *How I got there: Maria Otero. Newsweek,* October 24. Retrieved August 10, 2006 from http://www.msnbc.msn.com/id/9756481/site/newsweek/

Kark, R., Shamir, B., & Chen, G. (2003). The two faces of transformational leadership: Empowerment and dependency. *Journal of Applied Psychology, 88,* 246–255.

Lewis, J. J. (2004). Wangari Maathai: Women's history profile. Retrieved June 15, 2005 from http://womenshistory.about.com/od/wangarimaathai/p/wangari_maathai.htm

Lowe, K. B., Kroeck, K. G., & Sivasubramaniam, N. (1996). Effectiveness correlates of transformational and transactional leadership: A meta-analytic review of the MLQ literature. *Leadership Quarterly, 7,* 385–425.

McGinn, D. (March 27, 2005). Jack on Jack: His next chapter. Retrieved August 12, 2006 from http://www.msnbc.msn.com/id/7305758/site/newsweek/

Moraga, C. (1983). *Loving in the war years: Lo que nunca pasa por los labios.* Cambridge, MA: South End Press.

Morse, J. (2001). America's best: Campus crusader. *Time Magazine.* Sept. 17, 2001. Paragraph 1. Retrieved October 15, 2005 from http://www.time.com/time/archive/preview/0,10987,1000831,00.html

NewsSmith. (2001). *A woman for all seasons: Tributes to Ruth Simmons.* NewsSmith Internet. Retrieved October 15, 2004 from http://www.smith.edu/newssmith/NSSpr01/tributes.html

Robert, S. (2000). *Ruth J. Simmons is an inspiring intellectual leader of great integrity.* Brown University News Service, November 9, 2000. Retrieved October 18, 2004 from http://www.brown.edu/Administration/News_Bureau/2000-01/00-049b.html

Simmons, R. (1998). My mother's daughter: Lessons I learned in civility and authenticity. *Texas Journal of Ideas, History and Culture* (fall/winter) as cited in My Hero. Retrieved October 10, 2004 from http://myhero.com/myhero/hero.asp?hero=r_simmons

Simmons, R. (2001). *Remarks to the Brown community upon election as 18th president.* Retrieved August 11, 2004 from http://www.brown.edu/Administration/News_Bureau/2000-01/00-049r.html

Smith, B. (1981). *This bridge called my back.* New York: Kitchen Table Women of Color Press.

Tichy, N. M. (1997). *The leadership engine.* New York: Harper Business.

Yoder, J. D. (2001). Making leadership work more effectively for women. *Journal of Social Issues, 57,* 815–828.

Chapter 12

Feminist Leadership Among Latinas

Melba Vasquez and Lillian Comas-Díaz

In this chapter, we identify the increased presence of Latinas in various leadership roles, and the unique qualities and strengths that Latinas bring to their leadership roles. We describe the challenges and obstacles faced by Latinas, the effects of those on the identity of Latinas, and make re-commendations for workplace environments as well as for individuals in order to deal with those challenges.

Latinas belong to one of the fastest growing ethnic minority groups in the United States (U.S. Census Bureau, 2004, June, July). They com-prise a heterogeneous group of women who have been collectively termed Latinas, Hispanics, or Spanish speakers. Some self-identify as Mexican Americans, Chicanas, Cuban Americans, Puerto Ricans, NuYorican, Dominican, among other terms describing national origin. Still, some Latinas identify as "Americanas," embracing and celebrating the diversity and energy of the contemporary Latin American community wedded through a wealth of nationalities (Olmos, Ibarra, & Monterrey, 1999). The U.S. Census Bureau (2004, July) reported that the nation's Hispanic population reached 41.3 million, or approximately 14% of the U.S. population. The U.S. Census Bureau defines Hispanic as people whose origin are Mexican, Puerto Rican, Cuban, South or Central American, or other Hispanic/Latino, regardless of race. Hispanic populations are reported to continue to grow at much faster rates than the population as a whole (U.S. Census Bureau, 2004, June). The growth rate of 13% was almost four times that of the total population (3.3%). Latinos are now the largest ethnic minority group in the United States, and are projected to continue to grow in population due to large families and immigration patterns. For the purposes of this chapter we will use the term Latina to designate females from Latin American descent, either immigrant or several generations American.

Latinas' Contribution to Leadership in Society

Latinas are leaving their leadership mark in the professional panorama. Some magazines geared to Latina readers highlight Latinas in leadership roles. For example, *Latina Style* includes regular columns of "Latinas Today in the News," "Latina Leaders," "Latina Entrepreneurs," among others. The July/August 2004 *Latina Style* cover story was about the 50 best companies for Latinas to work for in the United States (Rosado & Ortuzar, 2004). The same issue carried an article on being a writer (Garcia-Aguilera, 2004) and another on "The Case for Latinas on Corporate Boards" (Riojas, 2004). Moreover, the September/October 2004 issue reported on the National Latina Symposium, the first national convention of Latina leaders, including influential Latinas in business, politics, and education (*Latina Style*, 2004).

Latinas have become increasingly active in various leadership roles such as advocacy, scholarship, and service in United States society. They have made significant strides and promoted change in U.S. society's institutions and workplaces. Many Hispanic women are now in leadership roles. Evidence reported by the U.S. Bureau of Labor Statistics, and interpreted by Hispanic Business Inc., indicate that Latinas have demonstrated increased leadership and impact in U.S. society. Hispanic women actually wield more power than Hispanic men both in proportion of professional or managerial positions (21.4% vs. 14% of the Hispanic workforce, respectively) and educational achievement (60% of bachelor's degrees awarded in 2000 to Hispanics went to women), according to a report (Research and Markets, 2004).

Hispanic women have indeed begun to make significant and rapid educational gains as well. While the number of bachelor's degrees conferred to U.S. residents increased 35% from 1976 to 2000, the number of bachelor's degrees earned by Hispanic women rose 430%. From 1997 to 2002, the number of Hispanic women-owned businesses surged 39%. In 2002, Hispanic women were estimated to own 470,344 firms, employing 198,000 people, and generating $24.9 billion in sales. And those numbers are projected to significantly increase: According to the Center for Women's Business Research (2006), the number of businesses owned by women of color of Hispanic origin is growing faster than the overall national rate for women-owned businesses.

Latina leadership has a central role in the community. For instance, the *promotoras* (peer advocates or women who promote a cause among Latinos) have contributed significantly to the development and sustenance of their community. Besides their organizational and leadership skills, *promotoras* act as community lay educators since they reside within the community they serve. For example, the National Council of La Raza recommended that culturally and linguistically appropriate programs recruit *promotoras* as peer educators to teach Latinos health promotion behaviors (Rios-Ellis, 2005).

Latina values

Although not all Latinas share the same values, there are a core set of Latino cultural values, including centrality of family, messages received about gender roles, and a collective identity that emphasizes social responsibility and service (Gomez et al., 2001). Some Latino cultural values seem to promote female leadership. For example, Latinas' relational style may explain the emerging success of Latina leaders. *Personalismo*, or the tendency to prefer personal relations to impersonal or institutional ones, can be an asset in business and professional roles (Comas-Díaz, 1997). Latinas use their interpersonal skills to further develop leadership qualities. The cultural concept of *familismo* refers to the tendency to extend kinship relationships beyond the nuclear family boundaries, leading to emotional proximity, affective resonance, interpersonal involvement, and cohesiveness (Falicov, 1982). Since *familismo* emphasizes interdependence over independence, affiliation over confrontation, and co-operation over competition, it may enhance Latinas' interpersonal relationships and leadership styles. Although there is controversy about gender differences in leadership style (Eagly & Johannesen-Schmidt, 2001), women's leadership styles, compared to that of male leaders, may be more interpersonally oriented, democratic, and transformational. On the whole, research on leadership style has very favorable implications for women's increasing representation in the ranks of leaders. Partly because of the perceived advantages of women's style of leadership, social and organizational changes place women, more often than men, in the position of being newer entrants into higher level managerial roles (Eagly & Johannesen-Schmidt, 2001). More research is needed to assess the leadership styles of Latinas, but one may predict that the intersection of gender and ethnicity results in leadership styles that generally are perceived to be valued and effective in organizations. Latinas have always exercised leadership, especially in families and communities. However, Latinas are just now beginning to achieve power and leadership in United States society.

Giving back to the community is an example of women of color's leadership (Comas-Díaz & Greene, 1994), and in particular, Latinas. Latina leaders identify early in their development the importance of belonging to a collaborative and supportive group. For example, Juana Bordas developed a Meztiza Leadership Institute where Latina leaders are trained, becoming members of the "Circle." Afterwards, they participate in Compaeras, a community-oriented extension of the Circle where the Latina leaders give back to the community by mentoring 12-year old Latinas (Scales, 2004).

The Latino collective concept of *comadres*—the relationship between a mother and the godmother of her child—has been extended beyond godmother to mean mentor, friend, and midwife. *Comadres* promote Latina leadership. Many Latina leaders use the concept of *comadres* to mentor other Latinas, in particular younger women. An illustration is Las Comadres para Las Americas (www.lascomadres.org), an informal internet-based group meeting monthly in several U.S. cities to provide support, build relationships, and conduct business. Another example of the concept of *comadres* to signify Latina leadership is developed by feminist women who are artists, curators, writers, performers, video artists, teachers, and students. This community focuses on feminism, multi-culturalism, and border issues (Berelowitz, 1998). Many Latinas feel that they will not be able to succeed without their *comadres'* help.

Challenges and Obstacles in Leadership for Latinas

What are the experiences of women of color in the various arenas in which they are leadership pioneers? What are the challenges? What are the obstacles? What are the unique strategies and contributions that Latinas make as we contribute to the increased presence of women's leadership in general? Although Latinas experience many similar experiences to other women, the intersection of gender and ethnicity makes for unique challenges and obstacles. The following are examples of experiences of successful Latina women who nonetheless experience obstacles and challenges in their endeavors. We've changed some identifying characteristics of these women, but all are women of color who have consulted with us in the past few months in the independent practices of the authors.

- A Latina, the only woman of color on the organizational management team of her corporation, whose employees number over 3,000, shows up at the annual board meeting to discover that her name has been left off the organizational chart of the annual report. This is one of many slights she has experienced since joining this firm.
- A highly accomplished Latina who is the only person of color among the vice-presidents of her corporation, who has won many awards and promotions, is still uncomfortable accepting social invitations to her colleagues' homes. The body language and mannerisms of most of her colleagues convey to her that she is only tolerated and not truly welcomed.
- A Latina, who serves on the national board of her nonprofit organization, experiences emotional pain and self-doubt in response to her colleagues' reactions about her strong stand to support a policy which she believes is important in promoting civil rights of employees of color.
- Another Latina is hired away from her position to join a corporation for a very substantial raise, only to discover on her third day on the job that the CEO has changed her title to a less prestigious one. Over the first few months, she perceives that her role is only that of a token, and that she is not getting the assignments and responsibilities that she expected, and of which she is capable.

What are the effects of these experiences? What are the effects on identity?

Defining Identity, its Relevance to Leadership, and Challenges to Identity for Latinas

Ethnic identity and gender identity are two major ways in which people define themselves and are defined by others (Garcia Coll, Cook-Nobles, & Surrey, 1995; Hughes, 2001). Identity is especially relevant because it influences our sense of self in regard to capabilities, motivations, and goals, all of which influence capacity for leadership.

What happens to the identities of Latinas and other women of color in this society? The way society constructs gender and ethnicity has major influence on the development of our identity. Specific experiences in family and community affect identity, as do the expectations in society. In our early development, girls and adolescents of color have to deal with several difficult issues not faced by majority adolescent girls, such as racist prejudicial attitudes, conflict between the values of our groups and those of larger society, and scarcity of high-achieving women of color in our group to serve as role models (Eccles, Wigfield, & Byrnes, 2003). Such difficulties can impede identity formation, leading to identity diffusion or inadequate exploration of different possible identities.

Cross (1991) argues that one must consider the development of both personal identities and racial/ethnic group identity. For example, a Latina may have a positive personal identity but be less positive of her ethnic group as a whole, or may have negative personal identities but have positive orientations toward her group. Ideally, we have both positive personal identities and positive group identities. In our society, it is a challenge to be positive about oneself and one's group unless we have messages within our families and communities about the positive nature of our ethnic groups. This kind of "inoculation" against the negative messages in society about our groups is critical to forming positive group identities.

Challenges to Positive Identity for Latinas

Four areas of social psychological research will be described to inform us of the current experiences of Latinas and other women of color that present challenges to a positive identity, and in effect, leadership roles, for Latinas.

Devaluation of women's work

In a review of various studies, Heilman (2001) concludes that because of gender stereotypes, ambiguity in evaluation criteria, lack of structure in evaluation processes, denial of credit for successes to women, women's performance is systematically evaluated with a negative bias and devalued. Even when women are accepted as competent, they may be penalized if they are violating gender expectations, or their successes may be attributed to special help or manipulations on the part of the women. Research suggests that people in society still assume that White males are more competent and worthy of high evaluations; people assign, probably unconsciously, higher evaluations to them, and devalue the exact same product of women and people of color (Heilman, 2001; Nieva & Gutek, 1980).

Aversive racism

Contemporary racism and discrimination are subtle. There is evidence that people of color are aware of it, but Whites who perpetrate it themselves are not aware of their behaviors. Social psychologists John Dovidio and Sam Gaertner (1996) have conducted research which indicates that although expressions of open hostility and clear dislike are not as evident on a daily basis as in the past, European Americans experience anxiety and uneasiness around people of color. In general, European American people consciously endorse egalitarian values and deny their negative feelings about people of color. As a consequence, they try to avoid direct and open discrimination. However, because of feelings of anxiety and uneasiness, they will discriminate, often unintentionally, when their behavior can be justified on the basis of some factor other than race or ethnicity (e.g., questionable qualifications). So they may have a nonprejudiced self-image, but also be engaging in discrimination. This is called "aversive racism."

One of our clients described her experience as continuously feeling on the "outer edge of the inner circle." Although she technically had the prestige, status, and even salary of an executive, she often felt that she was not really accorded the respect, value, and inclusion of her White male peers. She described their failure to make eye contact, failure to initiate interaction at key events, as well as continuously discovering that she did not get key informal information, and so forth. On the other hand, other employees in the organization, and not in the inner circle, called upon her constantly, and sought support from her as a role model.

Societal expectations/role restrictions for women of color

Societal expectations and role restrictions are also barriers for women of color. Ridgeway (2001) and Ridgeway and Walker (1995) draw from "expectation states theory" to describe how gender status beliefs create a network of constraining expectations and interpersonal reactions that is a major cause of the "glass ceiling." This theory assumes that the gender system is deeply entwined with social hierarchy and leadership because gender stereotypes contain status beliefs that associate greater status worthiness and competence with men than with women. Thus ability has very little to do with what happens to the identities of women and people of color.

What causes highly competent women of color to move away from nontraditional and toward more traditional pathways once they are in college? Arnold (1995) conducted a longitudinal study of high school valedictorians. Female high school valedictorians, around their second year of college, changed their aspirations for demanding careers and also began to think of themselves as not as smart as their male peers, despite continuing to perform as well. The college and career paths of the African American and Latina women in Arnold's study of valedictorians seemed to be even more affected by negative societal expectations.

Arnold (1995) saw two major problems among the women and men of color who were valedictorians, including lack of money and lack of deep knowledge about college and careers. These students took longer to complete college, averaging almost six years for their undergraduate degrees. The Caucasian valedictorians tended to complete college in four continuous years. The African American and Mexican American valedictorians were more likely than Caucasians to change institutions during their college careers (as cited in Scott-Jones and Takanishi, in press). Many women of color, influenced by stereotyped expectations of parents, teachers, and society, may often have abilities but experience confusing messages and expectations that contribute to the anxiety and fears of failure in areas of study related to nontraditional environments. These mixed and confusing messages seriously affect identity and consequently goals and motivations.

Stereotype threat

Claude Steele and his colleagues have identified a phenomenon that happens for people when they believe that there are certain negative stereotypes about their abilities—they tend to get threatened, anxious, and to underperform. Members of a group experience stereotype threat when they are evaluated in a domain in which they are regarded, on the basis of stereotype, as inferior (Steele, 1997; Steele & Aronson, 1995). In the face of threat to self-esteem, derived from this identification with the area in which they are both aspiring and at the same time expecting to be negatively regarded, they undergo "choking under pressure"

(Baumeister & Showers, 1984) and as a result, they commonly underperform. A person from the stereotyped group tends to become highly anxious, try harder (Steele, 1997), and obtain significantly lower scores than they would under nonthreatening conditions (Steele & Aronson, 1995).

Spencer, Steele, and Quinn (1999) carried out experiments to test the hypothesis that the negative stereotyping of women as inferior in math and science would lead to the effect of stereotype threat on women's performance in mathematics. The researchers tested a group of math-identified women compared to math-identified men, both groups equally qualified according to GPA and SAT scores (women and men who saw themselves as good in math). In the stereotype-threatening condition the women obtained significantly lower scores than the men. In the second condition, there was no difference between the women and men in test performance.

These studies have significant implications for the performance of women, women of color, and Latinas in particular. If the stereotypes based on sexist and racist ideologies tend to privilege White men in regard to ability, and are detrimental to women of color, then it follows that Latinas have more challenges in stereotype-threatening conditions. Pratto and Espinoza (2001) suggested that intersectional ethnic/gender stereotypes may be how mental images are organized, and emphasize the importance of studying the intersection of ethnicity and gender. In their study of college students who were asked to assign resumes of recent graduates to be the best person for various jobs, Pratto and Espinoza (2001) found that Whites, especially White men, were preferred for hierarchy-enhancing positions (high-power, highly paid jobs); Blacks and Hispanics, especially women, were more often assigned into hierarchy-attenuating positions (public defender's office, social service agencies, and charities). Stereotypes are thus detrimental to Latinas in that the expectations of others and of oneself can restrict expectations and opportunities.

Disidentification.   Students who face repeated anxiety and failure in school performance will eventually stop trying (Steele, 1997). Disidentification is a process whereby members of stereotyped groups, having experienced stereotype threat in their education, learn to protect themselves by avoiding and devaluing the associated academic activity.

Underperformance, that is, performing at a level lower than expected by GPA and entrance examinations, and disidentification may also be significant factors in women's avoidance of careers in math and science and other nontraditional careers. Steele (1997) comments:

272

when this threat becomes chronic in a situation, as for the woman who spends considerable time in a competitive, male-oriented math environment, it can pressure disidentification, a reconceptualization of the self and of one's values so as to remove the domain as a self-identity. (Steele, 1997, p. 614)

Especially with the paucity of Latinas in the powerful, high-status jobs, it is difficult for Latinas to try to maintain motivation to prevent the effects of bias and stereotypes on one's identity, goals, and expectations.

Even middle-class Black and Latino students may be less successful despite their families being relatively privileged. On the other hand, immigrant students of color, many of whom are from low-income families, are often academically successful. Immigrant students of color are largely immune to the insidious association between race and achievement that traps United States ethnic minorities. They were likely raised in societies where people of their race or ethnic group are in the majority, and thus have not been subjected to socialization processes that lead them to see themselves as members of subordinate or inferior groups. Thus immigrant students may be less likely to be affected by Steele's notion of "stereotype threat" (Noguera, 2001). They have not been socialized to see themselves as inferior, as have domestic ethnic minorities, so may be less threatened in engaging in the behaviors necessary for academic success. Middle-class Black and Latino students may be more likely to disidentify with the attitudes and behaviors necessary to achieve academic success if they perceive that as risking being ostracized for differentiating themselves from peers.

Organizational Strategies to Improve Identity and Opportunity for Leadership

What can organizations do to counteract these challenges to the identities, and thus positively affect the sense of capability, motivations, and leadership goals of Latinas and other women of color?

1. A critical factor in overcoming negative stereotyping is that supervisors and mentors must have optimism about women of color's potential, and that they communicate this fundamental, unambivalent belief in their employee's ability. Constructive criticism accompanied by the expectation of high standards is essential, along with

the expression of confidence in the person's ability to achieve excellence.

2. It is also important to understand or reconceptualize intelligence and related abilities as expandable or incremental qualities that are increased by training and experience (Dweck, 2002). Aronson (2002) found that students who were taught to consider intelligence expandable, who changed how they thought about intelligence in response to training, were able to increase their engagement in their education and thus to be more academically successful.

3. Create environments with an emphasis on co-operation, as contrasted with competition (Aronson, 2002). An emphasis on co-operation has been noted to be helpful for stereotyped college students renegotiating their identification with academia, and it should be equally helpful to women of color in a process of overcoming disidentification with nontraditional roles, created in the wake of earlier stereotype threat experiences in grade school, high school, or college classes. Working collaboratively and collectively is more congruent with the values of the cultural backgrounds of most Latinas.

4. Create an environment where diversity feels natural, and a Latina employee feels comfortable. Cultural differences should not only be tolerated, but respected and celebrated. Related to this concept is that those who own privilege, who are the power brokers and decision makers, must become comfortable with those different from them.

5. Be open to varied models of women's leadership. There is a natural tendency for decision makers to assume that those who get promoted into positions of leadership and responsibility should look and act like those who have been successful before them (usually White males). Latinas and other women of color are bypassed for higher roles because their styles sometimes appear different than those who have held those roles. Joyce Fletcher (2001) describes women's roles as potentially adding feminine wisdom and experience to organizational knowledge. Appropriate and relevant policies at all levels have tremendous impact on the identities of Latinas and other women. Sexual harassment policies, policies that encourage equity at all levels, for example, speak volumes in organizations. Government support of equity and diversity is critical to change in society. The July 23, 2003 U.S. Supreme Court decision that affirmed the use of race and diversity as a factor in evaluating

applicants has had a huge impact on our identities. Justice Sandra Day O'Connor's words were incredibly affirming: "In order to cultivate a set of leaders with legitimacy in the eyes of the citizenry, it is necessary that the path to leadership be visibly open to talented and qualified individuals of every race and ethnicity" (Jayson & Rodriguez, 2003, p. A-1). That is, universities are partly in the business of training a leadership corps for society, and a society with racial and ethnic tensions can benefit tremendously from having an integrated leadership (Lemann, 2003). This national consensus was articulated by a record number of policy briefs submitted to the Supreme Court by various organizations, universities, the military, and Fortune 500 companies.

Strategies for Latinas

What are the strategies recommended for individual Latinas who wish to develop skills and abilities to further develop leadership qualities and abilities?

1. Learn to assess "fit" for your values, skills, and capacity for challenge, both in terms of the job requirements and the degree of friendly versus nonfriendly environment for women of color. The "fit" ideally reflects work that fulfills a passionate, committed life purpose. Gomez et al. (2001) used qualitative methodology to investigate the career development of 20 notable Latinas, and found that participants' passion and commitment were significant personal characteristics.
2. Persistence is a very important variable in success. For example, it is the most important variable that determines whether someone will complete graduate school. Gomez et al. (2001) also found that the notable Latinas in their study felt a strong need to achieve their best in any situation by having a strong work ethic and often working "twice as hard" to prove themselves in the fact of sexism and racism. Knowing when to persist and when to adjust goals and expectancies becomes adaptive.
3. Take risks. Allow curiosity and energy to give direction to areas in which you wish to explore your power and salience. Risk takers often find that true fearlessness is not the elimination of fear, but the transcendence of fear, the movement through it and not against it.

275

Fearlessness means the willingness to lean into the anxiety and fear. Risk taking builds positive aspects of our identities.

4. Do not expect perfection from yourself; remember that mistakes are a part of life, everyone makes them. Steele's (1997) research on stereotype threat shows that marginalized people have a tendency to experience anxiety, stress, and threat at the notion that others have negative expectations about their performance. Thus Latinas and others may have a tendency to feel increased shame, anxiety, and humiliation when we are not perfect. A strategy to overcome this is to allow oneself to acknowledge and learn from mistakes, but not to allow them to be part of one's identity.

5. Transform hurt and rejection into anger, and use that anger in constructive ways. We can transform those feelings into healthy, assertive expressions that say, "We count," "I am to be respected," "You may not mistreat me," "I am deserving." Anger is a healthy signal that tells us as well as those around us where our boundaries are, what we instinctively feel is tolerable or intolerable, and can signal when those limits have been trespassed.

6. Immerse yourself into the positive aspects of your culture from time to time. For all women of color, and especially for those who suffer from disidentification, we encourage "immersion" into their ethnic group experiences.

7. Honor your identity as a multicultural one; that is, you are able to operate in several different contexts, which evoke different parts of yourself. Work on the delicate balance of knowing how and when various aspects of you will be most effective in what contexts. People of color are often multicultural and are able to develop skills of flexibility and adaptability to adjust to environments that are diverse and complex. Ramirez (1998) has long suggested that the complex immigration, international, intercultural, and multicultural experiences of persons of color lead to the development of complex interpersonal skills and abilities. The notable Latinas studied by Gomez et al. (2001) viewed themselves as bicultural or multicultural, meaning they could maneuver in both Anglo American and Hispanic culture. They often behaved differently in each world.

8. Observe role models and mentors; help to empower others. Mentors are scarce. Use them situationally, and at a distance if you have to. Observe skills and strengths of others and decide whether you wish to cultivate those as well. Be willing to mentor and support others. Empowering others can be the same as empowering

ourselves. The precious and powerful standing up for each other is one of the most exquisite gifts to give and to receive.

Conclusion

Workplace experts have said for years that plurality and diversity enhance creativity. If Latinas and women in general are ever to achieve the power and status that we deserve, we will have to participate equally in those contexts where the most important and far-reaching decisions are made. We must be present in sizeable numbers in these settings and must perform effectively in order to achieve a balance between male and female power (Carli & Eagly, 2001). Females account for 15.7% of the corporate officers in the Fortune 500 companies, and women of color comprise just 1.6% (Texeira, 2003). Latina women in the workforce will grow by 48% in the next decade, and groups such as *Hispanic Business* magazine are identifying Latina pioneers in the corporate world. These changes, with support from all sectors of society, are critical for the identities of Latinas and other women of color to allow for engagement in the complexities of the worlds in which people hold positions of leadership and power in organizations and governments. *Si se puede!* Yes we can!

References

Arnold, K. D. (1995). *Lives of promise: What becomes of high school valedictorians.* San Francisco: Jossey-Bass.

Aronson, J. (Ed.). (2002). *Improving academic achievement.* New York: Academic Press.

Baumeister, R. F., & Showers, C. J. (1984). A review of paradoxical performance effects: Choking under pressure in sports and mental tests. *European Journal of Social Psychology, 16,* 361–383.

Berelowitz, J.-A. (1998). Las Comadres: A feminist collective negotiates a new paradigm for women at the U.S./Mexico border. *Genders,* 28. Retrieved August 11, 2006 from http://www.genders.org/g28/g28_lascomadres.html

Carli, L. L., & Eagly, A. H. (2001). Gender, hierarchy, and leadership: An introduction. *Journal of Social Issues, 57,* 629–636.

Center for Women's Business Research. (2006). *Latinas and entrepreneurship.* Retrieved August 11, 2006 from http://www.nwbc.gov/ResearchPublications/documents/Latina_Factsheet_2006.pdf

Comas-Díaz, L. (1997). Mental health needs of Latinos with professional status. In J. García & M. C. Zea (Eds.), *Psychological interventions and research with Latino populations* (pp. 142–165). New York: Allyn & Bacon.

Comas-Díaz, L., & Greene, B. (1994). Women of color with professional status. In L. Comas-Díaz & B. Greene (Eds.), *Women of color: Integrating ethnic and gender identities in psychotherapy* (pp. 347–388). New York: Guilford Press.

Cross, W. E. Jr. (1991). *Shades of black: Diversity in African American identity.* Philadelphia, PA: Temple University Press.

Dovidio, J. F., & Gaertner, S. L. (1996). Affirmative action, unintentional racial biases, and intergroup relations. *Journal of Social Issues, 52,* 51–76.

Dweck, C. S. (2002). Messages that motivate: How praise molds students' beliefs, motivation, and performance (in surprising ways). In J. Aronson (Ed.), *Improving academic achievement* (pp. 38–61). New York: Academic Press.

Eagly, A. H., & Johannesen-Schmidt, M. C. (2001). The leadership styles of women and men. *Journal of Social Issues, 57,* 781–797.

Eccles, J. S., Wigfield, A., & Byrnes, J. (2003). Cognitive development in adolescence. In R. M. Lerner, M. A. Easterbrooks, & J. Mistry (Eds.), *Handbook of psychology volume 6, Developmental psychology* (pp. 325–350). Hoboken, NJ: John Wiley.

Falicov, C. J. (1982). Mexican families. In M. McGoldrick, J. K. Pearce, & J. Giordano (Eds.), *Ethnicity and family therapy* (pp. 134–163). New York: Guilford Press.

Fletcher, J. K. (2001). *Disappearing acts: Gender, power and relational practice at work.* Cambridge, MA: MIT Press.

Garcia-Aguilera, C. (2004). On being a writer. *Latina Style, 10*(4), 60.

Garcia Coll, C., Cook-Nobles, R., & Surrey, J. L. (1995). *Diversity at the core: Implications for relational theory.* Jean Baker Miller Training Institute Working Papers. Wellesley, MA: Wellesley Centers for Women.

Gomez, M. J., Fassinger, R. E., Prosser, J., Cooke, K., Mejia, B., & Luna, J. (2001). Voces abriendo caminos (voices forging paths): A qualitative study of the career development of notable Latinas. *Journal of Counseling Psychology. 48,* 286–300.

Heilman, M. E. (2001). Description and prescription: How gender stereotypes prevent women's ascent up the organizational ladder. *Journal of Social Issues, 57,* 657–674.

Hughes, D. (2001). Cultural and contextual correlates of involvement in family and community among urban Black and Latino Adults. In A. Rossi (Ed.), *Caring and doing for others: Social responsibility in domains of family, work, and community* (pp. 179–226). Chicago: University of Chicago Press.

Jayson, S., & Rodriguez, E. (2003, June 24). Affirmative action in colleges upheld: UT official hails ruling, saying "Hopwood is dead." *Austin American Statesman,* A1, A5.

Latina Style. (2004b). National Latina symposium, *10*(5), 20–22.

Lemann, N. (2003, June 29). A decision that universities can relate to. *New York Times*, 4–14.

Nieva, V. F., & Gutek, B. A. (1980). Sex effects on evaluation. *Academy of Management Review, 5*, 267–276.

Noguera, P. A. (2001, September). Racial politics and the elusive quest for excellence and equity in education. *In Motion Magazine.* Retrieved July 23, 2005 from http://www.inmotionmagazine.com/er/pnrp2.html

Olmos, E. J., Ybarra, L., & Monterrey, M. (Eds.). (1999). *Americanos: Latino Life in the United States/LA Vida Latina En Los Estados Unidos.* New York: Little Brown & Co.

Pratto, F., & Espinoza, P. (2001). Gender, ethnicity, and power. *Journal of Social Issues, 57*, 763–780.

Ramirez, M. (1998). *Multicultural/multiracial psychology.* Northvale, NJ: Jason Aranson.

Research and Markets. (2004). *U.S. Hispanic women in profile.* Retrieved August 11, 2006 from http://www.researchandmarkets.com/reports/75030/

Ridgeway, C. I. (2001). Gender, status and leadership. *Journal of Social Issues, 57*, 637–655.

Ridgeway, C. I., & Walker, H. (1995). Status structures. In K. Cook, G. Fine, & J. House (Eds.), *Sociological perspectives on social psychology* (pp. 281–310). New York: Allyn & Bacon.

Riojas, A. M. (2004a). The case for Latinas on corporate boards. *Latina Style, 10*(4), 80.

Rios-Ellis, B. (2005, September). *Critical disparities in Latino mental health: Transforming research into action.* Washington, DC: National Council of La Raza (NCLA) Institute for Hispanic Health.

Rosado, D., & Ortuzar, M. (2004, July/August). The 2004 Latina Style 50. *Latina Style, 10*(4), 25–36.

Scales, S. (2004, September/October). Leading others to leadership. *Latina Style, 10*(5), 8–9.

Scott-Jones, D., & Takanishi, R. (in press). Women, diversity and success in science and technology: Conceptualizing the issues. In N. Russo, (Ed.), *Women in science and technology.* Washington, DC: American Psychological Association.

Spencer, S. J., Steele, C. M., & Quinn, D. (1999). Stereotype threat and women's math performance. *Journal of Experimental Social Psychology, 35*, 4–28.

Steele, C. M. (1997). A threat in the air: How stereotypes shape intellectual identity and performance. *American Psychologist, 52*, 613–629.

Steele, C. M., & Aronson, J. (1995). Stereotype threat and the intellectual test performance of African Americans. *Journal of Personality and Social Psychology, 69*, 797–811.

Texeira, E. (2003, June/July). A delicate balance: Real life at work for women of color. *Working Mother*, 62–70, 117–118.

U.S. Census Bureau. (2004, June). Hispanics and Asian Americans increasing faster than overall population. *U.S. Census Bureau News*. Retrieved July 25, 2005 from http://www.census.gov/Press-Release/www/releases/archives/race/001839.html

U.S. Census Bureau. (2004, July). Hispanic population passes 40 million, Census Bureau reports. *U.S. Census Bureau News*. Retrieved July 25, 2005 from http://www.census.gov/Press-Release/www/releases/archives/population/005164.html

Chapter 13

Voices of Black Feminist Leaders: Making Spaces for Ourselves

Ruth L. Hall, BraVada Garrett-Akinsanya, and Michael Hucles

Black feminist leaders have always existed, even though the interest in, visibility of, and opportunities for them are a relatively recent phenomenon. Black women have maintained their voice despite efforts to silence them in the Black, feminist, and lesbian communities as well as the United States as a whole. Since Black women are classified as "other," they are not the focus of any movement's objectives. Black women are under pressure in the Black community to remain silent about sexism. Similarly, Black women are denied a full voice in the feminist and lesbian communities where the focus has been on White middle-class women. In sum, Black women have had to carve out spaces for themselves.

The purpose of this chapter is to discuss Black women leaders. We will begin with a working definition of Black feminism and Black feminist leadership, including how Black women leaders have evolved. Second, we will apply our definition of Black feminists to four historical periods: (a) slavery and Reconstruction; (b) the early 20th century (suffrage movement); (c) mid 20th century (civil rights, gay rights, and the women's rights movements); and (d) contemporary Black feminist leaders. These historical periods have been selected because of the major impact they had on shaping the lives of Black women in America and on Black feminist leadership.

Next, we will discuss the current status of Black women's leadership and include the strategies for and barriers to success. The chapter will conclude with recommendations for future directions for Black women's leadership.

Black Feminism and Life Along the Margins

First, we must answer the following questions: How do Black feminists differ from other feminists? How do Black feminist leaders distinguish themselves? Black feminism is the space where race, gender, class, and activism converge and emerge creating a positive and powerful multidimensional vision of how to implement strategies and opportunities for Black women. According to Beverly Guy-Sheftall (1986) our dual experiences with sexism and racism distinguish Black feminism. Similarly, Hill Collins (1990) states that "Black feminism [is] a process of self-conscious struggle that empowers women and men to actualize a humanist vision of community" (p. 39). Black feminism is inclusive in nature, recognizes that there is no hierarchy of oppressions (Lorde, 1983), and advocates that all oppressions must be eliminated. Alice Walker's (1983) concept of womanist (vs. feminist) conveys the full bodied expression of feminism, enhancing its substance and conceptually merging race and gender. Hooks (1984) echoes other Black feminists and states that her experience as an outsider with knowledge of the inside provides fodder for feminism. She asserts that "feminist theory lacks wholeness, lacks the broad analysis that could encompass a variety of human experiences . . . At its most visionary, it will emerge from individuals who have knowledge of both margin and center" (hooks, 1984, Preface).

Black women and Black feminists live on the margins of society which provides a unique perspective. Hill Collins (1990), Lorde (1984), and hooks (1984) address this marginal status as a source of creative measures that Black women can use to gain the benefits historically available to those inside the margin.

Others have parlayed the concept of margin/center status to one of positive marginality (Mayo, 1982). Hall and Fine (2005) state that "Positive marginality has been a cornerstone of the Black experience by providing psychological and political tools that are used to teach survival skills and coping styles generation after generation" (p. 177). The voices of Black women are active members in the chorus of gender and race. Black women have always been feminists but have been so in their own style and for their own survival.

Black Feminist Leadership

Black feminist leadership status is a designation that is accorded to a person—formally or informally. For the purpose of this chapter, our working definition of Black feminist leaders is: *Black women activists who, from the intersections of race and gender, develop paths, provide a direction, and give voice to Black women.* Black feminist leaders lead by example and generate opportunities for change, provide encouragement and skills to others, and ignite a desire in other Black women to create conditions for success. The ultimate goal of a Black feminist leader is to eliminate the multiple oppressions that compromise the lives of Black women. Race and gender anchor Black feminism and form the divining rod that makes Black feminist leadership unique.

Regardless of their community, class joins race and gender and completes the triad of the Black feminist leader's agenda. Many Black feminist leaders' roots are in low income families and poor communities. Consequently, Black feminist leaders have always recognized the compromising conditions facing a disproportionate number of poor Black women who lack access to resources (Reid, 1993). According to Roth (2004) the concerns of poor women were central to the Black feminist agenda in contrast to the White, middle-class feminist movement. Black liberationists also tend to ignore or marginalize gender and also marginalize the needs of the poor.

Historical Status of Black Women: Slavery and Reconstruction

We cannot underestimate the legacy of slavery and its influence on Blacks and Black feminist leadership. For Blacks, both feminist and antiracism agendas were part and parcel of their resistance to slavery. Even though Black women were disenfranchised from their native countries and the rights of humanity in this new land, informal Black feminist leadership was evident. Black women frequently served as the intermediary between the master and the slave population. Passive resistance was common for slave women who were well aware of their "duty." Many Black women, when possible, slowed down their work productivity or chose abortion rather than produce slaves. Other strategies were to poison the food of their masters if they were fortunate enough to be house slaves. Black women took control over an uncontrollable system any way that they could.

Black women's feminist leadership paired race with gender and class, as it is race that made these women slaves and gender that made them the target of both Black and White men (Davis, 1981; Giddings, 1984). Three women who played a large role in the struggle for Black freedom were Sojourner Truth, Harriet Tubman, and Maria Stewart. Orator Sojourner Truth articulated the needs and the strengths of Black and poor women who were marginalized in the suffragist movement. In her famous "Ain't I a Woman" speech at the 1851 women's convention in Akron, Ohio, Truth articulated how Blacks, including Black women, were deserving of equal rights and as valuable as White men and women (Truth, 1851).

Harriet Tubman's courageous journeys in the Underground Railroad are legendary. As a runaway herself, Tubman returned to the South 19 times over a 10-year period to assist family members and other slaves to freedom. Tubman fought for the right for Black women to be homemakers rather than having to work outside the home, a role denied to Black women by Whites.

Unlike Tubman and Truth, Maria Stewart was a free woman from Connecticut. Stewart became the first woman born in the United States to give public speeches (Lerner, 1972). She believed that there was no conflict between working and political activism. According to Giddings (1984), Stewart's speeches "articulated the precepts upon which the future activism of Black women would be based" (p. 50). Stewart felt that social conditions, rather than race and class, must be held accountable for the status of Black women. She objected to the inferior role of women popular in the day's religious communities and the use of religion to condone slavery or sexism (Giddings, 1984).

Sojourner Truth and Harriet Tubman had allies who included White abolitionists and Black and White men. These abolitionists included Lucretia Mott, a Quaker minister; South Carolinian feminist sisters Sara and Angelina Grimke, who were outspoken White women of their time; and Frederick Douglass, a legendary Black orator.

Reconstruction

Employment opportunities for Black women were usually limited to domestic work. Two Black women who were prominent in this period were Ida B. Wells and Mary Church Terrell. These women became active in the fight against lynching that had become epidemic in the late 19th century. Mary Church Terrell was the wealthy daughter of the first Black Southern millionaire. Memphis-raised Ida B. Wells sparked the campaign against lynching with her journalism and exposure of lynching in the South. College-educated as a teacher, Wells made her mark as a journalist and a newspaper owner. In 1892, Thomas Moss, a friend of Terrell and of Wells, was one of three men lynched in Memphis. Terrell used her wealth and influence to approach President Harrison with her antilynching agenda, to no avail. Wells's numerous articles and speeches eventually influenced the end of lynchings in Memphis. Clearly, both women were activists and examples of the interface of feminism and race.

Black women's clubs: National Association of Colored Women

Both Wells and Terrell became important to the organizational efforts leading to the formation of the National Association of Colored Women (NACW), founded in 1896. A White journalist was indirectly responsible for the formation of the NACW when he suggested that Black women were void of any redeeming value (Hendricks, 1993). This led Wells to found the NACW and both she and Terrell served as presidents (Jones, 1993). Wells and Terrell were part of a general pattern of many Black middle-class women in forming clubs during the late 19th century to address racism and sexism.

The Black women's club movement had a political agenda. Although these Black clubs were middle-class and the women identified as homemakers, their inclusive feminist borders addressed a commitment to assist poor Black women and to help all women achieve. For these club women, education should have no race or class boundaries and the home was viewed as a place of learning. Black women's clubs were a precursor to Black women's sororities. The two oldest Black women's sororities are Alpha Kappa Alpha and Delta Sigma Theta, founded in 1908 and 1913 respectively. Black feminist leaders grew in greater numbers through clubs and sororities and continued to maintain their agenda to eliminate racism, sexism, and classism.

Education has always been a cornerstone and a "way out" for Blacks, and educational opportunities for Black women increased during Reconstruction. Reconstruction saw the emergence of many strong feminist forces: historically Black colleges, Black sororities, and Black women's clubs. For example, Spelman College, a historically Black women's college, was founded in 1875.

The Early 20th Century

The early 20th century showed the continued forward movement of Black feminist leaders in politics, business and industry, education, and entertainment. Mary McLeod Bethune, Madam C. J. Walker, and blues singers Ma Rainey, Billie Holiday, and Bessie Smith represent the many forms of Black feminist leadership.

Politics

Mary McLeod Bethune founded the National Council of Negro Women (NCNW) in 1935 out of a growing concern that previous efforts did not go far enough to address the needs of working-class Black women. Bethune forced a re-evaluation of the focus of Black women's organizations. Too often, as Bettye Collier-Thomas (1993) noted, the efforts of these organizations were spent "raising money for male-dominated organizations and male-defined causes." The creation of a new organization "would forge new relationships among Black women" and "provide an unprecedented base of power for Black women" (p. 854). The NCNW has continued to be a viable and effective organization providing a vehicle for Black feminist concerns. Ms. Bethune also founded a training school for girls which eventually became Bethune-Cookman College, a four-year coeducational institution.

Industry

Until the arrival of Madam C. J. Walker, hair care products specifically for Black women were nonexistent. Married at 14, Madam Walker first worked on a Mississippi cotton field, became a washerwoman, and eventually moved to St. Louis to join her brothers who were barbers. While in St. Louis, Madam Walker joined the National Association of Colored Women. In order to help her daughter, who had developed a scalp problem, she began developing and marketing Black hair products (in partnership with Annie Malone) which blossomed into her own enterprise, Madam Walker's Wonderful Hair Grower. Her company focused on Black scalp and hair care products, cosmetics, and the permanent wave machine (invented by her employee, Marjorie Joyner). In 1908, she opened a beauty college in Pittsburgh. Madam Walker was the first Black female millionaire. Her business created employment opportunities for Black women and her philanthropic efforts included her involvement with the National Association of Colored Women (Bundles, 2001).

Medicine

Dr. Dorothy Ferebee, who graduated from Tufts University Medical School in 1924, noted the unique problems faced by Black women seeking medical degrees. She stated, "We women were always the last to get assignments in amphitheaters and clinics. And I? I was the last of the last because not only was I a woman, but a Negro, too" (Gamble, 1993, p. 926). Despite the barriers erected in the path of Black women's progress, many succeeded in becoming members of, and leaders within, the medical profession.

Entertainment

The Harlem Renaissance, the bosom of Black life and culture, served as a magnet for Black professionals and hopeful artists of all genres. According to Angela Davis (1998), the Black songstress Minnie Smith was the first to record a blues song in 1920. Although the success of Black women blues singers was eclipsed by Black men in the 1930s, the entertainment industry was fueled by the feminist leadership of Black women including Ma Rainey, Bessie Smith, and Billie Holiday. These women emerged from a Black male-dominated musical tradition—the blues and jazz—and carved out their own careers in a time when men reigned supreme. Submerged in their music were the life stories and struggles of poor and working-class women, a group of invisible women from whom they themselves emerged. These women paved the way for today's successful women in the music industry (Davis, 1998). For example, the legendary Ma Rainey is known as the "Mother of the Blues," and served as a mentor for younger singers including Bessie Smith.

Mid 20th Century and the Civil Rights Era

With the 1954 ruling in *Brown v. the Board of Education*, the mid 20th century launched the modern civil rights era. Newly formed Black professional organizations, such as the National Black Nurses Association, continued to emerge. Furthermore, the strength of the civil rights movement generated momentum that was enjoyed by other movements including the Black Power movement, the modern women's rights movement, and the modern gay rights movement. Like the suffragist movement that honed many feminist activist skills from the abolitionist movement, the contemporary feminist movement also benefited from the stage set by the civil rights era. The established pattern of the marginalization of Black women prevailed but Black feminist leaders were represented during these turbulent times in politics, activism, education, medicine, athletics, and entertainment. These Black women led by example and their leadership was evident in their roles in creating change for Black women.

Activism

Although there were countless figures who contributed their lives to the struggle, four names merit attention: Rosa Parks, Ella Baker, Fannie Lou Hamer, and Angela Davis.

Rosa Parks. Rosa Parks is often referred to as the Mother of the Civil Rights Movement. Historical records suggest that she was elected secretary of the National Association for the Advancement of Colored People (NAACP) at her first meeting because she was the only woman member. It was Rosa Parks's refusal to give up her seat on a bus to a White person that launched the Montgomery bus boycott and led to her arrest on December 1, 1955. Her bravery led to the U.S. Supreme Court's decision to make racial segregation on city buses illegal (Academy of Achievement, 2005).

Ella Baker. Following the 1955 Montgomery bus boycott, Ella Baker became the driving force behind the formation of the Southern

Christian Leadership Conference (SCLC). Baker brought her activist history and experiences with the NAACP to SCLC and was given the task of developing the organization (Giddings, 1984). Baker was instrumental in getting Black students involved in the civil rights movement through sit-ins and freedom rides which paved the way for the Student Nonviolent Coordinating Committee (SNCC).

Fannie Lou Hamer: "I'm sick and tired of being sick and tired." The development of SNCC led Fannie Lou Hamer to increased activism in the voter registration campaigns of the 1960s. A resident of Ruleville, Mississippi, Hamer lost her job and her home when she attempted to register to vote. Later, she was savagely beaten when she tried to help others register. Her SNCC activism led to her participation in the 1964 Mississippi Summer Project to register voters. Her efforts resulted in the policy by the National Democratic Party to exclude future delegations that discriminated against Blacks (Reed, 1993).

Angela Davis. Whether as a student, teacher, writer, scholar, or organizer, Angela Davis' history of activism spans several decades. She has been described as "a living witness to the historical struggles of the contemporary era" (Speak Out, 2005). Davis openly expressed her disappointment in the Black Nationalist movement's rejection of communism. In her opinion, nationalism was a barrier to addressing the underlying issue of capitalist domination of poor and working-class people of all races. Her history of activism led to her losing teaching positions, serving jail time, and being on the FBI's "Ten Most Wanted" list (although she was later acquitted of any crimes). Once again, using adversity to rally energy toward change, Angela Davis, a lesbian, feminist activist, cofounded the National Alliance Against Racism and Political Repression (Wikipedia, 2005).

Barbara Smith. A prominent lesbian activist, Barbara Smith has been a strong voice for Black women and for Black lesbians. Her voice and energy combined gender, race, sexual orientation, and activism. Smith's feminist work dates from the 1960s with her writings and activist politics (FemmeNoir, 2006). In 1981, Smith cofounded Kitchen Table: Women of Color Press, the first publishing company to focus on the writings of women of color. Through her writing and activism, she continues to be a voice that challenges all of us to appreciate that advancement comes with a realization that race, class, gender, and sexual orientation must be addressed in a political agenda.

Medical

Black women have long been associated with the health professions. In the South, Black women served as midwives from the colonial period to the 20th century. By the late 20th century, however, midwifery declined as hospitals were constructed and health insurance became more available (Seaholm, 1993). Moreover, the late 19th century saw the rise of a number of nursing training schools, usually for White women and usually attached to hospitals. Martha Franklin, a Black nurse, was the driving force behind the formation, in 1908, of the National Association of Colored Graduate Nurses (NACGN). By 1911, the American Nurses' Association (ANA) emerged, but the policies of racial exclusivity in training and organizations prompted Black nurses to form their own organization. The ANA ended its overtly discriminatory practices and opened its membership to Black nurses in 1948 (Hine, 1993).

Politics

Shirley Chisholm. In 1964, Shirley Chisholm became the first Black woman elected to Congress. She served seven terms in the House of Representatives and was a founding member of the Congressional Black Caucus. Her reign was filled with controversy and decisions based on personal beliefs rather than on their political correctness. Chisholm was quoted to have said during her 1972 presidential campaign: "Women have learned to flex their political muscles. You got to flex that muscle to get what you want" (Kaodik, 2005). Chisholm felt she was "guilty" of being an unabashedly gutsy politician who had learned to work within a system in order to advocate for those who had no voice (Brownmiller, 1970; Chisholm, 1970).

Patricia Roberts Harris. Patricia Roberts Harris is a Black feminist leader who represented her cultural and gender-based communities. Harris cochaired the National Women's Committee on Civil Rights during the Kennedy administration. In 1964, under the administration of President Lyndon Johnson, Harris became the first Black woman in the history of the United States to hold an ambassadorship. Later she was appointed to the office of Secretary of Housing and Urban Development by President Carter (1977) and to the office of Secretary of Health and Human Services in 1979. She was the first Black woman in history to serve on a president's cabinet (Famous Firsts, 2005).

Religion

Black women and men have always seen religion and spirituality as critical to their lives. Although Black women have participated in the formal process of religious worship they were not officially ordained until the late 19th and early 20th centuries with the Holiness and Pentecostal movements (Gilkes, 1993). More recently, other denominations have included Black women among the ordained. In 1977, after a long and distinguished career as an activist, lawyer, teacher, and poet, Pauli Murray became the first Black woman to be ordained as a priest in the Episcopal Church (Jacobs, 1993). Nearly 10 years later, in 1989, Barbara Harris became the first Black woman consecrated bishop in the Episcopal Church. Harris was a major voice in behalf of the poor, women, and minorities (Thompson, 1993).

Contemporary Black Feminist Leaders

Black women continue to be "firsts" in many fields and Black feminist leaders continue to grow in numbers and areas of influence. Clearly, today's Black feminist leaders are the recipients of the sacrifices and successes of our foremothers. Maya Angelou, poet, actress, and activist was invited to write and read an original piece of poetry for Clinton's Presidential Inauguration and was only the second poet asked to do so. Alice Walker was the first Black woman to win the Pulitzer Prize for fiction (1993). Ruth Simmons became the first Black president of an Ivy League school—Brown University—in 2000. Toni Morrison was the first Black American to win the Nobel Prize for literature in 1993 (Black women firsts, 1997; Famous Firsts, 2005). Clearly, Black women have garnered leadership positions and their successes are an incentive for the success of other Black feminist leaders.

Black feminist scholars

The Black feminist writers who have emerged to document our successes include Angela Davis, Patricia Hill Collins, Beverly Guy Sheftall, and Paula Giddings. One prevalent group of activist feminists is the Combahee River Collective in Boston, founded in 1974. The book, *All the Women are White and all the Blacks are Men, But Some of us are Brave* (Hull, Scott, & Smith, 1982), suggests that the battles fought by Black women and Black feminist leaders for race and gender equality and for social justice, although changed, continue to be a priority as the need to hear the collective voices of Black women heard continues.

The field of feminist psychology

A number of Black feminist psychologists have addressed the status of the psychology of Black women. Although our visibility continues to grow, there are still challenges. For example, many researchers and publications do not include Black women as participants and often categorize Black women as "noise" if they are few in number, and eliminate Black women from their analyses. Ironically, the conclusions drawn from these same studies are applied to everyone, regardless of race or gender. In addition, when Black women generate their own research, and do not include Whites in their analyses, they are often accused of a lack of objectivity even though White psychologists have been studying Whites for years and have not been similarly accused. Furthermore, if ethnic studies do not include Whites as the default group, the research is frequently not accepted for publication.

Black feminist leaders in psychology are too numerous to name but two "firsts" within feminist psychology organizations are of note. Pam Trotman Reid was the first Black president of Division 35 (Women) of the American Psychological Association and Ruth L. Hall (the first author of this chapter) was the first Black Collective Coordinator (president equivalent) of the Association for Women in Psychology. Black feminists within feminist and mainstream organizations have mentored others as they were mentored and, whenever possible, opened opportunities for success and achievement.

Current status of Black feminist leadership

Barriers. Many threads run through the lives of Black feminist leaders over the centuries but there is a remarkable consistency in the barriers that compromise forward momentum. The Big Four Barriers—racism, sexism, classism, heterosexism/homophobia—remain. America remains a privileged society and oppresses people of color, women, the poor, and lesbians.

Strengths. The context of leadership for Black women must occur within the framework of identity and culture. It is clear that, historically, Black women have survived because they have been able to adapt under adverse circumstances. Black women have adopted values, beliefs, and systems of activism that are addressed by Black feminist psychologists. A reality for Black feminists is that they must reject ascribed societal limitations. Whether our marginal status requires that we create a path for Black women where no path exists or take up the mantle with like-minded Black women, Black feminists have not only adapted but created systems for advancement. The perception of the margin as a position of strength allows Black women to feel in command of their lives rather than taking on a passive and ineffective stance.

A second strength and strategy for leadership among successful Black women is their congruent pattern of beliefs, attitudes, and behaviors that emphasize a connectedness with other people of African descent. It is the Black woman leader who displays a positive cultural consciousness of values and behaviors that promotes the survival of herself and her people (Kambon, 1992).

Life on the margins is embraced as a vantage point that offers possibilities rather than problems for Black women. Even with the limitations faced by Black women, more research about Black women is being conducted that focuses on our strengths rather than on pathological research agendas. Black feminist leaders have created innovative lines of research, have introduced new lines of inquiry, and sought out opportunities to examine several populations including Black lesbians (Hall & Fine, 2005; Hall & Greene, 2002), sexuality (Wyatt, 1997), and clinical work with Black women (Garrett-Akinsanya, 2000; Hall, 2001; Jackson & Greene, 2000; Sanchez-Hucles, 2000; Wyche & Crosby, 1996).

Our success is generated from the mentoring role played by Black women who have preceded us and by like-minded White allies and other women of color who have used their influence to fight for equality. As with Mott and the Grimke sisters, the support of allies is vital. The Black feminist agenda remains remarkably similar over the years but the foci are more refined and areas of success are more varied. The increased number of Black feminist leaders and of allies allows for a greater trajectory and impact.

Future Directions Created by Black Feminist Leadership

There is no shortage of talent or of Black feminist leaders within the Black feminist community. Black women leaders represent the potential that Black women have to remind the United States of its oppressive attitude toward Black women, and through their leadership create opportunities for themselves and for others. The women discussed in this chapter illustrate that Black feminist leaders have emerged and will continue to emerge despite adversity. The intersections of race, gender, and class consciousness define the Black feminist leader. Regardless of educational level, Black feminist leaders emerge and create opportunities. Slavery's signature is deep in the psyche of Black feminist leaders as they carry on a legacy built on independence and a need to care for others. For Black feminist leaders, Black womanhood is a definition created by their radical marginality and the knowledge of how to work within and outside of a system designed to oppress them. These women have gone against the odds and used their ingenuity, persuasiveness, and verve to channel their talent successfully. By default, the talent of Black women was transformed into leadership and opened opportunities for other men and women who saw them as heroines, mentors, and role models. Their legacy provides hope and the thought of possibilities to others. Following the African adage, "I am because we are," Black feminist leaders have always used their strength, enthusiasm, and persistence to benefit the advancement of Black womanhood. Our history is what drives us, carves out the path for Black feminist leaders, and makes their determination that much stronger.

There is no expiration date on leaders—those that came before us still hold those positions while others' leadership has yet to be acknowledged or emerge. The unique position of Black women allows them a freedom to understand privilege and oppression from multiple perspectives. Until the battle against oppression is won, Black feminist leaders will continue to come forward and be the voices of transformation.

References

Academy of Achievement. (2005). *Rosa Parks*. Retrieved April 25, 2005 from http://www.achievement.org/autodoc/page/par0pro-1

Black women firsts: Hidden gems of black history. (1997, April). *Ebony*. Retrieved April 22, 2005 from http://www.findarticles.com/p/articles/mi_m1077/is_n6_v52/ai_19279729

Brownmiller, S. (1970). *Shirley Chisholm*. Garden City, NY: Doubleday.

Bundles, A. P. (2001). *On her own ground: The life and times of Madam C. J. Walker*. New York: Scribner.

Chisholm, S. (1970). *Unbought and unbossed*. Boston: Houghton Mifflin.

Collier-Thomas, B. (1993). National Council of Negro Women. In D. C. Hine (Ed.), *Black women in America: An historical encyclopedia* (pp. 853–864). New York: Carlson Publishing.

Davis, A. Y. (1981). *Women, race, & class.* New York: Vintage Press.

Davis, A. Y. (1998). *Blues legacies and Black feminism: Gertrude "Ma" Rainey, Bessie Smith, and Billie Holiday.* New York: Pantheon.

Famous Firsts by African Americans. (2005). Retrieved April 23, 2005 from http://www.infoplease.com/spot/bhmfirsts.html

FemmeNoir. (2006). *Barbara Smith.* Retrieved August 14, 2006 from http://www.femmenoir.net/ll/2006/06/barbara_smith.php

Gamble, V. (1993). Physicians, twentieth century. In D. C. Hine (Ed.), *Black women in America: An historical encyclopedia* (pp. 926–928). New York: Carlson Publishing.

Garrett-Akinsanya, B. (2000, August). *Too legit to quit: A look at African American female leaders and African-centered wellness: Self-care as a success strategy for African American women.* Paper presented at the American Psychological Association national convention, Friday August 4, 2000.

Giddings, P. (1984). *When and where I enter: The impact of Black women on race and sex in America.* New York: Bantam Books.

Gilkes, C. T. (1993). Religion. In D. C. Hine (Ed.), *Black Women in America: An historical encyclopedia* (pp. 967–972). New York: Carlson Publishing.

Guy-Sheftall, B. (1986). Remembering Sojourner Truth: On Black feminism. *Catalyst, 1,* 54–57.

Hall, R. L. (2001). Shaking the foundation: Women of color in sport. *The Sport Psychologist, 15,* 386–400.

Hall, R. L., & Fine, M. (2005). The stories we tell: The lives and friendship of older Black lesbians. *Psychology of Women Quarterly, 29,* 177–187.

Hall, R. L., & Greene, B. (2002). Not any one thing: Multiple identities and complex legacies in African American lesbian relationships. *Journal of Lesbian Studies, 6*(1), 65–74.

Hendricks, W. (1993). Ida Bell Wells-Barnett. In D. C. Hine (Ed.), *Black women in America: An historical encyclopedia* (pp. 1242–1246). New York: Carlson Publishing.

Hill Collins, P. (1990). *Black feminist thought: Knowledge, consciousness, and the politics of empowerment.* New York: Routledge.

Hine, D. C. (1993). Nurses. In D. C. Hine (Ed.), *Black women in America: An historical encyclopedia* (pp. 887–891). New York: Carlson Publishing.

hooks, b. (1984). *Feminist theory: From margin to center.* Boston: South End Press.

Hull, G. T., Scott, P. B., & Smith, B. (Eds.). (1982). *But some of us are brave: Black women's studies.* New York: Feminist Press.

Jackson, L. C., & Greene, B. (Eds.). (2000). *Psychotherapy with Black women: Innovations in psychodynamic perspectives and practice.* New York: Guilford Press.

Jacobs, S. M. (1993). Pauli Murray. In D. C. Hine (Ed.), *Black women in America: An historical encyclopedia* (pp. 825–826). New York: Carlson Publishing.

Jones, B. (1993). Mary Eliza Church Terrell. In D. C. Hine (Ed.), *Black women in America: An historical encyclopedia* (pp. 1157–1159). New York: Carlson Publishing.

Kambon, K. K. (1992). *The African personality in America: An African-centered framework*. Tallahassee, FL: Nubian Nation Publications.

Kaodik. (2005). *"Reagan is the Pres but I voted for Shirley Chisholm" RIP*. SOHH.com Global Forum. Retrieved April 20, 2005 from http://www.sohh.com/forums/archive/index.php/t-533170.html

Lerner, G. (Ed.). (1972). *Black women in White America: A documentary history*. New York: Vantage Books.

Lorde, A. (1983). There is no hierarchy of oppressions. *Interracial Books for Children Bulletin, 14*(3&4), 9.

Lorde, A. (1984). *Sister outsider*. Trumansburg, NY: The Crossing Press.

Mayo, C. (1982). Training for positive marginality. In C. L. Bickman (Ed.), *Applied social psychology annual, vol. 3* (pp. 57–73). Beverly Hills, CA: Sage.

Reed, L. (1993). Fannie Lou Hamer. In D. C. Hine (Ed.), *Black women in America: An historical encyclopedia* (pp. 518–520). New York: Carlson Publishing.

Reid, P. T. (1993). Poor women in psychological research: Shut up and shut out. *Psychology of Women Quarterly, 17*, 133–150.

Roth, B. (2004). *Separate roads to feminism: Black, Chicana, and White feminist movements in America's second wave*. New York: Cambridge University Press.

Sanchez-Hucles, J. (2000). *The first session with African-Americans: A step by step guide*. San Francisco: Jossey-Bass.

Seaholm, M. (1993). Midwives. In D. C. Hine (Ed.), *Black women in America: An historical encyclopedia* (pp. 789–791). New York: Carlson Publishing.

Speak Out—Institute for Democratic Education and Culture. (2005). *Angela Davis*. Retrieved April 30, 2005 from http://www.speakoutnow.org/People/AngelaDavis.html

Thompson, K. (1993). Barbara Harris. In D. C. Hine (Ed.), *Black women in America: An historical encyclopedia* (pp. 537–538). New York: Carlson Publishing.

Truth, S. (1851) *Ain't I a woman?* Delivered at the Women's Convention in Akron, OH. Retrieved April 1, 2005 from http://eserver.org/race/aint-i-a-woman.html

Walker, A. (1983). *In search of our mothers' gardens: Womanist prose*. New York: Harcourt Brace.

Wikipedia (2005). *Angela Davis*. Retrieved April 30, 2005 from http://en.wikipedia.org/wiki/Angela_Davis

Wyatt, G. (1997). *Stolen women: Reclaiming our sexuality, taking back our lives*. New York: Wiley and Sons.

Wyche, K. F., & Crosby, F. J. (Eds.). (1996). *Women's ethnicities: Journeys through psychology*. Boulder, CO: Westview Press.

Chapter 14

Asian American Women Leaders: The Intersection of Race, Gender, and Leadership

Debra M. Kawahara, Edna M. Esnil, and Jeanette Hsu

The Asian American population is one of the fastest growing racial groups in the United States, comprising approximately 13.5 million individuals (U.S. Census Bureau, 2005) and representing over 34 different ethnic groups; an estimated 51% of this population are women (Nomura, 2003; True, 2000). However, little scholarship exists regarding the experiences of Asian American women compared to that of Euro American women. Available research has focused on topics such as familial roles and cultural values/beliefs, and has often perpetuated stereotypes of Asian American women as passive, exotic, or victims of a patriarchal "traditional" Asian culture. Research on leadership among Asian American women is even more sparse, despite the continued growth of the Asian American population, its diversity, and the rising visibility of Asian American women leaders.

This chapter explores the intersection between Asian American culture and gender in leadership. Beginning with a web-based discussion board, we interviewed several Asian American women viewed as leaders in their particular field or profession to explore and understand their diverse perspectives, examine their reflections about their paths to leadership and their current leadership roles, and understand the complex intersection of gender and race in their experiences. Core feminist concepts of resiliency and strength, empowerment, personal reflexivity, power relations, and connectedness are discussed in the context of Asian American women's development as leaders, as well as their styles and approaches to leadership. Examining leadership in the context of both gender and race is an important step toward developing new, more inclusive models of leadership, and we hope that this chapter will contribute to this valuable goal.

Brief Overview of Asian Women in America

Asian American women's leadership in the 21st century can be understood only in the context of Asian American women's history. Due to the combination of exclusion and antimiscegenation laws, the numbers of Asian women in America compared to Asian men remained suppressed as recently as the 1970 Census (Bradshaw, 1994).

Patterns of immigration

Women from Asian countries began immigrating to the United States in the mid 1800s with the first waves of voluntary immigration by Chinese seeking gold in the American West. The number of Chinese women was far below that of Chinese men and these women from China were often coerced to emigrate by false promises of wealthy marriages to countrymen already in America, sold by family members, or forcibly kidnapped to work in the sex industry among the primarily "bachelor" societies. Women who voluntarily emigrated, as well as those completing their indenture as prostitutes, often served in domestic roles, ran boarding houses or brothels, or served as cooks, laundresses, seamstresses, and other manual or semiskilled laborers (Bradshaw, 1994). While laws during the Chinese Exclusion period from 1882 to 1943 sought generally to control Asian immigration and status in American society, some exclusion laws targeted Asian women specifically, and was fueled primarily by negative stereotypes of Chinese women as "immoral" (Lee, 2003, p. 79).

Immigration of Chinese women was followed by that of Japanese women, typically arriving in America as "picture brides" of Japanese men between 1907 to 1924, forming functioning family units and developing Japanese family communities. Korean women were also classified as "Japanese" and were able to immigrate as picture brides before 1924. However, large-scale immigration of Korean women did not occur until after the Korean War (1950–65). In addition, the adoption of Korean children, mainly girls, also became a main route of Korean immigration. Another special population of Asian women immigrants included Asian women who married American servicemen stationed during American military involvements in the Pacific.

After the Immigration Act of 1965 eased restrictions on Asian immigration, women from China, Korea, South Asia, the Philippines, and Southeast Asia outnumbered that of Japanese women. These immigrants were also more highly educated, with Filipinas and South Asian women having the highest educational levels of all Asian immigrant groups (Bradshaw, 1994). These different circumstances have contributed to vastly different experiences for these women living in the US, and resulted in challenges for Asian American women as leaders in their ethnic communities and in American society.

Social activism

Many Asian American women have risen to leadership by addressing problems faced by their own ethnic communities, such as labor activism against sweatshop working environments, advocacy for children, and community education about domestic violence. Many Asian American women have worked in the public sphere to alleviate social problems such as poverty; to fight for equality and social justice; and to combat racism, sexism, and other forms of discrimination (Chow, 1989; Louie, 2000).

Despite the fact that Asian American women played increasingly greater leadership roles within their own ethnic communities, their presence and impact within the American women's movement has been inconsistent or conflictual at best, and nearly invisible at worst. Gender was the primary focus and category of analysis of the mainstream women's movement, ignoring or relegating to secondary consideration other dimensions of identity or experience such as race and ethnicity (Root, 1995). An essay by Mitsuye Yamada (1983) compellingly described the anger and frustration of Asian American women in what has generally been perceived as a feminist movement of White women. Asian American women have often found that White feminist organizations either ignored the needs and concerns of women of color, paid "lip service" to them, or "tokenized" the few women of color who attempted to influence these organizations from within. At the same time, Asian American women often found that identifying as a feminist or taking on leadership roles in the community was dissonant with community expectations and traditional cultural expectations for Asian women to be subservient, modest, and deferential (Bradshaw, 1994). Asian American women self-identifying as feminist sometimes found that they were characterized as "betraying" their ethnic identity by focusing on White women's concerns or appearing to prioritize sexism over racism. However, Yamada (1983) eloquently stated that "I have thought of myself as a feminist first, but my ethnicity cannot be separated from my feminism" (p. 73).

Following the lead of the civil rights movement and in alliance with other women of color, Asian American women have struggled against, and given voice to, the "dual oppression of racism and sexism" (Bradshaw, 1994, p. 93). Despite the challenges and conflicts of leadership for Asian American women in the women's movement, Root (1995, p. 274) noted that these women "laid an amazing political groundwork for future generations" in the male-dominated Asian American movement of the 1960s and 1970s, creating the first courses on Asian American women at California state universities, and publications on Asian American women's experiences. For Asian American women, developing a feminist agenda in the context of their communities was and is vital to affirming both gender and ethnicity in their own lives.

Biculturalism, Feminist Identity, and Leadership

Race and gender are dynamic and complex (Williams, McCandies, & Dunlap, 2002). The intersection of Asian American culture and gender on leadership may be influenced by one's biculturalism and feminist identity within different contexts. Bicultural competence (LaFromboise, Coleman, & Gerton, 1998) and feminist identity (Downing & Roush, 1985) are utilized to examine this intersection on leadership. Finally, a brief literature review on leadership that includes feminist models of leadership is described.

Biculturalism

LaFromboise et al. (1998) posited that psychological well-being involves developing and maintaining competence in both cultures. Based on their exhaustive literature review, LaFromboise et al. recommended six dimensions of bicultural competence. They consisted of: (a) an awareness, understanding, sensitivity, and appreciation of the social, historical, political, and psychological aspects of both cultures; (b) positive approaches toward both groups; (c) bicultural efficacy or the belief that one can live successfully within two cultures without compromising the meaning of their cultural identity; (d) ability to communicate cognitions and moods verbally and nonverbally; (e) role repertoire; and (f) being grounded with a well-developed social support network within both groups. This model illuminates the duality of "Americanness" and "Asianness."

Feminist identity

Hyde (2004) defined a feminist as a person who favors gender equality across multiple domains (e.g., political, economical, social). Therefore, a feminist supports changes (i.e., legally, socially) to achieve this equality. Feminist identity development has been delineated by Downing and Roush (1985), including the stages of (a) passive acceptance, (b) revelation, (c) embeddedness, (d) synthesis, and (e) active commitment. Based on women's life experiences, they indicated a cyclical model rather than a linear model. Fischer et al. (2000) found positive personal identity states with women in the last two stages. These studies support the idea that women in the latter two stages enjoy positive psychological experiences.

Becoming biculturally competent, transcending gender roles, and taking context into consideration may all impact an Asian American women's leadership style. The bicultural competence model is limited by not fully examining the development of one's feminist consciousness, while the feminist identity model does not address ethnic minority women's gender-related experiences both within the majority and minority groups. Neither model addresses the dualism of both race and gender in depth.

Impact of culture and gender on leadership styles and approaches

Early research on leadership characteristics included behavioral approaches, behavioral dimensions, and personality traits, but only studied male leaders. Contemporary research has focused on the intersection of leadership and gender, including an examination of theoretical frameworks and the strategies utilized by women to become leaders. However, few research studies have examined the intersection of gender and race in the context of leadership.

Appelbaum, Audet, and Miller's (2003) examination of gender and leadership indicated that women's leadership styles are typically different from men's and that both genders can integrate each other's typical styles. Further, women's styles are not less effective and tend to be more effective in team-based consensually driven organizational structures. Lastly, socialization drives the belief that women's leadership styles are less effective.

Researchers examining positive feminine leadership characteristics found that powerful feminist leaders showed a combination of agentic qualities such as directiveness and competence, and that communal qualities such as friendliness and warmth are characteristics (Eagly, Wood, & Diekman, 2000). Astin and Leland (1991) and Denmark (1993) studied successful feminist leaders and found empowerment strategies that included listening, communicating with others on their own level, employing strong people and not feeling threatened by them, giving positive feedback, and working through collegiality and consensus; thus a de-emphasis on power to control in favor of a leader's ability to empower others is recommended.

However, these models are limited by the exclusion of women's leadership within a cultural context. Darlington and Mulvaney (2003) examined leadership with a multicultural group of women by introducing a reciprocal empowerment model. The authors view reciprocal empowerment as aspirational, integrating "attributes of self determination, independence, knowledge, choice, and action" with qualities of empowerment such as "compassion, companionship, collectivity, consensus, and competence to enhance" self and others. The model embraces a democratic environment that fosters "mutual attention, mutual empathy, mutual engagement, and mutual responsiveness" (p. 3).

The literature review on bicultural competency, feminist identity, and leadership offered some insight in understanding the complex intersection between Asian American culture, gender, and leadership. However, these current models of ethnic, cultural, and feminist identity development do not yet account for the complexities of Asian American women's experiences.

Interview Study and Results

In order to gain greater understanding about the little-researched topic of Asian American women and leadership, we conducted interviews which allowed us to capture the multiple intersections of race, gender, and social locations. Interviews were conducted from July 2003 to August 2004 by the authors.

The participants were 12 women of Asian descent. A purposive sample was created to obtain a sample of diverse Asian ethnicities and professions. A diversity of professions was intentionally targeted to illuminate the common strengths, experiences, and skills of Asian American women leaders. All of the women selected were leaders and each was considered to be a high achiever in her respective field within a U.S. context. Table 14.1 shows demographic characteristics of the women in the sample.

Each of the women leaders was interviewed either in person or by phone. An interview guide consisting of five questions was developed. Avenues to recruit participants included: women from our professional network; women with known status, years of experience, job position, and work in their communities; and women referred by other women who participated in the study. Interviews lasted from 45 minutes to $2\frac{1}{2}$ hours in length. The interviews were then transcribed and analyzed for themes.

Emergent themes

Six themes emerged from the interviews. They were: (a) knowing oneself and doing something you believe in; (b) having a vision and inspiring others to work on that vision; (c) relational and collaborative leadership style; (d) taking on challenges, struggles, and conflicts; (e) dominant culture efficacy and biculturalism; and (f) support and encouragement.

Knowing oneself and doing something you believe in. Eight of the twelve women discussed their leadership roles as fitting with their personal values and interests. It was very important for the women to match their actions with their values. There was also an underlying passion, drive, and commitment:

> I would say just be involved, just be involved in whatever you are most passionate about whatever the issue might be because I think the leadership will come, you know, in a way will come naturally if you are committed to something, if you are willing to put in time. (Donna, public policy administrator, Chinese American)

303

Table 14.1 Interviewee demographics

Interviewee name[a]	Ethnicity	Natl. origin	Profession	Educ. level
Donna Tsui	Chinese American	US	Public policy administrator	Masters
Julianna Tang	Chinese American	US	Musician/artist	Unknown
Wendy Chen	Chinese American	US	University administrator	Ed.D.
Diane Liu	Chinese American	US	University administrator	Ed.D.
Sharon Lee	Chinese American	US	State legislator	Ph.D.
Jordan Nabe	Filipina	Philippines	Entrepreneur	College
Olivia Ramierez	Filipina	US	Director of university-based women's health program	Ph.D.
Ling Marsela	Filipina	Philippines	Magazine editor and founder	Masters
Tammie Fuji	Japanese	Japan	Psychologist	Ph.D.
Lynn Takasaki	Japanese American	US	Judge	J.D.
Katherine Bell	Japanese-African American	US	College administrator	Ph.D.
Sikha Mishra	South Asian	India	University professor	Ph.D.

[a] Actual names have been changed to pseudonyms.

It was consistent philosophically with me. So it felt right, you know, and it was the primary thing that drove me to all the things that I do because I have never stayed or been in positions and roles that I really didn't believe in . . . the things that I truly believed in, it fit with my values, my ideals . . . (Diane, university administrator, Chinese American)

See what there is out there first so that they know first of all what they believe in, you know, what gives them passion and then for them to see what it takes to fulfill their dreams. (Sharon, state legislator, Chinese American)

As a result of following their own path of self-discovery, many of the women were guided by their own interests and employment experiences which seemed to lead them to other opportunities. Unlike a more masculine approach of strategically planning one's career, many of the women found a more emergent, evolving process that weaved together their self-knowledge, growth, interests, and experiences. Further, many of the women did not actively pursue positions, but were asked and/or encouraged to apply to leadership and/or management positions because others recognized the superior work and abilities that the women possessed. However, the women had to be willing to apply.

After my doctorate one thing led to another and I started to work in the United States and then decided to stay here. . . . So I kind of came exploring my own status of being Asian in America and that got me more interested in the Asian American studies field . . . (Sikha, university professor, South Asian)

It's interesting. I never really asked for each position to move up, it's not like "oh, I have to be a dean" . . . I think in general I didn't really plan . . . (Wendy, university administrator, Chinese American)

Having a vision and inspiring others to work on the vision. One of the most prominent themes among the women was the belief that a leader has to have a vision and be able to inspire others to follow and act on the vision. Further, the leader has to convey excitement and enthusiasm about the vision and rally others' assistance to make it a reality.

I think that leadership is being able to lead I mean and have people follow whether it's following your vision or your direction and I think being able to command people to respect you and go with you . . . (Jordan, entrepreneur, Filipina)

. . . there is a shared value, shared agenda and that's all part of the vision piece. And I think it's the willingness and the ability to bring those pieces together and set the tone . . . (Diane, university administrator, Chinese American)

A leader must be able to do the position, and be able to sell the position to the followers. You must see where, when you start something, you must see where, be able to tell people, okay, 10 years down the road, this is where we want to be. So that sets a goal for people to strive for. And that's how we're going to get there. (Ling, magazine editor and founder, Filipina)

The vision seemed to embrace an entity larger than the women themselves. Seven of the women felt a deep sense of responsibility and commitment for social justice and advocacy. The impact of their work went beyond their own interests and career and more for others and communities who were in need. These women felt that they could be change agents and be activists for a greater good.

I think that getting involved in all these issues, getting into these positions of responsibility and feeling that I could make an impact on people's lives, and also actually feeling a sense of responsibility that I myself had to keep on going . . . (Sharon, state legislator, Chinese American)

I felt that as an administrator, I would actually be able to affect more students than I would have as a faculty member . . . I thought as an administrator I could actually change the system on a larger level. (Katherine, college administrator, Japanese-African American)

Relational and collaborative leadership style. Related to the leader's values, vision, and inspiration to others, eight of the twelve women discussed using a more decentralized and participatory leadership style. The women emphasized empowering others by sharing power and being willing to learn, work hard, and share through the process. Relationships among the group members seemed as important as the work itself. This type of leadership style seems to be influenced by both racial and gender socialization and influences.

Leadership, I think, reflects that sort of concern (co-operation, collaboration) for really bringing the group together and achieving the cohesiveness of the group to really move on some issues that we can really achieve consensus. (Tammie, psychologist, Japanese)

My leadership style is very reflective of Asian values. It's very relational, it's group oriented . . . it's about service . . . (Wendy, university administrator, Chinese American)

306

I try very hard to create an environment that is harmonious and feels like an effective good working environment so that different points of view can be heard. (Sikha, university professor, South Asian)

I believe that everybody within an organization and institution should be, is at the same level; I don't look down upon anybody just because of title and rank, but I see everybody very much collaborative and as peers even though I might have the title of executive director. So I do believe it's very relational, I do believe it's working together. (Donna, public policy administrator, Chinese American)

Taking on challenges, struggles, and conflicts.   As part of being a leader, the women had to be willing to step up when an opportunity arose or a problem was seen and take action. This meant that not only could the women identify problems or needs, but there was a willingness to become involved and do something about it.

I think just seeing a need that, especially in the Asian American community that there's so few people willing to step up to the plate really, so few people willing to take a leadership role. It's almost like if we don't do it, nobody's gonna do it . . . (Donna, public policy administrator, Chinese American)

I think that I could see a direction we needed to go in and most people didn't have a direction. And so I thought, "okay, what are we gonna do, what are we gonna do?" (Katherine, college administrator, Japanese-African American)

And I'm that type of person, if I see the need, I will create or do whatever's necessary for that because, it's my own comfort level . . . (Lynn, judge, Japanese American)

I decided I'm going to have to get back to the States and make sure that I do my part for this [Asian American lesbian] movement, which was that by the time the Asians get together and we get together . . . that's what led me then to organize and initiate. (Olivia, director of university-based women's health program, Filipina)

Some of the women spoke of challenging conventional cultural norms of Asian women being quiet and demure by speaking out and taking a stand on issues. Learning leadership skills such as communication and public speaking, listening, organizing, fund raising, educating, conflict resolution, and networking were essential for these women to be effective as leaders.

> I think that there is some reluctance or hesitance about challenging the cultural tradition. I think that there definitely was that and part of me I think certainly had that buy-in. (Tammie, psychologist, Japanese)

> I think that what I'm learning in this job is that I do need to speak up more and I need to challenge people more . . . (Wendy, university administrator, Chinese American)

> It made me realize you have to take a stand and you have to say "no, this is how I'm going to do it. I was raised in this country, given this freedom for a reason and if you don't like it, then too bad." (Julianna, musician/artist, Chinese American)

Dominant culture efficacy and biculturalism.   One of the prominent themes among the women was the necessity to work and be visible in multiple cultural settings, particularly the dominant culture. The ability to interact and connect within and outside one's own community seemed to be emphasized in order for barriers to be broken and alliances to be cultivated.

> All the speeches I give is talking about how important it is to be involved, whether it's to be involved in the Asian American community or mainstream and I say that it is extremely important for us to be more involved in the mainstream . . . (Donna, public policy administrator, Chinese American)

> I mean I'm glad that I'm in a key position to help Asian Americans because quite a few programs that were going to be cut originally, that would have affected Asian Americans. Yet, at the same time, I'm really honored and feel just so happy to be able to help a wider range of people. And I'm happy to be able to present a positive image of an Asian American leader to these people, who probably have not seen an Asian American woman this way before. (Sharon, state legislator, Chinese American)

> With non-Filipino organizations, it's a different matter, because I want to prove to the Asians, want to prove to mainstream that there are qualified Filipino leaders out there. (Ling, magazine editor and founder, Filipina)

Support and encouragement.   Eleven out of the twelve women discussed the importance of others for support, guidance, and mentoring. Some

308

found their own family members as influential in their leadership development; others had to find supporters along the way. Even for those who did not have their families' support or mentors within their field, the women found others who believed in them whom they could turn to for advice and who supported them through the setbacks and difficulties.

> I've been very fortunate in my entire career I've had tremendous role models and mentors throughout every stage of my development and from [my university] alumni to individuals in the Asian American community . . . (Donna, public policy administrator, Chinese American)

> If you don't have family support, you've got to create a surrogate family and don't just go looking for people that look like you 'cause you might not find it there . . . (Julianna, musician/artist, Chinese American)

> Well, first of all, having a partner, my husband I couldn't do it without family, just having a supportive family and having both immediate family and the parents just really to me is very very crucial in coping . . . (Jordan, entrepreneur, Filipina)

> I found that it was better for me for support . . . So I went to the lesbian community where all the secrets were out, whether that was alcohol or drugs, domestic violence, sexual abuse, rape, incest. (Olivia, director of university-based women's health program, Filipina)

Conclusion

Many Asian American women, and more specifically Asian American women leaders, do not fit the typical stereotype of Asian American women as passive, submissive, demure, and apolitical. This was clearly evident in both the web-based discussions and the interviews.

First, the women were active participants in the continual process of self-discovery. They seemed to know who they are, what they believe, and where they want to go. They are agents of their own lives and provide guidance for others to find their way. In effect, they are subjects of their own destiny, creating paths for themselves and others. Clearly, contextual dynamics and issues such as oppression and prejudice are a part of the path that these women negotiate. However, it appears that the women take charge of their realities as opposed to passively resigning, focusing on, or accepting them. As a result, the women appear to take their evolving sense of self and match it to the activities that they choose to engage in. This foundation of self gives them direction and allows them to inspire and engage others in that direction because their actions are driven by their values and passion.

Interestingly, the women seemed to have a sense of obligation and responsibility to the larger group that motivates their actions. Consistent with the historical literature reviewed earlier, many of the women's work and leadership involved the Asian and Asian American communities, but also embraced the larger society. Social advocacy and working toward social justice seemed to be important components of their vision. They could identify with those who were less visible, less heard, and less powerful in the system and wanted to change it for the betterment of society.

In order to do this, the women had to be willing to learn new skills and face challenges, struggles, and conflicts directly. For some, it required having the strength to defy conventional norms and expectations. Being communicative, managing conflicts, organizing rallies, and networking were abilities that the women developed and utilized to lead. In addition to these skills, the women recognized the need to be effective in interacting and working within the dominant culture. These leaders encouraged future leaders to be visible and to become involved in the mainstream community. Support from others assisted these women in facing the struggles, overcoming barriers, guiding them through the unknown, and providing them with a sense of belonging and acceptance.

These women used the values and behaviors of both the Asian and the dominant culture in order to achieve their goals, which are consistent with the literature on bicultural competence. Additionally, these actions suggest that these women fit the advanced stages of the feminist identity model.

Overall, the women's leadership style had a collectivistic view in what they were doing as well as the way that they lead, focusing on the group rather than the individual, and prioritizing relationships with others. Learning, sharing, including, and working together through empowerment appears to be important to many of the women. This collectivistic view is consistent with both Asian American cultural values and feminist values. From our interviews, it could not be ascertained whether this group orientation derives from their Asian American cultural heritage, their feminist perspective, their disposition, or a combination of factors.

What became clear in the process of examining these women's stories was their multidimensionality and complexity that was woven into their whole being. It was not that they were Asian, or that they were women, or that they were a professor, administrator, or musician that made them leaders. These multiple identity dimensions are intertwined with one another as well as with their unique life experiences. The experiences described by these women supported the assertion that it is impossible to examine one identity dimension at a time (e.g., race) separate from other dimensions (e.g., gender). It is imperative to develop new dynamic models to understand the intersections in their complexity, and with more specificity.

For instance, none of the models of biculturalism, feminist identity development, or leadership could fully capture or explain the experiences we were exploring because the models compartmentalize and separate the dimensions. Overall, they lacked the sophistication for what we were attempting to understand. We believe that more elaborate models must take into account the interactions and integration of the multiple, diverse identity dimensions.

The purpose of this research was to gain a better understanding of Asian American women leaders. Our research contains some limitations. First, we intentionally examined the two dimensions of race and gender. However, there are many other dimensions such as class, religion, time period, geographical location, age, sexual orientation, disabilities, and motherhood status that influence the women and their leadership that were not explored. Second, we asked certain questions and interacted in certain ways with the interviewees because of who we are and where we are in our own developmental journeys. This definitely influenced how the women we interviewed responded.

In sum, we believe that the greatest gift emerging from this project was the opportunity to share the rich stories and experiences that the women shared with us. They are truly awesome role models and doing wonderful things to inspire and motivate others to action. These women's lives highlight the accomplishments by Asian American women that are often overlooked or invisible to others because of stereotypes. Further, this work illustrates the strength, resilience, intelligence, and competence of these powerful Asian American women leaders. Our hope is that our research will continue to explore the complexity of these women's lives and leadership experiences and that others will join us in this endeavor.

References

Appelbaum, S. H., Audet, L., & Miller, J. C. (2003). Gender and leadership? Leadership and gender? A journey through the landscape of theories. *Leadership & Organization Development Journal, 24*(1), 43–51.

Astin, H. S., & Leland, C. (1991). *Women of influence, women of vision: A cross-generational study of leaders and social change.* San Francisco: Jossey-Bass.

Bradshaw, C. G. (1994). Asian and Asian American women: Historical and political considerations in psychotherapy. In L. Comas-Díaz & B. Greene (Eds.), *Women of color: Integrating ethnic and gender identities in psychotherapy* (pp. 72–113). New York: Guilford Press.

Chow, E. N. L. (1989). The feminist movement: Where are all the Asian American women? In Asian Women United of California (Ed.), *Making waves: An anthology of writings by and about Asian American women* (pp. 362–377). Boston: Beacon Press.

Darlington, P. S. E., & Mulvaney, B. M. (2003). *Women, power, and ethnicity: Working toward reciprocal empowerment.* Binghamton, NY: The Haworth Press.

Denmark, F. L. (1993). Women, leadership, and empowerment. *Psychology of Women Quarterly, 17,* 343–356.

Downing, N., & Roush, K. (1985). From passive acceptance to active commitment: A model of feminist identity development for women. *The Counseling Psychologist, 13,* 695–709.

Eagly, A. H., Wood, W., & Diekman, A. B. (2000). Social role theory of sex differences and similarities: A current appraisal. In T. Eckes & H. M. Trautner (Eds.), *The developmental social psychology of gender* (pp. 123–174). Mahwah, NJ: Erlbaum.

Fischer, A. R., Tokar, D. M., Mergl, M., Good, G. E., Hill, M. S., & Blum, S. A. (2000). Assessing women's feminist identity development: Studies of convergent, discriminant, and structural validity. *Psychology of Women Quarterly, 24,* 15–29.

Hyde, J. S. (2004). *Half the human experience: The psychology of women.* Boston: Houghton Mifflin.

LaFromboise, T., Coleman, H. L. K., & Gerton, J. (1998). Psychological impact of biculturalism: Evidence and theory. In P. B. Organista, K. M. Chun, & G. Marin (Eds.), *Readings in ethnic psychology* (pp. 123–155). New York: Routledge.

Lee, E. (2003). Exclusion acts: Chinese women during the Chinese Exclusion era, 1882–1943. In S. Hune & G. M. Nomura (Eds.), *Asian/Pacific Islander American women: A historical anthology* (pp. 77–89). New York: New York University Press.

Louie, K. B. (2000). Asian American women and social advocacy. In J. L. Chin (Ed.), *Relationships among Asian American women* (pp. 13–23). Washington, DC: American Psychological Association.

Nomura, G. M. (2003). On our terms: Definitions and context. In S. Hune & G. M. Nomura (Eds.), *Asian/Pacific Islander American women: A historical anthology* (pp. 16–22). New York: New York University Press.

Root, M. P. P. (1995). The psychology of Asian American women. In H. Landrine (Ed.), *Bringing cultural diversity to feminist psychology: Theory, research, and practice* (pp. 265–301). Washington, DC: American Psychological Association.

True, R. H. (2000). Foreword. In. J. L. Chin (Ed.), *Relationships among Asian American women* (pp. ix–x). Washington, DC: American Psychological Association.

U.S. Census Bureau. (2005, April 29). *Facts for features: Asian/Pacific American heritage month.* Retrieved May 4, 2005, from http://www.census.gov/Press-Release/www/releases/archives/facts_for_features_special_editions/004522.html

Williams, M. K., McCandies, T., & Dunlap, M. R. (2002). Women of color and feminist psychology: Moving from criticism and critique to integration and application. In L. H. Collins, M. R. Dunlap, & J. C. Chrisler (Eds.), *Charting a new course for feminist psychology* (pp. 65–89). Westport, CT: Praeger.

Yamada, M. (1983). Asian Pacific American women and feminism. In C. Moraga & G. Anzaldua (Eds.), *This bridge called my back: Writings by radical women of color* (pp. 71–75). New York: Kitchen Table Women of Color Press.

Chapter 15

Feminist Leadership Among American Indian Women

Clara Sue Kidwell, Diane J. Willis, Deborah Jones-Saumty, and Dolores S. Bigfoot

Vine Deloria, Jr., Standing Rock Sioux, in describing the trial of leaders of the American Indian Movement for the armed occupation of the village of Wounded Knee, South Dakota, in 1973, commented that while Indian male defendants and witnesses testified, they kept their eyes on a row of elderly Indian women seated in the back of the room (Deloria & Lytle, 1984). Whether this scenario represents a version of feminist leadership as conceptualized in this book may be debatable, but it definitely speaks to the role of American Indian women in their own communities as upholders of standards of moral order and responsibility. American Indian women occupy numerous roles in Native communities—caretakers and protectors as wives, mothers, and grandmothers; home-makers; participants in social and ceremonial events; managers of tribal programs; businesswomen; educators; members of tribal councils; and chiefs of Indian nations. Although American Indian women have taken on increasingly important roles of political leadership, little research has been done on what constitutes feminist leadership in Indian communities. In one study, many of the women surveyed identified American Indian men's leadership styles as more controlling, more concerned with self-interest, and more concerned with broad issues. They described their own styles as working to solve the problems of individuals, as being better listeners, as more objective, and as trying to get all points of view (McCoy, 1992).

In this chapter, we describe the cultural dimensions of traditional leadership in American Indian communities and how they affect the way that

Indian women exercise leadership. We will show how both culture and the unique political relationship of Indian tribes vis-à-vis the United States government affect the roles of women as leaders and how the objectives of Indian women leaders may differ from those of other feminist leaders. We argue that the value of inclusiveness, which is considered the key factor in feminist leadership in this book, is inherent in the nature of American Indian community life, where traditional decision making rested on consensus rather than majority rule. The challenges to Indian feminist leadership come not from hierarchical male/female power relationships in Indian communities, as is true for other groups, but from hierarchical structures of governance imposed on Indian communities as a result of their unique relationship with the federal government.

The Current Status of American Indian Nations

American Indian people in the United States today represent some 550 federally recognized tribes and Alaska Native villages throughout all 50 states. The term "American Indian" will be used throughout this chapter to encompass a number of terms—Native American, First Americans, First Nations, Native People, Native Alaskans, Eskimos, and Aleuts (Trimble, 2000). American Indian women resided on tribal lands and in urban areas, and with over 300 federally recognized tribes and 220 Alaska Native villages, the population and languages of American Indian women are as diverse as the tribes (Snipp, 1996; Trimble, 2000).

American Indians are a young population with an average age of 27.8 years, eight years younger than the mean age of the entire population of the US. Although Indians live all across the US, half reside in the western portion of the US. One half of American Indians now live in urban areas and have relocated to find work, to access educational opportunities, and to flee poverty (Willis & Bigfoot, 2003). American Indian communities exist in settings that range from remote, rural enclaves such as the Pine Point community on the White Earth Chippewa reservation in Minnesota, to relatively large communities like Window Rock on the Navajo reservation. There are relatively dispersed urban populations whose members congregate around an urban Indian center, such as the Chicago Indian Center. These communities are very diverse, but they are characterized by close kinship ties in rural communities,

315

tribal connections in larger towns, and by a more generalized sense of American Indian identity in urban communities.

Cultural Values and Women's Roles

What characterizes contemporary American Indian communities is a strong sense of egalitarianism among their members, a value stemming from the nature of precontact subsistence communities where all younger members of the community contributed in some way to the food supply and older people sustained the collective wisdom and experience of the group. The roles of men and women in such societies complemented each other—men hunted and women gave birth and raised children. Food collection and reproduction constituted the most basic elements of a social group. Each function was essential to the whole. The nature of leadership in tribal societies depended on individual achievement that gained the respect of members of the group. Feminist leadership in precontact American Indian communities was a natural state based on women's roles as mothers of children and their ability to make decisions that affected the well-being of those children. Women were particularly influential in matrilineal tribal societies where familial descent and inheritance of property were traced through the mother. Matrilineal systems were characteristic in the southeastern United States, particularly among the Cherokee, Chickasaw, Choctaw, Creek, and Seminole tribes. Women identified enemies and allies and chose mates for their children (Hudson, 1976). In Iroquois society in the Northeast, the women of the *Owachira* (female lineages) chose the men of the lineage who would occupy the role of *sachem*, the representatives of the family and tribe in the Grand Council of the League of the Iroquois (Fenton, 1998). Familial relationships were all-important. In matrilineal societies, a woman's children called her brothers "fathers," her sisters "mothers," and their children "brothers and sisters." Individuals could not marry a person who belonged to the same lineage or clan, even though that individual might be only a distant cousin by ordinary genetic standards (Hudson, 1976; Gilbert, 1943).

Men dealt with influences from outside the tribe, while women's control of food distribution and property provided stability within their lineages (Hudson, 1976; Ortner & Whitehead, 1981; Swanton, 1928). Over time, however, economic power in a money economy began to shift the roles of men and women in American Indian societies to reflect those of the European society (Willis, 1963). Although women might

316

play important roles in ceremonial activity, men made decisions that affected the group as a whole. Women were *influential* rather than *powerful* in tribal society (Corkran, 1967). They made the treaties with representatives of European governments and the United States that fostered the expansion of American economic power over Indian Nations with the fur trade and the introduction of new trade goods. Men largely controlled the trade, although women could often barter furs, hides, and agricultural goods with American traders. Men came to control property (Eggan, 1937; Kidwell, 1995).

The U.S. government attempted to break up tribal relations and impose private property on Indians in the General Allotment Act of 1887 and the Curtis Act of 1898. Congress dictated that Indian reservations would be divided into individual plots of land and allotted to Indian heads of families (who might, indeed, be women but were more likely to be men), their dependent children, and single individuals over the age of 18. Wives, per se, did not receive allotments (McDonnell, 1991). The General Allotment and Curtis Acts led to significant loss of property for American Indians. Between 1887 and 1934, the year in which a major shift of federal policy led to the ending of the allotment process, Indian-owned land shrank from approximately 138 million acres to approximately 52 million acres (Wilkinson, 2004). The suppression of American Indian cultures, the often forcible taking of Indian children to federal boarding schools, the failure of Indians to become self-sufficient farmers as the Allotment acts intended, all contributed to conditions of poverty and social breakdown in Indian communities. The government's attempt to turn men into farmers floundered due to a number of factors—traditional roles of men as hunters and women as farmers, the limitation on amounts of land allotted to Indians, and the harsh climatic conditions of the Great Plains that made subsistence farming difficult for even the best equipped White settler.

Federal policy used private property and boarding school education to try to reshape the basic values and gender roles of American Indian societies. In doing so, the government undermined both gender roles. Women were trained to be wives and homemakers and to have a civilizing influence on their husbands (Mihesuah, 1993). For men, their failure as farmers and providers for their families often forced women into those roles. The traditional, complementary nature of male and female roles was totally disrupted.

Clearly, the impact of such disruptive life influences was visited upon Indian women and has impacted their aspirations and responsibilities

317

toward accepting tribal and/or community leadership. Many American Indian communities in the 21st century are plagued by high rates of alcoholism and unemployment. Diabetes has replaced tuberculosis as a major health problem in Indian populations. Inadequate federal funding for the federal Indian Health Service denies Indians access to adequate health care, as do proposed cuts in the 2005 federal budget funding for the Bureau of Indian Affairs. High rates of spousal and child abuse in many reservation communities are indicative of the effects of past federal policies on Indian family life (Chester, Robin, Koss, Lopez, & Goldman, 1994; Norton & Manson, 1995; U.S. Department of Health and Human Services, 2001). Thus the nature and consequences of the numerous problems experienced by Indian people over the past 200 years have encouraged the emergence of women as leaders in tribal societies.

In contemporary American Indian communities, people can no longer depend on subsistence farming, and poverty is a fact of life for many Indian people in rural communities with no economic base (Bishaw & Iceland, 2003). Indian tribes have a unique (and often problematic) relationship with the United States government based on treaty rights and historical circumstances (Wilkins & Lomawaima, 2001). These economic and political circumstances affect women's roles in Indian communities today.

Contemporary Indian Feminist Leadership

Feminist leadership in American Indian communities today resides primarily in the political arena, that is, leadership which people exercise vis-à-vis organized governments that control economic resources and social services. It is a much different kind of leadership than that based in the traditional cultural values of Indian communities. The U.S. Supreme Court defined Indian tribes in 1901 as "a body of Indians of the same or similar race, united in community under one leadership or government, and inhabiting a particular though sometimes ill-defined territory" (Willis & Bigfoot, 2003, p. 83). Many, but not all, American Indian Nations now operate under constitutional forms of government, some adopted in the 1930s under the guidance of the Bureau of Indian Affairs (BIA) and others formulated in the era of tribal sovereignty ushered in by the Indian Self-Determination and Education Improvement Act passed by the United States Congress in 1975 (Deloria & Lytle,

1984). The issues that they deal with range from providing social services to their members to running business operations such as tribal casinos to generate income for the tribe.

Women have been elected to leadership roles in many Indian Nations and also function in national organizations that have formed as political lobbying groups to support Indian causes such as more federal funding for the Bureau of Indian Affairs and to fend off Congressional and state attacks on tribal sovereignty, that is, the rights of tribes to exercise internal self-governance over both members and land.

American Indian versus Feminist Issues: A Matter of Emphasis?

We have focused on defining "feminist" from an American Indian perspective, and we will define "leadership" within the contemporary political context of American Indian Nations. The White feminist movement of the 1960s emphasized women's demands for equal social status with men, equated with equal pay for equal work, equal employment opportunities, and control over their own fertility in the form of abortion rights. These demands had little resonance in American Indian communities where unemployment and poverty were the norm, where women were more likely than men to be hired for wage work because they were perceived to be more reliable workers than men, and where doctors in public health service hospitals sometime sterilized women on the grounds that they could not care for the children they already had (Lawrence, 2000).

In the era of Indian activism in the 1960s and 1970s that led to the takeovers of Alcatraz Island in San Francisco Bay (1969–71), the Bureau of Indian Affairs building in Washington, DC (1972), and the trading post at Wounded Knee on the Pine Ridge Reservation in South Dakota (1973), American Indian men and women joined to protest the oppressive treatment of Indian tribes by the United States government (Smith & Warrior, 1996). Although the confrontational and sometimes violent activism of that era has died out, Indian women generally see their energies directed toward American Indian issues rather than narrowly defined "feminist" issues.

In the broader sense that feminist values include social justice, Indian women are indeed feminist when as leaders they address issues of poverty, discrimination, and the effects of oppressive federal bureaucracy and

319

judicial actions in their communities. Their issues are not, however, those primarily associated with majority feminism. A survey of 36 Indian women elected tribal officials in the early 1990s revealed that their primary political agenda items were tribal economic development, health care, education, housing, and tribal/federal relations. In this regard, they shared these priorities with male leaders (McCoy, 1992).

The Challenges of Leadership in American Indian Communities

Any discussion of leadership in American Indian communities must be prefaced by the widely understood analogy of the crab bucket. When one crab tries to climb out of the bucket, the others hang on to it and try to pull it back into the bucket. When an individual in an Indian community appears to be making himself or herself better than others, especially if it seems to be at the expense of others, that individual is subjected to gossip, ridicule, and possible harassment. If inclusiveness is a characteristic of feminist leadership, then values of kinship ties and obligations to one's family first and the tribe second may work against inclusion of the whole community in tribal services. Leaders may be expected to favor their family and kinfolk over others in the community and this bias in favor of family can lead to factional divisions that undermine a leader's power to persuade people to follow his or her views.

The egalitarian values of past subsistence-based cultures persist; social pressure is to share resources with other community members rather than to use them for one's own benefit. Any attempt by an individual to control the behavior of others is met with resistance and resentment. In communities where elected tribal governments are viewed by some members as impositions by the federal government, tribal members simply opt not to participate at all in governmental functions such as council meetings, not to vote in elections, and to view with suspicion anything that elected tribal officials attempt to do. In this sense, true leadership is often exercised at an informal level, and very often by women who administer tribal programs that provide services for members. They become key communicators who create the information flow in a community and mobilize community resources—cook for senior citizens' centers, deliver meals, provide childcare, home health aids, and so forth.

In Indian communities, however, the crab analogy holds not only for individuals but also for family groups. Particularly in more remote Indian communities where kinship ties remain strong, family groups create factions within the community. Generally, some communal events—yearly powwows, rodeos, high school basketball games, and traditional ceremonial activities—hold the factions together in a social sense. But the economic power that can come to a tribal council through business development and administration of social service programs comes from outside the community in the form of grants or contracts from federal agencies such as the BIA, and control over this money requires that individuals who manage the programs favor their relatives by hiring them for jobs and distributing services. While non-Native society might call these practices "nepotism," American Indian society operates quite differently. Indeed, most tribal groups expect that those in positions of leadership will naturally favor family members. The foundation of this practice rests in the kinship system of Indian tribal society, which still persists to a remarkable degree. This situation pulls against the larger bonds of tribal identity, and the very family ties that have given women influence in their communities may cause political disruption within those communities.

Indian Women Leaders in Contemporary Society

Given the diversity of American Indian communities and their situations, we can focus on several Indian women who have become nationally recognized as women political leaders and look for commonalities and differences in their experiences as leaders. Wilma Mankiller, Ada Deer, LaDonna Harris, Annie Wauneka, Elouise Cobell, and Cecelia Fire Thunder, although not household names, demonstrate qualities of political leadership in contemporary Native America. Mankiller, Harris, and Wauneka achieved political prominence through their associations with powerful men, while Deer was influenced most strongly by her mother. Wauneka rose to political prominence in 1951 when she became the first woman elected to the Navajo Tribal Council. Her father had been the first chairman of the Council. Harris was in the vanguard of political activism in the early 1960s in Oklahoma as the wife of Senator Fred Harris from that state. Mankiller's career began in the mid 1980s with her work in the Cherokee tribal government, and she served as vice-chief under a powerful male chief, Ross Swimmer. Elouise Cobell took on the fight for Indian rights in 1996 as a result of her concern for her family. Cecelia Fire Thunder challenged a politically powerful Indian man—noted activist Russell Means—for the presidency of the Pine Ridge Sioux reservation in South Dakota in 2004. These women's stories demonstrate the scope of feminist leadership in the second half of the 20th century. The commonality in their experiences is that all worked at a grass-roots political level in their own communities before they went on to achieve national prominence.

Wilma Mankiller was elected Chief of the Cherokee Nation in Oklahoma in 1987. Born and raised near Tahlequah, in Northeastern Oklahoma, Mankiller spent part of her youth and early adulthood in the San Francisco Bay Area, where her family moved as a result of the federal government's program to relocate Indian people to urban areas for greater job opportunities. She became a social worker in Oakland before returning to Oklahoma in 1977. She had numerous family members in northeastern Oklahoma, and became involved in several projects to improve services in local communities. She was chosen by Ross Swimmer, the elected Chief of the Cherokee Nation, to serve as his running mate for vice-chief in 1983 and then ran on her own and was elected Chief in 1987. Her record of grass roots activism and her family's reputation were largely responsible for her success (Mankiller, 1993).

Ada Deer, a member of the Menominee Tribe in Wisconsin, was born on the tribe's reservation and became actively involved in the struggle to reverse the termination of her tribe in the 1960s. Termination was a federal policy of ending the government's relationship with American Indian tribes and the services to tribes that it entailed. The Menominee were the first tribe to be subjected to the policy, and as a result, high rates of poverty and unemployment came to prevail on the reservation, and tribal members lost educational and health care services. Deer's White mother, who had been a nurse, became an outspoken activist against termination, and Ada and her sister were aware of this activist struggle in their teens.

Ada went to college and ultimately to Columbia University for a master's degree in social work, but after working briefly in that field she enrolled in law school and began to work in Washington, DC, lobbying Congress to overturn the termination legislation and restore the Menominee to federal recognition. Her efforts helped foster the formation of a group of Menominees living in Milwaukee who joined the political efforts for restoration. She was ultimately elected as chair of the tribe after it regained recognition. She was appointed the first female Assistant Secretary for Indian Affairs in the Department of the Interior in 1993 but was asked to resign with the change of administration in 1997. Her decisions to recognize Alaska Native villages as tribal governments and to uphold the elected government of the Oneida Tribe in New York against a recall vote were controversial in Indian country, but her political connections in Congress benefited the Menominees and other Indian Nations across the country (Kidwell, 2001).

LaDonna Harris, Comanche, was born in a small community in Oklahoma to a White father and a Comanche mother. She was raised by her Comanche grandparents and married Fred Harris, a young man from her hometown who went to law school and engaged in a successful political career. Fred Harris was elected to the United States Senate, and LaDonna Harris was active in his campaign. As a Senator's wife, Harris also gained attention for her outspoken support of Lyndon B. Johnson's War on Poverty programs, particularly as they could benefit American Indian communities. She was the first Indian woman to testify before a senatorial committee when the Office of Equal Opportunity came under congressional attack. Using the resources of her husband's office and her own political savvy, she convened a meeting in 1963 that led to the founding of Oklahomans for Indian Opportunity (OIO), an organization that used federal grants to foster grass-roots community economic development activities in Indian communities in the state. Oklahomans for Indian Opportunity challenged the hold that the BIA had over tribal governments. Ultimately, LaDonna Harris established a similar organization in Washington, DC, Americans for Indian Opportunity, aimed at preparing Indian young people to take positions of political leadership in their own communities (Anderson, 2001).

Annie Wauneka, Navajo, was the daughter of Henry Chee Dodge, first chair of the Navajo tribal council. She was sent to an Indian boarding school where she had first-hand experience of the poor health conditions in such schools. The great influenza epidemic killed a number of students at the school, and later an epidemic of trachoma, an eye disease, struck. Wauneka completed the 11th grade at the school and then returned home. Her father discussed tribal issues with her, and she learned a great deal about the operation of the tribal government. She became an active crusader with the Public Health Service to improve health conditions on the Navajo reservation. She testified on numerous occasions before Congressional committees in Washington, DC, and she worked with a number of organizations, particularly ones involved in eradicating tuberculosis, which was a major health problem on the reservation. She was the first woman elected to the Navajo Tribal Council and remained active in promoting the betterment of Navajo health conditions until her death in 1997. Her leadership strategy was summed up in the title of her biography *I'll Go and Do More* (Niethammer, 2001).

Elouise Cobell was born on the Blackfeet Reservation in Montana. She attended Montana State University and has served as tribal treasurer of the Blackfeet tribal council. She and her husband operated a cattle ranch. At one point in the mid 1990s, she began to monitor the checks that she and family members received from the BIA for various leases and royalties on their lands and discovered that the amounts seemed not to correspond to the original agreements. In 1996 she filed a class action suit challenging the Department of the Interior and the BIA over the management of Individual Money Funds (IMF), that is, accounts maintained for individuals who had trust land that was leased to individuals or corporations or who drew royalties for resources taken from their lands. The suit has led to federal court judgments requiring the BIA to do a full accounting of the IMF system, which dates back to the allotment of Indian lands in the late 19th century. Cobell and supporters of the suit estimate that as much as $10 billion dollars was never paid to Indian account holders, while the Department of the Interior maintains that such an accounting is impossible because of inadequate record keeping. The case remains active in federal court, although some Indian leaders criticize Cobell for refusing to accept a negotiated settlement, fearing that Congress will find a way to dismiss the whole issue if it cannot be resolved. Cobell's name has, however, become associated with Indian demands for accountability on the part of the government toward individuals with whom it has a trust relationship (Hamilton, 2002–2003; Indian Trust, 2005).

Clad in a white buckskin dress with long fringe, an eagle feather wrapped in red tied in her hair, an eagle wing fan spread across her chest, and a hand held high in victory, Cecilia Fire Thunder took the oath of office as president of the Oglala Sioux Tribe on November 2, 2004. Fire Thunder defeated well-known activist Russell Means to be elected the first woman president of the Tribe, located on the Pine Ridge Reservation in South Dakota. Fire Thunder, a former licensed practical nurse, described herself as a grass roots activist. She spent several years in California as a labor organizer before returning to Pine Ridge. She ran a grass roots campaign, visiting communities across the reservation. Her special interests are health and language retention. Fire Thunder, known among her Lakota people as "Good Hearted Woman," leads a nation with a membership number of over 40,000 people. Her administration will be under high scrutiny because she is the first female leader of a strongly traditional society in which male leadership has been the norm (Indianz.com, 2004a, 2004b).

Mankiller, Deer, Harris, Wauneka, Cobell, and Fire Thunder come from different tribal backgrounds and have dealt with a range of issues. They have operated both in the arena of tribal government and in the halls of Congress. All have been strongly grounded in their own tribal communities, although they have sometimes been seen as distancing themselves from those communities by moving to the national level of political activism. All defy certain stereotypes of American Indian women that are still widely held in American society, that is, that Indian women are subservient to Indian men and that their place is in the home, not in public office.

Some American Indian men, influenced by generations of Christian missionary activity and government boarding schools, buy into these stereotypes, and they feel that Indian women are usurping power in contemporary society. Wilma Mankiller encountered this attitude in her time in office and countered it with the argument that sexism in Indian communities was a product of the imposition of Anglo-American values on Indians through Christian churches and formal education, not part of traditional Indian values. LaDonna Harris objected to the fact that her femininity was subsumed in media coverage that portrayed her as a painted Indian on the warpath.

Learning How to Lead

American Indian women continue to play important roles in the political struggles that tribes are waging to protect their right to self-government while demanding that the federal government lives up to its responsibility to protect the resources of tribes and provide adequate social services. Indian women more so than Indian men have honed skills of leadership through college education. The American Indian tribal colleges, currently some 35 in number, have given women access to higher education in unprecedented numbers, and women have served as presidents of many of those institutions since their inception—Janine Pease-Pretty on Top at Little Big Horn College in Montana and Phyllis Young at Fort Berthold Community College in North Dakota were among the early presidents of the American Indian Higher Education

Consortium, the colleges' professional association, which was established in 1973 (Benham & Stein, 2003).

In part because of their higher levels of education, American Indian women exercise leadership not only in national organizations such as the National Congress of American Indians, whose first executive director in 1944 was Helen Peterson, a Lakota woman (Cowger, 1999), but in the day-to-day operations of tribal governments. In the latter capacity, they are often directors of social services programs funded through the Bureau of Indian Affairs. For more affluent tribes, Indian women exercise a form of feminist leadership in these roles because they are viewed as providers of services through revenues generated by tribal businesses.

They have learned to exercise overt political power in relation to the federal government largely from the political activism of the 1960s and 1970s. Challenges remain, in that most federal and state politicians seem to view American Indians as a minority group that enjoys special privileges, that is, exemption from taxation and ability to run lucrative gambling operations, which are denied to other American citizens. The rhetoric of equal opportunity is now employed to demand that Indians be stripped of those privileges and denied their right of sovereignty and self-government.

Most politicians do not take Indian rights seriously, and federal court decisions have begun to swing against principles of tribal sovereignty in recent years. There are significant challenges ahead for Indian leaders, both men and women, to defend the treaty rights and sovereignty of Indian nations. They must become effective in lobbying Congress to shape legislation that affects Indian rights and argue in the courts to defend the right of tribes to govern their own affairs. They must become astute negotiators with state and local officials to establish clear understandings of the rights of Indian tribes to be free of external control, particularly in the area of taxation. In all of these areas, Indian women will also face the sexism that still exists in American society at large.

Conclusion

The practical and political concerns of American Indian communities override majority feminist issues. Women are currently confronted with much different circumstances than those that historically fostered the cultural traditions of egalitarianism. When their constituents see Indian tribal governments as puppets of the BIA rather than truly sovereign entities, feminist leadership in that arena is discredited. When women exercise their leadership as managers of social services programs or community events, they are generally overlooked. Here sexism clearly intersects with Indian identity.

An important research question that should be explored is: Where do Indian people in general look for leadership? Despite significant development of the political concept of tribal sovereignty since the Indian Self-Determination and Educational Improvement Act of 1975, there is still a great deal of development that needs to be done in many tribes to build strong, stable, and effective tribal councils. In many tribes, because there has been no governmental infrastructure to support political leadership, it has been exercised by charismatic men who dominated by sheer force of personality. Indian men and women need to work together in a common effort to achieve effective tribal governments. It behooves them to study how their own communities view leadership and how they value it.

The feminist movement and other salient women's issues have propelled many Indian women to the forefront of tribal politics, as well as state and local politics. In the 21st century, American Indian women will stand beside, rather than behind, men in their effort to preserve their tribes and treaty rights.

References

Anderson, G. (2001). LaDonna Harris/Comanche. In R. D. Edmunds (Ed.), *The new warriors* (pp. 123–144). Lincoln: University of Nebraska Press.

Benham, M. K. P., & Stein, W. J. (Eds.). (2003). *The renaissance of American Indian higher education: Capturing the dream.* Mahwah, NJ: Lawrence Erlbaum Associates.

Bishaw, L., & Iceland, J. N. (2003). Poverty: 1999. *Census 2000 brief.* Washington, DC: U.S. Department of Commerce, Economics and Statistics Administration.

Chester, B., Robin, R. W., Koss, M. P., Lopez, J., & Goldman, D. (1994). Grandmother dishonored: Violence against women by male partners in American Indian communities. *Violence & Victims, 9*(3), 249–258.

Corkran, David H. (1967). *The Creek frontier, 1540–1783.* Norman: University of Oklahoma Press.

Cowger, Thomas W. (1999). *The National Congress of American Indians: The founding years.* Lincoln: University of Nebraska Press.

Deloria, V., Jr., & Lytle, C. M. (1984). *The nations within: The past and future of American Indian sovereignty*. Austin: University of Texas Press.

Eggan, F. (1937). Historical changes in the Choctaw kinship system. *American Anthropologist, 39*, 34–52.

Fenton, W. N. (1998). *The great law and the longhouse: A political history of the Iroquois Confederacy*. Norman: University of Oklahoma Press.

Gilbert, W. H., Jr. (1943). The eastern Cherokees. *Bureau of American Ethnology Bulletin (No. 138)*.

Hamilton, J. T. (2002–2003). Progressing back: A tribal solution for a federal morass. *American Indian Law Review, XXVII*(2), 375–397.

Hudson, C. (1976). *The Southeastern Indians*. Knoxville: University of Tennessee Press.

Indian Trust. (2005). *Cobell v. Norton*. Retrieved March 1, 2006 from http://www.indiantrust.com/index.cfm

Indianz.com (2004a). *Cecelia Fire Thunder declared winner at Pine Ridge*. Indianz.com, November 3. Retrieved February 13, 2006 from http://www.indianz.com/News/2004/005169.asp

Indianz.com (2004b). *Pressure is on Fire Thunder as Pine Ridge President*. Indianz.com, November 15. Retrieved from http://www.indianz.com/News/2004/005350.asp

Kidwell, C. S. (1995). Choctaw women and cultural persistence in Mississippi. In N. Shoemaker (Ed.), *Negotiators of change: Historical perspectives on Native American women* (pp. 115–134). New York: Routledge.

Kidwell, C. S. (2001). Ada Deer. In R. D. Edmunds (Ed.), *The new warriors: Native American leaders since 1900* (pp. 239–260). Lincoln, NE: University of Nebraska Press.

Lawrence, J. (2000). The Indian health service and the sterilization of Native American women. *American Indian Quarterly, 24*(3), 400–419.

Mankiller, W. (1993). *Mankiller: A chief and her people*. New York: St. Martin's Griffin.

McCoy, M. (1992). Gender or ethnicity: What makes a difference? A study of women tribal leaders. *Women & Politics, 12*(3), 57–68.

McDonnell, J. A. (1991). *The dispossession of the American Indian 1887–1934*. Bloomington: Indiana University Press.

Mihesuah, D. A. (1993). *Cultivating the rosebuds: The education of women at the Cherokee Female Seminary, 1851–1909*. Urbana and Chicago: University of Illinois Press.

Niethammer, Carolyn J. (2001). *I'll go and do more: Annie Dodge Wauneka, Navajo leader and activist*. Lincoln: University of Nebraska Press.

Norton, I. M., & Manson, S. M. (1995). A silent minority: Battered American Indian women. *Journal of Family Violence, 10*(3), 307–318.

Ortner, S. B., & Whitehead, H. (Eds.). (1981). *Sexual meanings: The cultural construction of gender and sexuality*. Cambridge, UK: Cambridge University Press.

Smith, P. C., & Warrior, R. A. (1996). *Like a hurricane: The Indian movement from Alcatraz to Wounded Knee*. New York: The New Press.

Snipp, C. M. (1989). *American Indians: The first of this land.* New York: Russell Sage Foundation.

Swanton, J. R. (1928). Social organization and social usages of the Indians of the Creek Confederacy. In *42nd Annual report of the Bureau of American Ethnology, 1924–25* (pp. 279–325). Washington, DC.

Trimble, J. E. (2000). American Indian psychology. In A. E. Kazdin (Ed.), *Encyclopedia of psychology* (pp. 139–144). New York: Oxford University Press.

U.S. Department of Health and Human Services. (2001). *Strong heart study data book: A report to American Indian communities* (NIH Publication No. 01-3285). Washington, DC.

Wilkins, D. E., & Lomawaima, K. T. (2001). *Uneven ground: American Indian sovereignty and federal law.* Norman: University of Oklahoma Press.

Wilkinson, C. (2004). *Blood struggle: The rise of modern Indian nations.* New York: W. W. Norton and Company.

Willis, D. J., & Bigfoot, D. S. (2003). On Native soil. In J. D. Robinson & L. C. James (Eds.), *Diversity in human interactions* (pp. 77–91). New York: Oxford University Press.

Willis, W. S. (1963). Patrilineal institutions in southeastern North America. *Ethnohistory, 10,* 250–269.

Chapter 16

Leadership and Collaboration among Women with Disabilities

Martha E. Banks and Linda R. Mona[1]

The lack of discussion of leadership roles of women with disabilities cuts across disciplines. There is no literature on leadership styles, leadership and tokenism, and externally defined leadership with respect to women with disabilities. Due to the scarcity of literature in this area, this chapter reviews topics raised in a web-based discussion and provides suggestions for research.

Women with Disabilities, Leadership, and Feminism

Have women with disabilities registered on the feminist agenda? The answer to this question is rather complex. Although disability studies and medical anthropology scholars have been discussing the intersections between disability and feminism for the last several years, this trend has not been reflected in considerations of leadership. Interestingly, the lack of discussion of leadership roles of women with disabilities cuts across disciplines.

People with disabilities represent the largest nonmajority group in the United States with 28.6 million women (Jans & Stoddard, 1999) representing 53% of the entire group. Despite the large number of individuals with disabilities, only about 9.6% of people with disabilities attain college degrees. Thus the presence of women with disabilities is sparse in academic environments. In addition, those women who are employed in academic arenas may be less visible to others because they tend to be active solely within disability-related domains.

Only one qualitative study has focused on the career development of highly successful women with physical and sensory disabilities and also indirectly explored leadership themes within its investigation (Noonan et al., 2004). The results of this study suggest that highly achieving women with disabilities were passionate about their work, persevering in the face of internal and external barriers, self-confident and self-reliant, conscious of their coping strategies, internally motivated, and committed to helping others through their work.

Furthermore, the highly achieving women in Noonan et al.'s (2004) investigation reported using support systems for survival that are typical of nondisabled individuals (e.g., role models and mentors, networks of women, supportive colleagues, friends, and family). These women also appeared to be skilled at turning challenges into opportunities for personal and professional development. While this work does not focus specifically on the relationship between leadership and highly successful women with disabilities, the findings illustrate a number of empowering themes that may have relevance to women with disabilities, success, and leadership.

Identity Intersections

Although limited psychological literature is available on women with disabilities, leadership, and feminism, work completed within disability studies and other diversity-based writings address the complex social experiences of this community. The importance of empowering the voices of women with disabilities has been documented. Banks (2003) observed that "Therapists and other health professionals need to give women with disabilities greater priority in both clinical work and research" (p. xxxiii). To this end, the book included the voices of women with disabilities, so that the issues were in their words rather than merely interpreted. Of particular interest in Banks's (2003) work is the discussion of the intersection of identities that many women with disabilities experience.

Cultural issues can surface in the definition of disability and/or in self-identification for women with disabilities. For example, some women with disabilities choose not to identify themselves as having disabilities, due to a stereotype that acknowledgment of disability necessitates succumbing to disability and ending meaningful life activities. Feldman and Tegart (2003) found that, despite multiple disabling conditions which led to medical treatment and involvement in supportive psychotherapy groups, middle-aged and older African American women were reluctant to perceive themselves as having disabilities. This perhaps is related to the potential power loss resulting from adding disability to the already low social status of women of color (Corbett, 2003; Nabors & Pettee, 2003).

Family-related beliefs have also been addressed with regard to their impact on the life experiences of women with disabilities. Corbett (2003) noted that, in some instances, families are reluctant to acknowledge disabilities. She provided an example of a deaf woman whose mother modified her job applications to include fluency in Spanish and exclude fluency in American Sign Language, so that potential employers would not know that she was deaf. Similarly, Nabors and Pettee (2003) described women of color with acquired disabilities who had difficulty obtaining treatment from health professionals because their disabilities were not given credence or accommodation by family members who were dependent on them.

These unique social experiences of women with disabilities provoke much thought about the ways in which disability, gender, and leadership status function in relationship to one another. As part of Jean Lau Chin's Presidential Initiative on Feminist Leadership in the American Psychological Association's Society for the Psychology of Women, web-based discussions were launched to allow women around the world to dialogue about important issues and cross-currents in leadership. In the online environment, we aimed for rich discussion on disability, women, and leadership. Our goals were and remain to forge collaborations with other feminist groups. Participation from a broad group of women with feminist perspectives was desired so that cross-fertilization of ideas and groups could occur. We wanted to be recognized and heard and we needed partnership with others in order for this to occur because our numbers are small.

Core Questions and Themes

In developing a structure for the online discussion, the coauthors reviewed the literature and found little extant research. Therefore, they determined that an exploratory discussion was most appropriate. The initial core questions for discussion were:

- How do we identify early career women with disabilities to mentor for future leadership positions?
- What is the impact of disability identity on the pursuit of leadership opportunities for women with disabilities?
- How do women with disabilities avoid the trap of being perceived as potential leaders only within limited arenas (e.g., rehabilitation, disability advocacy)?
- What strategies exist for removing barriers to leadership for women with disabilities?
- What disability accommodations can be provided so that limitation and flexibility of tasks are possible without limiting leadership duties or losing leadership?

Unfortunately, there was little response to the initial questions posed. The coleaders attempted to generate more dialogue by posting questions and comments centered upon the core questions. However, as the online discussion progressed, related yet distinct themes emerged. Outlined below are the online themes provided by discussants along with explanations and/or examples.

- Leadership and tokenism: Women with disabilities are often tokens based on the premise that many people with disabilities represent extreme minorities in most social situations and there is a lack of literature on leadership for disenfranchised groups as they move from token positions to increased representation.
- Leadership is typically defined by others: Women with disabilities are often not considered to be leaders until other people acknowledge their leadership. For example, some discussants perceived themselves to be frequently sought experts in disability issues, but did not consider themselves to be leaders in general.
- Invisibility as leaders: For example, one discussant observed that, in a conference setting, although she was identified as a presenter by a ribbon on her name tag, she was not acknowledged professionally by other attendees until she actually presented her paper.
- Bearing additional responsibility for disability advocacy: In order to survive within organizations, women with disabilities often find themselves in the position of having to increase awareness of

disability concerns, such as appropriate accommodation and consideration of inclusion of a wide range of impairment types. These efforts often involve the development of skills that are not necessarily pertinent to the fulfillment of their assigned or designated roles within the organization.

• Disability disclosure and leadership potential: One discussant indicated that women with invisible disabilities may be viewed as competent, but if they reveal their disabilities, they are then confronted with obstacles to receiving accommodations and are stigmatized by an attitude that they are less competent than they were considered to be prior to such revelation.

• Ingroup–outgroup dynamics at disability conferences: Discussants indicated that at conferences focusing on disability, women with invisible disabilities are sometimes misperceived as not having disabilities and are not treated as women with disabilities until they make the effort to reveal their disabilities to other attendees.

• Differential impact of types of disabilities on leadership potential: Discussants pointed out that hierarchies seem to develop around the nature of disability (e.g., physical disability is considered more legitimate than mental disability) and duration of disability (e.g., lifelong disability is considered more significant than acquired disability).

The online discussion was extremely limited. Many questions were raised and discussed, as noted previously. However, the lack of scholarship on leadership that includes women with disabilities impeded the full answering and discussion of the questions raised. A major topic for discussion noted by some of the contributors was that they could not determine which social identities (e.g., disability status, gender, ethnicity) had immediate influence on their self-perceptions or the perceptions of others as leaders. For example, Gilkes (2001) described the conflict experienced by African American women leaders: "[Black] women themselves, knowing that their efficacy contradicts the dominant society's expectations of women, often refuse to acknowledge openly their own ability to make a difference" (p. 5). Even when these Black women accept their ability to make a difference, it is almost impossible to determine which social identity is most salient.

In addition to the minimal online discussion, as the collaborators on this project met in person or on conference calls with other participants in different areas, each question about feminist leadership and disability was met with silence. This is an area in which there is no scholarship.

Reasons for this might include the low social status accorded women with disabilities (Banks & Marshall, 2004), the considerable heterogeneity of disability, and the lack of diversity of ability status in most workplaces and organizations. One approach taken to examine the latter issue of the lack of diversity of ability status was an attempt to review the literature on leadership as disenfranchised groups moved from single token presence to critical masses. Unfortunately, the published literature in this area tends to be on the behavior of established leaders as they participate in efforts to increase diversity within their worksites or organizations (e.g., Bailey, 2001; Becker, Ayman, & Korabik, 2002; Boyce & Herd, 2003; Bullock, Ensing, Alloy, & Weddle, 2000).

Identifying Feminist Leaders with Disabilities

Some of the discussion participants are recognized as feminist leaders, but they are generally better known as leaders in the *disability field*. One of the goals of this project was to avoid marginalizing women with disabilities. We chose to identify women leaders overall, some of whom also have disabilities. It appears that viewing women with disabilities as leaders is still a novel idea. Not surprisingly, few disabled women are seen in leadership roles in mainstream society. And, of those we do see, they are typically in roles that focus on disability and/or the disability community. Three examples illustrate this notion.

Role model I

Judith E. Heumann served as Assistant Secretary for Special Education and Rehabilitative Services (OSERS) during the Clinton administration. Programs under her management included the Office of Special Education Programs, the Rehabilitation Services Administration, and the National Institute on Disability and Rehabilitation Research. She was among those who pioneered legislation recognizing that the U.S. Constitution guarantees equality of access and opportunity to persons with disabilities. Living with a disability since 18 months of age, Ms. Heumann served in various vital government roles including assisting with drafting the Americans with Disabilities Act, helping develop regulations for Section 504 of the Rehabilitation Act, and helping design federal and state legislation that led to the creation of more than 200 independent living centers nationwide. She was cofounder of the

World Institute on Disability (WID), the first research center devoted to disability issues (The Chelsea Forum, n.d.). Ms. Heumann received her Master of Public Health in 1975 from the University of California, an Honorary Doctor of Humane Letters in 1995 from Long Island University, Long Island, NY and an Honorary Degree of Doctor of Public Administration, in 2001 from the University of Illinois, Champaign, IL (Disability World, 2002).

Role model II

Dr. Susan Daniels contracted polio at six months of age. Though she spent much of her young life in rehabilitation institutes and hospitals, her parents strived for her full independence through ensuring that she attended a mainstream school. She went on to graduate summa cum laude from Marquette University (before campuses were wheelchair accessible), and received her Masters of Psychology from Mississippi State University and her Ph.D. in Psychology from the University of North Carolina.

As Chair of the Department of Rehabilitation Counseling at the Louisiana State University Medical Center, early in her career, Dr. Daniels developed a program to train individuals working with people with intellectual disabilities in community-based settings, which subsequently was a core element in that state's deinstitutionalization efforts. Dr. Daniels went on to hold a number of senior Federal positions, including Deputy Commissioner of the Rehabilitation Services Administration and Associate Commissioner for the Administration on Developmental Disabilities in the U.S. Department of Health and Human Services.

Perhaps Dr. Daniels' greatest accomplishment is the Ticket to Work and Work Incentive Improvement Act (TWWIIA). As Deputy Commissioner for Disability and Income Security Programs SSA, where she directed programs that serve more than 11 million people with disabilities, she worked tirelessly to lay the groundwork for TWWIIA. This legislation creates employment incentives for people with disabilities and removes the systemic barriers that have placed too many of this country's citizens with disabilities in the position of having to choose between health coverage and work (Bender, 2003).

Role model III

Dr. Carol J. Gill is a clinical and research psychologist specializing in health and disability. She is an Assistant Professor in the Department of Disability and Human Development at the University of Illinois at Chicago (UIC) where she teaches and provides leadership in disability studies curriculum development. She also directs the department's Chicago Center for Disability Research. Through this center, she and her colleagues conduct research, training, and community service projects in the social sciences. Their work emphasizes a disability studies approach and incorporates substantive direction by persons with disabilities at all levels. Since 1998, Dr. Gill has served as the Executive Officer of the Society for Disability Studies. Her research interests include disability identity development, health concerns and health service experiences of women with disabilities, disability bioethical issues, and professional training. Her conceptual and research articles have been widely published in both professional journals and in the popular disability press.

Dr. Gill's professional positions have included Director of Rehabilitation Psychology at Glendale Adventist Medical Center, Acting Director of the Program on Disability and Society at the University of Southern California, and Commissioner on Mental Health for the Los Angeles County Commission on Disabilities. She is currently President of the Chicago Institute of Disability Research, Adjunct Assistant Professor of Physical Medicine and Rehabilitation at Northwestern University Medical School, and Research Chair of the Health Resource Center for Women with Disabilities at the Rehabilitation Institute of Chicago (Disabled Women on the Web, 2004).

Promoting Leadership in Women with Disabilities

While the above examples shed some light into the kind of leadership roles held by members of this community, women with disabilities are all too often still viewed as tokens expending considerable energy advocating for inclusion. As noted above, virtually no information is available about leadership styles, and specifically about the application of feminist models of leadership by women with disabilities. Based upon these experiences and the lag in promoting women with disabilities on the feminist leadership agenda, it is unclear exactly what changes need to occur for advancing ideas about women, disability, and leadership. However, based upon disability literature and the discussions from the web-based discussion offered within this chapter, it is apparent that people studying women's experiences must become familiar with and embrace the diverse experiences of women with disabilities. When this happens, emerging leaders will seek mentorship and guidance from those already walking the path.

We believe that women with disabilities have not been given much consideration by feminist scholars because of three primary factors. First, the focus of feminism has been specifically on middle-class and upper-middle-class European American women, with little regard to the diversity of women. Women with disabilities have seldom been considered members of a particularly disenfranchised group. It is important that others working in the areas of feminism and leadership make concerted efforts to place issues pertinent to women with disabilities on their radar screens. This can be accomplished initially by acknowledging women with disabilities as a diverse group and making provisions for including this element of diversity in research, teaching, and advocacy work.

Second, feminism has primarily addressed the strengths of women as compared to men. As a consequence, there has been a focus away from women's "weaknesses," including those resulting in disabling conditions. In order for this mindset to change, disability needs to be defined much more broadly than by medical definitions that focus on impairment. Social definitions of the disability experience need to be clarified so that the complex life experience of living as a woman with a disability is explored and understood in its entirety.

Third, feminist advocacy has involved only the status of women. Similar to womanist advocacy exhibited by African American women (Gilkes, 2001), disability advocacy involves the betterment of the entire disability community, that is, women, men, and children. The expansion of this concept is necessary to better understand the goals of the disability community and where the efforts of women with disabilities may be focused within leadership roles.

Summary and Future Directions

This review has highlighted the urgent need for research on leadership and collaboration for women with disabilities. A proposed research agenda would examine three pressing issues. A basic need is the development of a model for leadership for women with disabilities. This must include attention to tokenism and the transition from tokenism to acceptance and respect, and would have to address stigma and ongoing appropriateness of accommodation. A second imperative is to ensure that women with disabilities are brought into center focus in all discussions of women and that the disenfranchisement of any women is no longer tolerated. Finally, the feminist research agenda must be expanded to include input from women leaders in the disability movement, but with the understanding that the potential contributions of those leaders consists of more than advocacy specific to disability issues.

Overall, it is our hope that issues surrounding leadership, feminism, and women with disabilities will become regularly included in discussions among theorists, educators, and researchers who explore general women's life experiences. We had originally hoped for a broader discussion on the mentorship of women with disabilities because it was thought that this type of relationship can be instrumental in developing leadership qualities among this group. We encourage those working in this area to reach out to this community through involvement with disability-related scholarly organizations. It is only when conversations among these entities truly begin that a more accurate knowledge base about the leadership styles and feministic principles of women with disabilities will be known.

Note

1   Contributors: Marlene Maheu, BraVada Garrett-Akinsanya, Rhoda Olkin, Rebecca P. Cameron.

References

Bailey, D. M. (2001). Labovian analysis of a manager's tale of distress: "It all worked out." *Occupational Therapy Journal of Research, 21*, 90–108.

Banks, M. E. (2003). Preface. In M. E. Banks & E. Kaschak (Eds.), *Women with visible and invisible disabilities: Multiple intersections, multiple issues, multiple therapies* (pp. xxi–xxxix). New York: Haworth Press.

Banks, M. E., & Marshall, C. A. (2004). Beyond the "triple whammy": Considering social class as one factor in discrimination against persons with disabilities. In J. L. Chin (Ed.), *The psychology of prejudice and discrimination: Volume 4: Disability, religion, physique, and other traits* (pp. 95–110). Westport, CT: Praeger.

Becker, J., Ayman, R., & Korabik, K. (2002). Discrepancies in self/subordinates' perceptions of leadership behavior: Leader's gender, organizational context and leader's self-monitoring. *Group & Organization Management, 27*, 226–244.

Bender Consulting Services. (2003). *Susan M. Daniels wins the 2003 Henry B. Betts Award.* Retrieved May 27, 2005 from http://www.benderconsult.com/news/press/20031218.html

Boyce, L. A., & Herd, A. M. (2003). The relationship between gender role stereotypes and requisite military leadership characteristics. *Sex Roles, 49,* 365–378.

Bullock, W. A., Ensing, D. S., Alloy, V. E., & Weddle, C. C. (2000). Leadership education: Evaluation of a program to promote recovery in persons with psychiatric disabilities. *Psychiatric Rehabilitation Journal, 24,* 3–12.

The Chelsea Forum. (n.d.). *Judith E. Heumann.* Retrieved May 27, 2005, from http://www.chelseaforum.com/speakers/Heumann.htm

Corbett, C. A. (2003). Special issues in psychotherapy for minority deaf women. In M. E. Banks & E. Kaschak (Eds.), *Women with visible and invisible disabilities: Multiple intersections, multiple issues, multiple therapies* (pp. 311–329). New York: Haworth Press.

Disability World. (2002). *World Bank appoints Judy Heumann to new disability adviser post.* Retrieved May 27, 2005 from http://www.disabilityworld.org/04-05_02/news/heumann.shtml

Disabled Women on the Web. (2004). *Carol Gill.* Retrieved May 27, 2005 from http://www.disabilityhistory.org/dwa/library_c.html#gill

Feldman, S. I., & Tegart, G. (2003). Keep moving: Conceptions of illness and disability of middle-aged African-American women with arthritis. In M. E. Banks & E. Kaschak (Eds.), *Women with visible and invisible disabilities: Multiple intersections, multiple issues, multiple therapies* (pp. 127–143). New York: Haworth Press.

Gilkes, C. T. (2001). *"If it wasn't for the women . . .": Black women's experience and womanist culture in church and community.* New York: Maryknoll.

Jans, L., & Stoddard, S. (1999). *Chartbook on women and disability in the United States.* An InfoUse Report. Washington, DC: U.S. National Institute on Disability and Rehabilitation Research.

Nabors, N. A., & Pettee, M. F. (2003). Womanist therapy with African American Women with Disabilities. In M. E. Banks & E. Kaschak (Eds.), *Women with visible and invisible disabilities: Multiple intersections, multiple issues, multiple therapies* (pp. 331–341). New York: Haworth Press.

Noonan, B. M., Gallor, S. M., Hensler-McGinnis, N. F., Fassinger, E. E., Wang, S., & Goodman, J. (2004). Challenges and successes: A qualitative study of the career development of highly achieving women with physical and sensory disabilities. *Journal of Counseling Psychology, 51*(1), 68–80.

Chapter 17

Lesbian Women and Leadership: Which Comes First?

Nancy L. Baker and Beverly Greene

This chapter discusses the phenomenon of lesbian leadership. One of the challenges in this discussion involves defining what we mean by lesbian leadership and what makes this kind of leadership different or similar to that of other women who are leaders. Lesbians are a heterogeneous group. However, they are often defined solely by the way they differ from heterosexual women. Differences notwithstanding, we may not be able to make presumptions about their similarities except in their mutual need to manage heterosexism.

This chapter focuses on the leadership by individuals who self-identify as lesbians or bisexual women involved in same-sex relationships. Lesbian leadership is defined as formal positions of organizational leadership held by lesbians in any organization, and individual actions by lesbians that provide leadership around confronting heterosexism or homophobia. This somewhat odd combination of leadership definitions is based, in part, on the discussion of the socially constructed nature of the label "lesbian." The basic difference between women who consider themselves heterosexual and those who consider themselves lesbians is their relationship to and experience of homophobia and heterosexism, so it makes sense to focus on individual actions that address homophobia and heterosexism. At the same time, given that the task of leadership creates challenges and choices that arise from heterosexism and homophobia, all leadership positions are relevant.

What Do We Mean by the Term Lesbian?

The first task in any discussion of lesbian leadership involves definitions. What do we mean when we say someone is a lesbian and what do we mean by the term lesbian leadership? Lesbian, like "homosexual" and "female," can be an imprecise term. The term "lesbian" was not used to refer to sexual behavior or love between two women until the late 1800s (Fletcher, 1990). Prior to that time, the term was a descriptor applied to individuals of either sex from the Greek island of Lesbos. The connection to women sexually involved with other women was made because Lesbos's arguably most famous citizen, Sappho, wrote intensely erotic poetry, some of which involved love between two women.

Generally when we refer to someone as a lesbian we are defining her as a woman whose erotic and sexual attractions are primarily to women. Both linguistically and conceptually, identifying or categorizing people on the basis of their sexual behavior or desire is a relatively recent social construction. There is ample evidence that human same-sex sexual interaction is at least as old as recorded history and is represented in most cultures.

However, the idea that people should be categorized based on the sex of the person(s) with whom they have sexual relationships did not develop until the late 19th century. Prior to that time, references to sexual acts between two people of the same sex were generally thought of and described as just that, behaviors people engage in, not individual identities. In other parts of the world people do not necessarily adopt an identity that is based on who they have sex with, but in the United States, gender normalcy is defined by erotic attraction to the other sex.

This conceptualization of same-sex attraction as psychologically inappropriate and morally incorrect creates a group of people who are socially marginalized, and their marginalization creates an identity based on their group membership. The degree to which such behavior was celebrated or persecuted, encouraged or demonized, has varied over time and culture, but it has not been universally deemed the central defining characteristic of an individual. In cultures that do not define gender as two dichotomous categories, as illustrated by some tribes of Native Americans, individuals that we might now label lesbian would have a role in the tribe that ranged from routine to honored and endowed with special talents.

Faderman (1992) writes of women living together without men during the 19th and 20th centuries in America. However, even this material tends to omit records of working-class and poor women. We feel that any discussion of lesbian leadership must include a consideration of the complexity in the lives of women who call themselves lesbians as well as the historical context of that label and its meaning.

The question of whether it is appropriate to think of lesbianism as an identity or a behavior is still part of an ongoing debate among feminist and gender or "queer" scholars. At the center of the issue is the question that Bohan (1993, 2002) raised: Is sexual orientation something a person discovers or one that society creates? This question is central to the issue of lesbian leadership.

Lesbians and Leadership

If we are creating a category or identity, how does that distinguish lesbian leadership or leadership by a lesbian from anything else? We do know that when social identities are constructed and social barriers become a part of that identity, there is a lived experience that becomes an intrinsic part of that identity. One of the questions raised by the position that sexual orientation is an intrinsic characteristic of the person is whether lesbianism is there from birth waiting to be discovered or developed over time. Once developed, is it fluid or stable? Further, is lesbianism "normal" or "pathological"? How lesbians are positioned with respect to their social privilege and disadvantage frames who lesbians are as leaders and how they are regarded in those positions.

Kitzinger (1987) argues that lesbianism is not a pathological deviation from normality but rather a radical act against male supremacy. Further, she and others argue that the construct reflects patriarchal assumptions about the necessity of linkages between physiology and "normal" sexual behavior, as well as the appropriateness of the nuclear family model for society.

Bohan (1993, 2002), while arguing that lesbianism is a socially constructed identity, reminds us that the virulence of homophobia and heterosexism make it a real factor in the lives of contemporary women. Being a lesbian and having a lesbian identity, regardless of its origins, is a reality created by a world committed to a heterosexist norm. In

343

a related vein, Hyde and Jaffee (2000), studying contemporary U.S. culture, found that prejudice against lesbians was a significant factor in encouraging the development of traditional female gender roles, including heterosexual identities. This finding provides support for the view that both heterosexual and lesbian identities are pieces of a socially constructed sexual orientation.

The degree to which lesbians are seen as traitors to their appropriate gender roles is relevant to a discussion of lesbian leadership in that leadership is considered a gendered quality. In Western culture, overt leadership is considered a male activity and women who exercise leadership in particular ways are seen as unfeminine, "wrong," and even castrating. The implication is that being a leader is something that no "normal" woman would want.

Scholars may disagree as to whether sexual orientation is a property of the person or represents social constructs that are a function of a heterosexist and patriarchal society, but there is recognition that it is a complex construct. The behaviors and feelings represented by the terms lesbian and heterosexual are neither one-dimensional nor discrete dichotomous categories (Peplau & Garnets, 2000). Sexual acts, desires, fantasies, and emotional and affectionate intimacy are all parts of what may be included as sexual orientation (Garnets, 2002).

Furthermore, while there is undoubtedly considerable correlation among these and other aspects of sexual identity, they can also be experienced and described as separate continuums along which an individual may vary. Furthermore, there is evidence that the development and maintenance of a lesbian identity is somewhat different from the development and maintenance of a male homosexual identity for the same reasons that heterosexual male and female identity differ (Bell, Weinberg, & Hammersmith, 1981; Peplau, Garnets, Spalding, Conley, & Veniegas, 1998).

This discussion attempts to underscore the difficulty in providing a clear or universally accepted definition of the term lesbian. It suggests that the issues that make lesbian leadership a unique issue for discussion are the challenges of heterosexism and homophobia. Further, given the difficulty in providing a definition or criteria for the term lesbian separate from the subjective experiences of individuals within a culture and historical context, it seems reasonable to define lesbians for our purposes as individuals who call or consider themselves lesbians and whose primary erotic attractions are to other women.

What is Lesbian Leadership?

Defining lesbian leadership proved challenging to us because there is limited formal literature that discusses lesbian leadership. Hence, definitions are based on the literature on lesbianism in general and the experiences and observations of the authors. First, we make a distinction between formal or organizational leadership and more informal leadership. There is also a distinction between lesbian leaders and leaders in the campaign for lesbian rights. In this chapter both formal and informal leadership roles by lesbians in any organizational context and the challenges those roles create are discussed. However, these categories will facilitate the identification of differences in the tasks and challenges faced by lesbian leaders.

Overall we do not view "lesbian leadership" as a specific constellation of qualities, characteristics, or descriptors that are specific to or limited to lesbians. Our conceptualization might be more accurately described as an understanding of lesbians in positions of leadership as well as lesbians who are openly identified as such and are celebrities. The latter, because of their notoriety, are often viewed as "leaders" because whatever they do garners public notice, hence drawing attention to that aspect of their identity. Their leadership is a function of their being viewed as leaders because of the paucity of lesbian role models; they are viewed as role models by both lesbians and others. Martina Navratilova, Rosie O'Donnell, Ellen DeGeneres, and others do not have occupations connected to their sexual orientation but their social status, coupled with their status as openly identified lesbians, makes them de facto leaders whether they choose to be or not.

A discussion of the leadership at an organizational level of the lesbian rights or antiheterosexism movement could also fall under the category of lesbian leadership, but it is not the focus of this discussion. Similarly, lesbians are not the only ones providing leadership in organizations directly supporting lesbian rights or exposing and challenging heterosexism and homophobia. However, the challenges faced by those not identifying as lesbians in supporting lesbian rights or opposing homophobia and heterosexism are beyond the scope of this chapter.

The preceding discussion makes it sound as if we can easily make dichotomous or at least discrete categories for organizations, along the dimension of the degree to which the issues being addressed by the organizations are directly related to combating heterosexism and homophobia. At one end of this imaginary continuum we could place organizations such as the National Center for Lesbian Rights. At the other end, we might place a business with one or more lesbians at the helm whose purpose is unrelated to the lesbian rights social movement, heterosexism, or homophobia.

Unfortunately, it is not quite that simple. Many of the lesbian or gay/lesbian organizations in the United States are professional, occupational, or workplace-based groups. Such organizations have a variety of functions that relate to the issue of lesbian rights or opposition to heterosexism and homophobia in a complex manner. Additionally, many organizations, particularly professional, academic, and social justice organizations that are not lesbian or gay/lesbian organizations, include opposition to homophobia and heterosexism in their mission. Nonetheless, some attention to the type of organization will help identify differences in the tasks and challenges facing lesbians in formal leadership roles.

In addition to the relatively obvious differences in the challenges to lesbian leaders operating in different types of organizations, there are also differences based on the social context in which the individual and organization operate. Within the United States there are significant differences in the degree to which lesbians are legally protected, or unprotected, from discrimination by individuals and employers, when compared to their heterosexual counterparts, and those differences vary in different parts of the country.

There are also differences in community norms concerning the acceptability of expressing and acting on heterosexist and homophobic attitudes and beliefs. In some states and locations, simply identifying publicly or even semipublicly as a lesbian can put an individual at risk for losing her job or having her parental and other basic civil rights challenged. Indeed, in the military such action is legally proscribed despite the fact that there are lesbians in this explicitly hierarchical institution where military rank is an overt sign of leadership. In these environments, lesbians are certainly providing leadership; however, their lesbian identity must remain invisible. Such environments would pose particular challenges to a lesbian seeking or maintaining a leadership position.

Beyond the borders of the United States, the levels of legal and religious prejudice and tolerance for lesbians varies tremendously, from full legal protection and equal legal status to areas where simply identifying as a lesbian is a serious crime. Even within the same geographic area, organizations or individuals linked to particular religious, cultural, or ethnic groups may face significantly different challenges and consequences than others. Thus, when we think of lesbian leadership, we must consider the geographical and social context in which these acts of leadership occur.

In addition to formal leadership, there is informal leadership. There are some places and contexts where simply attending an event of a lesbian social club or acknowledging one's own lesbianism may be a significant and courageous act of lesbian leadership. One may serve an important function as a role model. Given the relatively well-established finding that personal experience with lesbians and gay men reduces homophobia (Herek, 1989, 1990), it is reasonable to consider taking a public stance as a lesbian as an act of leadership.

The Public Lesbian

There are strains associated with being the public face for a stigmatized group. Safety becomes a potential issue for every woman whose lesbian identity is a public matter. Such concerns may affect the degree to which some women who are lesbians will be willing to pursue leadership positions, as their visibility makes them more vulnerable, even if their sexual orientation is not known. Their public visibility may increase the possibility that their sexual orientation will be discovered and revealed against their will.

The National Coalition of Anti-Violence Programs publishes an annual report with data on reported hate crimes against gays and lesbians. It covers about 30% of the country, the area where member groups monitor such violence. The report for 2003 documents hate crimes against gays and lesbians accounting for more than 10 murders and more than 750 serious violent assaults in each of the previous three years (Patton, 2004). Furthermore, although actual research is limited, there is some concern that violence is increased by hostile antigay rhetoric. In addition to physical attacks, lesbian leaders can also be the target for other expressions of bigotry such as hate mail and crank phone calls. Their very presence as leaders and their visibility may elicit more intense reactions from homophobes.

Concerns for personal safety that are a part of the role a public lesbian faces can exist whether the woman is a leader of a lesbian rights organization or the organizer of a lesbian bowling team. Additionally, the dangers of experiencing shunning and verbal attacks as a result of public identification as a lesbian can extend to the lesbian's children or other family members, especially if she lives in an area where homophobia is generally tolerated or encouraged. In addition to physical safety, there are potential concerns about economic safety for those who identify as lesbians. There is no national protection against discrimination in employment. Similarly, in many locations, discrimination against lesbians in housing is also acceptable.

Private experiences of homophobia and heterosexism can also result from public identification as a lesbian leader. There can be tension with family members who are not totally accepting of lesbians or lesbian rights or who may be embarrassed because the public lesbian "outs" her family as well. Many families and extended families deal with a family member's lesbianism by polite denial: everybody knows but nobody acknowledges that they know. Public recognition of an individual's lesbianism can make this polite denial impossible. This experience is particularly likely to occur for individuals who are leaders with mainstream media visibility or those whose employment is with an explicitly lesbian or gay organization. When a person's picture has been on TV or the response to where they work involves an explicitly lesbian or lesbian/gay organization, polite denial no longer works.

For women of color, being publicly acknowledged as a lesbian can also create tensions about acceptance in one's ethnic community. Because religion plays a significant role in many ethnic communities, the heterosexism and homophobia in many patriarchal religions have a greater possibility of creating problems for women of color with at least some part of their social support network. This issue is exacerbated in communities of recent immigrants from countries with no recent tradition of accepting lesbianism. Being identified as a lesbian is viewed as a rejection of the values of the country of origin, often a painful issue in immigrant communities. Yet being a lesbian does not prevent a woman of color from experiencing the consequences of racism or anti-immigrant sentiments in addition to homophobia.

Being the "Only One": Designated Hitter by Default

As many women of color have pointed out, being one of the few members of a stigmatized group in any particular environment creates the expectation that you are the representative of that group, the spokesperson, or the exemplar. This status confers a kind of implicit leadership whether one seeks it or not. This ranges from being expected to personally know "Ellen" or any other lesbian in the world, to being expected to have an opinion on every situation involving lesbians or lesbian rights anywhere.

Being "the lesbian" often also means that everything one does is seen and interpreted through that lens. This phenomenon is familiar to any woman who has been the only woman at her job. The loss of one's own unique individual identity is one of the well-researched consequences of being a member of a stigmatized group (Baker, 2002). If one is operating in a context where many people have prejudices against lesbians, this can result in a more negative evaluation of the lesbian's actions or views than would have occurred but for her lesbianism. Of course, as with other prejudices, research has demonstrated that the devaluing is rarely openly acknowledged as the result of prejudice. Instead, it is presented as an objective or legitimate evaluation (Deaux & LaFrance, 1998; Fiske, 1998; Hodson, Dovidio, & Gaertner, 2002; Rowe, 1990).

To some extent, this issue is more of a challenge for lesbians not directly involved with lesbian rights organizations. After all, although leaders of rights organizations are not necessarily more likely to know Ellen DeGeneres or somebody's cousin in Springfield, they are more likely to have a position on issues involving lesbian rights. Additionally, lesbians involved in the leadership of lesbian rights organizations may spend more of their time in circles where they are not "the only lesbian" in the room.

Another aspect of being "the lesbian" involves fear and curiosity about lesbian sexuality. Although this problem is likely being reduced by the increased visibility of lesbians both individually and in the media, status as the only lesbian can create potential misunderstandings about the meaning of friendly gestures or actions. It can make "the lesbian" the target of embarrassingly private questions about her sexuality or sexual behavior.

To Be Out or Closeted

The need to grapple with the question of whether or not to take on a public role, to "be out" as a lesbian, is relatively unusual (Frable, Blackstone, & Scherbaum, 1990). For members of most groups who are targets of bigotry and hate, group membership usually involves a visible attribute. However, lesbians, like other members of "invisible" groups, must make a decision about whether to challenge the culture's heterosexual assumption by being open about their lesbian status. This act can also be made difficult by the simple fact that announcing one's sexual orientation is unnecessary for those who identify as heterosexuals. In most contexts, one must formally "opt out" of heterosexual status or one is assumed to be heterosexual. Determining how and when to accomplish that opting out can be a challenge.

Although we are examining challenges, it is also important to note that many lesbians also receive significant social support and positive reactions as a result of public identification as a lesbian. This may come from other lesbians, but can also come from any individuals supportive of lesbian rights. Additionally, lesbians who make the decision to be open are freed from the necessity of hiding their personal lives from others and may experience considerable self-affirmation from this action.

Another, sometimes subtle, pressure is the burden of being viewed as the role-model. People are not perfect. None of us are immune from the possibility of poor judgment, a failed relationship, or a public faux pas. But people often hope or even demand that our leaders be free of human failings. Members of stigmatized groups, including lesbians, can feel a special desire that the faces known to the public reduce the negative image of their group, and can be harshly critical when that demand is not met. Obviously, although this pressure can be greatest for leaders of lesbian rights organizations, it also applies to any lesbian in a particularly public or leadership role including sports figures and "out" college professors.

The concerns about safety, social disapproval, and loss of individual identity are potentially relevant for all publicly open, "out" lesbians. Similarly, all "out" lesbians can experience a variety of positive benefits, from the reduction in the strain of hiding to the experience of reducing prejudice. However, as we have alluded to briefly, there are differences in how these more universal issues manifest as well as unique issues depending on the social and organizational context in which one is operating. These differences are worth exploring.

Leadership in Lesbian Rights Organizations

The role of leading a lesbian rights organization, especially one based in an area where the local social-political context is supportive of lesbians, can seem like an extremely desirable task. However, there are some pressures associated with being such a public face. As was discussed earlier, the public status can affect others in your life, including parents and children. It reduces the possibility of disapproval being cloaked in polite denial. This is especially true if the organization has visibility in the mainstream media. Such leaders are also extremely likely to experience role-model demands.

Business leaders

One of the more complex leadership challenges is for lesbians whose leadership role is unrelated to issues of sexual orientation or social justice. For these women, being a lesbian is, to some extent, an irrelevant fact. However, in a world where homophobia and heterosexism are real, a lesbian identity is never a totally irrelevant fact. As noted previously, a lesbian identity creates issues and challenges that must be addressed.

The challenges range from the almost trivial to the immense. Does one use the pronoun "we" when speaking about one's weekend activities, does one's put up a partner's picture on the desk or locker, does she come to the holiday party, does one invite colleagues to one's home, does one request domestic partner health benefits, who does one list as beneficiary for the retirement program, what label is used in response to the "relationship" query? If one is single, can one explore dating coworkers, and how does one respond to the offer by a colleague of a blind date with "a great guy"? Of course, at least some of these issues are also relevant for most other lesbians. However, when the relationship of the organization to the social-political issues involved is, at best, extraordinarily tenuous, there are fewer guideposts to aid the decision making. The resulting decisions are likely influenced greatly by factors that increase or decrease the consequences and benefits of the decision. Since many of those consequences and benefits are extremely individual, the decisions will also be individual.

Urban and rural settings

There are obviously different challenges in urban and rural settings. In urban settings it is possible to live and work in totally different locations, with overlap being extremely limited. In truly small towns and communities, it is hard to have a life without others being aware of your "private" activities. This makes some issues less a matter of choice; others may know with whom a person lives. However, it does not alter

351

the possibility that "polite denial" will operate, for example, "those two nice women live together in that one-bedroom apartment to help save money." Even for women in urban settings, being a member of a special community, whether it is a particular religious group, an ethnic group, or an avocation, can create many of the same issues as living in a rural area.

Summary

Barriers to lesbian leadership are numerous; however, they may all be viewed as a function of societal homophobia/heterosexism, sexism, and the degree to which these leaders' other identities further marginalize them. Whatever role the lesbian finds herself in, it always contains a requirement to manage social marginalization and its effects. These effects may be transformed by different roles and positions assumed by women who are lesbians, but are certainly intensified when a lesbian is in a position of leadership. Overcoming the barriers associated with homophobia/heterosexism is intrinsically connected to overcoming the barriers imposed by social marginalization. Clearly mentoring and support by women who are and are not lesbians are important for women who negotiate the challenges that are a function of this role.

We would like to think that such support would be naturally extended in feminist organizations as it is consistent with feminist goals. If such organizations are true to the mission of feminism they might be more supportive of lesbians in positions of leadership and enhance their capacity to exercise leadership relatively free of the need to defend themselves against homophobic bias.

Because of the invisibility of sexual orientation we may be blind to many women leaders who are lesbians but who are not open about their sexual orientation for fear of the situations we have discussed. As lesbians have historically been neglected in our scholarly endeavors, more research is warranted to give us additional information about the pleasures and challenges of lesbian leadership.

At one level, a discussion of lesbian leadership in the context of women's leadership is redundant. Lesbians, after all, are women. Different women make different choices and adopt different leadership styles and strategies. Although there is virtually no research on lesbian leadership styles, there is no compelling reason to believe that lesbians would be less variable than women in general on that dimension.

Nonetheless, this discussion may be of value. As was noted earlier, lesbians do experience the pressures and consequences of living in a heterosexist and homophobic society. Furthermore, in many locations those pressures are not limited by legal protection. On the contrary, homophobic and heterosexist views and values are, in many cases, inscribed in law. It is this reality that makes this discussion meaningful.

References

Baker, N. L. (2002). Despite our best intentions: Feminist psychology meets the legal system. *Psychology of Women Quarterly, 26,* 168–169.

Bell, A. P., Weinberg, M. S., & Hammersmith, S. K. (1981). *Sexual preference: Its development in men and women.* Bloomington: Indiana University Press.

Bohan, J. S. (1993). Regarding gender: Essentialism, constructionism, and feminist psychology. *Psychology of Women Quarterly, 17,* 5–21.

Bohan, J. S. (2002). Sex differences and/in the self: Classic themes, feminist variations, postmodern challenges. *Psychology of Women Quarterly, 26,* 74–88.

Deaux, K., & LaFrance, M. (1998). Gender. In D. T. Gilbert, S. T. Fiske, & G. Lindzey (Eds.), *The handbook of social psychology* (4th ed., pp. 788–827). New York: Oxford University Press.

Faderman, L. (1992). *Odd girls and twilight lovers: A history of lesbian life in twentieth-century America (between men–between women).* New York: Penguin Books.

Fiske, S. T. (1998). Stereotyping, prejudice, and discrimination. In D. T. Gilbert, S. T. Fiske, & G. Lindzey (Eds.), *The handbook of social psychology* (4th ed., pp. 357–414). New York: Oxford University Press.

Fletcher, L. (1990). *Lavender lists.* Boston: Alyson Publications.

Frable, D. E., Blackstone, T., & Scherbaum, C. (1990). Marginal and mindful: Deviants in social interactions. *Journal of Personality & Social Psychology, 59,* 140–149.

Garnets, L. D. (2002). Sexual orientations in perspective. *Cultural Diversity and Ethnic Minority Psychology, 8,* 115–129.

Herek, G. M. (1989). Hate crimes against lesbians and gay men: Issues for research and policy. *American Psychologist, 44,* 948–955.

Herek, C. M. (1990). The contents of anti-gay violence: Notes on cultural and psychological heterosexism. *Journal of Interpersonal Violence, 5,* 316–333.

Hodson, G., Dovidio, J. F., & Gaertner, S. L. (2002). Processes in racial discrimination: Differential weighting of conflicting information. *Personality & Social Psychology Bulletin, 28,* 460–471.

Hyde, J. S., & Jaffee, S. R. (2000). Becoming a heterosexual adult: The experiences of young women. *Journal of Social Issues, 56,* 283–296.

Kitzinger, C. (1987). *The social construction of lesbianism.* London and Beverly Hills, CA: Sage.

Patton, C. (2004). *National Coalition of Anti-Violence Programs Report.* New York: New York City Gay and Lesbian Anti-Violence Project.

Peplau, L. A., & Garnets, L. D. (2000). A new paradigm for understanding women's sexuality and sexual orientation. *Journal of Social Issues, 56,* 329–350.

Peplau, L. A., Garnets, L. D., Spalding, L. R., Conley, T. D., & Veniegas, R. C. (1998). A critique of Bem's "exotic becomes erotic" theory of sexual orientation. *Psychological Review, 105,* 387–394.

Rowe, M. (1990). Barriers to equality: The power of subtle discrimination to maintain unequal opportunity. *Employee Responsibilities and Rights Journal, 3,* 153–163.

Conclusion: Transforming Leadership with Diverse Feminist Voices

Jean Lau Chin

Most books and studies on leadership focus on leadership within corporations or within the public eye. Being a leader means having the corner office or being the chief executive. Women as CEOs in government, academia, corporations, and the workplace are still a relatively new phenomenon such that they make news just by holding the positions. Leadership theories and studies about good leadership and effective leadership styles seldom distinguish characteristics related to gender. Is there a difference between women and men as leaders? How do feminist values and principles apply to leadership? What is successful leadership?

Trait theories postulate characteristics about how leaders are born, or have charismatic personalities, to suggest that leaders lead separate from their contexts and environments. Case studies of successful leaders tend to study male leaders which results in attributing successful leadership to masculinized characteristics and traits. As we examined women and leadership in this book, I want to use the analogy of the carrot, the egg, and the coffee bean (Bainton, 2006). If we boil these ingredients, the hard carrot gets soft, the egg with hard but fragile shell gets hard, while the coffee bean transforms the water in which it is boiled; successful leadership is like boiling coffee, that is, transforming its environment while carrying out the functions of the organization.

Transforming Leadership

Transforming leadership models and incorporating the relevance of gender and diversity has been a goal of this book. Models of leadership now focus on transformational versus transactional leadership styles, and visionary versus task-oriented characteristics; there is data to suggest that women, especially feminist women, are more likely to be transformational in their leadership styles. While women are often described as more nurturing or collaborative in their styles, we are beginning to find that it is not as simplistic. Contexts, biases, perceptions, and values contribute immensely to differential notions of leadership and expectations of leadership behavior in men and women.

The experiences of women and men are often different. Iwasaki, MacKay, and Ristock (2004) explored the experiences of stress (e.g., negative and positive aspects of stress, different levels of stress, lack of sleep, pressure, financial stressors) among both female and male managers. In addition to substantial similarities, a number of important gender differences emerged. Gender continues to be socially constructed in society; specifically, there are differing gender role expectations and responsibilities for women and men. Female managers experienced "emotional stress," primarily because of the pressure to meet expectations of being responsible and caring for people both inside and outside of their home. In contrast, male managers tended to focus on themselves and regard other things as beyond their control or responsibility.

Many concepts have been proposed in this book to expand our theories and models of leadership to be relevant to women and responsive to gender. Many of the women leaders who contributed to this book identified social change, advocacy, policy and institutional transformation as motives for their seeking or attaining positions of leadership. Most viewed collaboration and inclusiveness as a value and a style of their leadership. While most identified feminist principles as contributing to their leadership behaviors, few felt that we have models of feminist leadership or leadership models that are inclusive of women.

To understand it, we needed to start from the experiences and case studies of women leaders or feminist leaders. To study it, we needed new concepts because existing ones did not capture the essence of leadership among women; some of those identified in this book are: coacted harmony, collaborative leadership, participatory leadership, empowerment leadership, servant leader, transformational leader, shared power, and positive marginality. All reflect the contexts in which leadership and leadership styles are exercised.

Women leaders more commonly lead in the context of a male advantage, that is, masculinized contexts; they are evaluated and perceived differently from men based on our current gender-related biases. Ethnic minority women leaders are often questioned in subtle and indirect manners that question their competence or assume they got to where they did because of affirmative action, not because they can do the job. Successful and effective leadership styles may differ depending on contexts—that is, masculinized contexts and crisis periods—and will change if and when our social institutions and organizations become more gender-equitable.

From this perspective, we view leadership as contextual, value driven, diversity-inclusive, and collaborative. We look to transform models of leadership—to identify diverse leadership styles across diverse groups, to embrace core values that motivate those in leadership roles, and to identify effective leadership styles for men and women to achieve the outcomes they envision for the organizations and institutions they lead.

The position of transforming leadership is not that men cannot or should not be leaders. It is that women can and should be effective leaders without needing to embrace those traits which are foreign, or to adopt those values which are not syntonic to their gender or culture. It is about using feminist models to promote the pathways to leadership, recognizing obstacles and drawing on strengths. It is about measuring and identifying effective leadership that is not simply based on male characteristics. It is about evaluating outcomes, not about identifying traits. It is about how issues of power, privilege, and hierarchy influence the contexts in which leadership is exercised.

Feminist Leadership

While we examined women and leadership in this book, we sought to identify and explicate new models of feminist leadership. How do women lead, and can women using feminist principles be effective leaders? An important distinction from the feminist literature was that being female and being feminist are not the same. We examined the experiences of feminist leaders. We identified women leaders who led with a feminist style. Both the literature and the experiences suggest that perceptions and expectations of women both demand and constrain them

357

in their roles as leaders; this makes for an environment for women as leaders that is different from that of men. Race and ethnicity interact with gender to shape how diverse women lead.

We conclude that *feminist leadership is a goal; and it is a style*. Feminist women who aspire to and end up in leadership positions bring to these positions values and characteristics that shape how they lead, but they are also shaped by the environments in which they find themselves. Based on feminist principles and values, it is a goal of feminist women that they apply these principles of collaboration, egalitarianism, and inclusiveness to leadership and to the positions of leadership in which they find themselves; therefore, it is a goal.

Eagly, Johannesen-Schmidt, and van Engen (2003) have found gender differences in how men and women lead that expand the notions of collaborative leadership styles. Eagly's studies also demonstrate the importance of perception and expectation on leadership styles, that is, bias toward expecting leaders to behave in roles congruent with their stereotyped views of gender styles. Women are more devalued in their leadership roles by men who occupy male-dominated roles (Eagly & Karau, 2002), and are evaluated more poorly in their performance as leaders (Eagly, Makhijani, & Klonsky, 1992).

Eagly and Karau (1991) studied the emergence of male and female leaders in initially leaderless groups. In these laboratory and field studies, men emerged as leaders to a greater extent than did women, particularly in short-term groups and in groups carrying out tasks that did not require complex social interaction. In contrast, women emerged as social leaders slightly more than did men. These findings were interpreted in terms of gender role theory, which maintains that societal gender roles influence group behavior, that is, role-induced tendencies resulted in men being more inclined than women to specialize in behaviors strictly oriented to their group's task and for women to specialize more than men in socially facilitative behaviors.

A feminist leadership perspective argues for gender-equitable environments and argues against masculinized contexts; it argues against women needing to act like men. The feminist leaders in this book view the importance of our social institutions and corporations evolving to become gender-equitable environments, and to achieve a yin–yang balance in the leadership styles of men and women.

A feminist leadership perspective introduces ethics, social justice, collaboration, and inclusiveness as key to their motivations for seeking positions of leadership. Feminist leaders in this book defined their leadership roles less as leaders of corporations and institutions, but more as leaders of thought and social change.

This book is the result of collaboration among many diverse feminist women psychologists who have served in leadership roles. We convened a dialogue on the www.feministleadership.com website to create a scholarly product on feminist leadership to expand and transform current theories and models of leadership. We intended to capture the experiences of feminist women leaders as case studies; their contributions include the critical thinking and analyses that apply feminist principles to current models of leadership. Many of the contributors were and are feminist leaders, who have been instrumental in the women's movement and battle for women's rights to get an equal place at the table.

Some of the contributors used historical accounts of leadership within racial/ethnic communities as their context, resulting in experiences and views of leadership that differ from those of White women. Their experiences lend credence to the intersection of identities as added dimensions to women in leadership role, that is, as leaders operating in both racialized and masculinized contexts. Contributors to this book expand our notions of leadership to be inclusive of roles in the public eye, national and corporate leadership, and those of community leadership. Contributors challenge historic models of leadership purporting to be genderless, but drawing primarily on the experiences of White men leading in contexts governed by male values and male norms.

Definitions of full-time work in the corporate world do not account for women being able to take time for child-rearing needs. Prescribed career paths for success do not factor in discontinuities because of pregnancy and childbirth. Rather, women's time away from their careers are viewed as reflecting a lesser commitment. Leadership styles too were evaluated from masculine traits and masculine perspective.

Many recognized the gender-role constraints on their leadership styles, and the masculinized contexts that influenced the ways in which they led—sometimes they were bound by them; other times, they sought to change them.

Diverse Leadership

By diverse leadership, we mean leadership roles, models, and styles that consider the diversity of women and men; of the range of racial,

359

ethnic, sexual orientation, and disability differences that contribute to effective leadership. While individual differences contribute greatly to how men and women lead, there are commonalities which bond the experiences of women, of racial/ethnic groups, of disability and lesbian groups, which contribute to how they aspire to and attain leadership roles. Our books and models on leadership typically define corporate leadership or management leadership as the sole domains of leadership. While this is leadership, our ethnic sisters remind us of leadership for the causes and needs of ethnic communities: advocacy leadership to effect social change and address issues of social justice as primary dimensions of leadership. Unlike the corporate leader who has embraced charitable causes, these community leaders define the ills in their communities as their primary role of leadership.

The diversity within these groups also contributes to differences in how they lead, which is both internal and external. Morrison and Von Glinow (1990) find that women and minorities face a "glass ceiling" that limits their advancement toward top management in organizations throughout U.S. society, that is, external limits and constraints on women and leadership. While women tend to use a collaborative style, collaboration alone is too simple to capture the styles of women leaders or feminist leaders. We must consider the historic experiences of women and racial/ethnic groups, and the contributions of culture to understand the confrontational and assertive styles of African American women, the attempts to achieve harmony and balance among Asian American women, and the stance of standing by their men as they take leadership among Native American women.

Think of our definitions of heroes and leaders, and how they are associated with "masculine" traits. Men who go into military battle are heroes and leaders. When roles are not public or associated with physical valor, our societies have tended not to view these roles as providing leadership. Our Native American sisters in this book urge us to rethink these associations of leadership. If we interpret them as ineffective or less valued as styles of leadership, we will have missed the point. If we define them from the perspectives of White middle-class society, we will continue to marginalize leaders from diverse groups. If we ignore the contexts in which these women leaders lead, which are reflected in our social and educational institutions, our corporate organizations, we will have committed the same errors found in the existing models of leadership we criticize.

What Next?

What do we do next? This book began a dialogue on women and leadership. We needed to start with the case studies and experiences of women leaders to understand effective leadership and the challenges faced by these women in institutions and society that have yet to accept the leadership of women on an equal basis with men. We needed to insert the goals and principles of feminism to construct and transform our existing models of leadership. The contributors to this book raise additional questions as they examine the issues of women and leadership and begin to deconstruct the principles and models of leadership. Some conclusions and questions to direct us to the next level include:

- Contexts: What are the contexts of leadership? How does the influence of masculinized contexts influence leadership and leadership style?
- Differences between men and women: Men and women may lead the same organization, but they do not share the same experience; gender-based biases influence the perceptions and expectations of the behaviors of women different from men.
- Why women lead: The purpose and outcomes of women as leaders often differ in their seeking or attaining leadership roles. Their concerns emphasize advocacy and social change compared to the concerns of men which emphasize being in charge; thus empowerment rather than "power over" might differentiate their motivations.
- Gender-equitable work environments: Existence of glass ceilings and the push for equal rights, equal pay, and mobility for women suggest that our work environments are not equitable. Evolution and advocacy to create gender-equitable environments and transform institutional cultures are needed.
- Mentoring and training: Consistent with feminist principles, we need to mentor and train new and emerging women leaders in ways that empower them to lead. We need to provide them with role models of a new generation of feminist leaders.

Our next steps will be based on what have we learned. The first step will be an e-publication that builds on this book, using technology to provide existing and emerging women leaders with a resource for dialogue and a tool to promote social change and transform our current

361

models of leadership. This is syntonic with feminist principles. In writing this book, we honor the feminist leaders who paved the way, and celebrate the strengths of women from diverse groups that bring us to this point in our thinking about women and leadership.

References

Bainton, D. (2006, March). *Navigating academic politics: Women in leadership.* Workshop at Where There's a Woman There's a Way: The Path to Leadership in Higher Education Conference, Office for Women in Higher Education, American Council on Education, San Francisco.

Eagly, A. H., Johannesen-Schmidt, M. C., & van Engen, M. L. (2003). Transformational, transactional, and laissez-faire leadership styles: A meta-analysis comparing women and men. *Psychological Bulletin, 129*(4), 569–591.

Eagly, A. H., & Karau, S. J. (1991). Gender and the emergence of leaders: A meta-analysis. *Journal of Personality & Social Psychology, 60*(5), 685–710.

Eagly, A. H., & Karau, S. J. (2002). Role congruity theory of prejudice toward female leaders. *Psychological Review, 109*(3), 573–598.

Eagly, A. H., Makhijani, M. G., & Klonsky, B. G. (1992). Gender and the evaluation of leaders: A meta-analysis. *Psychological Bulletin, 111*(1), 3–22.

Iwasaki, Y., MacKay, K. J., & Ristock, J. (2004). Gender-based analyses of stress among professional managers: An exploratory qualitative study. *International Journal of Stress Management, 11*(1), 56–79.

Morrison, A. M., & Von Glinow, M. A. (1990). Women and minorities in management. *American Psychologist, 45*(2), 200–208.

Index